The Other Worlds of Hector Berlioz

Berlioz frequently explored other worlds in his writings, from the imagined exotic enchantments of New Zealand to the rings of Saturn where Beethoven's spirit was said to reside. The sites at which his musical works are set are less remote, and his adventurousness has instead been located in his mastery of the orchestra, as both orchestrator and conductor. Inge van Rij's book takes a new approach to Berlioz's treatment of the orchestra by exploring the relationship between these two forms of control – the orchestra as abstract sound, and the orchestra as collective labour and instrumental technology. Van Rij reveals that the negotiation between worlds characteristic of Berlioz's writings also plays out in his music: orchestral technology may be concealed or ostentatiously displayed; musical instruments may be industrialised or exoticised; and the orchestral musicians themselves move between being a society of distinctive individuals and being a machine played by Berlioz himself.

INGE VAN RIJ is a Senior Lecturer in musicology at the New Zealand School of Music. Her first book, *Brahms's Song Collections*, was published by Cambridge University Press in 2006, having received substantial funding from a Marsden Grant from the Royal Society of New Zealand. She is a regular presenter at international conferences, including both the American Musicological Society and the Society for Ethnomusicology.

The Other Worlds of Hector Berlioz

Travels with the Orchestra

―――

INGE VAN RIJ

CAMBRIDGE
UNIVERSITY PRESS

University Printing House, Cambridge CB2 8BS, United Kingdom

One Liberty Plaza, 20th Floor, New York, NY 10006, USA

477 Williamstown Road, Port Melbourne, VIC 3207, Australia

314-321, 3rd Floor, Plot 3, Splendor Forum, Jasola District Centre, New Delhi - 110025, India

79 Anson Road, #06-04/06, Singapore 079906

Cambridge University Press is part of the University of Cambridge.

It furthers the University's mission by disseminating knowledge in the pursuit of education, learning and research at the highest international levels of excellence.

www.cambridge.org
Information on this title: www.cambridge.org/9781108814010

© Inge van Rij 2015

This publication is in copyright. Subject to statutory exception and to the provisions of relevant collective licensing agreements, no reproduction of any part may take place without the written permission of Cambridge University Press.

First published 2015
First paperback edition 2020

A catalogue record for this publication is available from the British Library

Library of Congress Cataloging in Publication data
Van Rij, Inge, author.
The other worlds of Hector Berlioz : travels with the orchestra / Inge van Rij.
  pages cm
ISBN 978-0-521-89646-7 (hardback)
1. Berlioz, Hector, 1803–1869. Orchestra music.   2. Orchestral music – 19th century – History and criticism.   I. Title.
ML410.B5V36 2015
780.92 – dc23   2014046697

ISBN 978-0-521-89646-7 Hardback
ISBN 978-1-108-81401-0 Paperback

Cambridge University Press has no responsibility for the persistence or accuracy of URLs for external or third-party internet websites referred to in this publication, and does not guarantee that any content on such websites is, or will remain, accurate or appropriate.

To Anneliese

Contents

List of figures   [*page* viii]
List of music examples   [ix]
Acknowledgements   [xi]

Introduction   [1]

1 Travels with the orchestra: Travel writing and Berlioz's *Orchestration Treatise*   [14]

2 Conquering Other worlds: Military metaphors, virtuosity, and subjectivity in *Symphonie funèbre et triomphale* and *Harold en Italie*   [70]

3 Visions of Other worlds: Sensing the supernatural in *Épisode de la vie d'un artiste* and *La nonne sanglante*   [127]

4 Back to (the music of) the future: Aesthetics of technology in Berlioz's *Euphonia* and *Damnation de Faust*   [193]

5 Exhibiting Other worlds: *Les Troyens*, museum culture, and human zoos   [245]

Epilogue   [320]

Select bibliography   [339]
Index   [351]

Figures

1.1 'Salut matinal.' [*page* 36]
2.1 Sketch of Paganini, by Boulanger c. 1840. [92]
2.2 Berlioz conducts with a mace. 'Satyrisches Bild' by Andreas Geiger, after Cajetan. [95]
4.1 'Mr Berlioz takes advantage of his "electric baton" to conduct an orchestra which will have members in every region of the globe.' [203]
4.2 Faber's 'Euphonia' automaton. [213]
4.3 Scene from 'Course à l'abîme', Salzburg Festspiel 1999, dir. Alex Olle and Carlos Padrissa. [230]
5.1 'Costumes des bayadères, Th. des Variétés', printed by Maison Martinet, No. 1223 of '1637 estampes coloriées représentant des acteurs en costumes de scène (1796–1843)'. [301]

Music examples

[All works are by Berlioz, unless otherwise stated.]

1.1	'L'île inconnue', bb. 62–81 [*page* 35]	
1.2	'La captive', first version [41]	
1.3	'La captive', bb. 17–24 [50]	
1.4	'La captive', bb. 71–4 [52]	
1.5	'La captive', bb. 103–6 [56]	
2.1	*Symphonie funèbre et triomphale* I 'Marche funèbre', bb. 62–8 [82]	
2.2	*Symphonie funèbre et triomphale* I 'Marche funèbre', bb. 175–82 [83]	
2.3	*Symphonie funèbre et triomphale* III 'Apothéose', bb. 1–19 [84]	
2.4	*Symphonie funèbre et triomphale* III 'Apothéose', bb. 218–21 [87]	
2.5	*Harold en Italie* II 'Marche des pèlerins', bb. 56–75 [107]	
2.6	*Harold en Italie* II 'Marche des pèlerins', bb. 169–85 [116]	
2.7	*Harold en Italie* III 'Sérénade', bb. 163–72 [120]	
2.8	*Harold en Italie* I 'Harold aux montagnes', bb. 124–34 [121]	
3.1	*Symphonie fantastique* I 'Rêveries – passions', bb. 358–75 [142]	
3.2	*Symphonie fantastique* IV 'Marche au supplice', bb. 109–13 [148]	
3.3	*Symphonie fantastique* V 'Songe d'une nuit de sabbat', bb. 456–87 [149]	
3.4	*Symphonie fantastique* II 'Un bal', bb. 120–39 [153]	
3.5	*Symphonie fantastique* II 'Un bal', bb. 281–8 [154]	
3.6	*Symphonie fantastique* II 'Un bal', bb. 300–321 [156]	
3.7	*Symphonie fantastique* V 'Songe d'une nuit de sabbat', bb. 414–20 [157]	
3.8	*Symphonie fantastique* I 'Rêveries – passions', bb. 410–15 [159]	
3.9	*Symphonie fantastique* V 'Songe d'une nuit de sabbat', bb. 31–9 [160]	
3.10a	*La nonne sanglante* 'Légende', Climax of first verse, bb. 184–90 [180]	
3.10b	*La nonne sanglante* 'Légende', Climax and continuation of second verse, bb. 217–25 [181]	
3.11	*La nonne sanglante* Duet, bb. 319–37 [187]	

3.12	*La nonne sanglante* Duet, bb. 350–70	[189]
4.1	*La damnation de Faust* 'Choeur d'étudiants et de soldats', bb. 132–49	[217]
4.2	*La damnation de Faust* opening, bb. 1–22	[221]
4.3	*La damnation de Faust* 'Le roi de Thulé: Chanson gothique', bb. 9–26	[223]
4.4	*La damnation de Faust* Marguerite's 'Romance', bb. 87–95	[224]
4.5	*La damnation de Faust* 'Sérénade de Méphistophélès', bb. 1–10	[227]
4.6	*La damnation de Faust* 'Évocation', bb. 41–5	[228]
4.7	*La damnation de Faust* 'La course à l'abîme', bb. 1–16	[233]
4.8	*La damnation de Faust* 'La course à l'abîme', bb. 90–104	[235]
5.1	*Les Troyens*, No. 29 'Chasse royale et orage', bb. 242–63	[257]
5.2	*Les Troyens* No. 11 'Marche troyenne', bb. 1–32	[261]
5.3	*Les Troyens* No. 18 'Chant national: Gloire à Didon', bb. 7–14	[266]
5.4	*Les Troyens* No. 12 Scène et récitatif, bb. 75–94	[275]
5.5	*Les Troyens* No. 12 Scène et récitatif, bb. 108–42	[278]
5.6	*Les Troyens* No. 42 Scène, bb. 1–15	[283]
5.7	*Les Troyens* No. 3 Duo, bb. 165–94	[288]
5.8	*Les Troyens* No. 3 Duo, bb. 101–64	[291]
5.9	*Les Troyens* No. 33c 'Pas d'esclaves nubiennes', bb. 1–12	[308]
5.10a	Auber, *L'enfant prodigue* Air de ballet No 1, 'Pas de séduction', bb. 1–7	[310]
5.10b	*Les Troyens* No. 33a, 'Pas des almées', bb. 1–7	[310]
6.1	Vincent Wallace, *Lurline* No. 3, 'The Naiad's Spell'	[326]

Acknowledgements

As Berlioz so elegantly illustrates in *Evenings with the Orchestra*, music criticism is ideally a form of dialogue between the author and fellow musicians, who may have quite distinct identities and ideologies, but who share the belief that music is worth debating and writing about. The 'dramatis personae' in my own musicological travels have played an invaluable role in the gestation of this book, even if I have not always followed their excellent advice. Davinia Caddy was the perfect 'Corsino', challenging me to address difficulties but doing so with friendship and flair. Vicki Cooper and Fleur Jones at Cambridge University Press have been a source of great support and patience, allowing me to pursue this research in directions I could not have anticipated when I first proposed the project. As copy editor, William H. Stoddard offered numerous invaluable suggestions, while Steven Huebner and Suzanne Aspden provided insightful editorial assistance on an earlier version of Chapter 4 (for *Cambridge Opera Journal*), as did several anonymous readers. Hugh Macdonald and Ralph Locke shared some of their profound knowledge of Berlioz and musical exoticism and offered encouragement on even earlier versions of various sections. And Emily Dolan and David Irving were kind enough to allow me access to preliminary versions or drafts of their own research. I hope my gratitude and debt to the publications of these and other scholars will be apparent within the book itself.

My past and present colleagues at the New Zealand School of Music and Victoria University have proved Wellington to be, in Berlioz's terms, 'a civilized town', and this book has greatly benefited from their responses to my various seminar presentations and drafts, as well as discussion of their own research. In particular, Elizabeth Hudson offered insight on innumerable occasions at every stage of the development of the project, repeatedly helping me to understand better what I was already thinking (or what I *should* have been thinking). Peter Walls brought his own multi-faceted knowledge of orchestras to bear on substantial sections of the manuscript; Keith Chapin provided illuminating editorial feedback on an earlier version of Chapter 5 (for *19th-Century Music*); Erin Helyard generously shared his Sibelius wizardry (and the occasional glass of Willy Gisselbrecht pinot gris); Douglas

Mews offered vital editorial assistance with the musical examples; Greer Garden advised on issues of French language, and Peter Russell on several passages of German; Stephan Prock helped me in working with film; and Ken Young and Margaret Medlyn enabled me to resurrect the duet from Berlioz's *La nonne sanglante* in performance.

I would also like to thank the students of the various special-topic classes I taught on aspects of this research since 2008, for their enthusiasm for Berlioz and their tolerance of the book that I was always 'just completing', and I have been privileged to supervise several postgraduate students who inspired me with their own developing research, including Frances Moore, who also offered valuable support as a research assistant. Lynne Wenden and Wendy Nolan Joyce provided vital further research assistance, in particular in relation to the musical examples and French translations, respectively. I am very grateful to Victoria University and the New Zealand School of Music, who supplied the funding for these research assistants, as well as several trips to Paris.

Finally, special thanks must go to my mother, Vivien van Rij, who offered a vital 'outsider' perspective on the manuscript; to Brian Diettrich, my Other half, both professionally and personally; and to our daughter Anneliese, for sometimes falling asleep to 'La captive'.

Introduction

> In a certain opera house of northern Europe, it is the custom among members of the orchestra, several of whom are cultivated men, to spend their time reading books – or even discussing matters literary and musical – whenever they perform any second-rate operas.
>
> Berlioz, *Evenings with the Orchestra*[1]

Reading Berlioz's *Evenings with the Orchestra* for the first time at a 'certain university' in the southern Pacific, I initially experienced no difficulty in engaging with its basic premise. Indeed, for a musicologist or orchestral musician, the subject position Berlioz assumes of his reader in northern Europe in 1852 is not difficult to adopt 150 years later on the other side of the world, in New Zealand, despite the historically and geographically encoded aesthetic assumptions this perspective entails. In *Evenings with the Orchestra* Berlioz presents his own music criticism as anecdotes recounted by the musicians of a fictional orchestra and overheard by the authorial persona, who engages in dialogue with the players and contributes additional stories of his own. By speaking directly to the orchestral musician, whose respect now – as then – Berlioz might count on having won through his compositions, he implicitly trusts the performer to share his own intelligence, taste, and understanding. Berlioz encourages his reader tacitly to concur with his distinctions between first- and second-rate works, between those individuals so powerfully moved by music as to die for it and those who applaud because they are paid to do so, and between the superficiality of music driven by ego or commerce and the magnificence of music that is seen to transcend such concerns. Where Berlioz's outlook might seem extreme and in danger of alienating the reader, he offers irony or acknowledges an element of exaggeration. Both the extremity and the irony are exemplified in the twelfth 'evening' of *Evenings with the Orchestra*, in which an ardent young man, reminiscent of Berlioz himself, commits a 'suicide from enthusiasm' over the music of Spontini. While such an act might seem

---

[1] Berlioz, *Les soirées de l'orchestre* (Paris: Michel Lévy frères, 1852), trans. Jacques Barzun, *Evenings with the Orchestra* (Chicago: University of Chicago Press, 1973), p. 5.

difficult to fathom, Berlioz acknowledges the improbability without wholly dismissing the possibility: 'Do you really believe such fanaticism possible?' the double bass player Dimsky asks, the evening after the story has been recounted in the pit; 'I don't believe it, but I've experienced it – often', is the reply.[2]

However, in the case of the final story of *Evenings with the Orchestra*, Berlioz's irony was insufficient to counter a jolt of alienation that thrust me completely outside the subject position I had adopted up to this point. The Second Epilogue of *Evenings* concludes with a story recounting 'The Adventures of Vincent Wallace in New Zealand'. While I had thus far recognised in Berlioz's orchestra and its (mostly) European world a precursor to my own musical experiences, the final story makes it clear that to Berlioz my homeland, New Zealand, was in every respect wholly foreign and Other, a land of cannibal warriors and alluring exotic maidens, threat and seduction, whose music is the complete antithesis of the European tradition represented by Berlioz, his fictional orchestra, and the Irish composer, Vincent Wallace, who enters this Other world.[3]

The fact that New Zealand in the mid nineteenth century was unlike Berlioz's Europe should not come as any surprise to a New Zealander. Indeed, the potential shock lies not so much in the setting as in the tone of the narrative, and what it assumes of its reader. In Berlioz's account, Vincent Wallace comes to New Zealand from Sydney to take part in a revenge attack on Māori.[4] After tricking a number of Māori into approaching their ship, Wallace and his fellow Europeans blow them 'sky high' with cannonballs, to shouts of 'God save the Queen'. The battle decisively won, Wallace goes ashore, where he is welcomed by the remnants of the tribe; he is worshipped by two young Māori girls, but his affections are inevitably drawn to the chief's daughter, Tatea, whom he eventually wins over with a keg of tobacco. After making love in the flax bushes and celebrating with a cannibal feast, Wallace is forced to leave this supposedly idyllic life when his ship returns

---

[2] Berlioz, *Evenings with the Orchestra*, p. 152.
[3] Although I capitalise 'Other', I intend no direct allusion to Lacan's 'Big Other', and draw more on postcolonialism and literary studies' 'turn to the other' than on psychological paradigms. Thomas Claviez, 'Done and Over With – Finally? Otherness, Metonymy, and the Ethics of Comparison', *PMLA* 128/3 (2013), 608.
[4] Berlioz actually uses the word 'New Zealander' rather than Māori, reflecting common usage at the time. Throughout this book I instead adopt modern practice and refer to the tangata whenua (the indigenous people of Aoteaora New Zealand) as Māori. In fact, this practice is itself anachronistic, as the tangata whenua did not identify as Māori but, rather, defined their identity through iwi (tribal) affiliations (as do many Māori today); but in the case of the Wallace narrative, the contradictory accounts of where he went within New Zealand make it difficult to establish which iwi he encountered.

to the bay. Tatea is distraught, carving her initial onto his chest in a form of tattoo, using the calligraphy Wallace has taught her. Wallace almost swims back to Tatea, but a chorus of 'Rule Britannia' aboard the ship gives him the requisite fortitude to sail onwards to 'civilisation'.

The flippant tone used to relate the attack on Māori and the exoticising sexualisation of their women are offensive, but Berlioz was aware of this and, as elsewhere in *Evenings*, he offers irony as a means of allowing his readers to distance themselves from the views expressed. Moreover, while the story is one of the few in *Evenings* that is attributed to Berlioz, rather than to one of his fictional orchestral musicians, he claims to have had it 'from Wallace himself',[5] and at times he interjects in the voice of his author persona to critique the attitudes assigned to Wallace. For example, when Wallace steps ashore after the massacre, Berlioz remarks: 'I must say [. . .] you both deserved to be roasted over a slow fire and eaten. Your folly and presumption are inconceivable!'[6] However, even allowing for irony, a subtly disturbing trace remains in the Wallace narrative, forcing the reader to question the subject position of the composer whose music (and, to some extent, aesthetics) are elsewhere so easily accepted as part of the western musicologist's or orchestral musician's broader cultural heritage. Berlioz uses New Zealand as a blank screen on which to project his own aesthetic outlook, safe in the assumption that his readers will view that screen from a perspective not so remote from his own. Such a position is clearly no longer tenable. The screen is not blank; it never was, of course, but now the projections shine onto readers who stare back at the phantasmagoric apparatus,[7] and what they see exposed is the assumptions behind the traditions of European art music itself.

In particular, Berlioz's Wallace narrative in *Evenings with the Orchestra* incites reflection on two ways in which western art music situates itself in the world. On one hand, Berlioz juxtaposes the world of his orchestral musicians against the exotic Other of remote New Zealand; but on the other hand, Berlioz implies that the great works in the repertoire of those orchestral musicians actually provide a means of imaginary transportation to Other worlds. Whereas New Zealand is defined by Berlioz in physical terms, as comprising places and bodies that can be conquered, seduced, or (as in the case of Wallace's tattoo) literally inscribed, the Other worlds of great art music are presented to us in *Evenings* as metaphysical ones. The chatter of the orchestra is silenced; no narrative is offered; the readers are told simply

---

[5] Berlioz, *Evenings with the Orchestra*, p. 366. [6] Ibid., pp. 369–70.
[7] On the phantasmagoria metaphor, see Chapter 3.

that the musicians are playing *Der Freischütz* or *Don Giovanni*, and if they wish to be transported with the musicians to those sublime realms they are left to construct the sights and sounds of the performance entirely in their heads. In other words, Berlioz's *Evenings with the Orchestra* sets up a relationship between great art music and exotic realms that is both complementary (each offers escape from the mundane reality of the present) and oppositional (the material, physical, and situated nature of exotic worlds – even if imagined – is juxtaposed against the metaphysical nature of the 'Other world' of western art music, envisaged as being beyond the physical altogether). While such distinctions are undoubtedly overdrawn, their tenacious legacy is still evident today, for example, whenever a division is made between western art music (or 'Classical music') and 'World music'.[8]

Of course, we do not need to read Berlioz's Wallace narrative to be critical of this mentality. 'Otherness' as a concept has been so well treated in the humanities as to appear almost hackneyed. And while my initial response to the Wallace story was as a New Zealander, the unease I have described is certainly nothing new to anyone who has confronted the possibility of racism in *Madame Butterfly*, the orientalism of *Aida* or the anti-Semitism of Wagner.[9] Although I am sympathetic to those who feel it is now time, as Thomas Claviez puts it, to 'lay to rest [the] spectral presence' of Otherness and alterity, I resist the return to 'sameness' or universalism that such a resistance implies.[10] Arguably race – the 'spectre in the house of music' long after it was confronted head-on in other disciplines, as Philip Bohlman and Ronald Radano pointed out in 2000 – is still not sufficiently acknowledged.[11] My approach is to historicise the concept of the racial Other in western art music by demonstrating how the dialectic between Otherness and universalism is germane to Berlioz's milieu, but I also broaden the definition of Otherness to encompass not only racial or ethnic identity, but also temporality and technology, as well as the supposed transcendence of western art music itself.

---

[8] Steven Feld, 'A Sweet Lullaby for World Music', *Public Culture* 12/1 (2000), 145–71. For more on the binaries of western music, see David R. M. Irving, *Colonial Counterpoint: Music in Early Modern Manila* (Oxford and New York: Oxford University Press, 2010), pp. 231–2.

[9] Roger Parker, 'One Fine Obscenity', *The Guardian*, 13 February 2007, www.theguardian.com/music/2007/feb/13/classicalmusicandopera.reviews, accessed 10 April 2014; Edward Said, *Culture and Imperialism* (New York: Random House, 1994), pp. 111–31; Marc A. Weiner, *Richard Wagner and the Anti-Semitic Imagination* (Lincoln: University of Nebraska Press, 1995).

[10] Claviez, 'Done and Over With', 608.

[11] Ronald Radano and Philip Bohlman, 'Introduction. Music and Race, Their Past, Their Presence', in *Music and the Racial Imagination* (Chicago: University of Chicago Press, 2000), pp. 1–45.

Particularly since the late 1980s, musicologists have been all too willing to expose, historicise, and deconstruct the ideological assumptions of western art music; both the paradigm that aligns western art music with remote Other geographic regions and the paradigm that locates such music beyond the physical world have been thoroughly interrogated. In the first category, studies of exoticism in western art music have examined the ways in which that music encodes thinking about Other peoples and places, not only in cases where the musical language conspicuously departs from 'unmarked' norms but also in those where it does not.[12] The all-too-close resemblance between Berlioz's telling of Vincent Wallace's narrative and the exotic opera plot archetype so vividly summarised by Ralph Locke reveals the significance of this body of literature to Berlioz's approach:

Young, tolerant, brave, possibly naïve, white-European tenor-hero intrudes, at risk of disloyalty to his own people and colonialist ethic, into mysterious, dark-skinned, colonised territory represented by alluring dancing girls and deeply affectionate, sensitive lyric soprano, incurring wrath of brutal, intransigent tribal chieftain (bass or bass-baritone) and blindly obedient chorus of male savages.[13]

Other musicologists have drawn on postcolonial scholarship, reception studies, or ethnographic work to consider ways in which Europe's supposed Others have themselves responded to this repertoire.[14] At the same time, the fundamental tenants of the most seemingly 'unmarked' western art music – even, or especially, works of the Austro-German instrumental canon – have themselves been subject to scrutiny.[15] In particular, Lydia Goehr's *The Imaginary Museum of Musical Works* revealed the extent to

---

[12] Ralph P. Locke, *Musical Exoticism: Images and Reflections* (Cambridge: Cambridge University Press, 2009).

[13] Ralph P. Locke, 'Constructing the Oriental "Other": Saint-Saëns's *Samson et Dalila*', *Cambridge Opera Journal* 3/3 (1991), 263.

[14] Bruno Nettl, *The Western Impact on World Music: Change, Adaptation, and Survival* (New York: Schirmer Books, 1985); Georgina Born (ed.), *Western Music and Its Others* (Berkeley: University of California Press, 2000); Radano and Bohlman (eds.), *Music and the Racial Imagination*; Mari Yoshihara, *Musicians from a Different Shore: Asians and Asian Americans in Classical Music* (Philadelphia: Temple University Press, 2007); Irving, *Colonial Counterpoint*; Irving, 'Others at the Opera: Emotional Responses of Non-Europeans to Music Drama in Early Modern Europe', paper presented at the annual conference of the Royal Musical Association, 19–23 September 2013.

[15] Susan McClary, 'Sexual Politics in Classical Music', *Feminine Endings: Music, Gender, and Sexuality* (Minneapolis: University of Minnesota Press, 1991), pp. 53–79; Nicholas Cook and Mark Everist (eds.), *Rethinking Music* (Oxford: Oxford University Press, 2001); Matthew Gelbart, *The Invention of 'Folk Music' and 'Art Music'* (Cambridge: Cambridge University Press, 2007).

which the timeless and universal pretensions of autonomous music were situated in a specific historical and geographical moment.[16]

In taking its cue from Berlioz's Wallace narrative and its telling in the pit of an imaginary orchestra, my primary purpose in this book is to interrogate Berlioz's conception of 'Other worlds' through a series of historically informed critical readings that uncover the tensions between the material and metaphysical realms in Berlioz's writings about and for the orchestra. I will be concerned not only with the complementary and contradictory relationships between western art music and Other worlds in and of themselves; rather, I am also interested in the ways those relationships shade into each other, in the tensions and ambiguities that arise as music is pulled between physical and metaphysical paradigms, and in the processes by which particular narratives became privileged.

Such issues have been addressed in a variety of ways by scholars in other contexts. For example, Vanessa Agnew has examined the role of travel and encounter – specifically the experiences of Charles Burney in Germany and James Cook (and Burney's son) in the Pacific – in redefining thinking about music's role, power, and universality and helping to shape thought around the work concept.[17] And Gary Tomlinson's work on *Music in Renaissance Magic* draws on anthropological methodology to 'approach Others' who were marginalised in the prevalent historical narratives of western art music.[18] Rather than focusing on racial alterity, Tomlinson's study locates Otherness in terms of the occult. Tomlinson thereby reflects a significant epistemological distinction between Renaissance and nineteenth-century thinking on Otherness, demonstrating that Renaissance thought is itself Other in ways traditional musicological scholarship had sometimes tended to overlook. Similarly, while studies of Otherness in nineteenth-century music have typically privileged the racial and ethnic difference that was a source of fascination in an age of increasing exploration, colonisation, imperialism, and tourism, musicologists have also uncovered ways in which

---

[16] Lydia Goehr, *The Imaginary Museum of Musical Works: An Essay in the Philosophy of Music* (Oxford: Oxford University Press, 1992; rev. 2007). Goehr's insistence on attributing the origins of the work concept to the social and contextual factors that clustered around the 'Beethoven paradigm', at the expense of earlier instantiations of the work concept, has laid her open to charges of imperialistic thinking of her own. See Reinhard Strohm, 'Looking Back at Ourselves: The Problem with the Musical Work-Concept', in Michael Talbot (ed.), *The Musical Work: Reality or Invention* (Liverpool: Liverpool University Press, 2000), pp. 128–52.

[17] Vanessa Agnew, *Enlightenment Orpheus: The Power of Music in Other Worlds* (Oxford: Oxford University Press, 2008).

[18] Gary Tomlinson, *Music in Renaissance Magic: Toward a Historiography of Others* (Chicago: Chicago University Press, 1993).

Otherness might be located in temporal terms. Indeed, nineteenth-century European thought aligned racial difference with temporality, by locating Europe's racial Others as occupying earlier stages on an evolutionary trajectory.[19] Additionally, Otherness in the nineteenth century (as in the Renaissance) can fruitfully be examined in relation to manifestations of supernatural or occult thought, which since the Enlightenment had been framed as reason's Other.

Berlioz's Vincent Wallace narrative is simply a final, and exaggerated, instance of the negotiations with a variety of forms of Otherness that occur throughout *Evenings with the Orchestra* and that are seen in Berlioz's writings more broadly. Berlioz readily explores Other worlds of the supernatural and of distant times, as well as distant places, and he does so in ways that might occasionally alienate modern readers, who are less accustomed to seeing our nineteenth-century ancestors as distanced from ourselves in the way we might with their Renaissance predecessors. Indeed, in exploring the 'Other worlds of Hector Berlioz', as with any historically inflected criticism, we are constantly reminded that just as the future, the supernatural, or New Zealand was Other to Berlioz, Berlioz's Paris is also Other to us.

A further way of exploring the sometimes contested nexus between the physical and metaphysical claims of western art music is found in the work of those scholars who have sought to give voice to the performers of this repertoire, for performers' perspectives and very presence had been similarly marginalised – or colonised – by an aesthetic which privileged musical autonomy and abstraction. Thus performer-centred perspectives have arisen in opera studies, where acknowledging the embodied creativity of the singer of Italian opera, in particular, has provided a powerful counternarrative to German metaphysics, sometimes drawing on feminist scholarship to acknowledge the gendered aspects of the familiar dialectic.[20] Alternative performer-centred models have been developed in relation to instrumental music. Elisabeth Le Guin explores a 'carnal musicology' that listens to and observes the modern performer's body (her own in particular) in dialogue with the (necessarily imagined) perspective of the

---

[19] Bernard McGrane, *Beyond Anthropology: Society and the Other* (New York: Columbia University Press, 1985), pp. 77–111; Rod Edmond, *Representing the South Pacific: Colonial Discourse from Cook to Gauguin* (Cambridge: Cambridge University Press, 1997), pp. 7–8.

[20] Mary Ann Smart, 'The Lost Voice of Rosine Stolz', *Cambridge Opera Journal* 6/1 (1994), 31–50; Carolyn Abbate, 'Opera; or, the Envoicing of Women', in Ruth A. Solie (ed.), *Musicology and Difference* (Berkeley: University of California Press, 1993), pp. 225–58; Michelle Duncan, 'The Operatic Scandal of the Singing Body: Voice, Presence, Performativity', *Cambridge Opera Journal* 16/3 (2004), 283–306; Clemens Risi, 'Opera in Performance – In Search of New Analytical Approaches', *The Opera Quarterly* 27/2–3 (2011), 283–95.

composer-performer Boccherini, and others have traced the importance of Liszt's or Paganini's physicality in their works.[21]

All these authors present powerful frameworks for considering tensions that underpin the process whereby western art music increasingly asserted its supposed independence from the concerns of the material or physical realm – the process whereby music moved from an alignment with physical worlds to one with metaphysical Other worlds. However, the focus of these texts is inevitably on individual performers (including composer-performers) and/or repertoire with prominent soloists. Berlioz occupies different territory. As a 'born virtuoso of the orchestra',[22] Berlioz's perspective was most obviously that of the composer or composer–conductor who oversees (and perhaps overrides) the individual subjectivities of the orchestral masses to unite them within his singular vision. Sceptical and at times downright hostile towards the aesthetics of Italian opera and the demands of divas and virtuosi, renowned primarily as a composer of instrumental music, and claiming to be three-quarters German,[23] Berlioz is not an obvious subject for an application of 'carnal musicology'. Indeed, Goehr cites Berlioz as an example of the privileging of text over performance, referring to his *Orchestration Treatise* (along with that of Czerny) as being 'written from a standpoint at which they were able to consider the complexities of instrumentation in abstraction from the demands and practical difficulties of actual performance', and alluding to the fact that Berlioz's Prix de Rome cantata on *Death of Orpheus* was declared unplayable.[24] But Berlioz's frustration on that occasion could also be interpreted as a sign of the opposite tendency – of an intense engagement with the materiality of the orchestra that was forced on this occasion to go unfulfilled, despite his conviction that his music *could* be played. Indeed, *Evenings with the Orchestra* tells a story subtly different to that promoted by Goehr, for it encourages us to view works, and Berlioz's musical aesthetic, through the eyes of the orchestral musicians, who are conceived as distinctive individuals. Those individuals

---

[21] Elisabeth Le Guin, *Boccherini's Body: An Essay in Carnal Musicology* (Berkeley: University of California Press, 2006); Dana Gooley, 'Warhorses: Liszt, Weber's "Konzertstück", and the Cult of Napoléon', *19th-Century Music* 24/1 (2000), 62–88; Jim Samson, *Virtuosity and the Musical Work: The Transcendental Studies of Liszt* (Cambridge: Cambridge University Press, 2003); Mai Kawabata, *Paganini: The 'Demonic Virtuoso'* (Woodbridge: The Boydell Press, 2013).

[22] Schumann, 'A Symphony by Berlioz', in Edward T. Cone (ed.), *Norton Critical Scores: Berlioz Fantastic Symphony* (New York: Norton, 1971), p. 243.

[23] Berlioz, *A travers chants* (Paris: Michel Lévy frères, 1862), trans. and ed. Elizabeth Csicsery-Rónay, *The Art of Music* (Bloomington and Indianapolis: Indiana University Press, 1994), p. 209.

[24] Goehr, *Imaginary Museum*, pp. 226–7, 231.

are silenced in the face of a masterwork, but Berlioz nevertheless gives us a sense of what it is that we must sacrifice for great art.

Certainly questions of agency and subjectivity in Berlioz's music are sometimes complex, but it is the claim of this book that the tension between a composer-oriented work concept and a performer-centred physicality is not only acknowledged but also actually *dramatised* as part of Berlioz's aesthetic vision. In this respect I might be seen to build upon recent studies of the orchestral body. For example, Emily I. Dolan has exposed the ways in which Haydn's music participated in an 'orchestral revolution', whereby the orchestra as an entity and the 'work' as a concept were actually interdependent. As Dolan points out, musicologists have been apprehensive of exploring the connection between the 'abundant materiality of the orchestra' and 'the notion of great musical works', for 'this inextricability of the orchestra from the "work" reverses the traditionally held values of the work concept. The great work is not ideal, but something immediate, sensuous, and bodily.'[25] Dolan positions Berlioz at the other end of this revolution: 'If the consolidation of the modern orchestra in the late eighteenth century liberated instruments, enabling composers to embrace their individual characters and expressive potential, the nineteenth century witnessed an attempt to circumscribe that freedom. To put it another way, Berlioz *re-instrumentalises the instruments of the orchestra*: they are obedient to his hand.'[26] If a new approach to Haydn's orchestra can thereby uncover the 'sensuous' and 'bodily' aspects of the orchestra, Dolan's language here suggests that Berlioz shifts the focus back to instruments as abstract entities, at the expense of the physicality both of the performers and of the instruments themselves – a suggestion this book will attempt to nuance.

Situating instruments in relation to technology opens up an additional, valuable line of enquiry and another potential form of Otherness: in Berlioz's era of accelerated industrial revolution and innovation, technology itself could be construed as exotic.[27] Moreover, technology intersects with – or is (in both senses of the word) instrumental to – all the Other worlds with which this book is concerned, as a powerful symbol of modernity, western civilisation, or masculine rationality against which a primitive, exotic, supernatural and/or female Other is juxtaposed, or through which that Other is contained. In exploring the role of technology, my book

---

[25] Emily I. Dolan, *The Orchestral Revolution: Haydn and the Technologies of Timbre* (Cambridge: Cambridge University Press, 2013), pp. 203, 202.
[26] Ibid., p. 219.
[27] Jeffrey Kallberg, 'Chopin's Music Box', in Artur Szklener (ed.), *Chopin's Musical Worlds: The 1840s* (Warsaw: Narodowy Instytut Fryderyka Chopina, 2008), pp. 89–202.

responds to a widespread growth of interest in the humanities in recent years in materiality rather than metaphysics – the 'material turn' which superseded the 'linguistic turn'.[28] This 'new materialism' has been eager to embrace 'the otherness of things'.[29] In terms of musicology, a number of scholars have steered a careful path through the risks of what Dolan warns can descend into 'weird musicology' in order to situate western art music in relation to contemporaneous technological paradigms, to 're-materialise' autonomous music and move 'beyond the *work*', or to validate the material dimension of maligned works whose reception was damaged by the rise of that aesthetic.[30] Berlioz, like Meyerbeer (a composer who has particularly benefited from this reevaluation), long suffered from being turned into Wagner's Other – not least of all by Wagner himself.

However, while I will repeatedly explore the concept of orchestra-as-technology in this book, I do not wish to lose sight of the bodies that wield that technology;[31] indeed, I argue throughout that the *sight* of the orchestra, as well as the negotiation between body and instrument, is integral to that same dialectic of Otherness which this book seeks to address. The ways in which the sights of the orchestra might either echo or obstruct the internal vision fostered by the instrumental ideal runs parallel to the similar negotiations of agency and subjectivity that attend the process whereby western art music positions itself in one world or an Other. And, on a larger level again, my book thus reinforces recent historiographical arguments that 'reassert the importance of the human' in the 'material turn'.[32]

While a number of concerns recur across the book, each chapter essentially examines the central dialectic between Berlioz's writings and music and Other worlds through an individual metaphor for the orchestra. Beginning with a close interrogation of Berlioz's Wallace narrative,

---

[28] Dan Hicks and Mary C. Beaudry, 'Introduction: Material Culture Studies: A Reactionary View', in Hicks and Beaudry (eds.), *The Oxford Handbook of Material Culture Studies* (Oxford: Oxford University Press, 2010), p. 1. On the importance of (material) 'presence' in the humanities, see also Hans Ulrich Gumbrecht, *The Production of Presence: What Meaning Cannot Convey* (Stanford: Stanford University Press, 2004).

[29] Bill Brown, 'Thing Theory', *Critical Inquiry* 28/1 (2001), 7, 12.

[30] Dolan, *Orchestral Revolution*, pp. 21, 20; Carolyn Abbate, 'Outside Ravel's Tomb', *Journal of the American Musicological Society* 52/3 (1999), 465–530; Cormac Newark, 'Metaphors for Meyerbeer', *Journal of the Royal Musical Association* 127/1 (2002), 23–43; Emily I. Dolan and John Tresch, 'A Sublime Invasion: Meyerbeer, Balzac, and the Opera Machine', *The Opera Quarterly* 27/1 (2011), 4–31.

[31] 'Why all the machines?' Carolyn Abbate asks, before pointing out how a focus on technology and mechanism at the expense of the 'drastic' elements of performance might mean 'relying on false Eros and synthetic carnality'; 'Music: Drastic or Gnostic?', *Critical Inquiry* 30/3 (2004), 528, 529.

[32] William Whyte, Review of *Oxford Handbook of Material Culture Studies*, in *The English Historical Review* 126/519 (2011), 514.

Chapter 1 focuses on the paradigm of travel writing. Through an exploration of the sources and critical ideology of Berlioz's account of New Zealand and other Pacific narratives, I directly confront Berlioz's attitude towards those geographically remote Others of my own world; I then explore ways in which that same ideology might be identified in Berlioz's treatment of the orchestra in his *Orchestration Treatise*, as well as in his song 'La captive', to identify how his distinctive conception of the orchestra *sui generis* positions his orchestral musicians as Others to be encountered and colonised.

Chapter 2 extends this image of colonisation by investigating military metaphors for the orchestra, revealing the imperial agendas characteristic of much exploration of 'Other worlds' – both musical and geographical. Orchestras were frequently likened to armies, and conductors to military generals. Berlioz himself employed military imagery when he toured Germany with his music in the early 1840s, likening his accounts of these endeavours to Napoleon's 'bulletins of the grande armée'. But Berlioz's metaphor raises key questions: given that Berlioz did not take an orchestra with him but instead had to 'conquer' local musicians each time he had his music performed, is it in fact the musical works themselves that represent his 'army'? And how do those works configure Berlioz's own role as military general (as composer or, especially, as conductor)? The two works examined in this chapter offer quite different answers to these questions. Berlioz's *Symphonie funèbre et triomphale*, originally written for a parading military band, provides a clear model of Berlioz writing for the orchestra in a literally militaristic manner, including ways in which music could be used to discipline minds and bodies, but in moving from the streets of Paris to the concert hall, Berlioz's fourth symphony also reveals some of the difficulties in reconciling physical space and imagined community within the musical work. By contrast with the overt militarism of *Symphonie funèbre et triomphale*, Berlioz's *Harold en Italie* (with solo viola) draws on models of subjectivity from Byron's poetic travel narrative and the Napoleonic legacy of the antihero to subvert the militaristic virtuosity typically associated with a soloist. But rather than forego military leadership altogether, Berlioz's second symphony shifts the focus to the composer's score and the new virtuosity of the conductor, which itself interacted with the military metaphor. Berlioz thereby positions the viola soloist at a significant juncture between assertion of individual physical presence and subservience to the composer's work.

Chapter 3 moves the focus from geographical Other worlds to the realm of the supernatural, examining how uncanny visions and ghosts were located on the margins between the physical and the metaphysical domains in ways that provide provocative paradigms for Berlioz's orchestral aesthetic. In

Berlioz's *Symphonie fantastique*, the orchestra is revealed to function similarly to the technologies of vision that were transforming how sight was constructed, thereby providing a new reading of the traditional discourse around the symphony's problematic programme and the accusations of materialism and Wagnerian phantasmagoria which it has long provoked. In contrast, in the ghost tale of his aborted opera, *La nonne sanglante*, Berlioz alludes to the operatic conventions associated with 'numinous intruders'; but his operatic supernatural is nevertheless vested in the orchestra in distinctive ways. The orchestra evokes technologies of disembodied communication such as the telegraph, employed in early séances, and the technological metaphor can be further enhanced by a consideration not only of the distinctive timbres Berlioz employs but also of the tactile experience of the players and the sight of the orchestra producing them. In both works, Berlioz's use of the orchestra thus not only reveals interconnections between the supernatural and psychological realms but also shows how narrow the gap was between the supernatural and the natural, the psychological and the physical, the sights of the orchestra or stage and the visions of the inner eye.

Chapter 4 similarly explores Berlioz's aesthetics of technology, but now from the perspective of temporality and, specifically, Berlioz's conception of the future; this chapter additionally addresses the roles of gender and genre in the technological Other. Set in the year 2344, Berlioz's novella *Euphonia* provides a potent illustration of these tendencies. This extended narrative from Berlioz's *Evenings with the Orchestra* exaggerates most explicitly the juxtaposition of Berlioz's own time between, on one hand, an idealised Germanic composer-centred tradition and, on the other, an Italianate idiom that emphasises what Berlioz perceived as an overemphasis on the singer's interests. Thus the female singer Mina seduces and then betrays two male composers before being crushed to death by the technology of a so-called orchestra piano. Berlioz's *La damnation de Faust* explores a similar dialectic of gender and genre; situated somewhere between symphony and opera, the work erases Marguerite's voice from its conclusion in order to privilege the orchestra and Faust himself (whose idiom is more 'symphonic'). While evoking the transformative impact of technology as associated with the future, Berlioz also anticipates and problematises the aesthetics of the so-called Wagnerian 'music of the future' that would overshadow his reception.

The fifth chapter introduces a final metaphor that connects Berlioz's orchestra and the concept of 'Other worlds': the exhibition, which – in another instance of the complex dialogue between the physical and metaphysical realms – intersects both with museum culture (whereby objects are displayed as symbolic of imagined histories) and with 'human zoos' (exhibiting living peoples). Berlioz was a judge of musical instruments at the first two international exhibitions in London and Paris in the 1850s. It was during and immediately after this period that he began to conceive his mighty opera, *Les Troyens*, in which Virgil's account of the fall of Troy, Aeneas's quest to found Italy, and the fates of Cassandra and Dido are infused with the imperial agendas enacted in the French and British exhibitions, and in the displaying of instruments as industrial or exotic objects. Taking its cue both from the exhibition metaphor and from the tableau structure of *Les Troyens* itself, the first half of this chapter assumes the form of a series of 'exhibits' recapitulating the orchestral metaphors of previous chapters to examine how the Other worlds of travel writing, military imperialism, the supernatural, and the technological and gendered dialectic of the future culminate in Berlioz's late opera, which repeatedly displays instruments in ways that evoke the exhibition context. The chapter concludes with an extended consideration of a different kind of exhibit: the performances of Indian dancers Berlioz encountered in Paris in the 1830s – veritable exhibits of a 'human zoo' – whom Berlioz thought to evoke in the Act IV ballets of his opera. Retracing this source of inspiration exposes conceptions of Otherness that are potent for the wider narrative of the work in performances to this day.

Finally, the Epilogue returns to Berlioz's Vincent Wallace narrative, which is revealed to anticipate aspects of the presentation of Otherness in *Les Troyens*. In both works, music serves alternately to exoticise the female love interest and to energise the male protagonist in specifically imperialistic terms. This connection between *Les Troyens* and the story told in Berlioz's Second Epilogue in *Evenings with the Orchestra* encourages a return to the self-reflexive mode of Berlioz's critical text. Where the orchestral musicians of Berlioz's 'civilised town' critique his narratives and juxtapose his stories against the works they perform, my book concludes by bringing Berlioz's narratives and music together. The Epilogue briefly examines how the music of Berlioz and of Vincent Wallace was subsequently employed as a 'civilising' force in New Zealand's colonial history, leading to an interrogation and reimagining of juxtapositions between Self and Other as manifested in western art music and a consideration of the implications of Berlioz's legacy today.

1 | Travels with the orchestra

Travel writing and Berlioz's *Orchestration Treatise*

> Where in Europe will you find this mysterious voice of a bird in love, whose secret murmuring made my whole being quiver with a new and fearful voluptuousness!
> Berlioz, 'The Adventures of Vincent Wallace in New Zealand'[1]

> [The orchestra] would evoke lamentation, murmuring, the mysterious sounds of virgin forests, it would sound the clamours, the prayers, the hymns of triumph or mourning of a people whose soul is magnanimous, whose heart is ardent and whose passions are fiery.
> Berlioz, *Orchestration Treatise*[2]

Berlioz ends *Evenings with the Orchestra* by regaling the musicians of his fictional orchestra with the improbable adventures of Vincent Wallace in New Zealand – an Other world he imagines populated with cannibals and seductive women. He begins his *Orchestration Treatise* with an introduction that situates the art of orchestration in historical context – as an Other world described as the 'Mediterraneans of music', which the composer must discover and then learn how to navigate.[3] Two different books; two different worlds; but connecting the two is the orchestra. In *Evenings with the Orchestra*, the orchestra is treated as a framework – or vessel – through which we explore Berlioz's diverse narratives. In contrast, in the *Orchestration Treatise* the orchestra is the destination itself. Indeed, in Berlioz's hands the orchestra is a world of delight and wonder awaiting the endeavours of the adventurous composer-explorer.

This chapter will extend the analogy between the orchestra and Other worlds by examining both Berlioz's accounts of foreign lands and his *Orchestration Treatise* through the lens of travel writing. Critical studies of European travel writing have revealed how the authors typically framed their accounts in ways that inform readers as much about their own culture

---

[1] Berlioz, *Evenings with the Orchestra*, p. 373.
[2] Berlioz, *Grand traité d'instrumentation et d'orchestration moderne* (Paris: Schoenberger; 1843/44, rev. 1855), trans. Hugh MacDonald, *Berlioz's Orchestration Treatise: A Translation and Commentary* (Cambridge: Cambridge University Press, 2002), p. 335.
[3] Macdonald, *Berlioz's Orchestration Treatise*, p. 4.

as about that of the Other. This self-reflexivity is apparent even – or especially – when the region explored is particularly remote. Thus, focussing primarily on Berlioz's account of New Zealand, as I do in the first section of this chapter, affords an opportunity to identify the ways in which Berlioz interacted with some of the central concerns of travel writing.

In the Vincent Wallace narrative Berlioz could not help but draw on the travel writing of other authors, since he had no personal experience of New Zealand. However, in writing of his own travels, also, Berlioz similarly echoes the intertextuality characteristic of travel narratives, and a brief examination of his accounts of his travels in Italy and the Germanic lands reveals how some of the key tropes of travel writing impacted on Berlioz's construction of societies closer to home. Questions of authorial voice and representation, scientific authority vs creative invention, conceptions of civilisation and barbarism, and evolutionary paradigms, all pertinent to accounts of those regions most foreign to Berlioz and his European contemporaries, are reframed in provocative ways in Berlioz's response to European countries, including his native France. Although Berlioz was widely read in travel writing, two authors in particular will be emphasised in this chapter – Dumont d'Urville and Alexander von Humboldt – as these two roughly contemporaneous explorers can be proven to have directly influenced Berlioz's writing in ways that are both contrasting and complementary.

In the final section of the chapter, I offer a critical reading of Berlioz's *Orchestration Treatise* to reveal how Berlioz treated the orchestra itself as a foreign destination. Berlioz gave his *Orchestration Treatise* an opus number, denoting the significance of the written text to his creative oeuvre. The primary mode of this chapter is thus textual criticism; I leave it to subsequent chapters to offer detailed instances of how Berlioz presents Others in musical terms. However, brief analytical consideration of two of Berlioz's songs that reference travel provides examples of how some of the points more specific to travel writing might translate into musical terms. For by viewing both Berlioz's Wallace narrative and his *Orchestration Treatise* in the context of travel writing, this chapter will examine the possibility that Berlioz's geographic and exotic Others are not always as remote from Corsino and his fellow European orchestral musicians in *Evenings* as Berlioz's narrative might encourage us to suppose.

Telling tales

Early in his *Memoirs*, Berlioz makes explicit that travel writing was one of his formative literary influences:

My interest in foreign countries, especially those in the other hemisphere, was whetted by reading all the books of travel, both ancient and modern, which I could lay hands on at home; and, had I chanced to live in a seaport town, I should certainly have run away to sea. My son has inherited my tastes. He is now in the navy, and I trust that he may distinguish himself in his profession.

Further acquaintance with La Fontaine and Virgil, however, caused my sea-dreams to pale before the beauties of poetry. The epic passion of the Latin poet first kindled my smouldering imagination.[4]

At its broadest, travel writing as a genre can encompass any text in which the author writes of, or from, an Other world that is foreign to the narrator and to his or her assumed reader. In his *Memoirs* Berlioz recounts how Virgil's *Aeneid* displaced 'sea-dreams' and love of travel writing in his youthful imagination, appearing to establish a juxtaposition between epic verse on the one hand and travel literature on the other. However, the *Aeneid* might itself be classed as travel writing, the Trojan hero's quest lending the additional Otherness of antiquity to those same 'sea-dreams'. Conversely, for Berlioz – who never travelled beyond Europe – travel writing of a more scientific nature about remote destinations was the stimulus for imaginary voyages that themselves could be laden with poetry. Nevertheless, while similar processes and ideologies can underpin even the most generically diverse forms of travel writing, in this book I will respect the distinction drawn by Berlioz, saving consideration of Virgil as well as of Byron's poetic travel narrative in *Childe Harold* for later chapters, and focussing in this chapter on travel narratives that fit into Berlioz's first category: accounts that are presented as factual, or whose rationale might be construed as primarily educational or scientific rather than literary or poetic. As we shall see, however, in travel writing science and poetry are often not easily separated.[5] Beginning with a consideration of the likely sources of Berlioz's narrative about New Zealand, including published accounts such as those he might have read as a child, as well as oral accounts by navigators who had travelled in the Pacific, we will see how Berlioz himself negotiated the ambiguous terrain between fact and fiction.

The first questions that arise in examining the nature of Berlioz's 'Adventures of Vincent Wallace in New Zealand' are ones of authorship, and these

---

[4] Berlioz, *Mémoires de Hector Berlioz* (Paris: Michel Lévy frères, 1870), annot. and rev. Ernest Newman, *Memoirs of Hector Berlioz*, trans. Rachel and Eleanor Holmes (New York: Knopf, 1932), pp. 6–7.

[5] See Casey Blanton, *Travel Writing: The Self and the World* (New York: Twayne Publishers, 1997), pp. 3–4.

questions in turn raise issues of appropriation and representation. Berlioz advised the fictional orchestra members of *Evenings* to 'Take [the details] for true, for I have them from Wallace himself, and he's much too lazy, in spite of his vagabond humor, to take the trouble of lying.'[6] Clearly Berlioz anticipated scepticism, and with good cause. While some scholars have assumed his New Zealand narrative is largely true, if embellished,[7] the story of the Irish musician who wreaks revenge on cannibal savages, goes ashore and romances the chief's daughter, and then answers the call of Queen and country to return to civilisation, accompanied by a chorus of 'Rule Britannia', sounds both implausibly exaggerated and suspiciously familiar. Indeed, Berlioz's narrative reads like the synopsis of an exotic fantasy that would seem most at home in the unabashedly implausible world of the opera stage – a world where Berlioz could regularly complain of violations of authenticity such as the presence of an organ in a Muslim temple ('c'est une faute de verité locale'),[8] a character with a 'comic' Alsatian accent in Russia, or window panes in Lahore.[9]

In contrast with the fanciful activities occurring on the stage, the preface to *Evenings with the Orchestra* appears to establish the sense and intellectual rigour of the orchestral musicians, who are closer – both literally and figuratively – to the composer-persona who eavesdrops on their conversations: they teach themselves English, and read the realist novels of Balzac, 'Dickens's enchanting pictures of social life', and, most significantly for this chapter, the first three volumes of Humboldt's *Cosmos* – a work which Humboldt described as '[t]he study of a science which promises to lead us over the wide range of creation', and which he suggested 'may be likened to a journey in a distant country'.[10] The stories the orchestral players tell each other in *Evenings* are mostly attributed by Berlioz to the players themselves, though the Wallace narrative takes the form of a letter Berlioz's authorial persona has supposedly sent to the orchestra to be read aloud by the musicians. Ultimately, of course, all the stories are his. The fact that Berlioz claims these texts are read by musicians *during* performances signals the exaggeration if not outright distortion of truth characteristic of the entire

---

[6] Berlioz, *Evenings with the Orchestra*, p. 366.
[7] Ibid., p. 366, n. 5; David Cairns, *Berlioz: Servitude and Greatness* (London: Penguin Books, 2000), p. 411.
[8] *Le Rénovateur*, 8 December 1833; *CM* I, p. 117.
[9] *Journal des débats*, 21 February 1854, p. 1; and 2–3 January 1861, p. 1.
[10] Alexander von Humboldt, *Cosmos: Sketch of a Physical Description of the Universe*, trans. Edward Sabine, 4 vols. (London: Longman, Brown, Green, and Longmans, and John Murray, 1847–58), vol. I, pp. 33–4.

premise.¹¹ Moreover, Berlioz introduces his orchestral characters in a list of 'Dramatis personae', implying that the activities of the pit are as much a dramatic fiction as the action on the opera stage.

However, if we simply accept the fictionalised aspects of Berlioz's premise we risk in turn obscuring more subtle and interesting questions of authorship. While many of the stories of Berlioz's *Evenings* had been published elsewhere under Berlioz's own name, the orchestral musicians to whom they are attributed in *Evenings* may have been based on particular individuals, and in some cases the stories could indeed have originated with them. Evidence of Berlioz's acts of appropriation can be found in the fourteenth 'evening' with the orchestra. Berlioz describes the third horn player, named Schmidt, as 'witty' and as one who 'can mimic like a professional comedian'. He attributes to Schmidt the story of 'A Visit to Tom Thumb', in which a provincial man is tricked into accepting that the generously proportioned individual before him (the singer Lablache, in Berlioz's account) is in fact the famous little person of the story's title, who supposedly assumes his full stature when he is relaxing at home.¹² A very similar anecdote was subsequently published by the horn player Eugène Vivier, whom Berlioz described as an 'ingenious trickster, an eccentric artist'.¹³ Vivier appears to have been somewhat annoyed by Berlioz's appropriation of his narrative, for the horn player prefaced his own publication of the anecdote with the words: 'Berlioz, having heard the following story being told, happily decided to reproduce it in one of his books, completely forgetting to name its author.'¹⁴ Such unattributed 'borrowings' are frequent in Berlioz's writings, but the Vivier case is symbolic, given that it is the 'voice' of an orchestral performer which Berlioz is appropriating. Berlioz dramatises Vivier as Schmidt and works the horn player's tale into his own literary fabric. As with Berlioz's use of the orchestral characters as mouthpieces for his own music criticism, this act of appropriation presents an apt metaphor for the process of orchestration itself, whereby the composer speaks through the performers in ways that necessarily curtail the authority of the individual performer-creator.

A different kind of question about authorship is to be found in the Wallace narrative. Berlioz attributes the details of the story to Wallace; he

---

11 Berlioz, *Evenings with the Orchestra*, p. 5.   12 Ibid., pp. 184–6.
13 Berlioz, *Mémoires* (Paris: Michel Lévy, 1870; reprinted Farnborough: Gregg International Publishers, 1969), p. 246.
14 E. Vivier, *De la Madeleine à la Bastille et, de là, chez Tom-Pouce* (Nice: J. Ventre, n.d.), p. 21. Did Berlioz learn his lesson? In the sequel to *Les soirées de l'orchestre* (*Les grotesques de la musique*, 1859), Berlioz allows Vivier to participate directly and under his own name in two anecdotes that he attributes to the horn player.

suggests they were then written in a letter from his authorial persona to the orchestra, and in this form read aloud by the violinist Corsino. However, in reality Berlioz appears to have constructed the Wallace narrative from unacknowledged additional sources of his own, and his authorial voice oversteps the role of mere editor.

Travel writing provides a useful paradigm for understanding Berlioz's approach to authorship in the Wallace story. In anticipating and addressing reader scepticism within the editorial frame, and urging readers to 'take [the details] for true', Berlioz was in fact employing a device common in travel narratives. Until the mid nineteenth century, creators of literary works did not themselves draw firm distinctions between their factual and fictional creations.[15] But authorial reliability was sometimes directly problematised in travel writing of a less literary nature. One such case is the so-called beachcomber genre, in which a European narrator (typically a man of somewhat questionable social status) goes ashore in a remote land, and, departing from the mores of his own society, 'goes native'. The beachcomber narrator's lack of institutional authority gives his narrative the appeal of raw immediacy but also invites anxiety around his potential unreliability.[16] Objectivity and credibility are typically restored through a framing scholarly editorial voice. Berlioz thus establishes Wallace as a 'beachcomber', positioning himself as the authoritative editor – though the beachcomber's liminal status as an outsider to his own society was one with which Berlioz himself might readily have identified.

So what exactly is 'true' in Berlioz's account of 'The Adventures of Vincent Wallace in New Zealand'? Addressing this question does more than merely satisfy positivist curiosity, for in unearthing the roots of the Wallace narrative in historical fact and fiction we learn about aspects of Berlioz's authorial process that are pertinent to his other writings also. Violinist and composer William Vincent Wallace (1812–1865), best known as the composer of the opera *Maritana*, was certainly a very well-travelled musician, having visited India, South America, Mexico, and the United

---

[15] See Tim Fulford, Debbie Lee, and Peter J. Kitson, *Literature, Science and Exploration in the Romantic Era: Bodies of Knowledge* (Cambridge: Cambridge University Press, 2004), pp. 4, 94.

[16] H. E. Maude, 'Beachcombers and Castaways', *The Journal of the Polynesian Society* 73/3 (1964), 254–93; Thomas Bargatzky, 'Beachcombers and Castaways as Innovators', *The Journal of Pacific History* 15/2 (1980), 93–102; Lydia Wevers, *Country of Writing: Travel Writing and New Zealand 1809–1900* (Auckland: Auckland University Press, 2002), pp. 92–3; I. C. Campbell, *'Gone Native' in Polynesia: Captivity Narratives and Experiences from the South Pacific* (Westport, CT: Greenwood Press, 1998); Susanne Williams Milcairns, *Native Strangers: Beachcombers, Renegades & Castaways in the South Seas* (Auckland: Penguin Books, 2006); Jonathan Lamb, 'History and Its Others', *The Journal of Pacific History* 42/3 (2007), 361–8.

States.[17] In 1835 Wallace travelled to Australia, where he earned the moniker 'the Australian Paganini'. He may indeed have visited New Zealand immediately after departing Australia: shipping records locate him on the ship *Neptune*, which docked in the Bay of Islands in New Zealand on 3 March 1838, en route for Valparaiso.[18] However, if Wallace did come ashore, it could not have been for more than eight weeks, and certainly not for the six months Berlioz suggests he spent in New Zealand, for there are records of Wallace performing in Chile at the beginning of June, just three months after he left Sydney.[19] The credibility of Berlioz's account is further undermined by an Australian newspaper report, which states that Wallace's motivation for coming to New Zealand was not, as Berlioz claims, to avenge a Māori attack on Europeans in New Zealand, but rather, to escape imprisonment for debt.[20]

Wallace himself may well have been the source of some of the untruths in Berlioz's account, for the evidence would suggest that, contrary to Berlioz's claim, Wallace was far from being 'too lazy [. . .] to take the trouble of lying'. In an interview with the New Orleans *Daily Picayune*, Wallace referred to spending four months in New Zealand (impossible, as we have seen). The obituary of Wallace written by his good friend Wellington Guernsey has Wallace twice narrowly escape death at the hands of the 'natives' – once on a whaling vessel and once when the chief's daughter pleaded his case. And an unpublished account left by Wallace's niece also suggests Wallace was involved with whaling, though this time the Māori girl nurses him through an unspecified illness rather than helping him escape death at the hands of her tribesmen.[21]

It is easy to imagine Wallace embellishing – or simply fabricating – stories of his travels as he and Berlioz spent what Berlioz describes as 'many a late

---

[17] Nicholas Temperley, 'Wallace, Vincent', *Grove Music Online. Oxford Music Online.* Oxford University Press, www.oxfordmusiconline.com/subscriber/article/grove/music/29838, accessed 10 April 2014; Andrew Lamb, *William Vincent Wallace: Composer, Virtuoso and Adventurer* (West Byfleet: Fullers Wood Press, 2012).

[18] 'Shipping Intelligence', *Sydney Herald*, 15 February 1838, n.p. The arrival of the ship in New Zealand is documented in Rhys Richards and Jocelyn Chisholm, *Bay of Islands Shipping Arrivals and Departures 1803–1840* (Wellington: Paremata Press, 1992).

[19] *El Mercurio* (Valparaiso), 4 June 1838, p. 3, refers to a performance by Wallace the night before. See also Kathleen Hellyar Myers, 'William Vincent Wallace: Life and Works', unpublished PhD dissertation, Bryn Mawr College (1980), p. 3.

[20] *Sydney Gazette and New South Wales Advertiser*, 17 February 1838, p. 2.

[21] Vincent Wallace, interview with *Daily Picayune*, 22 June 1842; Wellington Guernsey, obituary for Wallace, *The Musical World*, 21 October 1865; Annie de Meurant Mulligan, 'In Happy Moments', A1336 Item 19660, National Archives of Australia, Canberra, 1930. Mulligan's account will be revisited in the Epilogue.

night over a bowl of punch' in London,[22] and it may ultimately be impossible to know exactly what Wallace did when (or, indeed, if) he stepped ashore in New Zealand. This is likely to be a source of frustration to few people other than Wallace's own biographers or his descendants. However, there is evidence that at least part of the narrative was Berlioz's construction rather than Wallace's, and that Berlioz drew on several travel narratives of a more scholarly nature. This evidence has implications beyond the Wallace story itself, not only illuminating Berlioz's process in constructing his own travel narratives but also alerting us to the ideologies and approaches to travel writing that underpin his creative outlook more broadly. It is to this evidence that we now turn.

Sourcing the facts

The most compelling evidence for Berlioz having looked to other travel narratives when writing of Wallace's adventures is found in two passages in which Berlioz records words in what he terms the 'New Zealand language' (i.e., Māori). After Wallace has consummated his relationship with the chief's daughter Tatea, the two attend a cannibal feast at which Tatea sings to Wallace:

Tatea snuggled close to me, nonchalantly rested her head against mine, and sang into my ear, as if telling me a secret, three stanzas, of which this is the refrain; I shall never forget it:

> E takowe e o mo toku mei rangui
> Ka tai ki reira, aku rangui auraki.

(When you have reached the haven where you want me to go, my affectionate feelings will follow you.)[23]

As Andrew Lamb points out in his recent biography of Wallace, it is implausible that Wallace would have remembered 'the supposed benedictions in the Kanaki language'. Rather, it seems more likely that Berlioz was 'playing him at his own game' or, in words of particular resonance for this chapter, 'orchestrating Wallace's "Invitation to a Voyage"'.[24] The notion of a

---

[22] Berlioz, *Evenings with the Orchestra*, p. 367.   [23] Ibid., pp. 372–3.
[24] Lamb, *William Vincent Wallace*, pp. 29–30. While 'kanak' is an indigenous term for the people of New Caledonia, the term 'kanaka' denotes something of a stereotype, having been applied to labourers of Pacific origin on Australian plantations in the late nineteenth century. Berlioz reflects common usage in the nineteenth century, when the word could be applied to people of the Pacific more generally, or to the Hawaiian language specifically.

Māori girl singing to Wallace may have its origins in some actual incident (the girl in the account supplied by Wallace's niece also sings). However, unbeknownst to Lamb and Wallace's other biographers, the words of her song in Berlioz's retelling are lifted directly from a French text: the *Voyage de la corvette l'Astrolabe* by the French explorer Jules Sébastien César Dumont d'Urville.[25] While Dumont d'Urville appears to have had little direct impact on Berlioz's representation of Māori music, delving further into Dumont d'Urville's account of New Zealand reveals not only the ways in which his writings furnished details for Berlioz's imagining of that land but also ideological and formal aspects of travel writing that can be seen to frame both Berlioz's textual and musical representations of Others.

The song text appropriated by Berlioz from Dumont d'Urville was originally published in *A Grammar and Vocabulary of the Language of New Zealand*, compiled by the missionary Thomas Kendall and Professor Lee in 1820, but certain details of spelling and, in particular, the fact that Berlioz's French translation exactly matches that offered by Dumont d'Urville suggest that it was Dumont d'Urville's text that was Berlioz's immediate source. (See Table 1.1.)

Moreover, the text of the toast made to Wallace and the ship's surgeon at the cannibal feast is also taken directly from Dumont d'Urville's *Voyage de la corvette l'Astrolabe*. This text is not found in Kendall and Lee's *Grammar*, and Dumont d'Urville claims to have transcribed and translated the words himself when in New Zealand in 1824. The spelling of the Māori language is again almost identical, while the French translation in Berlioz's text simply replaces the third-person ('may *he* go well and be happy') with the second-person pronoun ('may *you* go well and be happy'), to suit his new narrative context. (See Table 1.2.)

Even if Wallace had dictated these particular texts to Berlioz from memory over a bowl of punch, the chance of the two musicians independently chancing on the same Māori spelling and French translations found in Dumont d'Urville's work is, to put it mildly, remote. Indeed, Dumont d'Urville himself comments on the approximate nature of the translation

---

[25] Jules Sébastien César Dumont d'Urville, *Voyage de la corvette l'Astrolabe*, 22 vols. (Paris: J. Tastu, 1830–1835). Few copies of *Voyage de la corvette l'Astrolabe* were printed, but an edition of the volumes comprising the 'Histoire du voyage' was produced by the publisher Roret in 1832–4, under the title *Voyage de découvertes autour du monde, et à la recherche de La Pérouse*. The content of *Voyage de découvertes* is identical to that of the first five volumes of *Voyage de la corvette l'Astrolabe* right down to the page numbering, and despite the different title should really be seen as an edition of the same text. Berlioz could have taken the Māori phrases from either source. Thus when I refer to *Voyage de la corvette l'Astrolabe* it should be understood to stand for both editions.

Table 1.1

Kendall and Lee (1820)[a]	Dumont d'Urville (1830–1833)[b]	Berlioz (1852)[c]
E takówe e ó mo tóku nei rángi,	E takowe e o mo tokou nei rangui,	E takowe e o mo tokou mei rangui
Ka tai ki reira, áku rángi auraki.	Ka tai ki reira, akou rangui auraki.	Ka tai Ki reira, akou rangui auraki.
When thou art arrived at thy intended port, my affections shall be there.	Quand tu seras arrivé au port où tu veux aller, mes affections y seront avec toi.	Quand tu seras arrivé au port où tu veux aller, mes affections y seront avec toi.

[a] Thomas Kendall and Professor Samuel Lee, *A Grammar and Vocabulary of the Language of New Zealand* (London: Watts, 1820), p. 107.
[b] Dumont d'Urville, *Voyage de la corvette l'Astrolabe*, vol. II, p. 504.
[c] Berlioz, *Les soirées de l'orchestre* (1852), ed. Léon Guichard (Paris: Gründ, 1968), p. 468.

Table 1.2

Dumont d'Urville (1830–1833)[a]	Berlioz (1852)[b]
Ko tinga na/hia ou we.	Ko tinga na, hia ou owe.
Puisse-t-il se bien porter,/être content.	(*Puisses-tu te bien porter, être content.*)

[a] Dumont d'Urville, *Voyage de la corvette l'Astrolabe*, vol. III, p. 683.
[b] Berlioz, *Soirés de l'orchestre*, p. 467.

of the second text, which he identifies not as a toast but as a baptismal blessing.[26]

Other relationships between Berlioz's account and Dumont d'Urville's *Voyage de la corvette l'Astrolabe* support the suggestion that Berlioz consulted Dumont d'Urville's work in preparing his account of 'The Adventures of Vincent Wallace in New Zealand'. In the *Voyage* Berlioz could have found details of Māori diet and cooking practices, canoes, and hongi (a form of greeting characterised by pressing noses and exchanging breath), as well as instances of cannibalism and the immolation of slaves.[27] In accounts printed within Dumont d'Urville's volumes, the crew of Dumont d'Urville's

[26] Dumont d'Urville, *Voyage de la corvette l'Astrolabe*, vol. III, p. 683.
[27] Citations of most of these topics are too numerous to cite individually, but on the immolation of slaves, see *Voyage de la corvette l'Astrolabe*, vol. II, p. 555.

expedition, like Berlioz, relate how women could be procured in exchange for gifts, and one describes the forcefulness of a Māori chief as he tries to persuade his reluctant young daughter to have sexual relations with a European – a possible model for the similar behaviour of Tatea and her father, as well as a signal of the potential for gendered aspects of Otherness common in the travel writing of male explorers.[28]

In Volume III of *Voyage de la corvette l'Astrolabe* Dumont d'Urville reproduces in French translation extensive sections from a number of mostly British sources relating to New Zealand. One of these is George L. Craik's *The New Zealanders*, which had only recently been published.[29] Craik's text presents an example of the beachcomber narrative: the story of the illiterate John Rutherford, who had lived in a Māori community for ten years, is framed by Craik's more scholarly editorial voice. In translating and incorporating Craik's text, Dumont d'Urville contributes his own additional editorial filter: in the preface to Volume III he makes claims typical of the editor persona, insisting on the veracity of the account and citing a certain roughness of style as evidence of the authenticity of its origins.[30]

The device of the editorial filter is found in 'The Adventures of Vincent Wallace', as we have seen, but the similarities between Dumont d'Urville's Rutherford narrative and Berlioz's account of Wallace in New Zealand extend well beyond this generic device. Both works relate the adventures of a European who falls under the protection of a Māori chief. Tellingly, in both accounts this Māori chief is called Emaï – Berlioz uses Dumont d'Urville's spelling of this name, which differs to that found in Craik's original ('Aimy'). And in both narratives the European marries the chief's daughter (the *two* daughters in Rutherford's case). Moreover, in both works the European cuts the buttons off his shirt and offers them to the chief's daughter (daughters). Similarly, the two accounts refer to a lack of jealousy amongst Māori women. Rutherford, like Berlioz, describes the killing and eating of a slave girl for a celebratory feast. Both detail the practice of Māori tattooing, and Rutherford, like Wallace, receives a tattoo on his chest.[31] While some of these details are the stuff of numerous exploration narratives, viewed together the sheer number of the parallels between Berlioz's narrative and Dumont d'Urville's *Voyage de la corvette l'Astrolabe* could make us wonder if Berlioz consulted any other source, and even whether there is any 'truth' in this story that emerged from Wallace himself.

---

[28] Ibid., vol. II, p. 257.
[29] George L. Craik, *The New Zealanders* (London: Charles Knight, 1830).
[30] Dumont d'Urville, *Voyage de la corvette l'Astrolabe.*, Preface to vol. III, p. 2.
[31] Ibid., vol. II, pp. 437, 266; and vol. III, pp. 739, 742, 749–50, 756, 764.

Berlioz knew Wallace, but we do not know what might have drawn Berlioz to Dumont d'Urville's hefty multivolume set – nor indeed how he came across it in the first place. Whether or not Berlioz ever met Dumont d'Urville in person, the explorer's name was certainly an evocative one to him. In 1842 Berlioz attended the navigator's funeral procession after Dumont d'Urville and his wife and son were, as Berlioz expressed it, 'so horrifically destroyed in the fire of the Versailles railway'.[32] The train crash gripped the public consciousness, and the funeral of Dumont d'Urville was a large-scale public event, laden with the sad irony that one of France's most famed explorers, who had several times circumnavigated the globe and explored Antarctica, had perished in a train just outside Paris.[33]

Berlioz may have accessed Dumont d'Urville's writings through other mutual contacts. As Berlioz mentions in his *Memoirs*, his son Louis entered the navy. To facilitate success in Louis's chosen profession, Berlioz employed two prominent figures in Pacific exploration as mentors: Admiral Jean Baptiste Thomas Medée Cécille and Captain Théogene-François Page. Berlioz met with each man several times in the years immediately preceding the construction of his Wallace narrative. Not only could Cécille and Page have given Berlioz access to Dumont d'Urville's texts, but also the two men may have inspired Berlioz with accounts of their own travels.

In the same year that Berlioz published his Wallace narrative (1852), he employed Admiral Cécille to act as Louis's patron. Cécille had himself captained his ship *Héroine* from Sydney to New Zealand's Bay of Islands in March 1838, two months after the *Neptune*, with Wallace on board, made the same trip. Whereas there is uncertainty about Wallace's experiences in New Zealand, we know beyond a doubt that Cécille encountered Māori directly, and indeed there are elements of Cécille's experiences that may have fed directly into Berlioz's Wallace narrative. While in New Zealand to document the success of various French whaling vessels in New Zealand waters, Cécille was sent to investigate a Māori attack on a French whaling crew in the Chatham Islands (six hundred kilometres southeast of the main islands of New Zealand) and to seek retribution. Further parallels with Wallace's adventures can be found in Cécille's use of tobacco to bargain with Māori, and in the way he disguised his ship as a 'dirty whaling ship' to enable him to approach the Māori without causing alarm. Similarly, in Berlioz's story the ship Wallace sails on is 'put into disorder' to 'give our

---

[32] *CG* II, p. 727.
[33] M. Matterer, *Notes nécrologiques et historiques sur M. le Contre-Amiral Dumont d'Urville* (Paris: Imprimerie Royale, 1842), p. 6.

frigate the appearance of a poor devil of a ship half disabled by a gale and no longer answering the helm'.[34]

The other maritime figure who supervised Berlioz's son, Captain (subsequently Vice-Admiral) Page, never went to New Zealand but he did play a significant role elsewhere in the Pacific. In the same year in which Berlioz published the Wallace story, Page arrived in Tahiti to take on the role of governor. Berlioz had hoped that Louis would accompany Page to Tahiti. Although this did not eventuate, Berlioz's thoughts were clearly with Page on this voyage even if his son was not. In what is ostensibly meant to be a review of a new *opéra comique* in the *Journal des débats* on 22 July 1852, Berlioz takes the opportunity instead to transport himself and his readers to Tahiti, as he imagines Page's arrival in that remote land.[35] In Berlioz's account, Page is greeted by two amorous young girls, the distant cousins, perhaps, of Meré and Moïanga, who follow Wallace 'like llamas'; moreover, Wallace, like Page, is described as using the 'Kanak language' to communicate with the 'native girls'.[36]

Barbarian ideology and civilising ideals

An investigation of the origins of the 'facts' of Berlioz's Vincent Wallace narrative reveals the complexities of Berlioz's claim that the details can be 'taken for true', and offers insight into Berlioz's process in constructing one individual story; but if we move beyond the facts to *the telling* of the facts, what begins to emerge is the agendas, ideologies, and themes that shape Berlioz's writings about Other worlds more broadly.

The travel narratives of Dumont d'Urville, Cécille, and Page must all be seen in the context of the official government business that their missions represented. In each case, the French navigator's presence in the Pacific inevitably framed indigenous peoples in the terms most amenable to the furtherance of French interests. Cécille's role in monitoring French whaling missions was of evident national purpose. Even more obviously, as governor of Tahiti, Page contributed to France's imperialist agenda. The newspaper *Messager de Tahiti* – established under Page's regime – reported

---

[34] See Caroline Cambridge and Peter Tremewan, 'L'affaire Jean Bart', *Canterbury Monographs for Teachers of French*, vol. 68 (Christchurch: University of Canterbury, 1998). Berlioz, *Evenings with the Orchestra*, p. 367.

[35] The story was reprinted in Berlioz, *Les grotesques de la musique* (Paris: A. Bourdilliat, 1859); trans. Alistair Bruce, *The Musical Madhouse* (Rochester, NY: University of Rochester Press, 2003), pp. 59–60.

[36] Berlioz, *The Musical Madhouse*, p. 59. Berlioz, *Evenings with the Orchestra*, p. 370. On the 'kanaka language', see note 24.

admiringly on the remarkable ease with which 'the [Tahitian] people bend their customs to our civilisation', watched over by the governor himself.[37] Similarly, Dumont d'Urville was serving his country when in New Zealand and in producing his account of his voyages he was in effect, writing for France – the *Voyage de la corvette l'Astrolabe* was, as the continuation of its full title states, 'exécuté par ordre du Roi'. In the 'Discours préliminaire' to the *Voyage de la corvette l'Astrolabe* Dumont d'Urville contextualises his account in relation to voyages since those of Columbus, but suggests that while earlier expeditions were often concerned with material gain and conquest, his own Pacific exploration reflects a more enlightened concern 'pour l'intérêt seul de la science et de l'humanité'.[38] Dumont d'Urville's purpose was thus ostensibly an extension of the same scientific humanism he noted admiringly in the accounts of Cook's voyages. However, Dumont d'Urville's description of the Pacific originates in the period where France was actively exploring the possibilities of trade, appropriation of resources, and actual colonisation within the Pacific, in direct rivalry with British concerns: British missionaries arrived in New Zealand in 1814, the French bishop Pompallier began promoting Catholicism from 1838, and whalers from both countries plundered the waters of New Zealand in the 1820s–40s. Dumont d'Urville's first voyage to New Zealand in 1824 represented the first time the French had gone ashore in that country in more than half a century, since the death in New Zealand in 1772 of the French captain Marion du Fresne and twenty-four of his crew at the hands of Māori – an event which had shocked France.

Dumont d'Urville's massive series needs to be seen in this wider context: it fulfilled his mission and made the remote region accessible to his readers – and employers – once more. He did not necessarily see the ultimate outcome of his voyages as the European colonisation of the lands he described. Indeed, Dumont d'Urville bemoaned the impact of British colonisation on New Zealand's Māori population and regretted the loss of local traditions. Nevertheless, his travel writing inevitably represents an appropriation of knowledge and a framing of the *idea* of Others that privileges the culture producing the texts. Dumont d'Urville effectively dictates the terms on which Berlioz represents New Zealand to his European readers. Berlioz's Wallace narrative mocks British imperialism ('The Union Jack flying at the mast produced on me the effect of Rinaldo's adamantine shield', Wallace claims, and Berlioz concludes with musings on the 'fanatical patriotism of

---

[37] *Messager de Tahiti*, 28 May 1854.
[38] Dumont d'Urville, *Voyage de la corvette l'Astrolabe*, vol. I, p. i.

the English'),[39] and Berlioz attributes the story's most problematic ideology (the grotesque pleasure of the Europeans when their superior weaponry brutally suppresses Māori resistance) to Wallace. But Berlioz himself enacts an intellectual colonisation through writing, whereby Māori become representatives of Europe's Other, with all the attendant appeal and threat, outdoing even the exoticism of the opera stage.

Anxieties over engagement with foreign peoples were also manifested in ideological discourse about the relationship between civilisation and barbarism. Civilisation could be presented as the ideal telos to which the supposedly barbaric or primitive Other can aspire to evolve, with assistance from, for example, enforced missionisation and subsequent colonisation.[40] But colonial domination over indigenous peoples was sometimes also perceived in negative terms as a process of degeneration from an idealised natural state. Indeed, as Rod Edmond points out, writings about the history of the Pacific region have tended to rehearse a periodised narrative.[41] According to this literature, admiration of the 'natural wisdom' of supposed savages and questioning of the 'civilized barbarity' of European culture (as in Diderot's 'Supplément au voyage de Bougainville') is succeeded by the quest to redeem the souls of the heathen populations. Finally, in the mid nineteenth century, the colonists begin to display regret for the loss of indigenous practices, at which point the 'fatal impact' theory takes hold. The explorer or travel writer could therefore seek to present and preserve colonised culture as initially encountered, though this mentality, too, was not without its problems, for it could freeze a living culture in an eternal and increasingly distant past, overlooking the dynamic ways in which indigenous peoples adapted to, mimicked, or challenged the culture of the colonists on their own terms.[42] This approach was evident when Dumont d'Urville made analogies between Māori and the heroes of Classical antiquity: though Dumont d'Urville (like Rousseau, Diderot, and countless others before him) considered his analogy to be a compliment, in subscribing to the trope of locating in New Zealand the 'cradle' of civilisation, Dumont d'Urville reveals that Māori resemble his readers only insofar as they represent an evolutionary infancy.[43]

---

[39] Berlioz, *Evenings with the Orchestra*, pp. 374, 375.
[40] Robert J. C. Young, *Colonial Desire: Hybridity in Theory, Culture and Race* (London: Routledge, 1995), p. 32.
[41] Edmond, *Representing the South Pacific*, pp. 8–15.
[42] James Clifford, *The Predicament of Culture: Twentieth-Century Ethnography, Literature, and Art* (Cambridge, MA: Harvard University Press, 1988), pp. 4–5, 16–17.
[43] On other instances of Classical analogies, see Irving, *Colonial Counterpoint*, p. 77; Bernard Smith, *Imagining the Pacific: In the Wake of the Cook Voyages* (Hong Kong: Melbourne University Press, 1992), p. 213.

A related outcome of the idealisation of the Other was to invert the primary paradigm and locate barbarism in one's own culture, reflecting the 'necessary interdependence and entanglement between civilization and barbarism in the mutually defining opposition that is supposed to set them apart'.[44] This was a sentiment expressed repeatedly in Berlioz's writings, particularly where he perceived commercial interests ruling over artistic ones:[45]

> I belong to a nation which has ceased to be interested in the nobler manifestations of intelligence, and whose only deity is the golden calf. The Parisians have become a barbarous people [...] The industrialism of art, followed by all the base instincts it flatters and caresses, marches at the head of an absurd procession, full of stupid disdain for its vanquished enemies.[46]

The 1848 revolution provoked an increase in the frequency of Berlioz's fantasies of leaving the 'barbarism' of Paris for idealised remote or exotic lands: he spoke of 'homesickness for distant lands', and of a desire to 'flee the old continent, to live with naïve and primitive savages', to undertake 'distant, very distant voyages', and to 'flee to the other hemisphere from this old, mad, cunning, enraged and stupid Europe, which I feel myself detesting heartily'.[47] This mentality is apparent in the Wallace narrative, with its exploration of competing conceptions of civilisation and barbarism, old world and new. It is the inferior opera on the stage, from which the orchestra of *Evenings* so desperately seeks diversion, that is barbaric, Berlioz implies, and he concludes his narrative by condemning Wallace for not returning to New Zealand but instead making money out of 'drawing-room compositions' in America, 'among people who are sunk in the deepest civilization'.[48]

Berlioz's attitudes to the relationship between barbarism and civilisation are also illustrated though his various writings about Tahiti. Berlioz often depicts Tahiti as a country of imaginative escape and release for the jaded critic, as in the account of Captain Page's arrival in Tahiti – a narrative which conveniently enables Berlioz to forestall discussion of the latest *opéra comique* by several columns.[49] The critic's duty of reviewing such

---

[44] Young, *Colonial Desire*, p. 32.
[45] Cécile Reynaud, 'Berlioz et l'Europe', in Alban Ramaut (ed.), *Hector Berlioz: Regards sur un dauphinois fantastique* (Saint-Étienne: Université de Saint-Étienne, 2005), p. 175.
[46] Berlioz, *Memoirs*, pp. 472–473. For a more detailed account of Berlioz's sentiments in 1848, see Peter Bloom, *The Life of Berlioz* (Cambridge: Cambridge University Press, 1998), pp. 117–22.
[47] CG III, pp. 654, 644, 721, 654.   [48] Berlioz, *Evenings with the Orchestra*, p. 376.
[49] *La croix de Marie* (with a libretto by Lockroy and Dennery and music by Maillart). The review was published in the *Journal des débats* on 22 July 1852 and the Tahitian section was subsequently reused in *Les grotesques de la musique*.

performances puts him in the position of the slave. The slave is a powerful symbol of Otherness whose individual subjectivity is suppressed to the point that he or she can be considered the property of another; but in Berlioz's account (as in the views of the abolitionists more generally) it is implicitly the slave-driver, not the enslaved, who is barbarous.[50] Berlioz makes this critique quite explicit, and attributes it to Page:

Monsieur Page sits on the starboard side of his ship and gazes at the wonderful view of this earthly paradise, where he is to live and rule for some years. He breathes in the intoxicating warm breeze which wafts from it, drinks from a fresh young coconut, and says, 'To think that in Paris at this moment the temperature is [35] degrees, and people are just entering the Opéra-Comique, where they'll stay cooped up until one o'clock in the morning to find out whether Pierrot will end up marrying Pierrette, to listen to the two little ninnies bawling their love to the accompaniment of a bass drum, and to be able to inform some newspaper's readers on the next day but one of the difficulties overcome by Pierrette in order to marry Pierrot! What rabid anti-abolitionists these newspaper proprietors are!'[51]

The same device – and the same destination – had been employed by Berlioz as early as 1840. In a review of another work at the Opéra-Comique, Berlioz describes Tahiti as an exotic paradise where weary Europeans should be able to go to escape from civilisation and seduce Queen Pomare.[52] Queen Pomare was a subject of great interest to the French at the time, and Berlioz's use of the image of seduction is significant, given that the competing attempts of the French and the British – the latter most commonly represented by the Anglican missionary George Pritchard – to win Pomare's political favours could be described as the attentions of rival suitors.[53] Elise Sergent, a prostitute described as having 'l'air sauvage', and who enjoyed a brief but sensational celebrity as a dance-hall personality in the early 1840s, went by the name 'la reine Pomaré', with her dance partner being dubbed Pritchard.[54] The French bid for Tahiti was ultimately the successful one, but Pritchard lived on – in person and in the French popular imagination – for some time. Berlioz uses the missionary Pritchard as an image of negative civilisation, depicting him as one who imposes puritanical morals – and

---

[50] Philip Gould, *Barbaric Traffic: Commerce and Antislavery in the 18th-Century Atlantic World* (Cambridge, MA: Harvard University Press, 2003), pp. 26–7, 30, 45.
[51] Berlioz, *Musical Madhouse*, p. 60.
[52] *Journal des débats*, 28 February 1840, p. 1; *CM* IV, p. 268.
[53] 'Les lamentations de Pritchard', *Charivari*, 19 August 1844, pp. 1–2.
[54] Tristan Rémy, *Elisa Sergent (La Reine Pomaré): Descendante des Franconi, amie de Baudelaire (1825–1847)* (Paris: Cirques, 1958), p. 11.

clothing – on the natural pleasures of the Tahitian paradise.[55] Indeed, for Berlioz, Tahiti's status is from the outset one of paradise jeopardised, if not quite paradise lost. His references to Queen Pomare become increasingly unflattering, perhaps fed by reports from Page. Thus by 1854 (two years after Page's arrival as governor), we hear from Berlioz of 'the massive Queen Pomaré growing ever fatter in her hut' – a reminder of how exotic fantasy could be eroded by having too much information about the Other.[56]

Revoicing the Other: The journey of a song

Although Berlioz does not derive details of Māori musical practices from Dumont d'Urville, the fraught nature of actual European engagement with the peoples of the Pacific, and the implications of this relationship for Berlioz's musical aesthetic, become apparent when we consider in more depth the journey of the Māori song Berlioz incorporates into his Wallace narrative. The first to transcribe the text was Thomas Kendall, who had arrived in the Ngāpuhi tribal region in the north of New Zealand in 1814 as one of the earliest missionaries sent to 'civilise' the Māori. The missionaries were naïve, and ill prepared for the formidable task they had set themselves.[57] To convert Ngāpuhi to Christianity, Kendall thought that it was first necessary to understand their language and culture from within; but isolated from the social and cultural structures that generated his Christian faith, Kendall found his own worldview increasingly jeopardised. In 1822 he took as a lover the daughter of a chief, and he became engrossed in Ngāpuhi spirituality. Though his Māori lover (like Tatea) was eventually forsaken, Kendall was nevertheless excommunicated, and was forced to leave New Zealand, confused and disillusioned.

Kendall's conversion to the Christian mission had begun when he heard the singing of psalms issuing from the open door of an evangelical church in London. In New Zealand, music was to be part of the process by which that same faith would be threatened, as Kendall revealed in a letter of 1818:

Time passes swift with me. I have been now nearly six years absent from my Native Land ... and during the last four years my eyes have been constantly fixed on scenes of human depravity and woe, and my ears have listened to, and been partly infected

---

[55] Berlioz, *Musical Madhouse*, p. 59. See also *Journal des débats*, 17 November 1849, p. 1, 13 November 1852, and 6 September 1854, as well as the review of 22 July 1852 and 'Diplomatic Correspondence', already cited.

[56] *Journal des débats*, 6 September 1854, and Berlioz, *Musical Madhouse*, p. 61.

[57] Judith Binney, *The Legacy of Guilt: A Life of Thomas Kendall* (Wellington: Bridget Williams Books, 2005).

with the profane and obscene rubbish contained in the heathen *Songs*. The latter I am under the necessity of attending to: For it greatly assists me in Learning the language, by writing down the themes of the natives, and studying their true meaning. The study is painful, and like the Study of the Metamorphoses of Ovid tends to injure the mind.[58]

Kendall's letter generates a number of polarities: not merely Self and Other, but also text and music, spirituality and sensuality, mind and body. In each case, Kendall implies that the integrity of the first concept is jeopardised by the second – sensual music enters via the ear to infect the mind and threaten the soul of the Christian missionary. While similar polarities frame many responses to music within European thought across the ages, Kendall's letter is helpful in highlighting ways in which responses to Europe's 'antipodean' Others could contribute to the terms of that discourse. Berlioz's own attitude to this polarity is made evident in his *Memoirs*: music is powerful because it 'speaks at once to the imagination, the mind, the heart, and the *senses*; and it is the reaction of the senses on the mind and heart, and *vice versa*, that produces the impressions felt by those who are gifted with the necessary organization, but of which *others* (the barbarians) can know nothing.'[59]

Two years after penning the letter cited above, Kendall sailed with two Ngāpuhi chiefs to England where they worked with Professor Lee of Cambridge University to produce *A Grammar and Vocabulary* – the first attempt to systematise the Māori language. The song text used by Berlioz is found in this volume, where it is accompanied by an English translation but presented without commentary, and with no reference to the musical features of the song. Reduced and codified as text, the song appears here as a tool for future missionaries and other visitors to help them apprehend the language, in the interests of their own cultural or religious goals.

When Dumont d'Urville takes up Kendall's text, he strips it of any remaining residue of its originating cultural milieu. Not a man likely to be 'infected' by music of any description (biographers note his puritanical upbringing and 'resistance to fine manners, the pleasures of society, conversation, music and dance'),[60] Dumont d'Urville presents the song text in a chapter laden with a full scholarly apparatus of footnotes, drawing heavily on the information provided by published accounts of previous explorations of New Zealand, and attributing this particular text to Kendall's *Grammar*.

---

[58] Ibid., p. 66. Emphasis in the original.   [59] Berlioz, *Memoirs*, p. 443. Emphasis in the original.
[60] M.- R.- P. Lesson, *Notice historique sur l'amiral Dumont d'Urville* (Rochefort: Henry Loustau et Cie., 1846), p. 8; Camille Vergniol, *La grande légende de la mer: Dumont d'Urville* (Paris: La Renaissance du Livre, 1930), p. 37.

Moreover, Dumont d'Urville's fleeting description of Māori music shelters him and his readers from possible threats of what Kendall termed 'infection' with a double negative: Māori music in general is, Dumont d'Urville writes, 'not lacking in harmony nor in inventiveness'.[61]

In its passage from the man of faith, to the man of science, to the man of art, this one Māori song becomes a symbol of European colonisation, anticipating the official colonisation of New Zealand, which began in the 1840s. In Kendall's and Dumont d'Urville's hands the recording of the song text represents the appropriation – and hopeful containment – of a Māori Other. Berlioz then takes the same seductive song and adapts it to a new purpose, the polarities of mind and body, Self and Other, sensuality and spirituality being reenacted on his own terms:

Where in Europe will you find this mysterious voice of a bird in love, whose secret murmuring made my whole being quiver with a new and fearful voluptuousness! What warblings of the harp can imitate it? What delicate web of upper harmonics can give an idea of it? And the sad refrain in which Tatea, associating by a strange whim the expression of her love with the thought of our separation, spoke to me of the far-off haven to which her affectionate feelings would follow me –

Beloved Tatea! Sweet bird! While singing like an Indian finch under the foliage at noon, she was with her left hand twining a long tress of her beautiful black hair about my neck, and with her right toying with the knuckle-bones of the slave's foot that she had just eaten. An enchanting blend of love, childishness, and reverie. Did the old world ever suspect such poetry? Shakespeare, Beethoven, Byron, Weber, Moore, Shelley, Tennyson, you are merely rough men of prose![62]

By the time Berlioz's story is read, the real woman who sang to Kendall – assuming there was one – has been silenced by three layers of European representation and construction. Placed in the mouth of a young Māori woman whose thoughts will follow her European coloniser on his journey back across the globe, the song now defines a European cultural identity by providing its antithesis: Tatea's song is described in terms of natural imagery, as birdsong. Berlioz refers to her 'enchanting [. . .] childishness', suggesting how he, like Dumont d'Urville, positions the Other as a less evolved version of the self. Tatea is also framed in terms suggestive of the Aeolian harp – the

---

[61] Dumont d'Urville, *Voyage de la corvette l'Astrolabe*, vol. II, p. 503. Dumont d'Urville footnotes this description with a reference to the account of Cook's first voyage, but it is now commonly believed that Māori did not sing in harmony during this period and that references to singing 'in parts' refer either to form or to 'faults'. See Mervyn McLean, *Maori Music* (Auckland: Auckland University Press, 1996), p. 34.

[62] Berlioz, *Evenings with the Orchestra*, p. 373.

upper harmonics stirred by the wind. The Māori woman is thus depicted as a musical instrument, stripped of human agency; she is a sounding body channelling nature's music rather than creating music of her own. However, while giving in to 'voluptuousness' is imagined as a source of pleasure for the listener, the reader is also prevented from falling too heavily under Tatea's spell and being seduced by Māori music, for Berlioz casually throws in a reference to the one thing no European could stomach: cannibalism. Tatea, we understand, is ultimately an exotic diversion, and her seductions cannot fully persuade Wallace – or his presumed readers – to give up the 'old world'.

'To the Pacific Ocean?' – the Pacific in Berlioz's music

While many of Berlioz's works are set in foreign lands, it is in vain that we look for an extended *musical* representation of the fascination with the Pacific evident in his Wallace narrative and his references in numerous columns to Tahiti. Perhaps Berlioz shared the view of Gautier, who commented that Tahiti was not an appropriate subject for the Parisian stage, for 'savages are not a success at the Opéra.'[63] It is the argument of this chapter that a consideration of Berlioz's *writing* about New Zealand might illuminate his music in subtle ways, in terms of revealing significant themes in Berlioz's attitudes to those he considered Other. Nevertheless, it is fruitful to give brief consideration to the two musical items in his oeuvre whose texts reference the Pacific.

The only overt reference to the Pacific in Berlioz's published music is in a line in the song 'L'île inconnue' – the final song of Berlioz's cycle *Les nuits d'été*, with texts by Gautier: 'Say, young beauty, where do you wish to go?' the narrator asks,

Is it to the Baltic?
To the Pacific Ocean?
To the island of Java?
Or is it in fact to Norway,
To gather the flower of the snow,
Or the flower of Angsoka?

The Pacific in Gautier's poem is one of several remote regions to which the narrator offers to transport the young woman, but the real destination (the 'unknown island' of the title Berlioz attached to the song) is the metaphorical

---

[63] Gautier, 'Opéra: *Ozaï*' *La Presse*, 3 May 1847. Quoted in *Gautier on Dance*, trans. and ed. Ivor Guest (London: Dance Books, 1986), p. 178.

Ex. 1.1 'L'île inconnue', bb. 62–81

'land of faithful love'. Like Gautier (who actually titled the poem 'Barcarolle', denoting a Venetian setting), Berlioz does nothing to make the Pacific a meaningful destination in its own right within the song: as seen in Ex. 1.1, the reference to the Pacific Ocean is set to an exact repeat of the previous phrase referring to the Baltic, and if the syncopated drone and string flourishes that punctuate each line are exotic markers (as might be implied by the return to harmonic momentum with the reference to the relatively familiar Norway), they thus reinforce a kind of generic Otherness. Certainly there is no evidence here of the scientific and philosophical curiosity Berlioz extended to his literary evocations of the Pacific.[64]

[64] Musical examples from Berlioz's works are adapted from *NBE*.

Fig. 1.1 'Salut matinal'. Reproduced from Jacques Barzun, *New Letters of Berlioz 1830–1868* (New York: Columbia University Press, 1954).

We might well imagine that the satirising irony of Berlioz's Pacific narratives would not have translated well into musical terms, while his simultaneous element of idealising fantasy would have been severely challenged had he attempted to replicate actual Pacific music. However, both the irony and the aural Otherness do find a place in the one instance in which Berlioz might be seen to attempt to suggest a Pacific sound: the 'Salut matinal' or, to give it its full (translated) title, 'Morning greeting improvised in the Kanak language and music by Hector Berlioz, master of the chapel of her gracious majesty, Aimata Pomaré, Queen of Tahiti, Eimeo [Moorea], Ouaheine [Vahine], Raiatea, Bora-Bora, Toubouai-Manou [Tubuai] and other islands, for the album of Mr Mendès, white man of Europe.' (See Fig. 1.1.)

The 'Salut matinal' is a mere seven-bar snippet Berlioz wrote into someone's album; moreover, the album has been lost and we cannot know for certain who Mr Mendès was, or when the 'Morning greeting' was written.[65] The text contains recognisable Tahitian words and could have been patched together or transcribed intact from some yet-to-be-identified source in travel writing. However, in musical terms it is really only the final note that

---

[65] Jacques Barzun, *New Letters of Berlioz 1803–1868* (New York: Columbia University Press, 1954), after p. 41; Peter Bloom, 'Introduction', *Cambridge Companion to Berlioz* (Cambridge: Cambridge University Press, 2000), pp. 1, 269 n. 1.

signals a possible attempt to evoke a foreign musical language. After six bars of relentlessly diatonic melody the sudden leap down a tritone to the accented $b^\flat$ is presumably a primitivism intended for comic purposes as much as an effort to capture an authentic Tahitian idiom. The tritone leap is the musical equivalent of the juxtaposition between the impressively long list of the possessions of 'her gracious majesty, Aimata Pomaré' and the final blunt mention of 'Mr Mendès, white man of Europe', and it represents another of the typical inversions we find in Berlioz's writings, whereby the Other (here Tahiti) is viewed as civilised and one's own society becomes barbaric. Alternatively – and depending when it was penned – the abrupt tritone could equally suggest the disillusionment that eventually tainted Berlioz's Tahitian fantasy. Further complicating the reading of the 'Salut matinal' is the possibility that the 'reine Pomaré' of Berlioz's dedication is not that Tahitian Queen but the prostitute Elise Sergent who appropriated her name; but in that instance the circumstances of the 'morning greeting' to the 'tayo' (friend) are perhaps best left obscure.[66]

For Berlioz, Tahiti (like New Zealand) was largely employed as a device to satirise European music, as is clear in a supposed letter written to Queen Pomare in pidgin French, which Berlioz published in a feuilleton of 1855 (and which he subsequently reprinted in *Les grotesques de la musique*). In an affectionate final gesture to Page, whose term in Tahiti had recently drawn to a rather uncomfortable close, Berlioz playfully intimates that the Queen enjoyed playing cards and drinking with the 'great, handsome (though French) captain who commanding [sic] Protectorate three years ago'.[67] The letter is interlaced with Tahitian words Berlioz may well have gleaned from Page (including 'tayo'), and the composer sets up his authorial persona as having an understanding of Tahiti superior to that of his fellow judges, including knowledge of Queen Pomare's proclivity for cigars – another possible model for Tatea's taste for tobacco?[68]

Berlioz's letter to Pomare is really a satire directed at the judging process of the 1855 International Exhibition. The judges of (European) musical instruments resist all attempts to bribe them, only to have their fair and informed decisions temporarily overturned on dubious grounds by the judges of other categories of objects. Berlioz's disillusionment becomes associated with France itself ('we again very irritated, upset, wanting get away from France and Exhibition').[69] The judges reconcile, and Berlioz's group in turn is called upon to endorse the judging of clubs, skirts, canoes, mats, and

---

[66] Bloom, *Cambridge Companion to Berlioz*, pp. 1–2.
[67] Berlioz, *Musical Madhouse*, p. 39.   [68] Ibid., p. 39.   [69] Ibid., p. 37.

crowns from Tahiti, leading to much speculation among the judges about Tahiti and the Queen whose crowns of arrowroot bark have been awarded the silver medal. The resulting contrasts and inversions of civilisation and savagery in a Pacific context will, by now, be familiar ones. What is of particular interest in this case is the way in which Berlioz specifically draws musical instruments into the discourse. The provocative juxtaposition in the letter between the natural produce of the colony and European instrumental technology reflects an ethos characteristic of the international exhibitions that I will explore in Chapter 5. In the second half of this chapter, the focus is instead on a different way in which the framing devices of (Pacific) Others encountered in this section can be applied to the discussion of instruments: a consideration of Berlioz's writing of his own travels provides a new reading of his *Orchestration Treatise* in the light of the cultural commentary enacted by travel narratives such as those of Dumont d'Urville and Page, revealing Berlioz's writings about European music and instruments to be underpinned by many of the same assumptions and framed by the same structures and strategies. Berlioz's orchestral instrumentalists are ultimately not so different to Tatea – sounding bodies which are rhapsodised, exoticised, adored... and controlled.

Travels with the composer 1: The captive in Italy

Berlioz never travelled to the Pacific himself – indeed, despite frequently expressing a longing to abandon 'the old world', he never left Europe at all. But some of the same techniques and ideologies of travel writing seen in Berlioz's Pacific sources can be found in the accounts of his travels in Europe, and a brief consideration of his Italian and Austro-German narratives provides important contextual information for the aesthetics of travel invoked in his *Orchestration Treatise*.

Berlioz's accounts of his major European excursions were published in serial form in journals before being reworked in his *Memoirs*. The *Memoirs* themselves have given rise to some of the same questions around veracity which characterise the Wallace narrative and travel writing more generally – indeed, Berlioz referred to his *Memoirs* as a whole in terms of travel writing: 'This, if I may use a nautical expression, is the log-book of my painful voyage.'[70] Moreover, Berlioz problematises the issue of veracity within the *Memoirs*. Writing of his adventures in the Abruzzi mountains, he claims to

---

[70] Quoted in Pierre Citron, 'The *Mémoires*', in Bloom (ed.), *Cambridge Companion to Berlioz*, pp. 133–4.

have given his peasant companion Crispino a sharp kick, but he reveals in a footnote that '[t]his is not true, and proceeds from the tendency which artists always have to write for effect. I never kicked Crispino.'[71] Reflecting on his experiences as a sort of self-exiled artist 'going native', Berlioz is here assuming the role of editor of his own 'beachcomber' style narrative, paradoxically reinforcing the reliability of the narrative facts by implying that he will alert us himself to any departures he makes from the truth. In general, however, Berlioz's European travels fall more obviously into the genre of travel writing about the Grand Tour than the beachcomber genre. In many accounts of the Grand Tour, the author (typically preserving a higher moral and social status than the average beachcomber) explores European destinations as the culmination of his (or her) education, encountering the 'cradle' of European civilisation in Italy, and models of industrial progress in Germany; the Grand Tour was concerned not so much with charting new territory as with reconciling the traveller's own experiences with those of the hordes of travel writers who had trodden the same ground before.[72]

Along with experiencing wonderment at beholding traces of classical antiquity and encountering Mediterranean culture, French and British visitors to Italy also frequently noted a sense of waste or loss, of a greatness consigned to the past, of monuments which were in decay or whose splendour was offset by the supposed indolence or disease brought on by the Mediterranean climate. As Stendhal put it, 'All is decadence here, all is mere memory, all is dead. Active life is in London or Paris... a stay here tends to weaken the soul, to plunge it into a stupor.'[73]

For Berlioz, both the educative elements and the sense of loss incurred by the Grand Tour's Italian stage were configured in specifically musical terms. His Italian sojourn fulfilled a core requirement of his success in the Prix de Rome in 1830, but Berlioz resented being exiled at this crucial stage of his compositional development to a country in which, he claimed, 'While the other arts are flourishing in all their vividness, grandeur, and majesty, music alone is degraded to the level of a poor hunted slave.'[74] Berlioz's strongest resistance to musical practices encountered in Italy was directed at Italian opera, at both the performers and their audiences. He concluded that 'the

---

[71] Berlioz, *Memoirs*, p. 152, fn. 2.
[72] Dennis Porter, *Haunted Journeys: Desire and Transgression in European Travel Writing* (Princeton, NJ: Princeton University Press, 1991), pp. 19, 35, 67, 72; Chloe Chard, *Pleasure and Guilt on the Grand Tour: Travel Writing and Imaginative Geography 1600–1830* (Manchester: Manchester University Press, 1999), p. 21.
[73] Quoted in Porter, *Haunted Journeys*, p. 134.   [74] Berlioz, *Memoirs*, p. 154.

Italians as a nation really appreciate only the material effects of music, and distinguish nothing but its exterior form [...] To the Italians music is a sensual pleasure, and nothing more.'[75]

In decrying the 'sensual pleasure' of Italian opera, in which he believed the composer's voice becomes a slave to the singer's physical indulgences, Berlioz creates a provocative alignment between performance and the foreign Other. Berlioz's response to Italian opera will be revisited in Chapter 4. The more obvious location for the exotic Italy in Berlioz's writings, of immediate interest in a consideration of his travel writing, is the Abruzzi mountains, where the composer sought refuge from Rome. In the fashion typical of accounts of 'primitive' music in travel narratives, Berlioz's comparative tendencies project the music of the peoples of this region into the past: the pfifferari of the Abruzzi are described as best heard amidst 'the mysterious monuments of a lost era' where it becomes 'easy to imagine oneself a contemporary of the ancient people among whom the arcadian Evander, the generous host of Aeneas, settled himself.[76]

The suggestion that the music of the pfifferari is best heard away from Rome stresses the importance to Berlioz of 'wild Italy' for the opportunities which it afforded him to free himself from civilisation altogether:

free to ignore the flight of time, to despise ambition, to laugh at glory, to discredit love, to wander north, south, east, or west, to sleep out of doors, to live on little, to wander at will, to dream, to lie exhausted and panting whole days in the soft, hot, murmuring sirocco wind! Perfectly, utterly, illimitably free! Oh, great, strong Italy! wild Italy! unheeding of artistic Italy, thy sister![77]

Berlioz's juxtaposition of 'artistic Italy' against 'wild Italy' is telling. The music of wild Italy is attractive, perhaps, in the same terms in which Tatea's song is attractive. It is so far removed from Berlioz's own musical world that it offers no threat to it – indeed, it is scarcely classed as 'art' at all, and can instead be mined for inspiration on his own terms. Berlioz's description of Italian musical practices functions in the manner of much travel writing: while ostensibly acting as a scientific account of foreign customs, it tells us more about Berlioz's own aesthetics. Italy serves in part as a foil to France, revealing an aspect of barbarism (in Berlioz's terms) that proves the relatively civilised nature of his native land.

Berlioz's status in Italy is symbolically captured in one of the few compositions he produced during his tenure in Rome: a setting of 'La captive', from Hugo's *Les Orientales* (Ex. 1.2). We will have recourse to 'La captive' several times in this chapter, for it provides a succinct illustration of multiple facets

---

[75] Ibid., p. 183.   [76] Ibid., p. 160.   [77] Ibid., p. 148.

Ex. 1.2 'La captive', first version

of the relationship between travel writing and orchestration. The poem is narrated from the perspective of a woman who has been captured and made part of a harem: 'If I were not a captive, I would love this country' she sings, as she details the exotic enchantments of her surroundings. The sentiment of 'La captive' is closely affiliated with Berlioz's own negotiations of the relationship between civilisation and barbarism.[78] In his original, simple strophic setting, Berlioz used only four of Hugo's nine verses, and those he selected – the first, second, third, and final verses – are where the thoughts of the homeland are strongest. There is little in his original setting to suggest markers of musical orientalism. Berlioz instead emphasises the emotional situation of his narrator, torn between resisting and succumbing to her exotic confinement, as emphasised by the yearning and sensuous sighs at the words 'captive' and 'plaintive' in the first verse. (See Ex. 1.2, bb. 7–8, 12–13.) After a climax on the tonic at the reference to the numberless stars (b. 16) – an image of the captive's new world associated with limitlessness and heights – she descends into the shadows of a low c' for the dark wall that confines her (b. 19), before a lilting dancelike arpeggiated figure suggests an embracing of the starry night and all it signifies. But at the end of the first verse (bb. 23–5), Berlioz introduces a slightly ominous chromatic figure that rises from the lower register of the piano (reinforced by the cello Berlioz subsequently added to the strophic setting), as if in response to the captive's reference to the 'sabre des Spahis' which polices the wall of the harem and reminds the narrator that she is there by force. The same low figure stirs at the end of each verse, emphasising the woman's confinement even when her text speaks of her new environment in wholly positive terms. The song in this original form encapsulates the pleasures and risks of Berlioz's own Italian captivity, but as we shall see later in this chapter, Berlioz subsequently drew on the resources of his native land to locate Otherness in the imaginary geography of the orchestra that accompanied this new version.

Travels with the composer 2: The German condor

While Berlioz's accounts of his travels in Austro-German lands could, like his Italian writings, be classed as part of an extended Grand Tour, they also fall into another category of travel writing, and one that connects more directly to the techniques identified in his writings about the New World. A letter from Berlioz to the Minister of the Interior reveals that on his first German tour the composer was fulfilling an official brief to obtain information

---

[78] Reynaud, 'Berlioz et l'Europe', pp. 177–8.

about German institutions for the benefit of France.[79] In writing for the nation, Berlioz thus loosely approximates the role of explorers such as Dumont d'Urville, whose writings he is known to have consulted. Moreover, the epistolary form Berlioz adopts for his accounts of the German tours, published upon his return in the style of open letters to various individuals, bears a resemblance to the technique of Dumont d'Urville's *récit du voyage*. As Dumont d'Urville pointed out, this style of narrative (as opposed to an organisation of material according to theme) gives the appearance of immediacy, thereby entailing an implicit authenticity as well as a strong sense of an individual narrative voice.[80] Berlioz's epistolary technique also potentially reveals some of the imperialising subtext of his travel writing. To the conductor, Girard, Berlioz writes in detail of the practices of the Stuttgart orchestra, the strengths and weaknesses of the individual players, and the layout and rehearsal techniques – as if preparing German territory for conquest by a fellow French conductor.

The imagined conquest of Germany by the French was provocatively matched by the ways in which Berlioz, like many writers of travel narratives, was also seduced by aspects of the Other culture he encountered. The final letter from the first German tour, addressed to the Irish pianist and composer George Osborne, is framed by Berlioz's 'vague uneasiness' at returning to Paris, where music 'is at once sublime and commonplace', and all too often enslaved to commerce.[81] Berlioz suggests that virtuosi like Osborne are less bound than he by commercial pressure, for they write for their own two hands rather than needing to assemble the massed forces of orchestra and chorus. Indeed, the whole letter to Osborne repeatedly returns to themes that cluster around questions of materiality and the relationship between composition and performance. Thus Osborne's Irish songs transport Berlioz to the composer's homeland and seem above commercial concerns; Berlioz has trouble convincing a postal worker in Magdeburg that he is the famous composer because he does not look sufficiently wealthy to fit that man's conception of his profession; the child prodigy Sophie Bohrer impresses but also scares Berlioz with her formidable memory, in which 'so many combinations of different kinds [are] engraving themselves', and he anticipates a successful future for her in Paris.[82]

However, it is Sophie's father, Antoine Bohrer, who inspires the most provocative passage of Berlioz's letter to Osborne. Berlioz relates how he

---

[79] Peter Bloom, 'La mission de Berlioz en Allemagne: un document inédit', *Revue de Musicologie*, 66/1 (1980), 70–85.
[80] Dumont d'Urville, *Voyage de la corvette l'Astrolabe*, vol. I, p. xxxi.
[81] Berlioz, *Memoirs*, pp. 333–4.   [82] Ibid., p. 339.

attended a performance of one of Beethoven's late quartets, led by Bohrer on the first violin. All four players are described as giving themselves over to the music in different ways, including the viola player Chrétien Urhan (the soloist in *Harold en Italie* at its first performance), who 'adored in silence; lowering his eyes, as though before the sun'. As for Antoine Bohrer himself:

> it was passion at its zenith, it was love in ecstasy. One evening, in one of those superhuman adagios where Beethoven's genius soars upwards, immense and solitary as the colossal bird of the snowy heights of Chimborazo, Bohrer's violin, whilst singing the sublime melody, seemed animated by epic inspiration; his tone acquired a twofold power of expression, and broke forth in accents unknown even to himself; inspiration shone out of the countenance of the virtuoso. We held our breath with swelling hearts, when Antoine, suddenly stopping short, laid down his fiery bow, and rushed into an adjoining room.[83]

This passage encapsulates the reason Berlioz could treat Germany as the 'oracle' – a land where music is venerated in religious terms.[84] In fact, the terms Berlioz employs here are also those of travel writing, as David Cairns points out: the reference to the 'colossal bird of the snowy heights of Chimborazo' was inspired by Alexander von Humboldt's *Tableaux de la nature* (1808; French translation 1828).[85] Pursuing this reference further is fruitful, for Humboldt provides an interesting counterbalance to Dumont d'Urville in a consideration of Berlioz's travel writing.

Berlioz consulted both the *Tableaux de la nature* and the first volume of Humboldt's monumental *Cosmos* in his father's library, and was also familiar with the second volume of *Cosmos*. Moreover, Humboldt facilitated Berlioz's first visit to Prussia, meeting with the composer before his departure from Paris: 'M. de Humboldt, who continues to scale the Cordilleras of science with the same courage as ever, showed a genuine interest in my artistic labours', Berlioz wrote to his father, perhaps hoping Dr Berlioz would find particular value in this endorsement from a fellow scientist.[86]

Humboldt provides a more obvious paradigm for Berlioz's writing style than Dumont d'Urville. 'Imagination rarely graces his tableaux', one of Dumont d'Urville's early biographers noted.[87] Berlioz described the second volume of *Cosmos* as 'an imperial and despotic read' – qualities for which

---

[83] Ibid., p. 338.   [84] Ibid., p. 344.
[85] David Cairns, 'Berlioz: Autobiography, Biography', in Peter Bloom (ed.), *Berlioz: Scenes from the Life and Work* (Rochester, NY: Rochester University Press, 2008), p. 229. Berlioz expands on the same image in his essay on the trios and sonatas of Beethoven, though this time speaking about works rather than specific performances. *The Art of Music*, p. 39.
[86] *CG* III, p. 98.   [87] Lesson, *Notice Historique*, p. 98.

he in other contexts expressed an only partially ironic admiration.⁸⁸ But while Humboldt achieved recognition as a scientist, and *Cosmos* matches Dumont d'Urville's multivolume travel account in ambition and scope, Humboldt's accounts of his travels, in stark contrast to those of Dumont d'Urville, are famed for the way in which they merge factual observation with a sense of the sublime more akin to Romantic poetry. Indeed, Humboldt is acknowledged to have made a significant contribution to literary Romanticism.⁸⁹ When Berlioz met him Humboldt had been appointed to a state position as counsellor to the King of Prussia; but in stark contrast to Dumont d'Urville's expeditions, Humboldt's travel in South America in the first years of the nineteenth century had been self-funded, and his numerous writings from this expedition convey a Romantic individualism relatively free from what Berlioz termed the 'sycophant's harness' of Humboldt's subsequent patronage.⁹⁰ *Tableaux de la nature* begins with a preface which reveals this conception of the individual impelled by nature:

> To contemplate the whole of nature, to capture the common action of all the forces which animate it, to renew the joy which the sight of tropical climes can never fail to stir in the sensitive man, that is the goal I propose [. . .] I hope that, despite these imperfections, my Tableaux of Nature [. . .] may offer those who read them some part of the joy which any sensitive soul experiences in contemplating directly the grand scenes which are retraced here!⁹¹

Humboldt's description of the condor displays his characteristic fusion of science and aesthetics to evoke the sublime transcendence of nature:

> Whenever man examines nature with his penetrating curiosity, or measures in his imagination the vast spaces of organic creation, of all the emotions which it stirs, the most powerful and the most profound is the sentiment inspired by the plenitude of life universally spread out. Everywhere, and even as far as the polar ice, the air rings out with the song of birds and the buzzing of insects. Life breathes not only in the lower layers of the atmosphere where the air is thicker, but also in the serene, ethereal regions. Whenever one has surmounted either the back of the Cordillères of Peru or, on the southern bank of Lake Geneva, the summit of Mont Blanc, one

---

⁸⁸ Cairns, 'Berlioz: Autobiography, Biography', p. 229; *CG* III, p. 655.
⁸⁹ Robert van Dusen, 'The Literary Ambitions and Achievements of Alexander von Humboldt', *European University Papers* (Bern: Herbert Lang, 1971); see also Mary Louise Pratt, *Imperial Eyes: Travel Writing and Transculturation*, 2nd edn (London: Routledge, 2008), pp. 118, 135; Nigel Leask, *Curiosity and the Aesthetics of Travel Writing, 1770–1840* (Oxford: Oxford University Press, 2002), p. 249.
⁹⁰ *CG* III, p. 98.
⁹¹ Alexander von Humboldt, *Ansichten der Natur* (1808), trans. Charles Galuski, *Tableaux de la nature* (Paris: Théodore Morgand, 1865), pp. 3–4.

finds in this isolation animate beings. We saw on Chimborazo, at a height almost 2,600 metres greater than the summit of Etna, butterflies and other winged insects. Perhaps they had been carried there by currents of rising air, and they wandered as foreigners in these regions where the timid steps of men were driven by the passion for knowledge; their presence nevertheless proves that, more flexible, the animal constitution can stand up to extremes where vegetation dies. We often saw the giant of the vultures, the condor, gliding over our heads, higher than the snowy saddle of the Pyrenees surmounted by the peak of Tenerife, higher than all the peaks of the Andes.[92]

Humboldt's condor is a resonant image for Berlioz's experience of Beethoven's music, albeit a complex one. Humboldt's Romanticism is entangled with colonialism, sometimes in problematic ways, for in anthropomorphising nature and the landscape, he often erases the human agency of the indigenous inhabitants of the lands in which he travels – inhabitants whose voices are thus rendered conveniently irrelevant to Europeans wishing to occupy their land, either physically or imaginatively.[93] In the extract cited above, Humboldt sweeps his reader onwards and upwards, from the general ('Whenever man examines nature...') to the specific (the condor), from the 'lower layers of the atmosphere' to ever higher mountains, from insects at high altitudes to the soaring condor. The rush of excitement Humboldt experienced at seeing the condor is relived in his prose, as Berlioz's excitement at the Beethoven performance is relived in his. We become fully absorbed in Humboldt's world, and his perspective, framed as an outlook that 'examines' and 'measures' nature, but whose own 'passion for knowledge' and perspective as a well-travelled and well-read European male frequently comes at the expense of indigenous knowledge and perspectives. Indeed, science itself was framed by Humboldt as a colonising enterprise: 'the scientific conqueror will never complain with the Macedonian, that there are no fresh worlds to subject to his dominion', Humboldt writes in *Cosmos*.[94]

Berlioz could not be accused of similarly erasing the identities of the German musicians he encountered on his travels – many are named, including all four players of Bohrer's string quartet. But Berlioz's use of Humboldt's image does raise questions about a kind of colonialism – the colonising of the player by the work – as well as the more obvious Romanticism of both his travel writing and his musical aesthetic. As Berlioz listens to the performance of Beethoven's quartet, it is the composer who is imagined as the condor of Chimborazo, soaring beyond the physical limits of the

---

[92] Ibid., pp. 331–2.   [93] Pratt, *Imperial Eyes*, pp. 123–32.   [94] Humboldt, *Cosmos*, vol. I, p. 22.

listeners and, presumably, the players. Bohrer is overcome in every sense. It is not Bohrer but his violin which is credited with the transcendent sounds 'unknown even to himself', until he is physically unable to take any more and rushes from the room. The 'terror' Berlioz experiences in witnessing Bohrer's twelve-year-old daughter 'engraving' masses of composers' works into her memory and fingers is not that distant in this scene, only here the terror is sublime. In Italy the composer is enslaved to the performer; in Germany the performer is colonised by the composer, and it is Berlioz's travel writing which, in common with the travel writing of his models, fuses science and aesthetics and creates the world anew for future travellers. But perhaps the ultimate colonisation of performer by composer occurs in the orchestra, where any 'imperial and despotic' tendencies of the individual instrumentalist are necessarily sacrificed to the composer's work. In turning now to Berlioz's *Orchestration Treatise* we shall see how the tropes of travel writing impact on Berlioz's conception of the Other world of the orchestra.

Discovering the orchestra: Berlioz's *Orchestration Treatise*

As Macdonald points out, in the *Orchestration Treatise* Berlioz writes about orchestration 'as though no one had ever discovered it before';[95] similarly, Fauquet suggests Berlioz 'breaks new ground'.[96] In other words, in producing what was the most influential treatise on the orchestra in the nineteenth century, Berlioz himself writes as a pioneering traveller. Berlioz's travels in Germany informed his final revisions to the *Treatise*, the first draft of which had been completed immediately prior to his departure. Berlioz refers several times in the *Treatise* to German practice, often comparing it to French procedures, to point out where France might be proud of her superiority or, alternatively, where she might learn from her neighbour. However, whilst Berlioz's musical examples are exclusively European, his *Treatise* also invokes the writing of more distant worlds. The introduction to the *Treatise* sets up the composer as a navigator of new terrain, and Berlioz closes the first edition with a description of the orchestra as a world of virgin forests and volcanoes. Throughout the *Treatise* Berlioz treats the world of the orchestra with the wonderment and passion for discovery characteristic of the travel writing that had fascinated him since his youth. While the

---

[95] Macdonald, *Berlioz's Orchestration Treatise*, p. xxxii.
[96] Joël-Marie Fauquet, 'The *Grand Traité d'instrumentation*', in Bloom (ed.), *The Cambridge Companion to Berlioz*, p. 167.

correspondences between Berlioz's *Treatise* and the writing of Dumont d'Urville or Humboldt are less direct than those seen in the Wallace narrative or his own European travel writing, an examination of the *Treatise* in relation to the techniques and ethos of travel writing reveals new perspectives on Berlioz's own navigations of the orchestral terrain and his encounters with its inhabitants.

As with the scientifically oriented writing of Dumont d'Urville and Humboldt (and unlike his own *Evenings with the Orchestra*), Berlioz's *Treatise* received an official state dedication, though not to the head of state of his own nation but, rather, to King Friedrich Wilhelm IV of Prussia. More significantly, the dedication was apparently facilitated by Humboldt, whose *Cosmos* was dedicated to the very same patron.[97] If the condor of Chimborazo signals Humboldt's impact on Berlioz's German travel writing, the *Treatise*, too, bears the imprint of the great German traveller and his sublime Romantic fusion of science and aesthetics. For Berlioz, as for Humboldt, colonisation lurks in the background, enabled by the writing if not overtly acknowledged within it. Addressing composers rather than players of the instruments he describes, Berlioz writes the orchestral world into existence and facilitates its conquest by other composers.

Of course, Berlioz was not actually the first to 'discover' either the art of orchestration or the art of writing about it. Perhaps the most significant precedent for Berlioz's *Treatise* is Georges Kastner's *Traité general d'instrumentation* (1837, rev. 1844) and his *Cours de l'instrumentation*, which followed in 1839 (rev. 1844). Berlioz's review of the latter played an important role in helping him to articulate his own developing thoughts on the subject, and may indeed have inspired him to publish his own treatise.[98] Much of the key technical information of Berlioz's work is anticipated by Kastner, but Berlioz effectively merges within a single text the science of Kastner's *Traité* with the poetics of his separate *Cours*. Moreover, Berlioz also takes a significantly broader stance towards orchestration than Kastner, for he effectively creates of the orchestra a world in itself. Citing Kastner's definition of orchestration as 'the art of applying appropriately the different types of instrument to a given melody', Berlioz offers an additional definition: 'it is also something else: it is the art of colouring with them the harmony and rhythm; even more than that, it is the art of moving people by the choice of timbre, independent of any effect of melody, rhythm or harmony.'[99] The same sentiment is found in the *Orchestration Treatise*, where Berlioz points out that the art of instrumentation can be

---

[97] *CG* III, p. 80.
[98] *Journal des débats*, 2 October 1839; *CM* IV, pp. 165–72.   [99] *CM* IV, p. 170.

used 'to create effects *sui generis*, with or without an expressive purpose and independent of any help from the other three great musical resources'.[100] Similarly, Berlioz elsewhere complained of the 'tyranny of keyboard habits' which caused so many composers to think at the piano and only subsequently orchestrate material.[101] If Kastner put the world of orchestration on the map, it is Berlioz who gives it an apparently independent existence.

'La captive' *sui generis*

Berlioz's conception of orchestration existing '*sui generis*' is strikingly illustrated in many of his compositions, including perhaps most famously *Symphonie fantastique*. That work will be examined in Chapter 3. Here, let us consider instead an example that, while less conspicuous in terms of its orchestration, resonates more directly with the themes of travel and travel writing explored in this chapter: 'La captive'. After initially conceiving the song in Italy for voice with simple piano accompaniment, Berlioz next added an optional cello line and then created several orchestral versions of the work, culminating in a performance for large festival ensemble organised by the transitional republican government in 1848. Berlioz specifically requested that the words of 'La captive' be printed and distributed on the day of this concert.[102] Indeed, the opening words 'Si je n'étais captive j'aimerais mieux ce pays' must have had a particular resonance for the composer in these circumstances, for the beauty of the musical landscape that the occasion enabled him to create came at the cost of artistic enslavement to the new political regime, which he considered especially 'barbarous'.

In reworking 'La captive' Berlioz did not simply 'orchestrate' or 'add colour' to preexisting material; rather, the whole song was reconceptualised through the orchestra in a process Holoman terms an illustration of 'Berlioz's creative world in microcosm'.[103] Although the melody of the originally strictly strophic song is stated in each verse, it is varied through both rhythm and orchestration to create a loose rondo structure. The second and fourth verses, where the woman's thoughts seem most removed from her current surroundings, form the contrasting sections, enclosed – or 'captured' – by those verses where she is drawn to her new environment. The ominous nature of this captivity is suggested by the orchestra. The timpani enter with a regular beat beneath her lilting melody at the words 'N'étincelait dans l'ombre le sabre du Spahis' (referring to the threat of the

---

[100] Macdonald, *Berlioz's Orchestration Treatise*, p. 6.
[101] Berlioz, *Memoirs*, p. 14. [102] *CG* III, p. 582.
[103] D. Kern Holoman, *Berlioz* (Cambridge, MA: Harvard University Press, 1989), p. 242.

Ex 1.3 'La captive', bb. 17–24

eunuch's sabre, gleaming in the shadows and defining her captivity) (see Ex. 1.3). Moreover, the low, rising chromatic figure that signalled the woman's confinement in the original version is preserved at the end of the first, third, and final stanzas (essentially the 'A' sections).

The second verse ('B' section) introduces a playful diminution and embroidered version of the melodic line as the narrator resists the assistance of a black eunuch to insist that she can tune her own guitar – an instrument which is instantly evoked by the introduction of pizzicato in the strings. When the wistful melody of the opening music returns ('Pourtant j'aime une rive...') it reinforces all the more strongly the contrast between the narrator's memory of the past, and the world in which she now finds herself.

It is in the final two verses of 'La captive' that the orchestra's position becomes most significant. Berlioz adds Hugo's eighth verse (not included in the piano version), in which the narrator mentions her pleasure at singing 'a Spanish song' to her light-footed companions as they dance. It has been observed that only in this verse does Berlioz introduce blatant exoticism, in his evocation of bolero rhythms and castanets in the orchestra. It has been further remarked that it is very revealing of Berlioz's aesthetic that it is Spain – the nearest and supposedly most familiar of the locales evoked by the song – that is the inspiration for this exoticising music.[104] What is less often noted, however, is the way in which Berlioz's bolero is rendered foreign in an additional sense by its orchestration. Berlioz instructs the upper strings, who carry the bolero rhythm, to play muted, *sul ponticello*, and pianissimo, which, along with the light-footed flourishes passed around the woodwinds, produces an airy effect strongly reminiscent of the fairies of Queen Mab in *Roméo et Juliette*. The physicality and sensuality of a 'genuine' bolero is thus rendered enchantingly unreal and fantastical. When the castanets are evoked by a low *d* in the timpani, retaining their characteristic percussive nature but with a conspicuously different colour, the effect of a distorted universe is timbrally reinforced. The registers and timbres of the bolero are inverted by Berlioz's orchestration. The cellos sing the main melody, but muted and in the low register associated with the ominous rising chromatic figure that encloses the earlier verses, and they occupy a different temporal world to the singer's lively new melody (Ex. 1.4). The overall effect is one of disorientation, as if the narrator is caught between worlds – those of her homeland and the present, but also those of fantasy and reality – and it is the orchestral timbre that enacts her state.

[104] Violaine Anger, 'Hector Berlioz et l'Orient', in *Berlioz et Hugo, fantasmes d'orient* (La Côte-Saint-André, Isère: Musée Hector-Berlioz, 2004), p. 23; Julian Rushton, *The Music of Berlioz* (Oxford: Oxford University Press, 2001), p. 149.

Ex. 1.4 'La captive', bb. 71–4

This effect of disorientation is sustained in Berlioz's orchestral setting of the final verse. Although the singer now returns to her opening melody in a final statement of the 'A' section, Berlioz subjects the material to a beautiful slow-motion disintegration. The section begins 'un poco più largo', and slows again several times as the verse continues. (See Ex. 1.5, in 'The Evolution of Orchestration'.) A second string orchestra is now employed (where forces permit) to provide a parallel version of the music of the first, perhaps suggesting in spatial terms the way in which the narrator is caught between two worlds. The introduction of tremolo contributes to the dreamlike state of the conclusion – indeed, at the end of the song Berlioz now has the singer repeat the words of the opening 'en rêvant' (dreaming): 'Si je n'êtais captive' she sighs, the fragments of the melody echoed by the cello and reinterpreted in the flutes, clarinets, and bassoons, before the violins pick up the lilting conclusion of her original theme, the singer is left repeating 'si je n'êtais captive' in a final descent to the tonic. Far from 'merely' orchestrating an existing song, Berlioz thus enables the orchestra to create the world of pleasurable captivity of Hugo's poem anew, the orchestra perfectly encapsulating the status of an Other world *sui generis*.

The composer and his informants

Kastner suggests in his preface that his *Traité* is intended above all to 'come to the aid of young composers'.[105] However, Kastner repeatedly displays

---

[105] Georges Kastner, *Traité général d'instrumentation* (Paris: Minier, c. 1840), n.p.

consideration for the player, and refers composers to manuals written by specialist performers of the instruments in question for further information. Fétis describes how, in addition to being proficient on piano and organ, Kastner thoroughly familiarised himself with a range of orchestral instruments when he became interested in composition, because he was 'convinced of the necessity to understand well the mechanism and resources of all instruments in order to make use of them appropriately'.[106] In contrast, Berlioz admitted he had learnt to play only the flageolet, flute, and guitar, commenting with heavy irony in the *Memoirs*: 'Does not this fortuitous choice look like the instinctive action of nature urging me towards the most powerful orchestral effects and the Michael Angelesque in music?... The flute, the guitar, and the flageolet!!!'[107] Berlioz's resistance to the 'tyranny of keyboard habits' also bespeaks an inability – which he strategically characterised as unwillingness – to compose through performance, through the motion of fingers at the keyboard. In his own orchestration treatise Berlioz only occasionally displays concern for the performer's perspective, and he seldom encourages the reader to consult the treatises of performers. His focus is more emphatically on the composer's requirements: musical instruments are defined in the treatise as 'every sounding body employed *by the composer*',[108] in an example of the 'imperial and despotic' tendencies Berlioz admired in Humboldt's *Cosmos*.

The one entry in Berlioz's *Treatise* that models quite a different stance is, significantly, the description of the guitar – Berlioz's 'own' instrument. He emphasises the fact that '[i]t is almost impossible to write well for the guitar unless one is a player oneself. Yet most composers who use it are far from any familiarity with it and write things of unnecessary difficulty with no sonority or effect.'[109] And again, a few pages later, 'I must emphasise again that one cannot write guitar pieces in several parts, full of passagework and using all the instrument's capabilities without playing it oneself. To get a good idea of what the great players can do in this sphere one must study the compositions of famous guitarists such as Zani de Ferranti, Huerta, Sor and others.'[110]

There is an unintended irony here, perhaps, in that Berlioz stresses the importance of expert or 'insider' knowledge most overtly in relation to one of the instruments least likely to concern the orchestral composer – 'I

---

[106] François-Joseph Fétis, *Biographie universelle des musiciens et bibliographie générale de la musique*, 8 vols. (Paris: Firmin-Didot, 1866–1868), vol. IV, p. 480.
[107] Berlioz, *Memoirs*, p. 13.
[108] Macdonald, *Berlioz's Orchestration Treatise*, p. 4 (emphasis added).
[109] Ibid., p. 80.   [110] Ibid., p. 86.

have always been attracted to terrible instruments', he writes elsewhere, with reference to the guitar.[111] His cited examples in the guitar entry are composed by famous performers on the instrument, unlike the examples he employs throughout the rest of the treatise, which are predominantly written by composers with no particular personal connection to the instrument whose idiom Berlioz suggests they exemplify.

When writing of orchestral instruments, Berlioz compensates for his lack of personal experience by drawing on what might be termed the indigenous perspectives of 'native informants'. In correcting some errors in Kastner's treatise he explains that he bases his own knowledge on a study of numerous individual instrument methods and has sat in on trombone lessons at the Conservatoire.[112] Berlioz is known to have positioned himself near or even within the orchestral pit during performances (possibly playing timpani in some performances of his own works), and to have had instrumentalists play through passages for him at his home.[113] George Osborne wrote of Berlioz, 'It was his constant habit to go into orchestras and sit with the different performers watching them and turning over the pages for them. In this way he learned the capacity of each instrument. Besides which he got several instrumentalists to come to his house where they played together little things which he wrote for them to see what they could accomplish.'[114] Similarly, *Evenings with the Orchestra* is predicated on the assumption that Berlioz's authorial persona is constantly close enough to the orchestra to eavesdrop on – or even take part in – their conversations, and at one point he finds a viola player's sleeping head resting on his shoulder.[115] However, in contrast with *Evenings*, in the *Treatise* the voices of these informants are typically not heard directly. In his account of his second tour of Germany, Berlioz claims, 'Instrumentation today is like a foreign language which has become fashionable. Many affect to speak it without having learnt to do so; consequently they speak it without understanding it properly and with a liberal admixture of barbarisms.'[116] The composer must learn the language of the orchestra that he explores in order to master it; but what is omitted in Berlioz's account here is the fact that the orchestra, too, must learn the composer's language in order for the music to sound. If Berlioz's *Treatise* outlines a form of 'encounter', we are – as in most travel narratives of the nineteenth century – seeing only one side.

[111] *Journal des débats*, 9 June 1855; quoted in Macdonald, *Berlioz's Orchestration Treatise*, p. 86.
[112] *CM* IV, p. 166.   [113] Macdonald, *Berlioz's Orchestration Treatise*, pp. xvi, 274.
[114] Quoted in Macdonald, *Berlioz's Orchestration Treatise*, p. xvi.
[115] Berlioz, *Evenings with the Orchestra*, p. 32.
[116] Quoted in Macdonald, *Berlioz's Orchestration Treatise*, p. xxiii.

The evolution of orchestration

Berlioz establishes the metaphor of the composer as explorer in the introduction to his *Orchestration Treatise*. After outlining how, one after the other across the centuries, melody, harmony, and modulation have undergone a process of exploration, Berlioz emphasises that it is now the turn of instrumentation, as well as expression and rhythm, 'to be discovered, dismissed, accepted, enslaved, liberated'.[117] He suggests that instrumentation is currently at the 'exaggeration' stage, before concluding: 'It takes a long while to discover the Mediterraneans of music, longer still to learn to navigate them'.[118]

Berlioz's description of the stages undergone in the exploration of the 'Mediterraneans of music' suggests a process of seafaring and exploration similar to that outlined in the introduction to the *Voyage de la corvette l'Astrolabe*, where Dumont d'Urville summarises the history of navigation since Columbus: the discovery of an Other world or people leads to an initial rejection of its foreignness or even denial of its very existence, followed by acceptance and, finally, the supposedly benevolent scientific humanism of Dumont d'Urville himself.[119] Berlioz's 'exaggeration' stage may seem difficult to situate in the context of geographical exploration, but it could suggest the paradoxical distancing effect of increasing familiarity that enabled exoticism to become ubiquitous on stage and in print back home, reduced to a set of stereotypical signifiers and used to reflect upon or ironise one's own culture. Indeed, Berlioz's Wallace narrative might itself be considered a prime example of the 'exaggeration' stage in the process of encountering Others.

The enslavement and exaggeration Berlioz describes in relation to the orchestra might seem to be a state of affairs far removed from the pleasurable captivity of 'La captive'. In fact, Berlioz turns the element of orchestral 'exaggeration' to good effect in that song. One of the most extreme examples of the enslavement and exaggeration of the orchestra offered in the *Treatise* comes in Berlioz's discussions of the bass drum, which, as he points out, is too often paired with cymbals, and leads to 'the most devastation and

---

[117] Berlioz, *Grand traité d'instrumentation et d'orchestration modernes*, ed. Peter Bloom, NBE vol. 24, p. 4.
[118] Macdonald, *Berlioz's Orchestration Treatise*, p. 4. On the trope of the exaggeration of orchestration, see Emily I. Dolan, *The Orchestral Revolution*, p. 219.
[119] Dumont d'Urville, *Voyage de la corvette l'Astrolabe*, vol. I, pp. II–III. Dumont d'Urville's humanism was not always benevolent: Melanesians in particular fared poorly in his racial hierarchy. Bronwen Douglas, 'In the Event: Indigenous Countersigns and the Ethnohistory of Voyaging', in Margaret Jolly, Serge Tcherkézoff, and Darrell Tyron (eds.), *Oceanic Encounters: Exchange, Desire, Violence* (Canberra: ANU Press, 2009), p. 182.

Ex. 1.5 'La captive', bb. 103–6

[...] the worst abuses and excesses of modern music': 'to write for it in [...] every ensemble, every finale, every little chorus, in ballets, even in cavatinas, is the ultimate in absurdity and – let's call things by their name – in brutality.'[120] Thus when the bass drum and cymbal mark the second half of each bar near the end of 'La captive' – a work texturally comparable to a delicate 'cavatina' and thus supposedly anathema to this medium – we are surely meant to notice them (Ex. 1.5). Fading from *pp* to *pppp*, the bass drum and cymbal offer both a magical reinvention or 'freeing' of this much-abused sonority, and, perhaps, a deliberate barbarism – a reminder of the state of captivity itself.

If Berlioz's model for the progress of orchestration can profitably be likened to European models of approaching Others, the particular paradigm he invokes is very much a nineteenth-century one, suggestive of evolutionary and dialectical thinking. Each musical element in turn is subjected to a process whereby it is introduced, debated, adopted, and then overused, before it finally becomes part of the poetic language to be employed in the service of beauty rather than simply for its own sake. The succession in which Berlioz tackles the musical elements in the Introduction to the *Orchestration Treatise* (first harmony, then melody, then modulation, followed by instrumentation, expression, and rhythm) suggests a form of teleological bias, reinforced elsewhere in the *Treatise* when he writes of the 'poverty of

---

[120] Macdonald, *Berlioz's Orchestration Treatise*, p. 280.

early music'.[121] It might seem momentarily odd that Berlioz would position harmony first in his evolutionary chain in the Introduction – rhythm was more commonly denoted the earliest or most 'primitive' aspect of musical practice. In fact, if these teleological processes are viewed in the context of the nineteenth-century conception of Otherness, the apparent contradiction is easily resolved. Just as newly discovered peoples were perceived to be less evolved, acting as 'our' metaphorical ancestors but with the capacity to be 'civilised' and modernised by Europeans, so too is rhythm at a primitive stage, only awaiting 'discovery' in order to begin its own evolutionary journey.

Berlioz's attitude, though directly concerned only with European instruments, reflects a broader ideology shared by his European peers regarding the relatively primitive status of the instruments most strongly associated with rhythm. Thus drums were commonly identified as symbolic of the least evolved musical cultures. Kastner, in his *Cours d'instrumentation*, lists drums, as well as flutes and zithers, as being among the first musical instruments to come into existence in antiquity.[122] And Chouquet, in compiling in 1875 a catalogue of the musical instrument museum of the Paris Conservatoire (of which Berlioz had earlier been the curator), commented that 'man, proceeding from simple to more complex states, contented himself with percussion instruments, then crude loud wind instruments before coming to conceive instruments where strings are plucked, hit, or rubbed.'[123] Berlioz makes a similar point in an article published after the first edition of the *Orchestration Treatise*: in the area of percussion, he writes, we are 'scarcely more advanced than the savages'.[124]

In contrast with rhythm, Berlioz suggests that instrumentation has already evolved to the 'exaggeration' stage. It has been 'discovered' by others, and is now subject to distortion and abuse, like the Pacific whose tropes Berlioz himself exaggerates in his writings. Berlioz's *Treatise*, he implies, will offer a truer understanding of the land of orchestration and help to free its inhabitants. But he cannot provide a guide to the whole 'world' of orchestration, for in the 'domain of inspiration [...] only genius may make discoveries and [...] only genius is allowed to tread'.[125]

---

[121] Ibid., p. 170.
[122] Georges Kastner, *Cours d'instrumentation* (Paris: A. Meissonnier & J. H. Heugel, 1844), p. 1.
[123] Gustave Chouquet, Avant-propos to 'Le musée de notre Conservatoire de Musique', reproduced in *Le Ménestrel*, 23 May 1875, pp. 197, 198.
[124] *Journal des débats*, 12 October 1847 *CM* VI, p. 331; Macdonald, *Berlioz's Orchestration Treatise*, p. 295.
[125] Macdonald, *Berlioz's Orchestration Treatise*, p. 6.

Civilised and barbaric instruments

Berlioz's *Treatise* makes few references to instruments associated with traditions outside western European art music, unless such instruments are already familiar in some form to his peers: thus the 'pavillon chinois' (or Turkish crescent) had been used in military bands, while the tambourine, which Berlioz associated with Italian peasants, had been absorbed into the orchestra by Berlioz himself to suggest *couleur locale* in *Benvenuto Cellini*. However, Berlioz uses the language of encounters with Others in describing some European instruments. Just as Dumont d'Urville and his peers perceived a hierarchy of peoples, in which some were more civilised than others, Berlioz discusses instruments in terms of barbarism and civilisation. Perhaps predictably, Berlioz associates barbarity with what he perceives to be an ugly sound – the 'cold, horrible bawling' of the serpent is described as 'fundamentally *barbarous*'. However, there is the suggestion that this ugliness is not simply inherent in the instrument, but also preserved through traditions that associate it with the (primitive) past. Berlioz complains that the serpent continues to be used in church music, but that its sound would be 'much more at home in the bloodthirsty rituals of the Druids than in those of the Catholic church'.[126] He notoriously subjects the serpent to his own 'exaggeration' in *Symphonie fantastique*.

However, conspicuous historicity is in itself certainly insufficient cause to condemn an instrument as barbarous. Berlioz elsewhere mentions antique cymbals which he saw in the Pompeii museum and which he had already employed in *Roméo et Juliette*. (He would subsequently use them again in *Les Troyens*, as we shall see in Chapter 5.) Perhaps the instrument that carries associations of the ancient world is appreciated for the way in which it gently reminds us of our supposed cultural origins, simultaneously exotic and familiar, as travellers to Italy on the Grand Tour commonly noted.

It is not only old instruments that can be barbarous, for Berlioz discusses newly invented instruments in terms that might suggest the potential barbarism of modernity. While he admires the instruments created by Alexandre and Sax, Berlioz excuses himself from discussing many other modern developments:

The author of this work is doubtless in no way obliged to mention the multitude of attempts of every kind that are made daily by manufacturers of musical instruments, their more or less unfortunate so-called inventions, nor to make known the pointless subjects whom they wish to introduce into the population of instruments.

[126] Ibid., p. 242.

But he must recommend and bring to the attention of composers the beautiful discoveries which have been made by ingenious artists, especially when the excellence of the result of these discoveries has been generally acknowledged, and when their implementation has already been accomplished in musical practice in part of Europe.[127]

Berlioz's language here reveals an interesting point of tension: new instruments are described again in the terms employed in the scientific studies of Other worlds – of the 'discovery' of peoples. But the metaphor sits awkwardly with the fact that these new specimens are the products of modern invention; they have been created by manufacturers rather than simply evolving naturally until they are 'discovered'. Moreover, Berlioz draws an important distinction between the 'ingenious artist' (Sax and Alexandre) and the 'manufacturer'. The implication is that the artist – assuming a God-like role – helps the race to evolve and follow its natural path. Humboldt, in the first volume of *Cosmos*, similarly urges his readers to embrace industry as a sign of natural progress fully compatible with art.[128] In contrast, the *manufacturer* fabricates rather than discovers, and is thus the creator of distorted (or exaggerated?) 'subjects'; he enacts a kind of genetic engineering *avant la lettre* suggestive of Frankenstein's monster.[129] Kastner suggests a similarly grotesque image for the failed inventions of instrument manufacturers, but without any of the connotations of travel and discovery: he likens these inventions to 'stillbirths'.[130]

The instrument builder who is an 'artist' is truly civilised because he is concerned with instruments not merely as technological ends in themselves, but rather as a means of gaining access to wondrous new sound worlds. However, ultimate authority must reside with the composer, for it is every 'sounding body employed *by the composer*' that can be defined as a musical instrument.[131] Once again, Berlioz appears to bypass the individuals who must intervene to convey the composer's work to the listener: the performers.

---

[127] Berlioz, *Grand traité*, p. 457. [128] Humboldt, *Cosmos*, vol. I, p. 38.
[129] David A. Hedrich Hirsch has demonstrated how Frankenstein's monster evokes anxiety about the colonial Other in a period of conflicting notions of what constituted 'fraternité' after the Revolution: 'Liberty, Equality, Monstrosity: Revolutionizing the Family in Mary Shelley's *Frankenstein*', in Jeffrey Jerome Cohen (ed.), *Monster Theory: Reading Culture* (Minneapolis: University of Minnesota Press, 1996), pp. 115–42.
[130] Patricia Jovanna Woodward, 'Jean-Georges Kastner's *Traité général d'instrumentation*: A Translation and Commentary', unpublished Master of Music thesis, University of Texas (2003), p. 285.
[131] Macdonald, *Berlioz's Orchestration Treatise*, p. 5. Emphasis added. See also Dolan, *The Orchestral Revolution*, p. 218.

Ideologies of classification

In structuring his *Treatise*, Berlioz follows the model laid out in Kastner's *Traité* rather than his subsequent *Cours*. After providing an account of the discipline of orchestration, Berlioz's treatise and Kastner's earlier work each give an overview of the instrument families, before proceeding to discuss the instruments individually. The act of classifying instruments is cross-cultural, but the nature of the classification system applied is culturally determined.[132] Not surprisingly, both Berlioz and Kastner reflect aspects of the classifying ideology that had underpinned European approaches for several centuries, prioritising physical characteristics of the instruments' constitution and/or means of sound production. Unlike classification systems based on the social context in which instruments were employed, the system of classification used by Kastner and Berlioz tends to objectify (in both senses) instruments. The system adopted by the two authors bears a resemblance to the Linnaean classification system being used by Dumont d'Urville and his contemporaries, whereby organisms are categorised into orders, families, genera, and species according to various physical attributes (a system problematically extended to the classification of humans in racial terms). This analogy is strengthened when Berlioz refers to instrumental families as 'races'. The trombone, for example, is 'true leader of the race of wind instruments'.[133]

Berlioz's classification system differs from Kastner's in several respects at the more detailed levels of division. Whereas Kastner classifies the organ as a keyboard instrument, Berlioz groups it with wind instruments. Kastner – an organist himself – thus classifies the instrument according to the feature most tangible to the performer, whereas Berlioz prioritises the sound production within the instrument itself. More radical is the way Berlioz, in contrast to Kastner, includes the voice in his section on wind instruments, which was criticised at the time: 'why are the voices placed in the section on wind instruments, after the serpent and ophicleide? Of course we know that the voice is, strictly speaking, a wind instrument, but we also think that its exceptional nature warrants the honour of a chapter of its own.'[134] Berlioz thereby reduces the human body itself to another 'sounding object', whose music is created by air passing through the chest and head cavities

---

[132] Margaret Kartomi, *On Concepts and Classifications of Musical Instruments* (Chicago: University of Chicago Press, 1990).
[133] Macdonald, *Berlioz's Orchestration Treatise*, 219.
[134] E. V., 'Grand traité d'instrumentation et d'orchestration modernes, par H. Berlioz', *Le Ménestrel*, 28 April 1844, n.p.

almost as if without any agency of the performer. It is not the individual performer who sings, but the 'orchestra', both its individual instruments and its collective body.

In 'La captive' Berlioz illustrates this conception of orchestral voice, and, interestingly, the impact it might have on the 'captivity' of the singer. While the original song (with piano) was so vocally gratifying that everyone from Berlioz's colleagues to the servants at the French Academy in Rome could not stop singing it, Berlioz felt that the orchestral version posed particular challenges to the singer.[135] To Liszt he wrote, 'It's quite difficult for the singer and it is necessary that she understand the conductor perfectly; otherwise it is nothing.'[136] And to Joachim Berlioz confessed, 'I love this piece but [...] it is very difficult to perform well because of the many nuances of movement and of reverie (exalted and voluptuous at the same time) where the singer must immerse herself entirely in order to be understood.'[137] Berlioz's suggestion that the reverie of 'La captive' is both 'exalted and voluptuous' describes the way in which the song is poised between memory of the past and the homeland, and the sensual comforts experienced by the body in the new land of the present. As we have seen, it is in the orchestra that this duality is most strongly felt, as Berlioz again emphasises the position of the composer as the navigator and writer of an orchestral world of his own creation – a world in which performers must be willing to give in to the dictates of the 'imperial and despotic' author who frames their world.

Science and art: Encountering the clarinet

Perhaps the most obvious difference between Kastner's and Berlioz's approaches to writing about orchestration is that, whereas Kastner separates his consideration of the 'science' and 'poetics' into the two volumes of the *Traité* and *Cours* respectively, Berlioz fuses the approaches within a single volume. But Berlioz also problematises the relationship between art and science. In his section on the concertina, Berlioz denigrates the 'scientists' absurd theories' about acoustics, questioning the practice of acousticians who argue that enharmonic differences should be observed even when equivalent notes are played simultaneously.[138] Berlioz thereby objects to academic knowledge based on theory rather than the evidence of the ears. Berlioz's own approach is, in contrast, founded on a detailed, practical study of the instruments themselves, and, like Humboldt's accounts of

---

[135] Berlioz, *Memoirs*, p. 161; *CG* I, pp. 538, 542.   [136] *CG* IV, p. 696.
[137] *CG* IV, p. 430.   [138] Macdonald, *Berlioz's Orchestration Treatise*, pp. 307–10.

the natural environment, is aimed at those who will interpret his (sonic) world through their ears and imaginations rather than exclusively through their intellect. Entries on individual instruments typically move from the factual, positivistic, or scientific (in this broader sense) to the poetic or aesthetic category. After opening with technical information about the range of the instrument in question, each entry moves to discussion of the emotive qualities of the instrument, before typically concluding with discussion of illustrative extracts from compositions. And just as Humboldt's depictions of foreign lands frequently bypass local human inhabitants, Berlioz's tendency to sweep from the scientific to the aesthetic suggests a move from composer to listener, and from instrument to ear, bypassing the agency of the performer, which must of necessity connect the two.

To understand the analogies between travel writing and Berlioz's *Treatise*, as well as the differences between the approaches of Berlioz and Kastner, let us examine Berlioz's entry on the clarinet, which can be considered both a typical entry and one in which certain distinctive features of Berlioz's *Treatise* receive particular emphasis.

The clarinet is the first single-reed instrument considered by both Berlioz and Kastner, who both begin by comparing the clarinet with the double-reed instruments of the previous section. Berlioz's emphasis is initially on technical or scientific observation. Thus the difference in sound quality between the clarinet's lowest notes and those of the bassoon is 'because of its coarser vibration pattern'.[139] And Berlioz's next paragraph categorises the ranges of the clarinet (incorrectly, as Macdonald points out), focussing here on technical issues of pitch and difficulty, and offering examples of the types of writing the composer should avoid when writing for instruments that have yet to adopt Sax's improvements. Both Berlioz and Kastner then proceed to discuss the best keys for the clarinet, and to consider the different clarinets available at the time of writing. But whereas Kastner suggests that the C, B♭, and A clarinets are all readily available in the orchestra, and that the composer should select the clarinet best suited to the key of the music, Berlioz puts considerably more emphasis on the different tone qualities of the full range of clarinets in existence and complains that too often players just play everything on the B♭ clarinet. In his own compositions Berlioz sometimes chose clarinets that were not the best 'fit' for the key, presumably to obtain the particular colour of the instrument in question, even at the expense of the player's comfort.[140] Berlioz cites his own use of the E♭ clarinet in *Symphonie fantastique* (without naming the symphony or acknowledging

---

[139] Ibid., p. 117.   [140] Ibid., p. 123.

his authorship) to 'parody, degrade and [...] brutalise' the theme, as an example of how this clarinet – never heard in the orchestra before – can be used to support the 'dramatic meaning of the work'. This leads to the directive that 'players should in general use only the instrument specified by the composer'.[141] Berlioz devotes a paragraph to the subject of fidelity to the composer, building, through admonition of increasing emphasis, on an issue that was important to him and that is central to the *Treatise*. Those 'notable players' who play everything on the B♭ clarinet are demonstrating 'inauthentic practice'. This 'infidelity' is particularly 'heinous' if transposing from the (readily available) A clarinet. The player will be forced to transpose some notes up an octave 'and ruin the effect the composer wanted – an intolerable state of affairs!'[142]

Kastner has no comparable paragraph. Indeed, where Berlioz makes his emphasis on the composer's perspective explicit, Kastner instead repeatedly displays concern for the performer, advising the composer to allow plenty of time for the player to switch from one clarinet to another within a work (something Berlioz does not take into account, either in the *Treatise* or in some of his own works),[143] and warning the composer not to entrust a solo to an instrument that has had insufficient opportunity to warm up. Moreover, Kastner goes on to imply that the composer must be careful not to tire his players.[144] Berlioz does display some interest in the performer's abilities when he advises the composer how to disguise difficult clarinet entries on high notes. But overall he seems almost to frame the performer here as an obstacle or inconvenience. Kastner, in contrast, concludes his entry with reference to the treatises of several clarinettists, thereby acknowledging their authority over their own instrument.

In the *Traité* Kastner offers brief information about how the clarinet might pair with other instruments in terms of different genres and functions, but he saves consideration of the affective qualities of specific ensemble writing for the *Cours*. Berlioz, on the other hand, moves into this affective discussion within the same volume. The diatribe on composer intent is immediately succeeded by a consideration of the qualities of the clarinet's different registers. This section initially adopts a more 'objective' tone. However, Berlioz quickly begins to introduce affective language, and the process of anthropomorphisation begins in earnest. The low clarinet's register produces 'icily menacing effects, those dark expressions of repressed fury' (something which Berlioz demonstrates in the descent of the clarinets at the reference to the dark wall of the harem that encloses 'La captive'); the top

---

[141] Ibid., p. 122.   [142] Ibid., p. 122.   [143] Ibid., p. 124.   [144] Kastner, *Traité general*, p. 39.

notes can sound as 'piercing shrieks'. But it is in the discussion of the middle register that Berlioz's own 'condor of Chimborazo' begins to soar. This register is characterised by 'haughtiness with intimations of tenderness and nobility', suited for 'the most poetic thoughts and feelings'; it is 'the voice of heroic love', the 'loved ones, wives and sweethearts, whose proud eyes and earnest passion exult to the sound of arms, who sing as they enter the fray and who crown their conquering heroes or die with the defeated'. Here Berlioz is so moved by the sonic world he contemplates that any pretence of scholarly distance is relinquished: 'I have never been able to hear the distant sound of military bands without being profoundly moved by this feminine quality in the clarinets and filled with images of this kind, as from reading the epic poetry of the ancients'.[145]

Many years later, Berlioz would embody the feminine mourning of the clarinet in the pantomime of Andromache in *Les Troyens*, inspired by Virgil's *Aeneid*. In the *Treatise*, Berlioz shows the earlier inspiration not only of that epic account of imperial travel, but perhaps also of the other kinds of travel writing that he was drawn to throughout his career. Compare, for example, Humboldt's movement back and forth from factual narration of detail to aestheticised and personal marvel at the bird that soared above him. This is evident in the passage already cited, where Humboldt first introduces the condor, but the process of interweaving scientific and aesthetic observation is extended and emphasised when Humboldt returns to the condor in the following chapter to offer a substantial discussion of the bird and its ability to thrive at high altitude. Humboldt outlines various names for the condor in local languages, as well as the scientific name designated by French zoologist Duméril, and works through other factual information about the bird's dimensions and habitat – just as Berlioz describes different forms of clarinet and their 'habitat' or characteristic uses. Again it is the notion of the condor surpassing normal limits which seems most to stimulate Humboldt's poetic imagination. After offering statistics about the extreme heights to which the condor soars, Humboldt continues, 'it is a striking physiological phenomenon to see the same bird which has been circling for whole hours in regions where the air is quite rarefied, suddenly swoop down on the shore of the sea, skimming (for example) the western slope of Pichincha, and in the space of a few hours traversing all climates.'[146] Humboldt's friend and colleague, the chemist Gay-Lussac (whose electrical demonstrations Berlioz attended with enthusiasm as a medical student) conducted an experiment

---

[145] Macdonald, *Berlioz's Orchestration Treatise*, p. 125.
[146] Humboldt, *Tableaux de la nature*, p. 385.

in breathing at high altitude, which demonstrated to Humboldt that man experiences anxiety and a painful exhaustion at much lower altitudes than those the condor can traverse with ease.[147] The condor thus surpasses human physical limitations; is it any wonder, then, that Berlioz employed the image for the ideal performance of Beethoven's quartet in which Bohrer's own physicality is erased?

The *Orchestration Treatise* reinforces the same perspective every time it bypasses performers and their bodily limitations to instead rhapsodise over the world of the composer's score. The entry on the clarinet concludes with some of the most ecstatic of those passages. The clarinet part in the overture to Weber's *Freischütz* provokes Berlioz to ask, 'Is this not the lonely virgin, the huntsman's fair bride, her eyes upturned to heaven, mingling her passionate plaint with the roar of the storm-wracked forest? . . . Oh Weber!!!'[148] The next example is from his own *Lélio*, where the muted clarinet (Berlioz encased it in a leather bag) is deemed even more powerful, and is compared to that ultimate Romantic instrument which has no performer at all – the Aeolian harp: 'it wrings the heart as much as even the trembling harmonies of the Aeolian harp itself'.[149] Again, as with Tatea's song, the Aeolian harp signals a sublime erasure of the agency of the performer.

Other examples Berlioz introduces to illustrate masterful writing for the clarinet include Beethoven's Seventh Symphony, as well as two curious cases (from Gluck's *Alceste* and Sacchini's *Oedipe à Colonne*) where the parts he associates with the clarinet were not actually included in the composers' original scores (or were given to another instrument), as Berlioz was aware, and thus cannot definitely be attributed to the composer in question. Coming so soon after Berlioz's caution always to obey the intentions of the composer, the effect is interesting – not only do performers get erased in great works, but where the world of the work is most powerful, even the composer might become secondary.

Other worlds, Other peoples?

Humboldt prefaced his *Tableaux*: 'Everywhere I refer to the eternal influence of physical nature on moral dispositions and on the fate of humanity. These pages are above all written for melancholy souls. He who wishes to escape the storms of life will gladly follow me into the depths of forests, across the immense steppes and to the heights of the Andes.'[150]

---

[147] Ibid., p. 386. [148] Macdonald, *Berlioz's Orchestration Treatise*, p. 126.
[149] Ibid., p. 127. [150] Humboldt, *Tableaux de la nature*, pp. 3–4.

Berlioz, too, invites the sensitive reader to follow him into a world of wonders – into the sublime extremes of the orchestral landscape of his ideal ensemble – and to contemplate the emotional impact on the listener of the physical nature of the orchestra. The passage that concluded the original edition of Berlioz's *Treatise* contains perhaps the strongest suggestion of Humboldt's aesthetics, as Berlioz contemplates the potential of a massive festival orchestra:

> [The orchestra's] repose would be as majestic as the ocean's slumber; its agitation would suggest a tropical hurricane, its explosions the fury of a volcano. It would evoke lamentation, murmuring, the mysterious sounds of virgin forests, it would sound the clamours, the prayers, the hymns of triumph or mourning of a people whose soul is magnanimous, whose heart is ardent and whose passions are fiery. The very solemnity of its silences would inspire fear, and the most rebellious beings would tremble to watch its crescendo swell and roar like an enormous, sublime conflagration![151]

Oceans, tropical hurricanes, volcanoes, and virgin forests are the stuff of the travel writing to which Berlioz was drawn. Not only Humboldt, but also Cooper's Leatherstocking novels, Chateaubriand's *Renée* and *Atala*, Bernardin de Saint-Pierre's *Paul et Virginie*, and the more scientifically oriented travel narratives of Levaillant or Volney could have stimulated Berlioz's metaphor. But it is Humboldt's characteristic romanticisation of the sublime terror and power of the natural world, in a context both scientific and aesthetic, which provides the most interesting parallel for Berlioz's *Treatise*. In the first volume of *Cosmos*, Humboldt speaks of Earth itself as a sounding body (if not an orchestra), with its atmosphere as '"the conveyer of sound"; the channel of the communication of ideas, the indispensable condition of all social life'.[152]

Berlioz's listener, like Humboldt's sympathetic imaginary traveller, seems almost physically overwhelmed by the sublime fear of beholding this massive force. Berlioz attributes at least part of this powerful sound world to the human voice (the 'clamours, prayers and hymns of triumph of a people . . .'). But it is unclear whether he is invoking the choral voices of his festival orchestra (classified as just more 'wind instruments' in the *Treatise*), or invoking a new metaphor for the voice of the orchestral body. The very ambiguity again suggests Humboldt's tendency to project agency onto the landscape at the expense of its human inhabitants.

---

[151] Macdonald, *Berlioz's Orchestration Treatise*, p. 335.   [152] Humboldt, *Cosmos*, vol. I, p. 305.

If it is the orchestral landscape that is Berlioz's ultimate destination, where does that leave the performer whose labour is necessary for that landscape to sound? Berlioz's performer occupies several subtly different positions. On one hand, Berlioz establishes the performer as a potential Other – a foreign entity whose subjectivity is quite different to his own, and who might even be barbarous if allowed to dominate, but whose identifying features, history, and character he can categorise in order to assist future composer-explorers to colonise their world. But mostly it is the instruments themselves that receive this categorisation and, indeed, humanisation. The orchestra can also suggest place (indeed, in Lichtenthal's musical dictionary – favourably reviewed by Berlioz – the word 'orchestre' retains as its primary definition the space occupied by the musicians in the theatre, and only secondarily refers to the players).[153] The performer is thereby often rendered invisible, albeit integral to the transportation of the listener to these sublime realms. In this respect, we might view the orchestral performers as occupying a role similar to that of the crew of Dumont d'Urville's ship.[154] The highly structured and efficient organisation of the crew, each assigned tasks under the ultimate authority of the captain, easily resonates with the image of an orchestra which operates under the authority of the composer (or the composer-conductor, as we shall see in the next chapter). Indeed, Berlioz drew the analogy himself, comparing the position of a festival conductor to that of the great eighteenth-century French naval commander Jean Bart, and comparing musicians to the crew of a ship entering the icy regions of the South Pole – an image likely heavily influenced by Dumont d'Urville's own Antarctic expedition.[155]

If in this metaphor the players are the crew, the musical instruments become objects that enable access to other worlds, and can thus be likened to the navigational and other scientific tools that facilitated exploratory voyages, including those of Dumont d'Urville. The nineteenth century saw changes in the way in which instruments – both scientific and musical – were perceived. Dumont d'Urville, in his preface, discusses ways in which developments in navigational equipment permitted ever easier exploration of new lands, so that in 1785 La Pérouse benefitted from the 'perfecting of instruments and methods' that had occurred since Cook's last voyage in 1776–9, and Dumont d'Urville later notes the continued improvement in

---

[153] Pierre Lichtenthal, *Dictionnaire de musique*, trans. Dominique Mondo (Paris: Troupenas, 1839), p. 123; *Journal des débats*, 18 October 1839. *CM* IV, pp. 189–91.
[154] On the division of labour in Cook's crew, see Porter, *Haunted Journeys*, p. 108.
[155] Berlioz, *Musical Madhouse*, pp. 75–8 and 189.

chronometers which had facilitated accuracy in navigators' observations.[156] There was also an increasing specialisation in the use of instruments in which the amateur scientist of Cook's era began to be replaced by the trained specialist. The same progression has been traced in music, with the increasing professionalism promoted by institutions such as the Paris Conservatoire. Indeed, the word 'virtuoso' encapsulates the difference; having earlier denoted a virtuous or generally skilled person (Joseph Banks was described as a virtuoso, as was his mentee Humboldt),[157] it came in the nineteenth century to denote someone with highly specialised technical skill in one particular field.

At the same time, this specialisation led to a model of divided labour in which individuals effectively became components of a machine, extensions of their instruments rather than agents in their own right. Where the eighteenth century treated man as a toolmaker, in the nineteenth century man was himself treated as the tool wielded by a higher authority.[158] We have already seen how Berlioz tends to treat the orchestral performers as extensions of their instruments, if they are mentioned at all. More subtly, he writes for the performers in such a way as to suggest the division of labour. Several times in the *Orchestration Treatise* Berlioz suggests ways that the composer might separate a single melodic line between different performers of the same or closely related instruments, to spare a single player or section from struggling to perform every note in a rapid line or to cover a wider range of pitches than can be attained from any one instrument. Berlioz offers examples where one woodwind instrument overlaps with another in realising a descending line, and where horns crooked in different keys between them provide all the chromatic notes of a single melody. The listener perceives a single melodic line, as the composer intends; but the players each have responsibility for only one 'component' of the 'final product'. Such a model might most obviously be likened to the factory workers of industrialised society, and we will revisit the implications of the mechanised model suggested by Berlioz's divided labour in further detail in Chapter 3. But the same specialisation was also characteristic of the ship's crew.

Viewing Berlioz's *Orchestration Treatise* through the lens of the nineteenth-century travel narratives to which the composer had access is not a matter of simple analogical transferral. However, it is perhaps in the

---

[156] Dumont d'Urville, *Voyage de la corvette l'Astrolabe*, vol. I, pp. xvi, xx.
[157] Porter, *Haunted Journeys*, p. 106. Pratt uses the word in relation to Humboldt, *Imperial Eyes* p. 122.
[158] Jonathan Crary, *Techniques of the Observer: On Vision and Modernity in the Nineteenth Century* (Cambridge, MA: MIT Press, 1990), p. 131.

resulting contradictions that the greatest interest lies. We have seen how, on one hand, Berlioz's approach to orchestral instruments (or their performers?) suggests a quasi-ethnographic approach to Others; but on the other hand, orchestral performers also become the hidden labourers of the ship's crew, the necessary components of the grand navigational machine upon whose work the voyage is dependent, but whose individual perspectives are almost irrelevant to the discovery of the new territory – the composer's work. In other words, there is a tension between the presence of the orchestra as an Other world in itself, and the orchestra as a tool wielded by the compositional 'self' in order to access that world. And there is a corresponding tension between the physical realities of the performers and their instruments, and the metaphysical world of the score. Negotiating – or navigating between – these worlds is a central concern of Berlioz's music, as we will see repeatedly in the chapters to come, where we journey through various works and worlds. Like the mutineers on Captain Bligh's *Bounty* (a story which Dumont d'Urville cites, and with which Berlioz was doubtless familiar), Berlioz's orchestral musicians do not simply resign themselves to quietly serving the work, and in the travels with the orchestra the physical and metaphysical worlds collide in provocative ways.

2 | Conquering Other worlds

Military metaphors, virtuosity, and subjectivity in *Symphonie funèbre et triomphale* and *Harold en Italie*

After three or four hours of such anti-harmonious *skirmishes*, not one single piece has been made intelligible. Everything is broken, inarticulate, out of tune, cold, commonplace, maddeningly discordant, hideous! [. . .] Once more his attention embraces everything; his eye is everywhere; with a glance he signals their entries to voice and instrument, up, down, to the right, to the left; with his right arm he flings forth terrible chords that burst in the distance like harmonious *projectiles*; then, on a pedal point, he arrests all this movement; rivets the attention of all; suspends every arm, every breath, listens for a moment to the silence . . . and then gives freer scope than ever to the whirlwind he has subdued [. . .] Then, when all is over, and success assured, his delight is intensified a hundredfold, since it is shared by the gratified self-love of all his *army*. You, you great virtuosi, are kings and princes by the grace of God, you are born on the steps of the throne; while composers have *to fight, to overcome, and to conquer*, in order that they may reign. But the very labours and dangers of the *struggle* only enhance the brilliancy and intoxication of their *victory*, and they might perhaps be even happier than you had they always *soldiers* at their command.

Berlioz, 'Letter III – To Liszt' (1843)[1]

Skirmishes, projectiles, armies, fighting, overcoming, conquering, victory, and soldiers . . . When Berlioz addressed an open letter to Liszt describing his experience as a touring composer–conductor in Austro-German lands in 1843, he made it clear that the composer's mission was a serious one. The militaristic metaphors for his Austro-German tour suggest an explicitly imperialistic framework for exploring Other worlds. For while Berlioz describes the virtuoso Liszt as a king, on account of his seemingly innate ability to command the audience, as the conductor Berlioz is a Napoleonic figure – a leader who must fight his way to the top and earn the respect of his troops in order to lead the army to victory. That Berlioz may have had Napoleon in mind is confirmed by the broader context for his letter

---

[1] Originally published in the *Journal des débats* 1843; reprinted in Berlioz's *Memoirs*, pp. 267–70. Emphasis added.

to Liszt. The letter was part of the series of columns outlining his tour that Berlioz published in the *Journal des débats*, and Berlioz described these missives, as well as correspondence with family and friends from this period, as his 'bulletins of the grande armée', thus likening his tour to the exploits of Napoleon's famed imperial army. Most tellingly, Berlioz used the same image when writing to his uncle Félix Marmion, who had been a soldier in the actual grande armée of Napoleon: 'You must have read in the newspapers of every stripe my bulletins of the grande armée.'[2]

But which is the empire that Berlioz's 'grande armée' was promoting? Which aspect of Napoleon's tours does Berlioz evoke in his use of the term? And indeed, who or what was Berlioz's 'grande armée'? In attempting to answer these questions, this chapter examines the application of military metaphors in two very different works by Berlioz, *Symphonie funèbre et triomphale* and *Harold en Italie*, with a focus on the issues of collective vs individual identity in the orchestra, the role of the conductor, and the relationship between the orchestra and the work concept.

Military metaphors and the orchestra

In the heated aesthetic debates of the nineteenth century (and earlier) it was not unusual for the imagery of warfare to be employed to suggest rival aesthetic outlooks. However, given Berlioz's sympathy for, and even veneration of, several German composers, it is not immediately apparent that the conflict he outlines in the opening quotation is an aesthetic one. Another common subject of military metaphors was the orchestra, but this interpretation of Berlioz's reference, too, poses some problems. John Spitzer suggests the military image was more typically employed in the eighteenth century when, indeed, it was the prevalent metaphor for the orchestra.[3] Both armies and orchestras were typically symbols of collective allegiance to a monarch. For this reason, according to Spitzer, militaristic imagery was less frequently applied to orchestras in the early nineteenth century: the Napoleonic wars saw the reconceptualisation of armies along nationalistic rather than monarchical lines, while at the same time orchestras came to be seen as civic institutions rather than as the loyal soldiers of a monarch.[4]

---

[2] *CG* VIII, p. 223. See also *CG* III, p. 80; *CG* III, p. 85.
[3] John Spitzer, 'Metaphors of the Orchestra – The Orchestra as Metaphor', *The Musical Quarterly* 80/2 (1996), 242–5.
[4] Ibid., p. 245.

New metaphors of nature and machine now gained favour over the military image so popular in the eighteenth century.

The fact that the supposed transformation in orchestral metaphors noted by Spitzer coincides with other commonly perceived musicological watersheds, and in particular Lydia Goehr's 'Beethoven paradigm', reveals the importance of changing perceptions of the orchestral body to the work concept. With the apparent demise of the military metaphor for the orchestra, the disciplined individual identities that combine to constitute an army were replaced by an image of a single entity (whether natural or mechanical) at the service of the composer's score – even if the materiality of instrumental sound actually played a more important role in the construction of the 'imaginary museum' than often assumed.[5]

Spitzer's reference to the Napoleonic wars also signals the deeper political resonance of this transitional moment. For Foucault, Napoleon is the key figure at 'the point of junction', not between military and nonmilitary models, but rather between 'the monarchical, ritual exercise of sovereignty and the hierarchical, permanent exercise of indefinite discipline' – discipline which, as Foucault demonstrates, permeated not only the army, but the school, hospital, monastery, prison, and indeed, society at large.[6] Each disciplinary institution, including the army, becomes, in this model, a machine that subjects the individual to discipline through surveillance. Critics of Foucault point out that he tends to treat the body in ahistorical terms, that he avoids the question of 'whose body?' and that, by treating the body as a metaphor and a site of discipline, he overlooks the power of the individual body to produce knowledge as well as being controlled by it.[7] Foucault does not mention the orchestra, but instrumentalists were certainly subject to variants of that same disciplining of 'docile bodies' through the various manifestations of what he terms 'the art of distributions' and 'the control of activity'. As I will demonstrate in this chapter, a consideration of the orchestra through this 'disciplinary' lens can be enriched fruitfully both by being historically situated and by acknowledging the embodied agency and knowledge of the disciplined performers in the orchestral 'army' – especially the 'army' of the composer whose

---

[5] Dolan, *The Orchestral Revolution*. Dolan also challenges aspects of the 'around 1800' paradigm – p. 6.

[6] Michel Foucault, *Surveiller et punir: Naissance de la prison* (Paris: Éditions Gallimard, 1975), trans. Alan Sheridan *Discipline and Punish: The Birth of the Prison* (London: Penguin, 1991), p. 217.

[7] Dorinda Outram, *The Body and the French Revolution: Sex, Class and Political Culture* (New Haven: Yale University Press, 1989), pp. 18–21.

Treatise, as Dolan suggests, 'marks the arrival of the modern discipline of the orchestra'.[8]

Spitzer identifies Berlioz as a composer who employs the new metaphors of nature or machine to suggest the force or collective identity of the orchestra. However, Berlioz did not actually abandon the military image for the orchestra. To take just one example, in a 'bulletin' to Heine, Berlioz referred to the orchestra of the Paris Conservatoire quite specifically as the 'young guard of the grande armée': 'I was each day more and more amazed at the rapid progress in the performance [of the Brunswick orchestra], and the impetuous assurance with which the whole body attacked difficulties that had long seemed formidable even to my Paris orchestra – that young guard of the grande armée.'[9] In the case of the Conservatoire, the military image could almost be taken literally, as a reflection of the early affiliation of the Paris Conservatoire with the revolutionary period and with Napoleon's rule. The 'grande armée' metaphor is stretched, however, when Berlioz applies the same concept to his travels in Germany, as he does in the open letter to Liszt. Unlike Napoleon, he is forced to leave behind his physical soldiers – his orchestra – when he heads out to conquer Germany. The only troops he brings with him are his scores, and by these means he must 'conscript' his battalion afresh each time he enters a new city. But if the identity of the soldiers of this 'grand armée' is ambiguous, there is no doubt who acts as their general: Berlioz, as conductor of his own music, fuses score and performers into one solid force. Moreover, that very ambiguity – between, on one hand, the orchestra as individual bodies and subjectivities and, on the other hand, the orchestra as a single body constructed through the score – is one that is explored reflexively in his writings and music. Revisiting that duality in this chapter through the lens of military metaphors reveals even more explicitly how Berlioz contributed to the disciplining of orchestral bodies in and through musical works, and how Other worlds were explored or constructed through negotiations between individual and collective forces.

Two symphonies will form the focus of this chapter: Berlioz's *Symphonie funèbre et triomphale* and *Harold en Italie*. Aside from the designation 'symphony' (his fourth and second respectively), the two works would appear to have little in common. Indeed, they could be seen as representing the two styles which Berlioz himself juxtaposes and contrasts in his *Memoirs*. *Symphonie funèbre et triomphale* is one of what he called his 'monumental' works, with 'strange gigantic physiognomy and colossal aspect' such that 'either one entirely misses the drift of the whole, or is crushed by a

---

[8] Dolan, *The Orchestral Revolution*, p. 216; see also p. 215. [9] Berlioz, *Memoirs*, p. 298.

tremendous emotion.'[10] In contrast, *Harold en Italie* fits into the second category, which Berlioz lays out in terms that are significant to the consideration of the role of performer subjectivity in orchestral works (as discussed later in this chapter):

As for such of my compositions as are conceived on an ordinary scale, and require no exceptional means of execution, it is just their inward fire, their expression, and their rhythmical originality, that have been most injurious to them, on account of the kind of execution they demand. To render them properly, the performers, and especially the conductor, ought to *feel* as I do. They require a combination of extreme precision and irresistible *verve*, a regulated vehemence, a dreamy tenderness, and an almost morbid melancholy, without which the principal features of my figures are either altered or completely effaced. It is therefore, as a rule, exceedingly painful to me to hear my compositions conducted by anyone but myself.[11]

Symphonie funèbre et triomphale embodies its military agenda overtly, having been conceived for a military band on the march in the 1840 ceremonies accompanying the transferral of the remains of the fallen revolutionaries of 1830 to the new commemorative Bastille column. However, the work's ultimate destination was not the column, but the concert hall, where it occupies a slightly uneasy position between occasional transience and canonic transcendence. In contrast, *Harold en Italie*, with its evocation of souvenirs from Berlioz's Italian sojourn and Byron's *Childe Harold's Pilgrimage*, superficially lacks suggestions of military imperialism. But it is actually *Harold en Italie* to which Berlioz refers in the letter to Liszt (cited at the opening of this chapter), when he finally turns from the militaristic imagery of his task as a composer on tour to discussion of the specific repertoire he performed, and it is the work that he discusses at the greatest length in the letter: 'I do not recollect the programme [in Mannheim]. I only know that I wanted to have my second symphony (*Harold*) in full.'[12] *Harold* was one of the most popular works on Berlioz's first German tour, and discussion of performances of this work features in several of his 'bulletins of the grande armée', along with references to much more obviously military-themed works, such as the cantata *Le cinq mai* (in which a soldier mourns Napoleon's death).

The aggressive imagery of Berlioz's account of rehearsals and performances of *Harold en Italie* is countered by the very different imagery stirred in listeners such as the Grand Duchess Amelia, who 'fancied she again beheld the calm peacefulness of the exquisite Italian nights'.[13] The best way to reconcile the contradiction would appear to be to subscribe to a

---

[10] Berlioz, *Memoirs*, p. 489.   [11] Ibid., p. 489.   [12] Ibid., p. 271.   [13] Ibid., p. 271.

separation between performer and listener that idealises the musical work as an abstract or metaphysical experience constructed by the listener in ignorance of the labour or battles upon which its impact is dependent. Certainly there are precedents for uncovering militaristic aspects in music that lacks explicit military themes or functions, as in the case of Liszt, whose performances and public persona were interpreted by contemporary audiences as embodying military aggression and heroism.[14] In Berlioz's case, also, a reconsideration of the act of performance helps us to understand the suitability of the military image for *Harold en Italie* on his German tour, and his description of his second stylistic group, above, makes it clear that the performance – and, indeed, the experience of the performers – is integral to the meaning of such works. However, a closer examination both of Berlioz's involvement with military matters and of *Harold en Italie* also reveals these battles to be woven into the composer's work more directly than we might assume.

Taking *Symphonie funèbre et triomphale* first, we will familiarise ourselves with Berlioz's attitudes to military music in the most literal sense, but we will also explore ways in which military paradigms might, like the symphony itself, move from the street to the concert hall. In the second half of this chapter, in contrast, we will effectively reverse the same process. Turning to *Harold en Italie* and its Byronic origins, as well as its relationship to Berlioz's Italian travels, we will consider its latent Napoleonic frameworks, and how they are both extended and contested through performance that sublimates individual bodies. What emerges through closer consideration of the militaristic aspects of both symphonies is a fundamental crux, both for Berlioz's music specifically, and for emerging notions of the work concept more generally, during a period in which battles over territory were being reimagined. From the Other worlds of imperial conquest in physical territories, to the Other worlds of rival subjectivity, just who was being fought, and how, become highly charged questions.

Symphonie funèbre et triomphale

From the battlefield to the streets of Paris: Berlioz and military bands

Berlioz himself had little personal experience of formal armed combat, but the 1830 revolution saw him experience other forms of military discipline

---

[14] Gooley, 'Warhorses', 62–88.

first hand. As he notes in the *Memoirs*, when violence broke out he was ensconced in the Institut in order to finish his Prix de Rome competition entry, with stray bullets flying overhead, and muskets protruding from doors to protect those who had taken shelter inside. Having completed his cantata, Berlioz took to the streets with a pistol, but rather than participating in the bloodshed he instead joined a group who were singing one of his own military-themed pieces – the 'Chant guerrier' from his op. 2 settings of texts by Thomas Moore. As crowds gathered around the singers, Berlioz describes the group as an 'armed force' (*force-armée*). Eventually he led the massed public audience to join in at the chorus of *La Marseillaise:* 'aux armes, citoyens!' which they did with such 'precision and power' that he was overwhelmed, and collapsed.[15] Without firing a single shot from his pistol, Berlioz instead presents himself to the reader as effectively marshalling the troops through music, uniting a disparate group of citizens into a collective and potentially deadly force. Not long after the days of revolution, Berlioz reveals how this alignment of music and military combat could be transferred directly to the orchestra. After a successful read-through of his 1830 Prix composition *Sardanaple*, he remarked, 'that which truly touched my heart was the emotion of *these old grognards* [soldiers of Napoleon's Old Guard] of the orchestra, who are usually moved by nothing and who stay at their desks like machines without feelings.'[16] In examining *Symphonie funèbre et triomphale* and *Harold en Italie* in this chapter, we will see two very different kinds of echoes or memories of the Napoleonic ideal as filtered through 1830 and embodied in the orchestra, each of which approaches the question of collective combat and musical weapons, but on its own terms.

Well before 1830 Berlioz – like most of his generation – had a wealth of experience of military music on which he might base his own images for the orchestra. Indeed, some of his earliest musical experiences of any kind are likely to have been through the military band of the local Garde Nationale, and one of his first music teachers conducted the band.[17] Military bands were an integral part of the musical landscape throughout Berlioz's career, and he worked directly with such bands on numerous occasions. For example, *Symphonie funèbre et triomphale* was written specifically for 210 regimental musicians, whom he referred to as 'cette armée musicale';[18] Berlioz used his first German tour to study the practices of the Prussian bands, carefully documenting differences in instruments and describing

---

[15] Berlioz, *Memoirs*, pp. 106–8. [16] *CG*, I p. 379. Emphasis in the original.
[17] Berlioz, *Memoirs*, p. 11. [18] *CG* II, p. 648.

their power in performance, and he drew on local regimental musicians for performances of sections of his *Requiem* in Berlin.

The availability of these military bands to interact with Berlioz's state-commissioned or occasional works reflects a general shift in employment during the first half of the nineteenth century, in which military bands became increasingly embedded in civilian life.[19] However, regimental musicians still went to war and served quite practical functions in coordinating combat, and music continued to be used to structure various phases in the soldiers' lives, from the reveille to the drum tattoos that identified opposing armies. As Kastner points out in his treatise on military music, music was a crucial means of maintaining order in the military 'machine', enabling soldiers to march together more efficiently and even overcoming natural fatigue, for it could override individual physicality in favour of the discipline of the collective body.[20] Kastner also tells how commanding officers often subjected their musicians to the same discipline as soldiers. In training sessions cries of 'Attention! Shoulder arms! Forward march!' competed with similarly aggressive commands to the musicians: 'Pay attention to your embouchure! Repeat the scale! Execute the double tonguing!'[21]

The use of audible signals to impose ever more numerous and precise forms of discipline on time and on bodies was transferred from the military (as well as the monastery) to the school, factory, and other institutions, and to other aspects of life beyond those institutions.[22] A striking example is found in Berlioz's novella *Euphonia*, where the highly regimented life of the titular utopian city of the future is, he tells us, 'governed in military fashion and subjected to a despotic regime'.[23] Residents of Euphonia, the 'musical city', live in sections of the city devoted to their instrument or voice type, and their musical education is compartmentalised in stages (first they learn rhythm, then solfeggio, then harmony, and finally expression). Their daily lives are disciplined not by a military trumpet but by signals from a giant 'steam organ'.

---

[19] Jeremy Montagu, et al. 'Military music', *Grove Music Online. Oxford Music Online*, Oxford University Press, www.oxfordmusiconline.com/subscriber/article/grove/music/44139, accessed 10 April 2014.
[20] Georges Kastner, *Manuel général de musique militaire à l'usage des armées françaises* (Geneva: Minkoff Reprint, 1848, 1973), p. 176.
[21] Ibid., p. 359.
[22] Michelle Perrot, 'The Three Ages of Industrial Discipline in Nineteenth-Century France', in John M. Merriam (ed.), *Consciousness and Class Experience in Nineteenth-Century France* (New York, London: Holme & Meier Publishers Inc., 1979), p. 160.
[23] Berlioz, *Evenings with the Orchestra*, p. 283.

Berlioz's military metaphors for instrumental music were underpinned by practical knowledge. Kastner's treatise on military music several times cites Berlioz as an important figure in the medium. And in 1845 (the year after *Euphonia* was written), Berlioz published two articles on the proposed reforms of military music in France, in which he reveals his sensitivity to the practical demands of military bands. Berlioz acknowledges that his own views about instrumental selection and balance in military bands are based on the understanding that they 'are in no way designed to be heard in concert rooms nor in theatres; it is in the open air that they must resound'. As he states, 'Armies manoeuvre in the open air, in the open countryside. Therefore orchestras who intend to make themselves heard in such a setting must be organised in quite a particular way to afford them the best possible chance of combatting these unfavourable circumstances.'[24] In contrast, on several other occasions Berlioz expressed his frustration about outdoor music – indeed, in the *Orchestration Treatise* he denounces the concept, stating that music 'en plein air' is not possible.[25] The battle for the military band is, in Berlioz's account, not conducted against an enemy army, but against the 'unfavourable circumstances' of the geography of warfare. The band needs to make itself heard by people other than the musicians themselves – it is for this reason that the lack of resonating space in the open field is problematic.

Performers, listeners, and muscular bonding

In expressing his frustration about 'musique en plein air', Berlioz was doubtless thinking of the recent problems posed by the performance of his *Symphonie funèbre et triomphale* in the streets of Paris. As he explains in his *Memoirs*, 'With the exception of what was played as we went along the Boulevard Poissonnière, where the big trees – still standing – served as a kind of reflector for the sound, all the rest was lost. On the Place de la Bastille it was still worse; scarcely anything could be distinguished even ten paces off.'[26]

Both in the *Orchestration Treatise* and in his account of *Symphonie funèbre et triomphale*, Berlioz makes it clear that the listeners with whom he is primarily concerned are the civic audience rather than the soldiers on the march. Similarly, the entry on the side drum in Berlioz's *Orchestration Treatise* reinforces the idea that his priority is the passive listener; for the

---

[24] *CM* VI, p. 20. [25] Macdonald, *Berlioz's Orchestration Treatise*, p. 319.
[26] Berlioz, *Memoirs*, p. 234.

marching soldier a single drum, so unsatisfactory in musical terms, would be sufficient: 'Simple rhythms which are without melody, harmony, tonality or anything that goes to make true music and which are intended simply to mark the pace of soldiers marching can be overwhelming when played by a body of forty or fifty side drums on their own.'[27]

Berlioz's distinction between the perspectives of soldier and civic listener is significant when we begin to consider the progress of *Symphonie funèbre* from street to concert hall. Berlioz's attitude reflects the increased civic function of bands during this period. While bands required a kind of listening different to that of the concert hall, their repertoire increasingly overlapped with those of both concert hall and opera house. Military bands sometimes performed as part of operas, and popular operatic arias would be arranged for military band, with a solo instrument taking the melodic line. Berlioz's *Symphonie funèbre et triomphale* evokes the vocal idioms increasingly common in regimental band repertoire, particularly in the extended recitative for solo trombone of the central 'Oraison funèbre'.

Given that Berlioz eventually made the finale of his symphony a choral one, the inspiration for using instrumental recitative may have come most directly from Beethoven's Ninth Symphony, which itself evokes military contexts through its suggestion of janissary bands.[28] Indeed, cross-fertilisation between the opera house or concert hall and military bands was common, and a 'militaristic style' was more important to early Romantic music than the familiar narratives of absolute music generally acknowledge.[29] What today appears as a clear practical and aesthetic distinction between the orchestra and military band was, for many in the nineteenth century, much less obvious, with considerable overlap between both performers and repertoire.[30]

Symphonie funèbre et triomphale illustrates the close relationship between battlefield and concert hall in a particularly obvious way. Though it was commissioned for performance 'en plein air' in the streets of Paris, Berlioz felt that the 'real performance' was the public rehearsal in the Salle Vivienne.[31] There is a strong hint of irony when Berlioz tells his father that the performance on the streets was 'l'exécution en scène' (the performance 'on stage'),

---

[27] Macdonald, *Berlioz's Orchestration Treatise*, p. 288.
[28] Of course, janissary idioms were evoked in earlier repertoire also, including Mozart's *Die Entführung aus dem Serail*.
[29] Dolan, *The Orchestral Revolution*, p. 228.
[30] Lawrence Levine, *Highbrow/Lowbrow: The Emergence of Cultural Hierarchy in America* (Cambridge, MA: Harvard University Press, 1988), pp. 104–7.
[31] Berlioz, *Memoirs*, p. 234.

for it failed as a *musical* performance precisely because the streets of Paris lacked the acoustic properties of the concert-hall stage.[32]

Symphonie funèbre et triomphale was never music to be played in battle. However, it is important to note that, even if military bands were increasingly experienced in civilian contexts rather than primarily on the battlefield, they retained key aspects of military discipline. Moreover, listeners were not necessarily passive recipients of musical works, but could – like soldiers on the battlefield – be physically influenced by what they heard and saw in band performances. In other words, music need not have been written for performance on the battlefield in order to serve a military agenda. William H. McNeill has written of the 'muscular bonding' stimulated by both dancing and military drilling in different periods and cultures, whereby collective bodies were disciplined into cohesive units, experiencing the pleasure of a common purpose.[33]

Berlioz speaks of the powerful effect such 'muscular bonding' could have on a listener in an explicitly militaristic context. In his *Orchestration Treatise*, Berlioz recommends employing more than one side drum, as we have seen. He continues,

> Perhaps this is a good place to mention the peculiar but very real charm for the ear that results from a mass unison or the simultaneous sounding of a very large number of instruments of the same type, regardless of what kind of noise they produce. This may have been noted when attending the drill of infantry soldiers: at the commands to 'slope arms' and 'lay down arms', the little crack of the rifle band and the dull whack of the butt hitting the ground carry no significant meaning when one, two, three, or even ten or twenty men make the sound; but when the manoeuver is made by a thousand men, the unison of a thousand sounds that were insignificant in themselves create a brilliant ensemble which *attracts and captures your attention involuntarily*, which gives pleasure, and in which I even find vague and mysterious harmonies.[34]

The muscular bonding of the infantry is explicit; but what is interesting is how Berlioz conceives the infantry as performers whose coordinated bodies and weapons are discussed in a treatise on writing for the orchestra, and whose impact on the *listener* is foremost in Berlioz's mind. The listener's attention is captured by the 'vague, mysterious harmony', but the captivity is pleasurable. Images of violent militarism in music could evoke what

---

[32] *CG* II p. 648.
[33] William H. McNeill, *Keeping Together in Time: Dance and Drill in Human History* (Cambridge, MA: Harvard University Press, 1995).
[34] Berlioz, *Grand traité*, p. 450. Emphasis added.

Gooley (following Peter Gay) calls the 'cultivated aggression' that enabled the bourgeoisie to release tensions under the guise of an 'alibi' – in this case, the fact that the violence is offset by the 'civilizing or cultivating effects' associated with art.[35]

Berlioz's *Symphonie funèbre et triomphale* belongs to a genre of funereal and commemorative works, but while it might thus serve to mourn the consequences of physical aggression, that very act of mourning is itself configured in terms guaranteed to bind performers and audience together physically and emotionally in a virtual army, subject to disciplined control. For those performing *Symphonie funèbre et triomphale* on the streets of Paris, 'muscular bonding' would be most likely to have occurred in the marches of the first and final movements, which were repeated six times as Berlioz and his regimental bands processed slowly from Saint-Germain-l'Auxerrois to the Bastille column.

In the opening funeral march, Berlioz disciplines both performers and listeners through timbre. Repeated abrupt tonal shifts are accompanied by a sudden return of instruments, including the side drums and trumpets (Ex. 2.1). These instruments, long associated with European military music in the field, were precisely the instruments Berlioz positioned closest to himself when on the march, as extensions of his own disciplinary authority. And he seems to have been intent on preserving this element of spatial authority when the work moved to the concert hall: the side drums are to be placed at one extremity of the orchestra, the rest of the percussion at the other, thus framing and containing the other instruments.

The reflective central movement explores the rhythmic freedom of recitativo style through the individual (and, presumably, more self-directed) voice of the solo trombone. Described by Berlioz as 'the true leader of the race of wind instruments', the trombone is subtly individualised within the first movement also: in the closing repetition of the main march material, the trombone has a new countermelody, but one which sounds 'trapped' within the predetermined texture (Ex. 2.2).[36] It is this entrapment from which the ode releases the trombone into relative freedom, before the final movement celebrates the apotheosis of the souls of the dead and unites the bodies of the living in a stirring march.

While the listeners who lined the path of the procession could not have heard more than a small section of the symphony as the musicians paraded past them, Berlioz implies that those gathered in front of the column might have experienced an extended form of embodied response akin to 'muscular

---

[35] Gooley, 'Warhorses', p. 81.   [36] Rushton, *The Music of Berlioz*, p. 217.

Ex. 2.1 *Symphonie funèbre et triomphale* I 'Marche funèbre', bb. 62–8

bonding'. After the trombone recitative of the 'Oraison funèbre', where we might imagine heads bowed as the remains were blessed, the tomb was sealed. The concluding 'Apothéose' opens with a fanfare that directs the eyes upwards to the new commemorative column. The gradual upward sweep of the gaze simultaneously enacts a looking back in time: at the base of the column is inscribed the year 1830; above this the names of the dead are listed in three partitioned sections, one for each of the 'Three Days' of July, in reverse order from bottom to top – 29–28–27 July; finally the eye comes to rest on the golden figure of Liberty in flight at the top. Berlioz embodies this physical movement in the music. He described the final movement as 'a hymn of praise [. . .] an apotheosis when, after the sealing of the tomb, the attention should be concentrated on the column alone, surmounted by the figure of Liberty, with her wings outstretched to heaven, like the souls of those who had died for her'.[37] The fanfare that introduces

[37] Berlioz, *Memoirs*, p. 232.

Ex. 2.2 *Symphonie funèbre et triomphale* I 'Marche funèbre', bb. 175–82

this 'Apothéose' was conceived as rising 'by degrees from the very depths of the orchestra to the high note where the apotheosis breaks in'.[38] After two bars of drumroll (perhaps coinciding with the sound of stone grating upon stone as the tomb was closed), the fanfare rises through three sections of arpeggiations, each successively prolonging another note of the triad – and perhaps accompanying the gaze upwards to another segment of the column. Finally the whole orchestra unites in the cathartic release of the

---

[38] Ibid., p. 233. Berlioz here appears to offer a perspective contradictory to the one expressed in 'High and low sounds', where he ridicules the association between pitch and vertical space. *The Art of Music*, pp. 150–51.

Ex. 2.3 *Symphonie funèbre et triomphale* III 'Apothéose', bb. 1–19

fortissimo opening of the march as the collective gaze of the attendees might be imagined arriving at the figure of Liberty (Ex. 2.3).

When the *Symphonie funèbre* was performed at the Bastille column Berlioz's intended effect was lost, for, as he tells it, '[a]s a finishing stroke, the National Guard, impatient at having to stand so long under arms in the blazing sun, began to march off to the sound of fifty drums, which continued to beat relentlessly through the whole of the apotheosis, so that not one note of it could be heard.'[39] There was thus a direct clash between two conceptions of military music – between the drums of the National Garde, and the military band of Berlioz's more civic-focussed symphony. The immediate physical connection of listener and place was then sacrificed when the work moved from the column to the concert hall – in the absence of the Bastille column, the gaze was necessarily directed inward, rather than upward.

[39] Berlioz, *Memoirs*, p. 234.

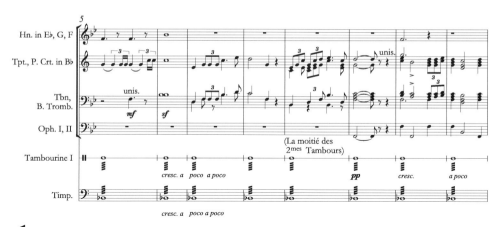

Ex. 2.3 (*cont.*)

For subsequent performances Berlioz helped to engage listeners by adding voices at the climax, as well as strings. While strings played little role in military bands, their introduction is not incompatible with military-style 'muscular bonding'. Berlioz wrote of violin sections: '[a] slight movement of the arm, an imperceptible nuance of feeling which would have no visible effect in the hands of a single violinist, these can generate a magnificent and irresistible flow of feeling when multiplied by a cluster of unisons, and strike to the heart of one's very being.'[40] Berlioz here suggests the listener's pleasure in witnessing a kind of military precision in his discussion of the violin section where, again, collective, coordinated effort is at the heart of the impact on the listener. Indeed, Berlioz's listener almost becomes part of the drill, bonding with the group in a manner that borders on the physical. The violins (and violas) are saved for the third and final movement of *Symphonie funèbre et triomphale* – the first movement has

[40] Macdonald, *Berlioz's Orchestration Treatise*, p. 34.

Ex. 2.3 (*cont.*)

only celli and basses, and the central movement has no strings at all. They are thus introduced as a reinforcement of the music of 'glory' and victory, making their first appearance at the tutti release that follows the fanfare and culminating at the final climax with string crossing that creates bow movement suggestive of the parrying of swords, as the 'sublime victims' of the revolution are acknowledged (Ex. 2.4).

Regiments of musicians: Viewing the orchestral army

Aspects of military discipline could be located in musical bodies with no direct connection to military contexts, including the orchestra. For example, Berlioz's second article on the review of military bands concludes:

Ex. 2.4 *Symphonie funèbre et triomphale* III 'Apothéose', bb. 218–21

We can only wish that soon other branches of music, which are languishing under the rust of prejudice and routine, will benefit from the kind of attention that the Minister of War, guided by his extensive experience and his deep love of everything concerned with the glory of the army, has just given to regimental music. So many important institutions for the arts of peace could be directed militarily![41]

Elsewhere, Berlioz implies that the act of performing music itself might instil a kind of civic unity – perhaps even a military cohesion. Joseph d'Ortigue suggested that Berlioz shared the view that collective instruction in music was the most effective means of 'maintaining discipline among soldiers' and of 'making them humane and honest, saving them from idleness and vice'.[42] But Berlioz also recommended that music should be taught in schools as a way of 'civilising' the general population, for 'of all the means of civilising, music is one of the most effective, one of the quickest and least dangerous'.[43]

---

[41] *CM* VI, p. 127.

[42] Joseph d'Ortigue, 'Des Sociétés Philharmoniques dans le midi de la France', *Gazette Musicale de Paris* 48 (30 November 1834), p. 382. See also Katherine Kolb Reeve, 'The Poetics of the Orchestra in the Writings of Hector Berlioz', unpublished PhD thesis, Yale University (1978), p. 137.

[43] *CM* II, p. 549. Reeve, 'The Poetics of the Orchestra', p. 137.

The military discipline of Berlioz's utopian city Euphonia penetrates from the macrocosm of the city to the microcosm of the musical bodies within it: both Foucault's 'art of distributions' and his 'control of activity' are manifest in rehearsals and performances, which break down the orchestral or choral unit into parts, and take the regulation of the performers to an extreme degree:

> Any marking of the rhythm by bodily movements during the singing is strictly forbidden to the choristers. They are also trained to silence, a silence so absolute and profound that if three thousand Euphonian choristers were assembled in the amphitheatre or in any other resonant place, one could still hear the buzzing of an insect, and a blind man in their midst might think he was quite alone.[44]

Similarly, in the *Orchestration Treatise* Berlioz writes, 'the noise of instruments warming up and playing during the interval is deeply offensive to sensitive listeners.'[45] Silence is taken as the ultimate ideal of discipline in the school, army, and prison of the era.[46] The potentially paradoxical emphasis Berlioz places on silence in Euphonia and on the rigid control of physical movement in a body whose purpose is to make music hints at the dystopian element of his vision – one which I will explore further in Chapter 4. This is 'muscular bonding' of an extreme kind.

The inspiration for Euphonia's regimentation may have come from Berlioz's experience of Prussian military bands, which he described as 'regiments of musicians, rather than musicians of regiments.'[47] Berlioz's account of the performance of 320 of these musicians, assembled by their band leader Wilhelm Wiprecht to perform for him and a small audience at the home of the Crown Prince of Prussia, emphasises the importance of physical discipline and coordination, critical not just to the military drill, but also to effective orchestral performance. Indeed, the first music performed was an arrangement of Berlioz's own overture *Les francs-juges*:

> I was astonished at not seeing the orchestra; no sound betrayed its presence, when a slow phrase in F minor, well known to both you and me, made me turn my head towards the largest room in the palace, which was concealed from our sight by an immense curtain [...] and difficult as the music was they performed it with

---

[44] Berlioz, *Evenings with the Orchestra*, p. 286.
[45] Macdonald, *Berlioz's Orchestration Treatise*, p. 362.
[46] Foucault lists silence among the 'instruments' of the new form of discipline. *Discipline and Punish*, p. 128.
[47] Berlioz, *Memoirs*, p. 325.

marvellous exactness, and that furious fire with which you of the Conservatoire perform it on your great days of enthusiasm and ardour.[48]

The concealment of Wiprecht's band behind a curtain is also highly suggestive of a new kind of musical listening, one that would appear to be in direct opposition to the more typical context for military bands. In military drilling and many civic ceremonies, the visual aspect of the band often played a vital role, for audiences of military music 'hear with their eyes'.[49] Berlioz remarked upon the effectiveness of this visual element in relation to the 1846 performance of military bands at the Hippodrome (the highlight of which was, according to Kastner, the 'Apothéose' of the *Symphonie funèbre et triomphale*).[50] While the loss of sound in the outdoor setting gave rise to one of his diatribes about 'musique en plein air', Berlioz was favourably impressed with the visual spectacle:

[T]he staging was otherwise very beautiful and admirably organised; the uniforms of various colours and forms, grouped in ordered units, the flags, the sparkling helmets, that hive of brass instruments reflecting the rays of the sun, and around them the huge crowds of people who filled the terraces and part of the Hippodrome's arena – all this formed a magnificent scene.[51]

Visual spectacle was also integral to the initial ceremonial performance of the complete *Symphonie funèbre et triomphale*. Berlioz was instructed to ensure that all two hundred musicians of the military band he employed for the *Symphonie funèbre et triomphale* were in uniform, 'to avoid an unsuitable multicoloured effect and in order to give the cortege of the 28th the necessary character'.[52] In fact, it was not only musicians in military bands who performed in uniform. Costuming is another area in which we may see the traces of military discipline in orchestral practice, from the livery and swords of the orchestras of Louis XIV or Napoleon[53] to the uniform worn by students of the Conservatoire and the obligatory white cravats of the Opéra orchestra, as satirised by Berlioz.[54] The military connotations of orchestral dress were

---

[48] Ibid., pp. 325–6.
[49] Roland Bannister, 'How Are We to Write Our History? Perspectives on the Historiography of Military Music', *Musicology Australia* 25 (2002), 17.
[50] Kastner, *Manuel général de musique militaire*, p. 329.
[51] *Journal des débats* 29 July 1846. *CM* VI, pp. 189–90.   [52] *CG* II, p. 646.
[53] Spitzer and Zaslaw, *The Birth of the Orchestra: History of an Institution, 1650–1815* (Oxford: Oxford University Press, 2004), p. 75; Adam Carse, *The Orchestra from Beethoven to Berlioz* (Cambridge: W. Heffer & Sons Ltd., 1948), p. 68.
[54] 'Arrêté concernant l'Habillement', 12 January 1808, in Constant Pierre (ed.), *Le Conservatoire National de Musique et de Déclamation: Documents historiques et administratifs* (Paris: Imprimérie nationale, 1900), p. 294; Berlioz, *The Musical Madhouse*, pp. 4–5.

seemingly heightened by the physical coordination of string players, at least for some viewers. Chorley, writing in 1844, commented admiringly of the Paris Conservatoire orchestra, 'You may see the phalanx of bows plying up and down the strings with a mechanical consent and parallelism.'[55]

Indeed, if the physical movements of musicians could be likened to those of soldiers, their instruments were sometimes compared to weapons. As Maiko Kawabata has pointed out, the bows of violin concerto soloists were often likened to swords.[56] And developments in wind and (in particular) brass instruments could suggest the hardware of modern warfare.[57] The general analogy between instruments and weapons is recognised by Berlioz in one of the articles he published on the proposed reforms of military music in France. After discussing the need to allow the instrumental technology in wind and brass employed in military bands to evolve, Berlioz concludes: 'to cite an example that is close to the subject with which we are concerned, did it not take years of debate before percussion-guns could be replaced with flintlock rifles? And was there not earlier even more effort involved in substituting the latter for wheel-lock and matchlock muskets?'[58] Berlioz is clearly employing an analogy here, albeit a highly suggestive one. But he also points out how Sax, whose instruments and instrumental innovations he praised, was directly sponsored by the Minister of War.[59] Moreover, in the *Orchestration Treatise*, he suggests a particularly close affiliation between the visual and aural aspects of brass and of the armour worn in battle: 'the massed brass in large military bands bring to mind a regiment in shining armour marching to glory or to death'.[60]

Berlioz was inevitably frustrated when the conditions of the performance of his *Symphonie funèbre et triomphale* rendered much of the work inaudible to the crowds, but his conclusion suggests that the root cause was a preference in France for the visual at the expense of the aural: 'Music is always thus respected in France at all fêtes or public rejoicings, where they think it ought to figure . . . to the eye.'[61] Indeed, he had written the work specifically to cater for this context. To his father, he claimed, 'this time I wrote so large that even those with myopia could read me'.[62] And he reinforced the visual metaphor: 'it is a billboard, a colossal inscription which the whole world

---

[55] Quoted in Elliot W. Galkin, *A History of Orchestral Conducting in Theory and Practice* (New York: Pendragon Press, 1988), p. 617.
[56] Maiko Kawabata, 'Virtuoso Codes of Violin Performance: Power, Military Heroism, and Gender (1789–1830)', *19th-Century Music* 28/2 (2004), 100–103.
[57] Newark, 'Metaphors for Meyerbeer', 32.   [58] *CM* VI, p. 19.
[59] *CM* VI, p. 127. Also Berlioz, *Memoirs*, p. 308.
[60] Macdonald, *Berlioz's Orchestration Treatise*, p. 125.
[61] Berlioz, *Memoirs*, p. 234.   [62] *CG* II, p. 649.

saw.'[63] The visual element was important to Berlioz's music, but it needed to be enacted on his terms, as we shall see in the next chapter.

Conducting the orchestral army

If an orchestra could be likened to an army, whose authority do they serve? In the performances on Berlioz's tour, the roles and authority of composer and conductor were crucially merged, for Berlioz conducted performances of his own music, in a move he himself considered unusual: 'A composer touring Germany to put on and conduct himself concerts dedicated to the performance of his own works is something that has never been seen before.'[64] Berlioz's own references to his German tour as the equivalent of the tour of Napoleon's 'grande armée' reflect the importance of the composer–conductor gaining new territory in German lands.

The use of military imagery for conductors was actually quite common during this period. Indeed, comparisons between conductors and generals or military commanders highlight a crucial transformation of the conductor's role – a transformation in which Berlioz played an important part. The shift from conductor-as-timekeeper to conductor-as-interpreter vested considerable authority in the individual, while the growth in size of the orchestral forces under his command and the complexity of the musical demands of many of the works performed meant that even basic coordination and timekeeping required increasing authority and a disciplined approach to rehearsals.

Berlioz's *Symphonie funèbre et triomphale* was conducted at the ceremonial premiere by the composer himself, marching backwards at the head of the band. While suggestions that Berlioz conducted with a sword are unfounded,[65] the composer's baton itself conveyed a powerful military symbolism. Both the baton and the bow (which was preferred by most conductors in France in Berlioz's time) had military associations. The analogy between the violin soloist's bow and the sword could be extended when the violinist conducted, thrusting the bow in the air rather than drawing it across the strings, and images of violinists in the act of conducting sometimes suggest a kind of sword play. Paganini, in particular, cut a Napoleonic figure at the head of the orchestra.[66] (See Fig. 2.1.) The violinist-conductors conveyed the authority of one who had 'risen from the troops' and could

---

[63] *CG* II, p. 649.   [64] *CG* III, p. 98.
[65] He mentions to his father that he conducted with a baton. *CG* II, p. 648; Hugh Macdonald (ed.), *NBE* vol. 19, p. VIII.
[66] Kawabata, *Paganini: The 'Demonic' Virtuoso*, p. 88.

Fig. 2.1 Sketch of Paganini, by Boulanger c. 1840. Library of Congress, Music division, Gertrude Clarke Whittall Collection.

himself join as well as lead the fray.⁶⁷ When Berlioz praised Habeneck, in his all-important performances of Beethoven's symphonies in Paris in 1829, he spoke admiringly of the way Habeneck, as a violinist, could quickly demonstrate things to the other violinists. Moreover, a Napoleonic dimension to Habeneck's authority is implied when Berlioz likens the discovery of Beethoven's symphonies to the discovery by 'notre armée d'Égypte' of the pyramids: 'The leader [*chef*] who guides these musicians in the discovery of a new world of music is fully worthy of his mission.'⁶⁸

Berlioz would later come to express more critical perspectives on Habeneck as a conductor, proclaiming after the latter's unsuccessful performances of *Benvenuto Cellini*, 'Unhappy composers! learn how to conduct, and how to conduct yourselves well (with or without the pun), for do not forget that the most dangerous of your interpreters is the conductor himself.'⁶⁹ And when Berlioz took to the podium, it was with the baton rather than the bow in his hand. 'I have never touched a bow in my life', he told one paterfamilias in Breslau, who was intent on having Berlioz instruct his son

---

⁶⁷ See, for example, the description of Pugnani in Galkin, *A History of Orchestral Conducting*, p. 468.
⁶⁸ *CM* I p. 43. ⁶⁹ Berlioz, *Memoirs*, p. 223.

on the violin: '"I am giving a concert, but I shall not play the violin myself." "Then what will you do?" "*I shall have the violin played*, and shall conduct the orchestra."'[70] With no ability as a violinist himself, Berlioz was certainly not in a position to demonstrate to the orchestra on the violin in the fashion prevalent in Paris, and he also saw the bow as inferior to the baton, especially for rapid movements.[71] Whereas the violinist–conductor is one of the troops, the baton conductor represents the authority of the general who must stay out of the fray in order to govern. As one critic wrote, 'a general should direct his army, and rarely fight himself.'[72] If the bow is the symbol of the soldier's sword (or rifle), the baton is the symbolic authority of the marshal's staff, and may have made its way to the orchestra via marching bands.[73]

Accounts abound of the military authority of the baton conductor, particularly in Germany. In the first of the open letters reporting on his German travels, Berlioz commented on German approaches to conducting, quite different to those he had encountered in France (where bow conducting was still being defended as late as 1878).[74] Berlioz points out that in Germany there were several sources of authority; ideally the composer would conduct his own works, but the Kapellmeister would usually conduct 'the principal operas and all important musical works of which the authors are either absent or dead'. Moreover, the Kapellmeister was usually an able composer and 'always conducts with a baton'.[75] In contrast, the leader would deal with the 'material details of the studies', including the demonstration on his violin of the bowing or phrasing. This division of roles reinforced a split between the composer–conductor's spiritual authority and the materiality of performance.

Other accounts emphasise the militaristic associations of German baton conductors. Weber was described as 'lead[ing] his army to the musical fray',[76] while Spontini (in Wagner's words) gripped his baton 'as a marshal's staff and used it, not for beating time with, but commanding'.[77] According to Moritz Hanemann, Spontini would assume the 'field-marshal's position' and viewed his instruments as 'heavy artillery'.[78] Berlioz, as a baton

---

[70] Ibid., p. 429. [71] Macdonald, *Berlioz's Orchestration Treatise*, p. 340.
[72] Paris correspondent of *Harmonicon* June 1825, p. 103; quoted in Carse, *The Orchestra from Beethoven to Berlioz*, p. 312.
[73] José Antonio Bowen, 'The Rise of Conducting', in José Antonio Bowen (ed.), *The Cambridge Companion to Conducting* (Cambridge: Cambridge University Press, 2003), p. 94.
[74] David Cairns, 'The French tradition', in Bowen (ed.), *The Cambridge Companion to Conducting*, p. 138.
[75] Berlioz, *Memoirs*, p. 246. [76] Quoted in Galkin, *A History of Orchestral Conducting*, p. 505.
[77] Quoted in Carse, *The Orchestra from Beethoven to Berlioz*, p. 300. [78] Ibid., p. 345.

conductor himself, was similarly described in military terms. Gautier referred to Berlioz's orchestra at the Cirque Olympique concert of January 1845 as 'the army of general Berlioz'.[79] To Hallé, Berlioz was 'the most perfect conductor I have ever set eyes upon, one who held absolute sway over his troops'.[80] And Vladimir Stasov employs the military image to suggest the dynamic power of Berlioz's conducting: 'Leading [the orchestra], Berlioz is a veritable general, adored by all his forces, inspiring them by some kind of extraordinary power to accomplish unprecedented feats.'[81]

Berlioz himself likened the conductor's baton to weaponry when, exchanging batons with Mendelssohn on his German tour in a gesture of solidarity, he referred to the two men as chiefs exchanging tomahawks. He described his own compositions several times as 'bordées' (rounds of cannon fire) – an image propagated by a popular lithograph showing him as conductor directing an orchestra comprising cannons.[82] Some versions of this image show Berlioz to be conducting not with a baton, but with a mace, further reinforcing the military nature of his authority (Fig. 2.2). Berlioz's rehearsal practice emphasised a new kind of authority akin to military and other 'disciplines'. He was among the first to institute sectional rehearsals – an approach that reflects both the greater division and specialisation of the Napoleonic army (broken into units coordinated and overseen by their general) and the division and surveillance of labour more broadly in the modern era.[83] Moreover, Berlioz conducted from the full score, unlike many of the violinist conductors who would use a specially prepared version that had the first violin line, a bass line, and only select other staves. He thus embodied Napoleon's perspective, for the latter claimed, 'my great talent, the one that distinguishes me the most, is to see the entire picture distinctly'.[84]

The disciplinary control of the baton conductor occasionally met with scepticism or resistance, particularly in the early years of its establishment. For some, the military associations of the baton suggested a dictatorship that was felt to harm rather than benefit music. Moritz Hauptmann, in the *Neue Zeitschrift für Musik* in 1836, complained about Spohr's use of 'the cursed little white stick [...] domineering over the whole orchestra'.[85] Similarly,

---

[79] Gautier, *La Presse*, 6 January 1845 Quoted *CG* III, p. 219, fn 1.
[80] Quoted in Galkin, *A History of Orchestral Conducting*, p. 555.
[81] Quoted in Macdonald, *Berlioz's Orchestration Treatise*, p. 364.
[82] *CG* I, pp. 96, 518, 524; *CG* II, p. 22.   [83] Foucault, *Discipline and Punish*.
[84] Quoted in Geoffrey Ellis, *The Napoleonic Empire*, 2nd edn (Basingstoke: Palgrave Macmillan, 2003), p. 76.
[85] Quoted Carse, *The Orchestra from Beethoven to Berlioz*, p. 304.

Fig. 2.2 Berlioz conducts with a mace. 'Satyrisches Bild' by Andreas Geiger, after Cajetan. Reproduction courtesy of Erich Lessing Culture and Fine Arts Archive.

when Mendelssohn introduced baton conducting in Leipzig, Schumann protested, 'For my part, I disliked the conductor's stick in the overture as in the symphony. I sounded Florestan, who remarked that the orchestra should stand like a republic in a symphony, refusing to acknowledge a superior.'[86]

[86] Ibid., p. 305.

The victory of the score?

If a conductor's authority could suggest a military dictatorship, whose individuality was at stake? Despite the similarity of their objections to the baton, Hauptmann and Schumann represent subtly different perspectives: Hauptmann speaks as a former member of Spohr's orchestra, Schumann as a member of Mendelssohn's audience. While the conductor must first win over the orchestra, like new conscripts, to respect his authority, there is a sense in which it is ultimately the audience that is being fought against through the successful mastery (or conquest?) of a new score by the performers. When Berlioz himself employs the military metaphor, this is often his meaning. For example, at a performance in Berlin he had to take extra measures to prepare his orchestra and chorus, since Meyerbeer (their usual conductor) and Elssler (the choirmaster) were both ill during the final rehearsals. After stirring his troops with a speech, Berlioz describes the performance as a victorious battle:

> our forces [were] reanimated, full of courage, and enchanted at not having lost a battle in which both their honour and mine were at stake. On the contrary, we gained a brilliant victory [...] I should, as soldiers say, have turned up my eyes in a most absurd manner. The first volley once endured, the rest was mere play [...]. When the concert was over [...] Wiprecht alone, with an embrace like that of a cuirassier, had the power to make me come to.[87]

Berlioz gave similar accounts of his physical exhaustion after conducting the ceremonial performance of *Symphonie funèbre et triomphale*, though after four hours of walking backwards conducting his 210 musicians, such physical strain was inevitable. He told his father two days later that he was still worn out, and that the day before 'I could scarcely write, so much had the movement of my arm and the pressure of the baton tired the muscles of my hand'.[88]

Elsewhere it is the performers themselves who are treated as the target of Berlioz's assault. In his *Memoirs* Berlioz summarises his battles with various sectors of the musical world, first and foremost 'the Parisian public', but also those musicians wounded by his reviews, and other conductors. 'You will admit that I have had a fine phalanx to fight', he concludes, 'without mentioning the singers and the virtuosi, whom I always call brusquely to order when they take irreverent liberties with the music, or the envious beings who are always ready to be exasperated at anything more brilliant than themselves.'[89]

---

[87] Berlioz, *Memoirs*, p. 331.   [88] *CG* II, p. 648.   [89] Berlioz, *Memoirs*, pp. 485–6.

The performers Berlioz cites as those he must battle against are those who pit their 'voices' against his own. Here Berlioz speaks more as a composer than as a conductor. It is his music that is 'more brilliant' than the very different creativity of the virtuosi or the singers who depart from his scores.[90] Elsewhere Berlioz implies a sublimation of performer into score in the ideal musical work, for example in a letter he sent to his sister in 1830, as he contemplated his *Symphonie fantastique*:

Ah, my sister, you cannot imagine the pleasure of a composer writing freely under the direct influence of his will alone. When I have sketched the first bracket [*accolade*] of my score, where my instruments of different ranks are arranged in battle formation, when I think of this virgin field of chords that scholastic prejudice has preserved untouched until now, and which, since I have been freed, I regard as my domain, I rush forward with a kind of frenzy to forage there; sometimes I address my soldiers: 'you, coarse folk, who until now spouted nothing but foolish remarks, come and allow me to teach you how to speak; all of you, graceful musical will-o'-the-wisps, whom routine has filed in the dusty cabinets of wise theoreticians, come and dance before me and show that you are good for something better than acoustical experiments; and above all,' I say to my army, 'you must forget the songs of the guardroom and the habits of the barracks.'[91]

While Berlioz is concerned with new harmonies – an aspect that can be located in the score – he also makes clear to his sister that the orchestra and the performance are central to his aesthetic. It is through the orchestra that he will explore and conquer these 'virgin territories' of music. But just as in the *Orchestration Treatise* we saw how Berlioz tends to personify instruments rather than discuss the people who play them, here again it is his *instruments* he imagines arranged in battalions. Orchestral performers occupy a slightly uneasy position in his conception of his works.

Berlioz's use of military metaphors for the orchestra becomes particularly significant in this context, for unlike the new collective metaphors of machine and nature, which generally erase individual identities,[92] the military metaphor acknowledges the presence of individuals within a collective. Moreover, the mechanical and military images are not necessarily mutually exclusive, but can work in tandem, as revealed in Chorley's comment about the '*phalanx* of bows' of the Paris Conservatoire orchestra, 'plying up and down the strings with a *mechanical* consent and parallelism'.[93] The almost

---

[90] Holoman, *Berlioz*, p. 356. [91] *CG* I, pp. 303–4.
[92] Spitzer, 'Metaphors of the Orchestra', p. 248; and Goehr, *Imaginary Museum of Musical Works*, p. 274.
[93] Quoted in Galkin, *A History of Orchestral Conducting*, p. 617. Emphasis added.

dehumanising effect, in which individual players are overlooked in favour of their instruments and become part of the collective 'orchestral machine' or 'grande armée' that realises the composer's work, takes on a particularly unsettling meaning when viewed in light of the horrors of modern warfare. Less radically, we might at least acknowledge that Berlioz's employment of the military metaphor reflects tensions around the work concept and the relative authority of the composer and conductor, the conductor and the orchestra, and the orchestral players and the listeners in the realisation of the music. But these tensions could be productive, or pleasurable rather than destructive.

With its employment of an actual military band, its use of muscular bonding, and its combination of civic function and Napoleonic aura, *Symphonie funèbre et triomphale* demonstrates obvious ways in which the military metaphor might be invoked. Katherine Kolb Reeve describes the symphony as Berlioz's 'most specifically popular work', demonstrating him to have been 'the first of Napoleonic stature to undertake such ventures, and to make of the social statement a lasting work of art'.[94] Berlioz himself described the *Symphonie funèbre et triomphale* as being among the works that demonstrate 'a class of ideas which I have been almost the only modern composer to deal with, and the mere import of which has entirely escaped the older writers'.[95] However, he did not make the *Symphonie funèbre* part of his 'grande armée' when he toured Germany two years later, despite the availability of the renowned Prussian regimental musicians. Perhaps he felt the work was too explicitly connected to its French context. Wagner, who greatly admired the *Symphonie funèbre et triomphale* when he heard it in Paris, remarked that the symphony would 'live and be an inspiration as long as there is a nation called France'.[96]

Berlioz did include in the musical arsenal he took to Germany movements of his *Requiem* (which resulted from a commission that similarly connects the work with those who gave their lives in the 1830 revolution, though it was performed for those who gave their lives for a different French victory – the Siege of Constantine); he also took the explicitly Napoleonic cantata *Le cinq mai*. Perhaps Berlioz considered those works less bound to a specifically Parisian 'stage' – to the streets and column that were evoked

---

[94] Kolb Reeve, 'The Poetics of the Orchestra', pp. 132, 133. See also Cairns, *Servitude and Greatness*, pp. 209–10.
[95] Berlioz, *Memoirs*, p. 488.
[96] From an essay in the Dresden *Abendzeitung* 5 May 1841; cited in Cairns, *Servitude and Greatness*, p. 210.

even when *Symphonie funèbre et triomphale* moved into the concert hall. However, rather than examine the German reception of the *Requiem* or *Le cinq mai*, let us instead now turn to *Harold en Italie*, a work which occupied a central role in Berlioz's German battalion, but whose military and Napoleonic elements are heavily concealed. Where *Symphonie funèbre et triomphale* is blatantly heroic, conceived to commemorate and celebrate the dead of the July revolution (and perhaps also their Napoleonic predecessors) through the sights and sounds of a military band, *Harold en Italie* has been persuasively described as 'anti-heroic',[97] with a reclusive individualistic protagonist who avoids conflict, embodied on the concert platform by a viola soloist whose idiom and instrument seem directly to counter any suggestion of the military. However, antiheroism is defined by its relationship to heroism, and an understanding of the military contexts for *Harold en Italie* enables us better to appreciate the way in which the work is defined through this act of negation. Both works also stage worlds, or 'Other worlds', in the concert hall – the Parisian streets of *Symphonie funèbre et triomphale* are matched by the Italian landscapes signalled by the title and embodied musically in Berlioz's second symphony. Indeed, both works may on some level have originated in Italy, with Berlioz's earliest conceptions for a military symphony (which was intended to commemorate those who died on Napoleon's Italian campaign and celebrate the general's return to Paris) occurring as Berlioz retraced Napoleon's steps at the end of his Italian sojourn. Sketches for this work and an ode to the dead Napoleon frame the first sketches for *Harold en Italie*.[98] Perhaps the most significant difference between the two works is the ways in which they model subjectivity, from the implicit collective response of *Symphonie funèbre et triomphale* to the individualism of *Harold*. More subtly, these differences are enacted through the position and subjectivity of the performers themselves – through the agency of the disciplined body.

---

[97] Mark Evan Bonds, 'Sinfonia Anti-eroica: Berlioz's Harold en Italie and the Anxiety of Beethoven's Influence,' *The Journal of Musicology* 10/4 (1992), 417–63.

[98] D. Kern Holoman, 'The Berlioz Sketchbook Recovered', *19th-Century Music* 7/3 (1984), 290–91 and 292–6. Holoman challenges Tiersot's assumption that the sketches for *Harold* date to the same period as the initial sketches for a military symphony. Moreover, the sketches for the military symphony contain no thematic material connected to the *Symphonie funèbre et triomphale*, though Berlioz may have planned to put some of these ideas to use in the *Fête musicale funèbre* he planned in 1835, and Holoman speculates that he might subsequently have used material from the *Fête musicale funèbre* in the *Symphonie funèbre et triomphale*: Holoman, *Catalogue of the Works of Hector Berlioz* (Kassel: Bärenreiter, 1987), p. 151. Thus while the thematic sketches for *Harold en Italie* and the *Symphonie funèbre* are not exactly on 'two sides of the same page', their originating conceptions may have been.

Harold en Italie

Berlioz in Italy

Little of *Harold in Italy* was actually written in Italy, and when Paganini commissioned a work to show off his new viola, it appears to have been Britain rather than Italy to which Berlioz turned for inspiration. A newspaper announced the theme was to be 'les derniers instants de Marie-Stuart'.[99] Moreover, two of the musical themes (including the *idée fixe* itself) originated in Berlioz's treatment of a Scottish topic: Rob Roy, as represented in the overture of the same name, which Berlioz had initially conceived in Italy but later abandoned. Nevertheless, in understanding the military dimension of *Harold in Italy* and the way Other worlds are embodied in this work, it is useful to begin in Italy, and in particular with Berlioz's experience of Napoleonic and military frameworks in this context.

Berlioz departed from Paris for Italy in December 1830 during a period when Napoleonic fever was rampant. Theatre listings were dominated by works with titles such as *Le petit Corporal, Joséphine, Le Lieutenant d'artillerie,* and *Napoléon en paradis.*[100] Arriving in Italy after a couple of months in La Côte, Berlioz was thus primed to respond to the traces of Napoleon's imperial legacy in the lands which had been the site of some of Napoleon's formative conquests. The Villa Medici in Rome, where Berlioz was obliged to reside for at least part of his tenure as a Prix de Rome recipient, bore the inscription 'À Napoléon le Grand, les Arts reconnaissants',[101] and it was Napoleon who had set up the French Academy in this new accommodation in 1803, safeguarding it from permanent closure after the French Revolution.

Moreover, Napoleon was admired not only by many in Paris and Germany, but also by certain factions in Italy, for his conquest of the Austrians on Italian soil and the subsequent period of Napoleonic rule of the Kingdoms of Italy and Sardinia helped to foster the ideology and infrastructure of a united nation.[102] Although Austrian rule in the north was reasserted after Napoleon's fall, and the kingdoms were redivided along old

---

[99] See the announcement in *Gazette musicale* 26 January 1834; cited in Holoman, *Catalogue of the Works*, p. 144.

[100] Titles taken from the theatre listings in *Figaro*, 7 December 1830 – and there were several more similarly titled plays all advertised on the same day.

[101] Ruth Berges, 'That Elusive Prix de Rome' *Music Review* 55/2 (May 1994), 146.

[102] Alexander Grab, 'The Napoleonic Legacy in Italy', in Deborah Burton, Susan Vandiver Nicassio, and Agostino Ziino (eds.), *Tosca's Prism: Three Moments of Western Cultural History* (Boston: Northeastern University Press, 2004), pp. 3–18.

lines, some Carbonari identified Napoleon as the symbolic leader of their own resistance.

Berlioz experienced first-hand the associations between the French and the Carbonari, when on several occasions he encountered official suspicion that he was part of the resistance. One of his travelling companions on the journey to Italy was subsequently killed with Menotti in the uprising against the Duke of Modena, and Berlioz remarks in the *Memoirs* that the time of his arrival 'was a most unfavourable one'. He explains, 'as a Frenchman coming from Paris, I had the greatest difficulty in getting into the Papal States. The officials refused to *viser* my passport, as the Academy students were suspected of having fomented the insurrection of the Piazza Colonna, and the Pope by no means desired an increase of the little revolutionary colony.'[103] Berlioz later comments that the police 'saw a revolutionist in every Frenchman'.[104] Moreover, the Italian uprisings of 1831 were connected in Berlioz's imagination to the image of Napoleon through the participation of his nephews. In Florence, Berlioz attended the funeral service for Napoléon Louis Bonaparte, the one-time heir to Napoleon who had with his brother (the future Napoleon III) fought amongst the Carbonari in northern Italy: 'Bonaparte! *His* name; *his* nephew; almost *his* grandson; dead at twenty'.[105] Similarly, when returning to France at the end of his tenure, Berlioz retraced Napoleon's steps, powerfully moved by 'awe-inspiring tracks which I followed as far as the Alps when on my way back to France'.[106] Berlioz passed through Lodi: 'I took care to see the famous bridge, and could even fancy that I heard the thunder of Bonaparte's grape-shot and the cries of the flying Austrians.'[107] And he contemplated a visit to Elba, Corsica and St Helena 'to gorge [himself] on Napoleonic memories'.[108] It was during this period that Berlioz sketched the earliest material for his 'military symphony' on Napoleon's return from Italy; the next sketch he would enter into the same notebook (even if two years later, as is now assumed) was for *Harold en Italie*.[109]

Italian responses to Napoleon's rule and legacy are too complex to examine in depth here. In any case, what is more directly relevant to Berlioz's *Harold en Italie* is the French perception of Italy during this era. The fact that Napoleon's armies had been able to occupy and colonise Italian territories was often attributed to defects in the Italian character, rather than to the fact that Italy was already divided and subject to foreign rule.[110] When Berlioz

---

[103] Berlioz, *Memoirs*, p. 120.   [104] Ibid., p. 128.   [105] Ibid., p. 135.
[106] *CG* II, pp. 24–5.   [107] Berlioz, *Memoirs*, p. 182.   [108] *CG* I, p. 539.
[109] Holoman, 'The Berlioz Sketchbook Recovered', 291.
[110] Chard, *Pleasure and Guilt on the Grand Tour*, p. 236.

complains that '[t]o the Italians music is a sensual pleasure, and nothing more',[111] his attitude might thus be seen in relation to Italy as a subject of military conquest. Moreover, the fact that Italian traditions were most obviously embodied in the voice, and in particular in opera, reinforced this military rhetoric. '[I]nstrumental music is almost unknown' in Italy, Berlioz claimed, and after hearing an orchestra in Rome, he commented that it was 'about as imposing and formidable as the Prince of Monaco's army'.[112]

Berlioz himself felt that in Italy 'the anti-musical state had reduced me to a state in which it was almost impossible to compose. I wrote only three or four pieces all the time I was at the Academy.'[113] Rather than entering a creative dialogue with the traditions he encountered in Italy and learning from its masterworks (as the painters, sculptors, and architects were expected to do), he treated Italy almost as a form of *couleur locale*, or even of musical exoticism in which it is the setting, not the style nor technique, which is appropriated by the composer.[114] As with much musical exoticism, there is a strong sense in which Berlioz's use of Italian subjects, in both his writings and his music, might thereby be seen to enact a kind of imperialism, all the more striking given the strength of the Italian operatic tradition in his own land. In employing Italian idioms and subjects within contexts wholly antithetical to those in which he had encountered them, Berlioz was effectively conquering the land for his own artistic vision. For example, his *Roméo et Juliette* is in many respects the antithesis of Bellini's operatic treatment of the same subject, which he saw in Florence. Berlioz condemned the singers who took on the roles of Bellini's 'Juliet (who was played by a fat woman) and Romeo (by a small thin one)'.[115] In contrast, Berlioz's lovers are voiced by instruments.

As an operatic work on an Italian subject, *Benvenuto Cellini* might have provided Berlioz with an opportunity to enter into dialogue with some of the traditions of 'artistic Italy' as he had encountered them a few years earlier during his Italian residency. The fact that he refused to do so may be behind the hostile reception of the opera in England by what Berlioz described as 'a society of *Italiens*' who deliberately agitated against the work.[116] It was 'not only a question of a musical vendetta, but a question of nationality. The Italians at Covent-Garden are furious to see themselves outflanked by *foreigners*'.[117] Far from dialoguing with Italian operatic practices, Berlioz almost seems to subvert or critique them in his music (as he did many times

---

[111] Berlioz, *Memoirs*, p. 183. [112] Ibid., p. 158. [113] Ibid., p. 160.
[114] Locke, *Musical Exoticism*, p. 43. [115] Berlioz, *Memoirs*, p. 134.
[116] *CG* IV, p. 330. [117] *CG* IV, p. 335.

in his music criticism). For example, in the carnival pantomime, the boisterous on-stage audience responds to two 'singers', Arlequin ('premier ténor romain'), who carries a lyre, and Pierrot or Pasquarello ('un chanteur de la Toscane'), who carries a small bass drum – an instrument associated with barbarism in the *Treatise*, as we have seen. Moreover, rather than exploring the innate vocal sensuality of an Italianate performance, Berlioz places both 'voices' in the orchestra – their 'vocal' music is actually sounded by the cor anglais and ophicleide, respectively. The play-within-a-play effect here highlights not only the immediate narrative context of the scene (Arlequin is a parallel of the artist figure Benvenuto, while Pierrot is the bumbling Balducci who stifles his creativity), but also that of the opera itself in relation to Berlioz's idealised audience.

In *Harold*, too, vocal idioms are given orchestral voice. Here, however, the idiom is not that of opera (as commonly invoked in concerto central movements); rather, Berlioz employs the idioms of what he described as 'wild Italy'. The second movement of *Harold en Italie* suggests the 'soft litanies' of the gleaners of Subiaco, returning home 'to the accompaniment of the sad tinkling of the distant convent bell',[118] and the third movement recalls Berlioz's experience of the rustic serenade of his peasant companion Crispino.[119] The final movement becomes fully absorbed in 'wild Italy', evoking the fearsome vitality and turbulence of the brigands. Like many a traveller imaginatively colonising a foreign region, Berlioz uses Italy as a site for self-reflection. But to understand the nature of this approach, we first need to examine the role of the key figure who mediates Berlioz's reception of Napoleon's Italian legacy: Byron, who had himself been involved with the Carbonari in the early 1820s.

Byron in Italy

If Berlioz retraced Napoleon's footsteps on the trip home, it was Byron who was in his mind as he sailed to Italy during the height of French infatuation with the poet. One of the crew claimed to have voyaged with Byron in the Adriatic and Greece, and although Berlioz was somewhat sceptical of his account, the composer 'was too much pleased to find myself with a man who had possibly shared Childe Harold's Pilgrimage to question his veracity'.[120] However, it has been customary to compare Berlioz's programmatic framework in *Harold en Italie* with the scenarios outlined in Byron's poem (and particularly its Fourth Canto), and to find the points of

---

[118] Berlioz, *Memoirs*, p. 147. [119] Ibid., pp. 149–50. [120] Ibid., p. 118.

resemblance few and far between. As Tovey puts it, 'no definite elements of Byron's poem have penetrated the impregnable fortress of Berlioz's encyclopaedic inattention'.[121] Comparisons of Berlioz's symphony and Byron's poem tend to focus instead on the character of the protagonist, which furnished Berlioz with a model in which to fashion himself as a kind of antihero; but the relationship between the two works extends further,[122] and exploring this relationship helps to elucidate the role of Napoleon and militarism in the antiheroic ideal.

The Byronic antihero was defined by Lord Macaulay as 'a man proud, moody, cynical, with defiance on his brow and misery in his heart, a scorner of his kind, implacable in revenge, yet capable of deep and strong affection'.[123] As Robert Pascall suggests, Nietzsche and others in the nineteenth century attributed the rise of the antihero at least in part to a response to the Napoleonic age and its aftermath, for even Byron felt like 'a worm compared to such a being' as Napoleon.[124] Berlioz's generation similarly displayed an ironising awareness of their inevitable inability to experience for themselves the now legendary power of the Napoleonic image. Berlioz revealed this awareness when he heard that Napoleon's body was to be returned to Paris some months after his *Symphonie funèbre et triomphale* had accompanied the remains of the fallen of 1830 to the Bastille column: 'I'm really mad to have written this triumphal march for our little July heroes when it could almost have done for the great hero.'[125]

However, the Napoleonic image was not an unambiguously heroic one, particularly for Byron's generation in Britain. During his reign and afterwards, Napoleon functioned as a symbol with multiple meanings depending on who was invoking him, and when. As Simon Bainbridge suggests, for the English Romantic poets, Napoleon was both 'an *Other* against which they could define themselves' and a figure with whom they could identify – 'the supreme embodiment of the hero in an age in which the artist was increasingly seen as heroic'.[126] But among his British peers, Byron's overt admiration of Napoleon during the period of the Napoleonic wars was a provocative declaration of his own antiheroic status, for Napoleon was

---

[121] Donald Francis Tovey, 'Berlioz: "Harold in Italy", Symphony with Viola Obbligato, Op. 16', in *Essays in Musical Analysis*, 7 vols., London: Oxford University Press, 1936, vol. IV, p. 74.

[122] Paul Banks has demonstrated that Byron's influence extends beyond what Tovey implies. See 'Harold, de Byron à Berlioz' in Christian Wasselin and Pierre-René Serna (eds.), *Hector Berlioz* (Paris: Éditions de l'Herne, 2003), pp. 152–61.

[123] Quoted in Robert Pascall, 'Those Grand Heroics Acted as a Spell: Aspects of Byron's Influence on Music in Nineteenth-Century Europe', *Renaissance and Modern Studies* 32/1 (1988), 128.

[124] Ibid., p. 128. [125] *CG* II, pp. 649–50.

[126] Simon Bainbridge, *Napoleon and English Romanticism* (Cambridge: Cambridge University Press, 1995), pp. 1–2.

often demonised in the British press.[127] Byron made explicit reference to his own Napoleonic status, not only in his heroic political aspirations for Greece, but also as a poet. He famously claimed in *Don Juan* that he was 'the grand Napoleon of the realms of rhyme'.[128] And *Childe Harold* is infused with Napoleonic references as Byron's protagonist visits sites that bear the imprint of Napoleonic memory, sometimes provoking extended reflections on the Napoleonic hero.

Significantly, however, it is not a Napoleonic hero that Byron portrays in *Childe Harold*, but a Napoleonic *anti* hero. Harold himself is quite specifically defined in terms that oppose military heroism: 'he would not delight ... /In themes of bloody fray, or gallant fight,/But loathed the bravo's trade, and laughed at martial wight.'[129] And Canto III shifts some of this antiheroism to Napoleon himself, when Harold visits '[t]he grave of France, the deadly Waterloo!'[130] Napoleon's defeat had occurred after the publication of the first two Cantos, and its shattering impact on Byron can be felt not only in Canto III, in the extended reflection provoked by the visit to Waterloo, but also in the account of Harold's Italian travels in Canto IV. The Napoleon of the final two Cantos is both great and fundamentally flawed, a man '[w]hose spirit antithetically mixed/One moment of the mightiest, and again/On little objects with like firmness fixed'.[131] Similarly, in Canto IV Napoleon is a fatally self-defeating hero, 'vanquished by himself, to his own slaves a slave'.[132] Indeed, Byron presents the post-Waterloo Napoleon as himself an antihero.[133]

Both Byron's gloomy stance towards Napoleon's defeat at Waterloo and the type of antihero embodied in *Childe Harold* were in some ways more easily embraced by French readers than by readers in Byron's England. Generally sympathetic to Byron's works from the time they first started appearing in French translation in 1818, the French also believed that they would have been more accepting of the author's morals, which, in Britain, were sometimes condemned.[134] Indeed, Edmond Estève suggested that, to the French, Byron 'gave us back the greatest portion of ourselves'.[135]

---

[127] Ibid., pp. 10–13.   [128] Ibid., p. 2.
[129] Byron, *Childe Harold's Pilgrimage* [canto] II [verse] 40, in Jerome McGann (ed.), *Lord Byron: The Major Works* (Oxford: Oxford University Press, 2000), p. 64. Subsequent page numbers for *Childe Harold* refer to this edition.
[130] *Childe Harold* III 18, p. 109.   [131] *Childe Harold* III 36, p. 114.
[132] *Childe Harold* IV 89, p. 174.   [133] Bainbridge, *Napoleon and English Romanticism*, p. 181.
[134] Joanne Wilkes, 'Byron and Nineteenth-Century French Readers', in Richard A. Cardwell (ed.), *The Reception of Byron in Europe* (London: Thoemmes Continuum, 2004), p. 14.
[135] Quoted in Peter Cochran 'From Pichot to Stendhal to Musset: Byron's Progress through Early Nineteenth-Century French Literature' in Cardwell (ed), *The Reception of Byron in Europe*, p. 39.

Berlioz's *Memoirs* present the composer as fuelling his own antiheroic misanthropy through his 'companion', Byron. He recounts how he would sit in St Peters reading *The Corsair*: 'I adored that inexorable yet tender nature – pitiless, yet generous – a strange combination of apparently contradictory feelings: love of woman, hatred of mankind [. . .] I sought on the pavement for traces of the noble poet's footsteps.'[136] Berlioz then proceeds to demonstrate his own 'hatred of mankind' when his reverie is interrupted by a peasant arriving to pray: 'What is art to you? A means of materialising the objects of your worship, and exciting you to dance or laughter.'[137]

Berlioz's description of his treatment of the character of Harold crucially reveals how he translated aspects of the Byronic antihero into musical terms:

> I conceived the idea of writing a series of scenes for the orchestra, in which the viola should find itself mixed up, like a person more or less in action, always preserving his own individuality. The background I formed from my recollections of my wanderings in the Abruzzi, introducing the viola as a sort of melancholy dreamer, in the style of Byron's *Childe Harold*. Hence the title of the symphony, *Harold in Italy*. As in the *Symphonie fantastique*, one principal theme (the first strain of the viola) is reproduced throughout the work, but with this difference, that in the *Symphonie fantastique* the theme – the *idée fixe* – obtrudes itself obstinately, like a passionately episodic figure, into scenes wholly foreign to it, whilst Harold's strain is super-added to the other orchestral strains, with which it contrasts both in movement and character, without hindering their development.[138]

Berlioz's description emphasises the wilful isolation of Harold in Byron's work: 'Childe Harold at a little distance stood,/And viewed, but not displeased, the revelrie'.[139] Indeed, Berlioz asked that the viola stand apart from the orchestra, exaggerating the thematic separation inherent in his conception.[140]

The way in which Berlioz superimposes the viola's melody over characteristic themes in each movement means that, rather than leading the orchestra, the Harold figure shapes and reshapes the way we listen to that other material. Thus, for example, in the second movement Berlioz uses the orchestra to depict a procession of pilgrims. The orchestral strings engage in a call and response. When the viola enters with the *idée fixe* it is superimposed, implying a quite different metre, and reframing the continuing statements of the pilgrims' chant (Ex. 2.5). The listener's experience is shaped through this imaginary identification, as is emphasised by the fact that we hear the pilgrims approach and then recede into the distance

---

[136] Berlioz, *Memoirs*, p. 139. [137] Ibid., p. 140. [138] Berlioz, *Memoirs*, pp. 202–3.
[139] *Childe Harold* II 72, p. 73. [140] *NBE* vol. 17, p. 4.

Ex. 2.5 *Harold en Italie* II 'Marche des pèlerins', bb. 56–75

in a large-scale hairpin crescendo–decrescendo across the movement; our subject position is Harold's, not that of the pilgrims.

Kawabata has likened *Harold en Italie* to eighteenth- and nineteenth-century travel writing, because of this positioning of the protagonist in relation to the external scenes. She further points out the viola's 'utter sonic dissimilarity' from 'any sound coded as Italian', suggesting that it functions as a 'vehicle for subjectivity' whereby the 'composer-as-traveller "speaks" through the solo viola'.[141] But this distance should not be understood in terms of the 'detached observation and comparison' prioritised in travel writing before the late eighteenth century and still plainly apparent in Dumont d'Urville's texts.[142] Rather, Byron's *Childe Harold* reflects the tendency of Romantic travel writing to stage tableaux, in which the viewer becomes absorbed by, and within, his or her surroundings, before breaking the spell to resume the journey – a tendency also evident in Humboldt's significantly titled *Tableaux de la nature*. In Byron's work, the Waterloo scene

---

[141] Maiko Kawabata, 'The Concerto That Wasn't: Paganini, Urhan and Harold in Italy', *Nineteenth-Century Music Review* 1/1 (2004), 83, 74.

[142] Chard, *Pleasure and Guilt on the Grand Tour*, p 184.

of Canto III, for example, is effectively a tableau – an extended reflection on Napoleonic subjects inspired by the site of the battlefield. Only after twenty-nine verses do we return to Harold himself.

Byron attributes the sentiments about Waterloo to Harold, as his character's reported thoughts ('Thus Harold inly said').[143] However, often it is Byron's own authorial persona who becomes absorbed in the scenes he describes. In becoming engrossed in the 'peopled desert Past', particularly at Waterloo, or in sites of Napoleonic memory in Italy, Byron thus also approaches a kind of imaginative fusion with Napoleon himself, who (as we have seen) is made over in the Byronic antihero image. The Harold persona is the means whereby this imaginative absorption is achieved:

'Tis to create, and in creating live
A being more intense, that we endow
With form our fancy, gaining as we give
The life we live, even as I do now.
What am I? Nothing: but not so art thou,
Soul of my thought! With whom I traverse earth,
Invisible but gazing, as I glow
Mixed with thy spirit, blended with thy birth,
And feeling still with thee in my crushed feelings' dearth.[144]

Byron thus provides a model for Berlioz's own imaginative fusion with Napoleon, as well as a particular model of subjectivity. But how might we reconcile this Napoleonic persona with the obvious and persistent personification of Harold-as-viola (at least in the first three movements of Berlioz's work), as well as Berlioz's statements emphasising the viola's separateness from the scenes described? To understand this, we need to consider further how Byron treats the Harold character.

In the first two Cantos, Byron preserves a superficial distinction between Harold and his own authorial voice. This use of the Harold persona was not universally admired. One reviewer complained: 'We deem the introduction of the character altogether reprehensible... the mischief lies in foisting him where he has no business'.[145] It was by no means uncommon to have more than one authorial voice in a travel narrative – indeed, as we saw in the previous chapter, the use of a framing or omniscient editorial voice was often

---

[143] *Childe Harold* III 52, p. 119.   [144] Ibid. III 6, pp. 105–6.
[145] William Roberts, *The British Review* 3 (June 1812), 285–6. Quoted in Jane Stabler, 'Byron's Digressive Journey', in Amanda Gilroy (ed.), *Romantic Geographies: Discourses of Travel 1775–1844* (Manchester: Manchester University Press, 2000), p. 224.

used to offset an unreliable narrator and lend the travel narrative a credibility that countered the wondrous nature of the unfamiliar places or events described. Byron himself employs this 'editorialising' tone, particularly in his supplementary notes.[146] In the third canto, Byron still refers to Harold by name as a separate character. Significantly, though, Harold is named for the final time at Waterloo.[147] After this point, Byron increasingly uses the first person: 'I live not in myself, but I become/Portion of that around me', he suggests.[148] It is as if Harold, too, becomes erased at Waterloo. The closing verses of the poem present a final glimpse of Harold, whose very existence as an entity independent of Byron himself is now questioned:

But where is he, the pilgrim of my song,
The being who upheld it through the past?
Methinks he cometh late and tarries long.
He is no more – these breathings are his last;
His wanderings done, his visions ebbing fast,
And he himself as nothing: – if he was
Aught but a phantasy, and could be classed
With forms which live and suffer – let that pass –
His shadow fades away into Destruction's mass.[149]

This is more than just a simple acknowledgement that Harold was, all along, an autobiographical construction. As Byron tells us, it is through the creation of Harold – through art itself – that he lives a life 'more intense'. But the device also imperils the very genre of travel writing. Whereas the typical trajectory of the travelogue saw digressions curtailed, and the omniscient editorial authority reasserted, Byron's *Childe Harold* absorbs the authorial voice into the character, and concludes with both voices literally 'at sea'.

Berlioz's own tendencies towards generic destabilisation are apparent in his treatment of the viola in *Harold en Italie*, which evokes expectations of the concerto only to subvert them. Presented as the protagonist (by Berlioz's admission), the viola's position apart from the orchestra is suggestive of a concerto soloist, and its first entrance is prepared with all the ceremonies of a concerto sonata-form exposition. But the very choice of the viola, typically an instrument taken up only by 'discarded violinists', as Berlioz puts it,[150] and the way Berlioz writes for it combine to challenge concerto expectations.

---

[146] Ibid., p. 230.   [147] *Childe Harold* III 52, p. 119.   [148] Ibid. III 72, p. 125.
[149] Ibid. IV 164, p. 195.   [150] Macdonald, *Berlioz's Orchestration Treatise*, p. 35.

If Berlioz uses the viola to suggest the character of Byron's Harold, how – if at all – does his destabilisation of genre recreate Byron's distinctive fusion of character and authorial persona? The most obvious answer would be that it is *as composer* that Berlioz captures Byron's role as author. Near the conclusion of the fourth and final Canto, Byron provides a direct model for Berlioz's approach to musical voice:

other days come back on me
With recollected music, though the tone
Is changed and solemn, like the cloudy groan
Of dying thunder on the distant wind[151]

The passage is suggestive of the opening of the fourth movement of Berlioz's *Harold en Italie*. Berlioz has the viola recall characteristic themes from each of the first three movements, now inflected with its melancholy and fragmented, for each time the recalled theme is forcibly overwhelmed by the brash music of the brigands. The device is usually seen as deriving from Beethoven's Ninth Symphony, thus directing the listener to the particular nature of the heroic models with which Berlioz himself, as a composer, was wrestling.[152] The Beethovenian allusion is unmistakable, but recognising that the device may simultaneously derive from Byron in no way lessens its importance. The opening of the fourth movement foregrounds Berlioz's own authorial voice (the anxiety of Beethovenian influence finally being addressed head on), but does so through the 'character' of the viola. In other words, authorial persona and character are fused.

The viola's near disappearance from the remainder of the movement, in which the raucous brigands dominate, could also be seen to echo Byron's poem. The brigands' violence enacts a kind of Waterloo for Berlioz's Harold, as we have seen. Indeed, Byron's description of the battle of Waterloo opens with alternating juxtapositions of the music and sounds of peace with those of war in another possible analogy with Berlioz's aggressive statements of the brigands' music:

Music arose with its voluptuous swell,
Soft eyes looked love to eyes which spake again,
And all went merry as a marriage bell;
But hush! hark! a deep sound strikes like a rising knell!
Did ye not hear it? – No; 'twas but the wind,
Or the car rattling o'er the stony street;

---

[151] *Childe Harold* IV 104, p. 178.   [152] Bonds, '*Sinfonia Anti-eroica*', 418.

On with the dance! let joy be unconfined;
No sleep till morn, when Youth and Pleasure meet
To chase the glowing Hours with flying feet.
But hark! – that heavy sound breaks in once more,
As if the clouds its echo would repeat;
And nearer, clearer, deadlier than before!
Arm! arm! it is – it is – the cannon's opening roar![153]

Virtuosity and militarism: Paganini and Liszt

By virtually eliminating the viola from the final movement of *Harold en Italie*, Berlioz might suggest a kind of triumph of the composer's work over the virtuosity of contemporaneous concerto paradigms. This would present a particularly provocative response to Italian idioms represented not just by singer and audience-focussed opera, but also by Paganini, who had originally commissioned the work. But such a view does not fully do justice to Berlioz's vision. Returning to Berlioz's own description of nonmonumental works such as *Harold*, we are reminded that he places a lot of emphasis on the performers – on the orchestra, and in particular on the *conductor*: 'especially the conductor, ought to *feel* as I do'.[154] Far from locating the impact of works like *Harold en Italie* exclusively in the score, Berlioz here appears to see performance as central – not only as a way of giving aural realisation to his conception, but also as a forum in which the performers' own subjectivity is critical to the effect. Thus, it is not Berlioz-as-composer, but Berlioz-as-composer–*conductor* who represents the Byronic authorial persona within *Harold en Italie*. And it is by situating *Harold en Italie* within both the militaristic associations of the new conducting traditions and the heroic virtuoso traditions represented by Liszt and Paganini that we really come to appreciate both the Byronic resonance and the extent of Berlioz's originality.

In the case of Paganini, the fact that it was his commission that originally instigated the work, and that he famously then refused to play it, means that his model of heroism helps to define the ways in which Berlioz's conception is understood as *anti* heroic. The choice of the viola was Paganini's, but it appears that he wanted music that was at least closer in idiom to the concertos for which he was famous as a violinist. As we have seen, analogies were drawn between the violinist's bow and the soldier's sword, particularly in virtuosic concerti where the relationship between the soloist

[153] *Childe Harold* III 21–2, p. 110.   [154] Berlioz, *Memoirs*, p. 489.

and the orchestra furthermore suggested a model of Napoleonic leadership and charismatic domination.[155] As Kawabata points out, 'Paganini was understood as "heroic" not only because he resembled Byron but because he wielded his bow like a weapon, commanded orchestras like an army general, and played military music that seemed to glorify the foregrounded individual. To many, Paganini seemed to emblematise military, not Romantic, heroism'.[156] (See Fig. 2.1, above.) For Berlioz, the military associations of the violin could also have been reinforced by his admired Uncle Marmion, the soldier who, in addition to having been 'deep in the brilliant vortex of the great Emperor', also 'played the violin admirably'.[157]

Part of Paganini's public persona as a performer was inflected by the Byronic antihero, due to his supposed sexual excess and features of his appearance and personality that he was thought to share with Byron's characters.[158] If we recall how Byron himself drew Napoleon into the antihero type, we can see how Paganini could invoke both military associations and the antiheroic elements of a Harold figure. Berlioz himself connected Paganini's rise to Napoleon, almost suggesting that the famous violinist had taken up Napoleon's mantle: 'his career began at the court of one of Napoleon's sisters, at the most solemn hour of the Empire he was making a triumphant tour though Germany just as the giant was going to his grave.'[159] As Kawabata illustrates, Paganini's Napoleonic credentials were consolidated during this period, based not only on the visual militarism of Paganini's performances, but also on his ability to conquer both audiences and orchestras across Europe.[160]

In writing for the viola, Berlioz could draw on all the visual heroic associations of Paganini's violin, but these served only to highlight how the nature of Berlioz's writing for the viola was antiheroic. Where the violin soloist of a typical concerto was accustomed to lead his troops into metaphorical battle with a flourish of the bow, and beat them into submission with his virtuosity, Berlioz's viola finds itself 'mixed up' in the orchestral 'scenes', more observer than leader, '*without hindering* their development'.[161]

An even more powerful source of Napoleonic imagery than Paganini was Liszt. While Paganini was clearly an important factor in the initial

---

[155] Maiko Kawabata, 'Virtuoso Codes of Violin Performance', 101.
[156] Ibid., 89.   [157] Berlioz, *Memoirs*, p. 8.
[158] Kawabata, 'Virtuosity, the Violin, the Devil... What *Really* Made Paganini "Demonic"?' *Current Musicology* 83 (2007), 97.
[159] Berlioz, *Evenings with the Orchestra*, p. 194.
[160] Kawabata, *Paganini: The 'Demonic' Virtuoso*, pp. 49, 86–7.
[161] Berlioz, *Memoirs*, p. 203; italics added.

conception of *Harold en Italie*, Liszt became bound up in the work's reception, using Berlioz's symphony as the basis for an extended article on programme music in 1854, and creating his own transcription of the work for piano and viola, as well as producing a transcription of the 'Marche des pèlerins' for piano solo. In fact, the idea of Liszt as a performer may have informed Berlioz's conception of *Harold en Italie* in subtle ways. The two composers had been forming a friendship in the four years prior to the composition of *Harold en Italie*, culminating in Liszt's participation in benefit concerts for Berlioz and Harriet Smithson.[162] Even if the influence was not a conscious one, a brief consideration of Liszt's own performer persona highlights several issues that are crucial to *Harold en Italie:* the relationship between military imagery and the role of subjectivity, especially in works for soloist and orchestra, and questions about the ways in which virtuosity impacts on the ideals associated with the musical work.

Whereas Paganini's rise coincided with Napoleon's fall, Liszt's rise coincided with the flourishing of the cult of Napoleon that swept through Paris and Germany in the build up to and aftermath of the 1830 revolution.[163] Dana Gooley has traced the way Liszt as a performer invoked a Napoleonic and/or militaristic image to audiences, from his tendency to wear a sword, to the specific details of his characteristic technique, such as the use of vertical motion that suggested an 'attack' on the keyboard. Berlioz was witness to the way in which Liszt could physically overcome an audience in performance, writing in 1833, 'His features are so dazzling, his endings so frightfully forceful and precise, his embellishments so delicate and in such a new style, that in truth it is sometimes impossible to applaud him for he has petrified you.'[164] And he later wrote that Liszt (like Ernst) 'never seems so powerful as when he has two thousand listeners to subdue'.[165]

Liszt's militaristic persona could be viewed as purely despotic, but this overlooks the ways in which military strength could be associated with acts of liberation – a concept fresh in people's minds after the 1830 revolution.[166] Furthermore, part of Liszt's appeal was that he was able both to rule over his audiences and to appear to have arisen from them, as Lawrence Kramer points out. Heine was disturbed when Liszt placed a red camellia in his lapel during the rapturous applause that followed his performance, for the

---

[162] Kregor, 'Collaboration and Content in the *Symphonie fantastique* Transcription', The *Journal of Musicology*, 24/2 (2007) 195–236.
[163] Gooley, 'Warhorses', pp. 67–8.   [164] *Le Rénovateur*, 19 December 1833; *CM* I, p. 119.
[165] Berlioz, *Memoirs*, p. 443.
[166] James Deaville, 'The Politics of Liszt's Virtuosity: New Light on the Dialectics of a Cultural Phenomenon', in Michael Saffle and Rossana Dalmonte (eds.), *Liszt and the Birth of Modern Europe* (Hillsdale, NY: Pendragon Press, 2003), pp. 115–42.

same flower was worn on the breasts of soldiers in the audience who had recently returned from combat in Africa; to Heine, the implication that Liszt, rather than the soldiers, was the successor of Napoleon's military heroism was problematic. Kramer suggests that the camellia simultaneously evoked military heroism and the desire of the audience to penetrate to the inner self. The camellia thus symbolised Liszt's willingness to allow himself effectively to be wounded, to display a suggestion of interiority despite or through the visual excess of his performance.[167]

If Liszt's relationship with his audience was complex, so too was his relationship with compositional authority. Liszt's rise coincided with a backlash against virtuosity by German critics in the 1830s and 1840s, partly because of the way virtuosity seemed antithetical to interiority. But while Liszt was a prime candidate for the suspicions surrounding the travelling foreign virtuoso, he was sometimes able to persuade critics that he attained an ideal relationship with the musical works he performed. This relationship was achieved not through a suppression of his self as a performer, nor through any conception of *Werktreue*, but rather by giving the impression that through performance he entered 'the spirit of the creator and blend[ed] his own genius with it', thereby revealing the subjective identity of the work.[168] Liszt was thus a powerful figure in the imperialism of the musical work. Through his Napoleonic persona, Liszt forcibly beat instruments and audiences into a form of submission not only to himself as performer, but also to the works of other composers.

Gooley's discussion of Liszt's performance of Weber's *Konzertstück* illustrates several of these themes and also raises questions relevant to Berlioz's *Harold in Italie*. *Konzertstück* was a 'warhorse' in Liszt's repertoire, Gooley suggests, not only because it was performed more frequently than any other work in his concerts of the 1830s but also because it exemplified Liszt's role as a Napoleonic military figure.[169] In the final section of Weber's programmatic concerto, the orchestra makes three statements of a march, each one louder than the one before, to suggest the approach of the hero who has returned from the crusade. In Weber's original version, the piano

---

[167] Lawrence Kramer, 'Franz Liszt and the Virtuoso Public Sphere: Sight and Sound in the Rise of Mass Entertainment', in *Musical Meaning: Toward a Critical History* (Berkeley: University of California Press, 2002), p. 75.

[168] Gooley, 'The Battle against Instrumental Virtuosity in the Early Nineteenth Century', in Christopher H. Gibbs and Dana Gooley (eds.), *Franz Liszt and His World* (Princeton, NJ: Princeton University Press, 2006), p. 104. See also Mary Hunter, '"To Play as If from the Soul of the Composer": The Idea of the Performer in Early Romantic Aesthetics', *Journal of the American Musicological Society* 58/2 (2005), 357–98.

[169] Gooley, 'Warhorses', 73.

enters triumphantly with the third and loudest statement, but shortly afterwards it gives way to the orchestra, for the soloist and the orchestra tell the story together. However, as Gooley points out, for his own performances Liszt altered the piano part so that the soloist enters with distinct thematic material that clearly differentiates it from the orchestra; he then rewrites the piano part at the third statement of the march so that the piano has a sustained and dominating presence. In other words, Liszt makes the piano – or rather, himself as pianist – represent the military hero protagonist within the narrative. It is through his performance, in visual terms and through the alterations to the score, that Liszt embodies a Napoleonic character that is not necessarily self-evident in Weber's work alone, and he does so by modelling himself as the centre of subjectivity in the work.

Embodying antivirtuosity

Designated a symphony by its composer, Berlioz's *Harold en Italie* could be expected to occupy a very different position in the dialectics of work and virtuosity, as well as in terms of subjectivity and military imagery, to that modelled in the warhorses of Paganini and Liszt. Indeed, Gooley demonstrates how the self-contained orchestra of the symphonic genre was viewed by German theorists of the time as an egalitarian entity whose collective identity enabled a focus both on the work and on interiority in ways that were diametrically opposed to the suspicious display of the virtuoso concerto.[170] Similarly, while Kramer acknowledges that symphonies, too, could be theatrical and virtuosic, he suggests that these qualities were vested in the composer (primarily through the use of programmes) rather than being situated in the performance itself.[171]

The solo viola of *Harold en Italie* inevitably invokes certain associations with the virtuoso concerto, even if only to invert them. When Liszt transcribed the work for viola and piano, he augmented the viola's role, interestingly doing to the *other* instrument's part what he did for the piano in Weber's *Konzertstück*. But Berlioz reprimanded him:

On the other hand, don't you think that the part you're giving the viola – which is bigger than that which it has in the score – changes the physiognomy of the work? ... The viola must only play the role in the piano score that it plays in the other edition. The piano here represents the orchestra, and the viola must remain

---

[170] Gooley, 'The Battle against Instrumental Virtuosity', pp. 77–9; 93.
[171] Kramer, 'Franz Liszt and the Virtuoso Public Sphere', p. 81.

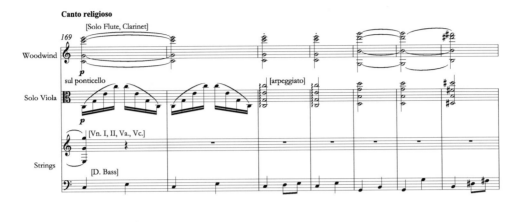

Ex. 2.6 *Harold en Italie* II 'Marche des pèlerins', bb. 169–85

apart and retreat into its sentimental nonsense; everything else is foreign to it, it *witnesses* the action but never takes part.[172]

Nevertheless, *Harold en Italie* also demonstrates how individual performers and performance might play a significant role in modelling a particular kind of subjectivity akin to that seen in Liszt's performance of Weber's *Konzertstück*. Indeed, the second movement suggests Liszt's performance of Weber's work quite directly. The pilgrims' music is heard approaching and then retreating through the lens of the soloist, who, as in Liszt's version of the *Konzertstück*, joins the march near its dynamic peak. Interestingly, Berlioz's music at this point is at its most virtuosic. In the section titled 'Canto Religioso', the soloist has a lengthy passage of arpeggiated chords (Ex. 2.6). The passage is not particularly challenging technically, but in another context it might have afforded the soloist an opportunity to indulge in idiomatic display. Indeed, Liszt cites this passage as evoking Paganini: 'The viola accompanies clear flowing harmonies with arpeggiated chords of the

---

[172] Berlioz to Liszt, 3 or 4 June 1852. *CG* IV, p. 183.

kind Paganini first applied, and which sound wonderful here.'[173] However, Berlioz asks that the viola play *sul ponticello* (over the bridge). This prevents the strings from fully resonating, producing a wispy or even rasping sound. The colour is distinctive (it was only very rarely indicated by Paganini in his own scores) and could be interpreted as Berlioz's sacrifice of soloistic brilliance to the composer's colouristic conception of the whole. Indeed, the passage forces the player into a situation of mild discomfort. The bow does not naturally want to rest near the bridge, and viola players tend to cast their gaze down to the strings, as if to check the bow's position in what Elisabeth Le Guin, with reference to Boccherini, describes as 'scripted gestural constraint or awkwardness'.[174]

However, the physicality of the soloist is also significant in its own right. The gesture of the repeated string crossing, causing the bow to rise and fall on the beat, is a form of 'conducting' the rest of the orchestra and is a motion that, in a different context, might evoke the sweeping of a sword, as we have seen.[175] For the string player there can also be a profoundly meditative quality to this repetition in the section Berlioz describes as a 'religious song', for the rising and falling of the arm has something of the feel of breathing about it. The violist's self-consciousness – the need to monitor the position of the bow near the bridge – might in this respect be seen as an indication of Harold's inability fully to relinquish his own subject position even in this moment where his close identification with the pilgrims might tempt him to, in Byron's terms, be 'purifie[d] from self'.[176] As Le Guin and others have pointed out, one need not be a player of an instrument oneself to respond with innate bodily sympathy to the physical gestures of the performer, and there is a sense here in which Berlioz again uses the viola to draw the listener into his narrative.[177] Indeed, the suppression of overt virtuosity in this work only renders sympathy with the viola protagonist more likely, for we are not distanced by feats of seeming impossibility.

The rare gestures towards virtuosity in *Harold en Italie* paradoxically serve to heighten the work's departure from the violin concerto paradigm, or from Liszt's extravagant performance of Weber's *Konzertstück*. Indeed, the viola players who took on the solo role generally represented the antithesis of the Paganini/Liszt tradition. They were sometimes orchestral viola players (whose solo role might thus have retained elements of the egalitarian, collective interiority associated with the Germanic symphonic ideal),

---

[173] Liszt, 'Berlioz und seine "Harold Symphonie"', in L. Ramann (ed.), *Gesammelte Schriften von Franz Liszt*, 6 vols. (Leipzig: Breitkopf und Härtel, 1882), vol. IV, p. 83.
[174] Le Guin, *Boccherini's Body*, p. 127. [175] Ibid., p. 36.
[176] *Childe Harold* III 90, p. 131. [177] Ibid., p. 24.

or sometimes virtuosi such as Chrétien Urhan or Joseph Joachim who were renowned for espousing ideals of *Werktreue*.[178] But paradoxically, moments such as the 'Canto Religioso' are also the moments in which we might come closest to experiencing the performer's subjectivity *as performer* rather than as a voice for the composer's persona.

The relationship of Berlioz's viola to the Liszt or Paganini performance archetype is primarily an antithetical one, despite the occasional provocative similarities. Berlioz does use the viola line in ways that suggest an individual subjectivity, particularly through the employment of the *idée fixe*; but ultimately he could be seen to reinforce his own authorial control as composer over the whole. To his bitter regret, Berlioz never actually saw Paganini perform. To Berlioz, Paganini-as-performer thus remained an idea or persona, and if he referenced that idea in *Harold en Italie* he necessarily did so in abstract terms. Moreover, as Berlioz was not himself a viola player, his conception of the viola-protagonist was inevitably crafted from a composer's perspective.

However, there *is* a way in which Berlioz may be seen to write himself into the music as a performer: he positions himself within the score as a conductor. If, in considering *Harold en Italie* as subverting the military associations of its soloist, we have thus far ultimately reinforced some of the basic tropes of existing readings of the symphony, examining the role of the conductor provides an opportunity to invert the inversion and effectively remilitarise the work in a particularly interesting way. While it is commonly recognised that the viola part in *Harold en Italie* challenges models of heroism and virtuosity, what no one seems to remark is that this same heroism and virtuosity are still present in the conductor's role.

Victory of the conductor

We have seen how Berlioz as a conductor was frequently likened to a military figure, leading his troops into battle with inspirational discipline and charisma. However, *Harold en Italie* presents a particularly interesting case. It was specifically after sitting through botched performances of *Harold en Italie* that Berlioz resolved always to conduct his own works in future. Similarly, he resisted publishing the score and parts of *Harold* until after his return from the first two tours of Austro-German lands, as he wished to establish direct authorial control over performances of the work.[179] In an

---

[178] Kawabata discusses Urhan's relationship to the work; see 'The Concerto That Wasn't', 95–108.
[179] Banks and Macdonald, 'Foreword' to Berlioz, *Harold en Italie*, NBE vol. 17, p. X.

essay on Paganini, Berlioz compared the notion of the composer controlling his own works to the role of the virtuoso performer: the 'performing instinct cannot be transfixed' and '[t]hat is the reason not only why the works of the great virtuoso inventors suffer more or less from not being played by their composers, but also why those of original and expressive composers retain only a part of their power when the author does not preside over their performance.'[180]

Moreover, it is *Harold en Italie* that Berlioz uses in his conducting treatise to illustrate the quite particular challenges of conducting an orchestral force of separate contrasting units. In the third movement, which depicts the serenade of a mountaineer to his mistress, Berlioz juxtaposes two different blocks of music, centred respectively on the principal serenade theme and a rustic dance. Towards the conclusion of the movement, Berlioz brings the two together simultaneously. The lively beat and drone of the dance continue in the orchestral violas, while the melody of the serenade is stated over the top by the solo viola. Meanwhile, the viola's *idée fixe* is actually sounded by the flute. (See Ex. 2.7.) Not only melodies but tempi are combined. For the serenade and *idée fixe* the primary tempo shifts to half the speed of the previous section; but Berlioz bars the orchestral violas and dance beat separately to indicate that they continue in a 6/8 that is twice as fast as the rest of the orchestra.

This metrical convergence could have originated in overtly military contexts. Kastner (citing Castil-Blaze) writes of how the quick march (*marche double* or *pas redoublé*) of the military band would sometimes combine with the regular beat at half the speed of separate troops in the field: 'this effect is not without charm for a trained ear.'[181] In Berlioz's setting, the military authority of the conductor's leadership is crucial. This is more than simply giving cues and beating time; it is a matter of coordinating two distinctly opposing forces.

Berlioz reveals his own tactics in the conducting treatise, indicating how the conductor might give a sub-beat for the first bar. Girard, the conductor of the first performances, was unable to negotiate the transition, as Berlioz explains:

at the fourth performance of *Harold* he made so serious a mistake at the end of the serenade (where, if one part of the orchestra does not double its speed, the other part cannot go on, because the whole bar of the former corresponds to the half bar

---

[180] Berlioz, *Evenings with the Orchestra*, p. 199.
[181] Georges Kastner, *Manuel général de musique militaire à l'usage des armées françaises* (Geneva: Minkoff Reprint, 1848, repr. 1973), p. 335.

Ex. 2.7 *Harold en Italie* III 'Sérénade', bb. 163–72

of the latter) that, seeing at last that there was no hope of his working up the end of the allegro properly, I resolved in future to conduct myself, and not allow anyone else to communicate my ideas to the performers.[182]

It is hard for us now to understand the complexity of this passage, which demanded what was at the time a new kind of conductor.[183] According to Liszt, the cross rhythms of the third movement are more easily appreciated in the score than in performance, as a manifestation of the composer's craft.[184]

Berlioz situates virtuosity and authority in the conductor – or the composer–conductor – rather than the soloist. Indeed, if *Harold en Italie*

---

[182] Berlioz, *Memoirs*, p. 204. [183] Galkin, *A History of Orchestral Conducting*, p. 405.
[184] Liszt, 'Berlioz und seine "Harold Symphonie"', p. 87.

Ex. 2.8 *Harold en Italie* I 'Harold aux montagnes', bb. 124–34

sets up Harold as a kind of antihero, it seems also to set up the viola as an anticonductor, juxtaposed against the 'real' leadership of the baton-wielding composer. 'Ha, ha, ha! haro! haro! *Harold!*' read a satirical critique of the work, cited by Berlioz himself in his *Memoirs*.[185] The stuttering attempts to pronounce the viola's name suggest the stumbling false entries of the Allegro theme of the first movement, where the viola might be expected to take charge in leading the orchestra into the main body of the movement. At this crucial moment the viola falters and it is instead left to the conductor to get things moving (Ex. 2.8).

In this early negotiation over leadership, the conductor stakes his claim as the authority. The same message becomes even more obvious in the final movement, the 'Orgy of the Brigands', where the viola soloist sits out a large part of the movement that is the most technically demanding and potentially militaristic sounding of the whole symphony – Liszt suggested that the movement has a 'warlike character',[186] and his piano transcription of the orchestral part contains some of the most aggressive 'vertical' movement of fingers into the keys characteristic of Liszt's own militarist persona.[187] In

---

[185] Berlioz, *Memoirs*, p. 204.   [186] Liszt, 'Berlioz und seine "Harold Symphonie"', p. 92.
[187] Gooley, 'Warhorses', 76.

Berlioz's original, orchestral version it is the conductor who commands our attention.[188]

Of course, many concertos might evoke this idea of divided leadership, but what makes *Harold en Italie* so interesting is a confluence of several factors: its role in Berlioz's own thinking as a conductor; its subversion of virtuosity; and the fact that the work is, after all, titled a symphony. We might account for the divided leadership by returning to Berlioz's Byronic source, where the omniscient Byron-persona (like the conductor) frames and controls the Harold persona (the viola) before the author–narrator (Berlioz) acknowledges that Harold is, after all, an extension of himself. However, in performance, moments such as the *sul ponticello* passage highlight the physical reality of the Harold persona, giving it a presence that cannot be erased or fully assimilated even when the instrument is silenced for much of the final movement.

Similarly, the divided leadership of Berlioz's work might evoke the two aspects of the Napoleonic persona adopted by Liszt. The conductor is the 'despot' Napoleon, while the viola is the 'liberator'. Through the viola persona, the audience experiences both the pleasure of being overpowered by the virtuoso and the introspection of the liberator who 'frees and elevates the soul'.[189] Like Liszt with his Napoleonic persona, Berlioz in *Harold en Italie* is thus able to foreground a kind of virtuoso subjectivity that is in dialogue with the composer's work. But when both the virtuoso and the composer were Berlioz himself, that military authority ran perilously close to the accusations against virtuoso indulgence sometimes incurred by Liszt. And when Berlioz took this work to Germany on his tour of the 'grande armée', such accusations risked being levelled not only at the suspicious figure of the touring virtuoso, but against the work itself. Indeed, a brief consideration of Berlioz's Harold *en Allemagne* reveals how the relationship between performance and score in this work invoked both the positive and negative aspects of military virtuosity.

Harold in Germany

In a very tangible way, when Berlioz toured Germany, his scores were like his battalions. He makes several references in his letters and so-called 'bulletins of the grande armée' to the logistics and expense of transporting the stacks of

---

[188] In relation to the similarly visually spectacular sections of Liszt's transcription of *Symphonie fantastique*, Kregor suggests that Liszt becomes an 'ersatz conductor': 'Collaboration and Content in the *Symphonie fantastique* Transcription', 227.

[189] Franz von Schober, quoted in Deaville, 'The Politics of Liszt's Virtuosity', p. 124.

scores and parts around Germany: they required a whole separate stagecoach of their own. Berlioz would often arrive in a new town unannounced, but bearing a letter of introduction to this or that Prince, Duke, or Kapellmeister. He would then undergo a battle to assemble an orchestra from the local musicians and adapt his music to the available resources, as he told Liszt, having to reorchestrate or cut movements to take account of local resources. The orchestral musicians in these early stages could sometimes present themselves to Berlioz as an opposing force to be conquered. He describes the scepticism and suspicion that sometimes greeted him as a foreigner in Germany, and the difficulties of dealing with orchestral players as wilful individuals. This was not unique to Germany. In Paris in 1843, shortly before departing for his German tour, Berlioz conducted the Conservatoire orchestra in a festival concert at the Opéra, commenting on how many orchestra members owed allegiance to their regular conductor, Habeneck, whom he describes as their 'old general'. In most cases, however, Berlioz found that the local German musicians would gradually warm to his music, sometimes becoming passionately committed advocates. In Braunschweig, Berlioz describes how, like soldiers, the players would incur physical injury to serve his music. In the final movement of *Harold en Italie*, he writes, 'Schmidt (an astounding double-bass) tore the skin off the forefinger of his right hand at the beginning of the pizzicato passage of the *Orgy*; but he went on, not thinking of stopping for such a trifle, or caring for its bleeding, merely contenting himself with changing the finger.'[190] Moreover, successful concerts were described in terms of military victories: players would lay wreaths on Berlioz's scores – a symbolic triumph of his works through the efforts of the performers.[191]

Clearly the performers were won over to Berlioz's mission. And Liszt, in his essay on *Harold en Italie*, suggests that this was Berlioz's best known work in Paris and in Germany to both artists and amateurs (*Künstlern und Liebhabern*).[192] But what about the critics, responding to Berlioz's music from the audience rather than as new orchestral conscripts under the direct power of his baton? Here, too, there were occasional celebratory wreaths, but for the most part German critics articulated a greater distance – to them, Berlioz was an 'Other', particularly in terms of his national identity. The melodies of *Harold* were 'of a French character and therefore appear to us to border on the trivial; in vain does one seek German depth and interiority'. Yet, as Hermann Hirschbach, writing for the *Neue Zeitschrift für*

---

[190] Berlioz, *Memoirs*, p. 299.   [191] Ibid., p. 301.
[192] Liszt, 'Berlioz und seine "Harold Symphonie"', p. 70.

Musik, continued, '[e]ven his most unjust opponents must at least acknowledge his incredible talent for instrumentation.'[193] As a travelling performer touring his own music, Berlioz might be seen to have occupied territory similar to that of the foreign virtuoso – a position treated with suspicion by German critics, as Gooley has pointed out.[194] In Berlioz's case, that virtuosity was sometimes understood as having been vested in the score by the composer. Schumann's famous description of Berlioz as 'a born virtuoso of the orchestra' – based on a perusal of a score (Liszt's piano reduction, no less) of *Symphonie fantastique* rather than experience of Berlioz as a conductor – was echoed on Berlioz's German tour by the critic for the *Allgemeine musikalische Zeitung*, who praised the 'great energy and *virtuosity* of depiction in the character pictures'.[195] But some also noted Berlioz's skill as a conductor. Thus Johann Philipp Samuel Schmidt (writing for the *Allgemeine Wiener Musik Zeitung*) stated, 'As conductor of his extraordinarily difficult compositions Berlioz demonstrates particularly through a high degree of care, how the powerful bodies hold together.'[196]

Perhaps most interesting in relation to Berlioz's virtuosity is the review by Bartholf Senff for *Signale*: 'In any case it seems to us to be a more magnificent achievement to stake all on the whole orchestra – and this is a whole unlike any other – than on a single instrument. Alongside Berlioz the virtuosi of single instruments idle through the countryside like so many poor itinerant sword-wielding journeymen [*arme fechtende Handwerksburschen*].'[197] Senff's imagery suggests the orchestral mastery of both composer and conductor. Moreover, the reference to instrumental virtuosi appearing by comparison to be 'poor itinerant sword-wielding journeymen' resonates with the swordplay of the solo violinist (and violinist-conductor), beside whom Berlioz had attained the status of a master swordsman. In other words, work and performance, composer and conductor, the world of the European tour and the worlds conjured by the score, were brought together under Berlioz's baton.

Brought together, but not fused. For while *Harold en Italie* reflects aspects of the work concept that might have been sympathetic to German critics on Berlioz's tour, it is important to note the ways in which Berlioz and his work also resisted the complete domination of work over performers – or

---

[193] Quoted in Gunther Braam and Arnold Jacobshagen (eds.), *Hector Berlioz in Deutschland: Texte und Dokumente zur Deutschen Berlioz-Rezeption (1829–1843)* (Gottingen: Hainholz, 2002), p. 524.
[194] Gooley, 'The Battle against Instrumental Virtuosity', pp. 89–90.
[195] Braam and Jacobshagen (eds.), *Hector Berlioz in Deutschland*, pp. 535–6. Emphasis added.
[196] Ibid., p. 555.
[197] Ibid., p. 521. Thanks to Roger Hillman (ANU) for assistance in translating this passage.

listeners. On one hand, Berlioz's German travels instilled or reinforced in him particular aspects that might be seen to strengthen the work concept. Thus it was *Harold en Italie* that provoked him to conclude that works should be performed complete. While the second movement was usually the most popular one, he remarks that it was less successful when performed in isolation, concluding that this offered 'a fresh proof of the necessity of not breaking up certain compositions, and of only producing them at the proper time and from the suitable standpoint.'[198] Similarly, Berlioz admired the respect with which German audiences treated musical works, praising behaviour that Goehr identifies as reflective of the emerging work concept.[199] On the other hand, he was also 'afraid of being respected' himself, writing (after a performance of Beethoven's music in Breslau in 1846):

[T]he public [. . .] admire that masterpiece as much as it can be imagined, and if they do not applaud, it is *from respect*. I must confess that this word, which would have had so deep a meaning in Paris, and in all places where the disgraceful manoeuvres of the claqueurs are prevalent, made me feel very anxious. I was dreadfully afraid of being respected. Happily this was not at all the case.[200]

Moreover, *Harold en Italie* demonstrates the importance of performer virtuosity in a way that directly challenges another aspect of the work concept: the very fact that Berlioz felt he himself needed to be present to conduct the work at each performance violates the idea that all elements necessary for the successful realisation of the work were contained within the score.[201]

Later, when offered a position conducting the imperial orchestra in Vienna, Berlioz turned it down, writing that he made the 'curious discovery that Paris truly holds my heart' and that Paris was 'an electric city which attracts and repels in turn but towards which it is ultimately always necessary to return if one has ever lived there, and especially when one is French.'[202] It would be a truism to suggest that Berlioz was a perennial outsider – an Other whether in Italy, Germany, or France. Perhaps more interesting is the way in which Berlioz scripts this Otherness into his works and realises it in performance. While the collective reflection and muscular bonding of *Symphonie funèbre et triomphale* spoke to Berlioz's ideal of monumentality, it is the negotiation of Other worlds in *Harold en Italie* that made this work both closer to his heart and better able to travel. Whether

---

[198] Berlioz, *Memoirs*, p. 262. Compare Goehr, *Imaginary Museum*, p. 240.
[199] Goehr, *Imaginary Museum*, p. 236. See also James H. Johnson, *Listening in Paris: A Cultural History* (Berkeley: University of California Press, 1995).
[200] Berlioz, *Memoirs*, p. 417.   [201] Goehr, *Imaginary Museum*, pp. 224–7.
[202] *CG* III, p. 366.

it is Harold, Napoleon, Byron, or Berlioz in Italy, what matters is less the Otherness of the Italian setting itself than the subjective identification of listener with soloist and conductor in a world of shifting relationships between autonomy and authority. That such relationships were enacted through both scores and performances that were deemed to threaten German 'depth and interiority' may not seem surprising, since such terms became prevalent in responses to Berlioz's music and to attempts to define Germanness in music more broadly. The seemingly opposing aesthetics of (German) interiority and (French) spectacle will be revisited in the next chapter, where Berlioz's manipulation of the visual dimension within the score and in performance will be reconfigured in terms of 'Other worlds' of the supernatural, which straddle the division between physical and imaginary in even more potent ways. Again, it is through competing conceptions of the orchestra that Berlioz explores the tension.

3 | Visions of Other worlds

Sensing the supernatural in *Épisode de la vie d'un artiste* and *La nonne sanglante*

It has become almost a truism to suggest that the Paris of Berlioz's era was a culture of spectacle, as manifested in everything from the rise of the illustrated novel to the development of photography, and from the parading of the *flâneur* to the displays of the new department store windows.[1] In musical terms, this spectacle has been most easily traced in opera, where lavish sets, costumes, special effects, and dance enticed audiences' eyes to the stage, and audience members themselves could court the gaze of admirers in the illuminated auditorium. In fact, concert performances, too, were advertised as '*spectacles*' (i.e., 'sights' as well as 'shows'), and Paganini and Liszt owed at least some of the power of their performer personae to the circulation of images capturing their virtuosic prowess. However, at the same time, a contrasting instrumental aesthetic arose in which the focus shifted to the work of the composer, which was felt to be better understood if the eyes were closed altogether. German emphasis on 'Innigkeit' stressed the power of instrumental music, in particular, to redirect the gaze inwards; the visualisation stimulated by hearing was imagined as internal and deep and was juxtaposed against the supposed externality and materiality of sight.[2] Although Wagner drew on the spectacle of French grand opera for aspects of his staging, he famously dimmed the lights in the auditorium to focus attention on his works, and he espoused the value of 'Innigkeit'. Even dimmed lights were not enough for devotees like Bruckner, who supposedly only opened his eyes towards the end of *Götterdämmerung* to enquire, 'why did they burn the woman at the end?'[3] The legacy of these aesthetics is a

---

[1] Walter Benjamin, *Passagenwerk* (1927–940), ed. Rolf Tiedemann, trans. Howard Eiland and Kevin McLaughlin, *The Arcades Project* (New York: Belknap Press, 2002); Guy Debord, *La société du spectacle* (Paris: Buchet-Chastel, 1967); Martin Jay, *Downcast Eyes: The Denigration of Vision in Twentieth-Century French Thought* (Berkeley: University of California Press, 1993); Ségolène Le Men, *La cathédrale illustrée de Hugo à Monet: Regard romantique et modernité* (Paris: CNRS Éditions, 1998).

[2] Friedrich Geiger, '"Innigkeit" und "Tiefe" als komplementäre Kriterien der Bewertung von Musik', *Archiv für Musikwissenschaft* 60/4 (2003), 265–78. On the stereotypical juxtapositions of internal listening and superficial vision, see also Jonathan Sterne, *Audible Past: Cultural Origins of Sound Reproduction* (Durham, NC: Duke University Press, 2003), p. 15.

[3] Keith William Kinder, *The Wind and Wind-Chorus Music of Anton Bruckner*. Westport, Connecticut: Greenwood Publishing Group, 2000), p. 51, n. 14.

powerful one. As Elisabeth Le Guin points out, the visual aspect of instrumental performance tends to be problematised even today: 'Our disdain of theatricalization and visualization in instrumental performance runs deep, a legacy of [...] German idealism [...] and of the powerful notion of absolute music that emerged from it; more even than physical sensation, the notion of visual effect as intrinsic to the instrumental work is likely to seem excessive, even repellent.'[4]

Berlioz occupies a fascinating position in relation to the dialectics of visual culture. Repeatedly condemned by German critics for a lack of 'Innigkeit' and for an excess of the materiality that was associated by those critics with French visual culture, Berlioz nevertheless articulated resistance to the dominance of vision, and to the French desire for music that figured first and foremost 'to the eye'.[5] In later years he criticised the emphasis on visual spectacle at the opera house: 'The Opéra has been transformed into a Diorama theatre; you go there to *see* the last act of the ballet *Le Corsaire*; as for the music, it's the last thing anyone cares about.'[6] Moreover, Berlioz confessed to being powerfully moved by Liszt's performance of Beethoven's 'Moonlight' sonata when the lights had gone out and he thus could not see the charismatic performer. Liszt, symbolically enough, also took the opportunity on that occasion to present a rendition that was much more faithful to Beethoven's text, stripped of all the interpolated embellishments he was accustomed to adding in performances where his own pianism was on display.[7]

In this chapter we will examine two works that deal with the question of musical vision: *Épisode de la vie d'un artiste* (the collective title Berlioz gave to *Symphonie fantastique* and its sequel *Le retour à la vie*, subsequently titled *Lélio*),[8] and the duet from his abandoned opera *La nonne sanglante*. Significantly, both works raise questions about supernatural realms, and the 'Other worlds' explored are those of dreams and the ghostly apparitions which give rise to questions about the nature of sight itself. In moving from the geographical worlds of travel writing and military conquest to what Hamlet (quoted in *Lélio*) describes as 'The undiscovered Country, from whose bourn/No traveller returns' (3.1.78–9), we will nevertheless find that several of the concerns of previous chapters pertain. In particular, an investigation of the internalisation of vision and the psychologising of the supernatural provides an opportunity to explore further the relationship

---

[4] Le Guin, *Boccherini's Body*, p. 35.   [5] Berlioz, *Memoirs*, p. 234.
[6] *CG* V, p. 294.   [7] Berlioz, *The Art of Music*, pp. 39–40.
[8] Peter Bloom, 'A Return to Berlioz's "Retour à la Vie"', *The Musical Quarterly* 64/3 (1978), 361–3.

between the tangibility and transcendence of the musical work. Again, the orchestra itself acts as a means of navigating between worlds. In both *Épisode* and *La nonne sanglante*, supernatural sights are embodied sonically by the orchestra rather than realised visually on the stage, but the sight of the orchestra itself becomes part of that navigation. *Épisode de la vie d'un artiste* discloses new thinking about vision that challenges the familiar discourse of programme music, at a time when the understanding of sight was being both reembodied and internalised. In contrast, *La nonne sanglante* invokes familiar operatic conventions of spectral visitation, but it, too, draws on the sounds, sights, and perhaps also tactility of its orchestra to conjure Other worlds for the listener.

Épisode de la vie d'un artiste

'With the ear, the eye'

The very conception of Berlioz's *Symphonie fantastique* was associated by his contemporaries with visual idioms. Joseph d'Ortigue suggested that Berlioz had created this dramatic symphony in lieu of an opera. The Opéra is 'the theatre of magic and illusion', d'Ortigue writes, where 'imaginary divinities come from the head of poets and take on voice and form'. But young composers like Berlioz struggle to gain entry to the Opéra, d'Ortigue tells us. Moreover, Berlioz wanted to speak to the soul and not just the senses. He has taken the forms and colours of opera and enriched them; he has, d'Ortigue writes, 'replaced sight with sound'.[9]

Berlioz himself prefaced the programme of *Symphonie fantastique* by suggesting it is like 'the spoken text of an opera, serving to introduce the musical movements, whose character and expression it motivates'.[10] Indeed, the programme presents many vivid images that might conjure the spectacle of the stage. The young artist becomes obsessed with a woman commonly understood to be based on the Irish actress Harriet Smithson, the object of Berlioz's fixation during the period of the symphony's conception. Smithson's performances in Shakespeare's plays in Paris in 1827 had themselves relied heavily on the visual language of gesture since much of the audience, including Berlioz, had only a limited understanding of English. Similarly,

---

[9] *National*, 15 December 1832, p. 1.
[10] Berlioz, First programme, in Edward T. Cone (ed.), *Norton Critical Scores: Berlioz Fantastic Symphony* (New York: Norton, 1971), p. 21. The comment does not appear in the subsequent programme he prepared for performances which also incorporated *Lélio*, which he describes as being executed 'dramatically'. See Cone (ed.), *Norton Critical Scores*, p. 31.

the ball of the second movement suggests a type of event that was typically dominated by visual spectacle, with attendees gazing not only at the display of dancing couples but also at the dance orchestra and their leader.[11] The country scene of Berlioz's third movement suggests opera or landscape painting, though it has an even more striking visual analogy in the diorama (a visual medium which drew on both theatrical sets and landscape painting), as we shall see shortly. The march to the scaffold of Berlioz's fourth movement falls within the genre of the military processional, with its attendant appeal to the eye. And although the concluding execution by guillotine represents an occasion whose entertainment value had subsided somewhat since the Terror, it, too, suggests a form of public spectacle. Finally, Berlioz's witches' Sabbath represents a different kind of visual medium. The movement evokes the 'Walpurgisnacht' scene of Goethe's *Faust* – a work which was familiar to many due to a widely circulated series of lithographs by Delacroix in 1828 that helped to popularise and propagate the medium.[12]

In *Lélio*, conceived as a continuation of *Symphonie fantastique*, the evocation of dramatic spectacle is even more direct. An actor now represents the musician who, awakening from his nightmare, seeks consolation in his art. He imagines and remembers music in his mind, before finally overcoming his demons by composing and staging a fantasy on Shakespeare's *Tempest*. However, while the presence of the actor creates a visual realisation of the scenario, the fact that the artist in *Lélio* only 'imagines and remembers' the music that he presents to us is significant. Moreover, Berlioz requested that when *Symphonie fantastique* was performed with *Lélio* the orchestra should be concealed behind a curtain for both works until the concluding 'Tempest fantasy': 'The following programme should be distributed to the audience whenever the Fantastic Symphony is executed *dramatically* and consequently followed by the monodrama *Lelio*, which finishes and completes the *Episode from the Life of an Artist*. In such cases, the orchestra should be unseen, placed on the stage of a theatre behind the lowered curtain.'[13]

The music is thus to be construed as emanating from the artist's head, and the visual dimension is largely internalised. The plan to conceal the orchestra was not realised until 1855, when the work was performed in Weimar. Nevertheless, critical responses to earlier performances frequently point to a distinctive treatment of the visual dimension in Berlioz's symphony. Although vision is internalised, many critics felt that the symphony

---

[11] Eric McKee, *Decorum of the Minuet, Delirium of the Waltz: A Study of Dance–Music Relations in 3/4 Time* (Bloomington: Indiana University Press, 2012), pp. 90–128.
[12] Jay, *Downcast Eyes*, p. 121.   [13] Cone (ed.), *Norton Critical Scores*, p. 31.

translated that vision too literally, and that the aura of materiality of objects perceived by the eye persisted. Whereas earlier in the century, French critics could praise '[t]he magical power of the musical art [which] forces us... to translate fugitive sounds into images',[14] *Épisode de la vie d'un artiste* was created at a time when Romantic critical discourse increasingly privileged music that eschewed a connection to definite images or text. It was on these terms that Paul Scudo, one of Berlioz's most vehement detractors, objected to the symphony: 'No, music is not intended to paint material sounds for the ear';[15] and another reviewer reprimanded Berlioz for 'writing on the notice all that he intended to paint'.[16]

Unsurprisingly, German critics were equally disparaging, but they often attributed the visuality of Berlioz's programme specifically to his French nationality:

Undoubtedly an equivalent German composer would have given us something at the same time more artistic and more natural, and less prone to losing itself in objective descriptions. But the author is French, and here we reach the important point, that the judgment of his life and works take place first and foremost before the eye.[17]

Schumann, too, attributed his reservations about Berlioz's programme to France: 'Berlioz was writing primarily for his French compatriots, who are not greatly impressed by refinements of modesty. I can imagine them, leaflet in hand, reading and applauding their countryman who has depicted it all so well; the music by itself does not interest them.'[18] However, Schumann himself adopts visual language in his analysis of Berlioz's work. In interpreting the first movement Schumann employs an architectural metaphor: 'We have often read of those old Scottish castles, [...] and in our mind's eye have enjoyed the randomly placed windows and the boldly jutting towers. Look at our symphony in the same way.'[19] Moreover, Schumann concluded that it was wrong to be anxious about the visual dimension of music *per se*:

Along with the musical imagination there is often an idea unconsciously at work; along with the ear, the eye; and this ever-active organ, in the midst of sounds and tones, holds fast to certain outlines that can solidify and take clear shape as the music develops. The greater the number of musical analogues suggested by the thoughts

---

[14] Quatremière de Quincy, quoted in James H. Johnson, *Listening in Paris* (Berkeley: University of California Press, 1995), p. 207.
[15] Quoted in Johnson, *Listening in Paris*, p. 272.   [16] Ibid., p. 272.
[17] Quoted in Gunther Braam and Arnold Jacobshagen (eds.), *Hector Berlioz in Deutschland*, pp. 523–4.
[18] Cone (ed.), *Norton Critical Scores*, p. 246.   [19] Ibid., p. 228.

or pictures to be produced in tone, the more poetic or plastic in expression the composition will be.[20]

Schumann is not talking about abstract images or sensations, for he goes on to recount how he and a friend both spontaneously visualised the same detailed scenes of historic Seville when listening to a Schubert march.[21] Clearly Schumann's objection to *Symphonie fantastique* does not reflect antipathy for the process of visualisation itself. Rather, Schumann takes issue with the fact that it is Berlioz's programme rather than the music that dictates the nature of the content to be visualised.

More virulent in his condemnation of the visual dimension of Berlioz's symphony was Wagner. In his opinion, Berlioz had been dazzled by the sight of the score of Beethoven's Ninth Symphony, yielding to 'a purblind polyopia'.[22] In trying to recapture Beethoven's vision Berlioz was only able to reproduce the bizarre surface, Wagner suggests. Berlioz 'must sink as artist into mechanism, as supernatural, fantastic dreamer into an all-devouring materialism' – he is buried 'beneath the desert waste of his machines'.[23]

Critical questions and concerns around the nature and role of programme music as represented by Berlioz also lingered well into the twentieth century.[24] However, instead of refuting such accusations, either through recourse to formalist analytical approaches or, conversely, by defending the significance of the programme, in this chapter I shall instead take a new approach and confront and embrace the visual and supposedly materialistic dimension of Berlioz's *Épisode de la vie d'un artiste* by exploring how his work reflects crucial changes in the perception of vision occurring during the same era.

Berlioz's programme itself points to the way the ear and eye work together in his conception. As he tells us, '[b]y a strange quirk, the beloved image only presents itself to the artist's mind united with a musical thought in which he finds a certain character – passionate, but noble and timid – like that of the one he loves. This melodic reflection and its model pursue him incessantly like a double *idée fixe*.'[25] The so-called *idée fixe* is thus both a

---

[20] Ibid., p. 247.   [21] Ibid., p. 247.

[22] Wagner, *Opera and Drama,* trans. William Ashton Ellis, *Richard Wagner Prose Works*, 8 vols. (New York: Broude Brothers, 1966), vol. II, p. 75.

[23] Ibid., p. 77.

[24] See, for example, Katherine Kolb Reeve's summary and problematising of twentieth-century manifestations of the absolute versus programme debate in her review of David Cairns, *The Making of an Artist* and D. Kern Holoman, *Berlioz* in *Journal of the American Musicological Society*, 45/1 (1992), 134–6.

[25] Author's own translation from the French in Cone (ed.), *Norton Critical Scores*, p. 22.

melody that is heard in each movement of *Symphonie fantastique* (and that returns twice in the sequel *Lélio*), and a vision of the woman herself – but one accessible only to the 'artist's *mind*'. Berlioz's interest in this form of internal visualisation was subsequently articulated in an essay on musical imitation: 'music can act by its own means upon the imagination in such a way as to engender sensations analogous to those produced by the graphic arts.'[26]

Approaches to Berlioz's later symphonies and symphonic dramas that treat them as 'covert opera' (in Rushton's words) or 'semi-operas' offer ready paradigms for framing *Épisode de la vie d'un artiste* as a kind of opera without the stage.[27] But opera is not the only paradigm for Berlioz's symphony and its sequel. When Berlioz's *Épisode de la vie d'un artiste* was advertised in the 'Spectacles' section of the *Courrier français* on 13 December 1832, it was positioned not only with opera and balls, but also with several other genres grounded in visual display, including a diorama showing 'views' of Mont Blanc, Napoleon's tomb, and the city of Edinburgh; a neorama showing scenes of Westminster Abbey and St Peter's in Rome; and a toporama in honour of Walter Scott. The 'orama' craze, in which spectators experienced massive painted scenes in purpose-built theatres, was at its peak in the years surrounding *Symphonie fantastique*. These visual displays will be revisited shortly. However, *Épisode de la vie d'un artiste* benefits from being situated in relation to a wider array of visual technologies, including inventions that were intended more for the scientific community and/or for domestic entertainment.

The comments already cited by Wagner, Schumann, d'Ortigue, and Berlioz himself all point to a kind of internalisation of vision. Music stimulates mental images that speak to the inner eye – the eye that sees most clearly when the 'real' eyes are closed or in darkness. Leon Botstein has called for more attention to be paid to this kind of internal visualisation stimulated by instrumental music in the nineteenth century, suggesting that '[t]he role of the visual imagination in listening to music during the nineteenth century remains quite unexplored.'[28] Botstein's call has, in part, been answered by scholars who have explored the relationships between instrumental music and the fine arts.[29] Berlioz was somewhat

---

[26] Berlioz, 'On imitation in music', in Cone (ed.), *Norton Critical Scores*, p. 37.
[27] Julian Rushton, *Berlioz: Roméo et Juliette* (Cambridge: Cambridge University Press, 1994), pp. 80–86; Daniel Albright, *Berlioz's Semi-operas* (Rochester, NY: University of Rochester Press, 2001).
[28] Leon Botstein, 'Hearing Is Seeing: Thoughts on the History of Music and the Imagination', *Musical Quarterly* 79/4 (1995), 582.
[29] Thomas S. Grey, 'Tableaux vivants: Landscape, History Painting, and the Visual Imagination in Mendelssohn's Orchestral Music', *19th-Century Music* 21/1 (1997), 38–76; Marsha L. Morton

dismissive of the importance of visual arts to composition, claiming that 'painting [...] cannot encroach on the domain of music',[30] but his stance need not prevent fruitful analogies being drawn between his music and this or that contemporary painter.[31] However, the question of Berlioz's visual conceptions can be approached profitably from a different angle. Rather than concentrating exclusively on the *products* of vision, or *what* is seen, we should also think about the process and idea of vision itself. The period in which *Symphonie fantastique* was conceived and performed was actually a crucial turning point in the way the viewing subject was constructed. Jonathan Crary has argued that it was in the 1820s and 1830s, rather than with impressionism and later abstract art at the end of the century, that the modern understanding of vision was radically transformed, and that this transformation can be best understood not only through contemplation of art, but through the technologies that were developed to study and entertain the eyes.[32] It is these technologies that will provide the framework for the reconsideration of *Épisode de la vie d'un artiste* in this chapter.

Berlioz may have had direct experience of the science behind the changing conceptions of vision. For many years he counted a noted ophthalmologist, Jules Sichel, among his friends (referring Vincent Wallace to Sichel when Wallace suffered an acute inflammation of the eye).[33] But I am less concerned with proving direct influence than with suggesting the synchronicity between Berlioz's work and the technologies of vision which point to the wider transformation of perception that was happening during this period. The initial focus will be on technologies such as the panorama, diorama, and phantasmagoria that connect primarily to the programmatic content of the *Symphonie fantastique* – to the internal *mise-en-scène* and its relationship to musical sound. However, my subsequent examples of visual technology move the focus to a more exclusively musical element, with a consideration of how technologies of colour and vision relate to Berlioz's use of the orchestra.

---

and Peter L. Schmunk (eds.), *The Arts Entwined: Music and Painting in the Nineteenth Century* (New York and London: Garland, 2000).

[30] Berlioz, 'On imitation in music', in Cone (ed.), *Norton Critical Scores*, p. 37.

[31] Karen Joan Rosell, 'Color: A credible link between the paintings of Eugène Delacroix and the music of Hector Berlioz?' unpublished PhD dissertation, Ohio University (1986); Robert Henri Tissot (ed.), *John Martin, Hector Berlioz: Une esthétique romantique du sublime et de l'insolite* (Grenoble: CRHIPA, 2009).

[32] Jonathan Crary, *Techniques of the Observer* (Cambridge, MA: MIT Press, 1990).

[33] Berlioz, *Evenings with the Orchestra*, p. 376.

Camera obscura

In the eighteenth century the most emblematic visual technology was the camera obscura.[34] Literally a 'dark room' or box, the camera obscura enabled the viewer to see a miniature image of the outside world reproduced within the enclosure by light coming in through a small opening. The camera obscura was considered to symbolise the natural process of human vision. The darkened box itself was thought to be analogous to the mind, receiving light through the opening of the eye and forming a mental image that directly reproduces a fixed external reality. A related device, the camera lucida, was controversially used by artists, including Berlioz's peers in Rome, to facilitate accuracy.[35] But the camera lucida, as the name implies, did not project an image into a darkened chamber – rather, it enacted a direct transferral from the world to the canvas or page.

It was the camera obscura's emphasis on literal and exact reproduction *within the mind* that often lay behind its metaphorical applications. For example, Berlioz's colleague Jules Janin commented on the developing role of the theatre director: 'Before the drama erupts, the *metteur-en-scène* has visualised the whole play in the camera obscura of his mind.'[36] Janin's metaphor suggests a vision that exists initially or exclusively within the darkened chamber of the director's mind and is only subsequently projected onto the stage – in other words, Janin proposes a reversal of the usual process by which the image originates in external reality. Nevertheless, the emphasis on a direct correlation between inner and outer vision is characteristic of the camera obscura model, and it is here that the metaphor is ill-suited to the kind of inner vision suggested by instrumental music such as *Épisode de la vie d'un artiste*. As Berlioz wrote, direct imitation in music must be used sparingly, as a means rather than an end, and should 'not reproduce its sound exactly as it is in nature'. Rather, ideal imitation would 'merely trace the outline of its subject, and touch it with delicate colour'.[37]

While Berlioz's image of tracery seems suggestive of the camera lucida as used by artists, he clearly distinguishes the musical process from the

---

[34] Crary, *Techniques of the Observer*, p. 27; Donata Pesenti Campagnoni, 'Les machines d'optique comme métaphore de l'esprit', in Campagnoni and Paolo Tortonese (eds.), *Les arts de l'hallucination* (Paris: Presses de la Sorbonne Nouvelle, 2001), pp. 111–40.

[35] Barry Bergdoll, *Léon Vaudoyer: Historicism in the Age of Industry* (Cambridge, MA: MIT Press, 1994), p. 77.

[36] Quoted in Donald Roy (ed.), *Romantic and Revolutionary Theatre, 1789–1860* (Cambridge: Cambridge University Press, 2003), p. 383.

[37] Berlioz, 'On imitation in music', in Cone (ed.), *Norton Critical Scores*, p. 43.

approach of the painter, for the transferral of the visual image to the aural imitation can only take place in the mind. Moreover, the camera obscura model for vision was itself increasingly being challenged or supplanted during the period in which he conceived *Symphonie fantastique*. It is usually the daguerreotype and the photographic camera itself that are seen as the logical successors to both the camera obscura and camera lucida. However, as Crary has argued, the more radical challenges to the camera obscura paradigm were actually found in other technologies of vision in the first decades of the nineteenth century. It is by situating Berlioz's *Épisode de la vie d'un artiste* in relation to some of these other visual technologies with which it is contemporaneous that we can best begin to understand the nature of the internal visualisation of instrumental music.

Panorama

The earliest visual medium that provides a fruitful paradigm is one to which Berlioz himself refers directly in his essay on musical imitation: the panorama. Writing of so-called 'indirect or emotional imitation' in music, Berlioz discusses the impact of compositions that suggest breadth and powerful majesty:

> one may say that they represent a broad expanse or infinity itself, because the composer has been able to suggest to the ear, through the breadth of his melodies, the grandeur and clarity of the harmony and the majesty of the rhythm – all of these being set off by contrary effects – impressions analogous to those a climber might feel on the summit of a mountain when beholding in space the splendid panorama suddenly unrolled *before his eyes*. And here, too, the truth of the *image* will appear only if the listener has taken pains to inform himself ahead of time about the subject treated by the musician.[38]

Berlioz's use of the word 'panorama' denotes a wide-ranging perspective, much in the sense in which we most commonly use the term today, but the description of the image as being 'unrolled' hints at the original usage of the word 'panorama'. Arising in the late eighteenth century but continuing to flourish in the first decades of the nineteenth, panoramas were huge 360-degree paintings mounted on the circular walls of custom-built rooms and were viewed from special platforms within the centre of the space. Artists used *trompe l'oeil* effects to fool the eye and create the illusion of reality, enabling the viewers to feel as if they were situated within landscapes and

---

[38] Ibid., p. 45. Italicised emphasis in original.

scenes from often remote places. Berlioz's use of the panorama image to suggest a vast, seemingly unbounded vista reflects a popular type of panorama scene, and it also points to a distinguishing feature of the panorama entertainments: though the illusion was of distant perspectives, the viewer was actually fully enclosed.

The panorama arose around the same time as the panopticon – the structure envisaged by Jeremy Bentham and discussed by Foucault, where a central viewing tower would give prison guards the ability to watch any prisoner, while remaining unseen themselves.[39] The panorama responds to a similar climate of surveillance and control in the late eighteenth century.[40] The panopticon was envisaged as a way of controlling prisoners or workers, who could not know when they were being watched, and were thus forced to moderate their own behaviour continuously. Similarly, the panorama had early military applications, deriving in part from the use of observational towers to take in the lay of the land in order to facilitate conquest or governmental control.[41] Subsequent panoramas sometimes depicted the scenes of battles or the lands of colonial occupation. Repackaged for the predominantly middle class viewers 'back home', panoramas of New Zealand, India, or Egypt enabled a kind of virtual tourism where the perspective was safely framed, the literal centrality of the viewer guaranteed, and the 'Other world' could be experienced without any of the inconveniences or dangers of actual travel that might imperil the traveller's sense of self.[42] Witness the language with which a panorama of Wellington, New Zealand, was promoted in Britain in the early years of colonial settlement in 1849:

to the emigrant, above all men, 'knowledge is power,' the want of it a fatal weakness. As an emigrant colony, New Zealand is fast rising in importance, and it therefore affords us much pleasure to be able to direct the attention of our readers to a means whereby they may attain a clear, practical, matter-of-fact view of that country and its resources.[43]

In suggesting that imitative instrumental music might invoke a panorama, Berlioz thereby raises questions of a controlling subjectivity or perspective. He suggests a 'world' of sound which encloses the listener within the ideology of the composer's persona.

---

[39] Foucault, *Discipline and Punish*, pp. 195–228.   [40] Le Men, *La cathédrale illustrée*, p. 97.
[41] Michael Charlesworth, *Landscape and Vision in Nineteenth-Century Britain and France* (Aldershot: Ashgate, 2008), pp. 9–13.
[42] Stephan Oettermann, *The Panorama: History of a Mass Medium*, trans. Deborah Lucas Schneider (New York: Zone Books, 1997), p. 7.
[43] *Brighton Guardian* 28 November 1849, as reported in *New Zealand Spectator, and Cook Strait Guardian*, 24 April, 1850.

Humboldt in *Cosmos* praises the panorama genre as 'a substitute for travelling through different regions'.[44] He expands, 'Panoramas are more productive of effect than scenic decorations, since the spectator, enclosed as it were within a magical circle, and wholly removed from all the disturbing influences of reality, may the more easily fancy that he is actually surrounded by a foreign scene.'[45] Panoramas could thereby 'raise the feeling of admiration for nature', but Humboldt implies that nature, when encountered by the viewer subsequently, was perceived to imitate art. It was the aesthetic contemplation of the original panorama, 'removed from all the disturbing influence of reality', that instilled the deepest response. Berlioz's use of the panorama image conflates the natural and the aesthetic into a single moment: the climber views the landscape as if it is 'unrolled' – as if it is a panorama.

The effect of the quasi-realism of the panorama could be uncanny. Viewers sometimes suffered from nausea or vertigo, or imagined they heard the sounds of the scene before them or detected movement. Significantly, though, while the panorama simulated reality, unlike the camera obscura it represented a vision mediated by art – indeed, it was perhaps the slight disjunction between the image and reality that caused the physical unease of the spectator.[46] In explaining his mental state when conceiving *Symphonie fantastique*, Berlioz seems to invoke these uncanny aspects of the panorama, in which the spectator's commanding position at the centre of the sphere can also be an alienating one: 'I feel as if I'm at the centre of a circle whose circumference is for ever growing; the physical and mental worlds feel as if they are on that circumference, which constantly moves further away, and I remain alone with a memory, in ever greater isolation.'[47]

Diorama

When Berlioz complains that the Opéra had become a 'diorama' where audiences went only to *see* works, he reveals an interesting analogy between the two media: the diorama was originally created by Louis Daguerre, who before he pioneered and lent his name to the daguerreotype had been an operatic set designer. Daguerre's diorama employed the same *trompe l'oeil* effects as the panorama and as his opera sets, but there were no actors visible in Daguerre's dioramas. Clever lighting effects were sometimes used

---

[44] Humboldt, *Cosmos*, vol. 2, p. 457.   [45] Ibid., p. 457.
[46] Oettermann, *The Panorama*, pp. 12–13; 78–9.   [47] *CG* I, p. 238.

not only to evoke changing times of day but also to suggest animation. As with the panorama, the settings were actual places.

Two popular dioramas captured Swiss scenes suggestive of the third movement of Berlioz's *Symphonie fantastique*. *The Valley of Sarnen* was exhibited frequently in Paris and in London after its creation in 1822. An article in *The Times* describes the 'striking effect' of the changing light which depicted an approaching storm: 'a murky, tempestuous blackness – discolours every object, making us listen almost for the thunder which is to growl in the distance.'[48] A second Swiss diorama scene created in the early 1830s, *The Valley of Chamonix*, introduced alphorns playing the *ranz des vaches* – the shepherd's call evoked by Berlioz in *Symphonie fantastique*.[49]

While approaching storms and shepherds' calls are common enough in Romantic landscapes, the significance of the resemblance of these dioramas to Berlioz's work lies not merely in the theme treated, but also in the way this theme is presented and in the nature of the audience's responses to it. In the position of the diorama somewhere between art and nature, between imitation and reality, *The Valley of Chamonix* was seen to have gone too far. One visitor commented: 'Here is an extraordinary mixture of art and nature, producing the most astonishing effect, so that one cannot decide where nature ceases and art begins.'[50] Berlioz faced similar accusations in *Symphonie fantastique*, of which Schumann said that it 'cannot be called a work of art, any more than Nature itself without human cultivation'.[51] In fact, it could be argued that Berlioz's symphony benefits from the unease inspired by the diorama, whose extreme realism made the absence of actual life seem uncanny. The writer for *The Times* comments how, in the *Valley of Sarnen* diorama,

The whole field is peopled: a house, at which you really expect to see persons look out of the window every moment [...]; and yet, in the midst of all this crowd of animation, there is a stillness, which is the stillness of the grave. The idea produced is that of a region – of a world – desolated; of living nature at an end; of the last day past and over.[52]

---

[48] Quoted in Helmut and Alison Gernsheim, *L.J.M. Daguerre: The History of the Diorama and the Daguerreotype* (London: Secker & Warburg, 1956), pp. 15–16.
[49] Anthony Newcomb has pointed out this possible connection between *Symphonie fantastique* and the diorama: 'New Light(s) on Weber's Wolf's Glen Scene', in Thomas and Marita Petzoldt McClymonds Bauman (eds.), *Opera and the Enlightenment* (Cambridge: Cambridge University Press, 1995), p. 75. See also John Tresch, *The Romantic Machine: Utopian Science and Technology After Napoleon* (Chicago: University of Chicago Press, 2012), p. 143.
[50] Newcomb, p. 29.
[51] Schumann, 'A Symphony by Berlioz', in Cone (ed.), *Norton Critical Scores*, p. 223.
[52] Quoted in Gernsheim, *L.J.M. Daguerre*, pp. 15–16.

Visions of Other worlds

The third movement of *Symphonie fantastique* concludes with a similar emphasis on uncanny isolation and stillness. According to Berlioz's programme, 'one of the shepherds again takes up the *ranz des vaches*; the other no longer replies.... Distant sound of thunder... loneliness... silence.'[53] For a listener familiar with the diorama, the sense of eerie absence is only heightened when listening to Berlioz's work, which is like a memory of absence; the desired object is doubly distanced from us. Daguerre effectively removed real actors' bodies from his theatrical sets in order to create the diorama, but Berlioz went one step further towards the uncanny in removing the sets themselves and speaking directly to the inner eye.

Phantasmagoria

While eeriness and unease were an occasional consequence of the panorama and diorama, with the phantasmagoria they were its primary objective. Developed by Belgian showman and amateur physicist Étienne-Gaspard Robertson in 1798, the phantasmagoria used a moving magic lantern to project images onto smoke and invisible screens to create the sensation of ghosts and other supernatural figures. Although Robertson claimed to be serving science, he concealed the technology of his apparatus, and terrified his audiences with seemingly inexplicable images of death and the supernatural.

Created in the aftermath of the Terror, the phantasmagoria shows purported to raise the ghosts of those who had been guillotined. The macabre fascination with this mode of execution perhaps lingers in the fourth movement of Berlioz's *Symphonie fantastique*, with its march to the Scaffold.[54] But the most obvious thematic connection between the phantasmagoria and Berlioz's *Symphonie fantastique* is the show described as 'Preparations for the Sabbath', which depicts a grotesque ritual complete with witches, bats, skulls, and will-o'-the-wisps strongly suggestive of Berlioz's fifth movement:

A clock strikes midnight: a witch, her nose in a book, raises her arm three times. The moon descends in front of her and becomes blood red; the witch strikes it with her wand and cuts it in two. She raises her left hand for the third time and cats,

---

[53] Berlioz, First programme, adapted from Cone (ed.), *Norton Critical Scores*, p. 25.
[54] A more direct antecedent for that movement is Victor Hugo's *Le dernier jour d'un condamné*, which itself uses the word 'phantasmagoria' to suggest the visions that haunt the condemned man before his execution. Hugo, *Le dernier jour d'un condamné* (Paris: Charles Gosselin, 1829), pp. 6, 90.

bats and skulls fly by with will-o-the-wisps. In the middle of a magic circle appear the words: departure for the SABBATH. A woman arrives astride a broomstick and flies into the air.[55]

The phantasmagoria shows also prominently featured rapid and unexpected transformations: a beautiful woman would abruptly become a skeleton, ghoul, or monster. Berlioz's manipulation of the *idée fixe*, from a 'noble' melody to a 'mean, trivial and grotesque' parody is a kind of aural equivalent. More subtly, when he offers fragmented distortions of the *idée fixe* in the first movement in (as seen Ex. 3.1), he evokes the smoky manifestations of the phantasmagoria show – or at least, such is suggested by Schumann's description of the passage: 'little by little the shadowy outlines assume living form [...] Now the entire first theme, in terrifying splendour [...]; and now completely fantastic shapes, which remind us of familiar ones only once, and then as if smashed to pieces. All vanishes.'[56]

Robertson's memoirs reveal the importance of music and sound to the whole phantasmagoria enterprise:[57] he employed wind machines, hail and rain machines, the glass harmonica, and strategically placed strikes on a gong at moments of maximum tension or to mark sudden changes. Berlioz's use of unusual orchestral colours in the final movement of *Symphonie fantastique* may have evoked some of these sounds to his early audiences: the bouncing of the wood of bows upon strings, wind glissandi, and the striking of off-stage bells that herald changes of scene would certainly have been more at home in the popular spectral entertainments than in the usual symphonic fare.

The concealed orchestra of *Lélio* may also be seen to build on the phantasmagoria. The actor who embodies the artist protagonist seems to conjure forth and discuss sounds whose sources are hidden from view, just as Robertson hid the actual sources of the sounds of his phantasmagoria shows. Richard Leppert points out that, before recording technology was available and disembodied sound became familiarised, concealing the source of music was typically done for the purposes of 'magic and mystery'.[58] But Berlioz's invisible orchestra goes further, to suggest the psychologising of the uncanny that was taking place during this period: the sounds are

---

[55] E. G. Robertson, *Mémoires récréatifs, scientifiques et anecdotiques d'un physicien-aéronaute* (Langres: Clima, 1985), p. 171.
[56] Schumann, 'A Symphony by Berlioz', p. 230.   [57] Robertson, *Mémoires*, pp. 203–4.
[58] Richard Leppert, *Sight of Sound: Music, Representation, and the History of the Body* (Berkeley: University of California Press, 1993), pp. xix–xx.

Ex. 3.1 *Symphonie fantastique* I 'Rêveries – passions', bb. 358–75

imagined as inside the head of the protagonist: 'I hear music around me... What can that singular faculty be which thus substitutes reality through the imagination?... What ideal orchestra is that playing within me?'[59]

Visual metaphors and the inner eye

There is a crucial and obvious distinction to be made between Berlioz's use of concealed musicians and that found in the phantasmagoria. Where the sounds of the phantasmagoria were secondary to the fantastical apparitions that they accompanied, in *Symphonie fantastique* and *Lélio* the sounds appear to emanate from the protagonist's mind, and the only visions in Berlioz's works are internal ones. However, a shift in emphasis from the outer to the inner eye was actually highly characteristic in the usage of the word 'phantasmagoria', and it was precisely at the time Berlioz conceived *Symphonie fantastique* that the transformation of the concept was occurring.

The metaphorical application of visual technology was anticipated by the panorama. In addition to its sense of a painted scene, and its more familiar modern meaning of a wide-ranging view over an actual location, the word 'panorama' could be used to suggest an internalised vision (or, as the *Oxford English Dictionary* defines it, 'a mental vision in which a series of images passes before the *mind's* eye'). 'Ma mémoire est un panorama', Chateaubriand suggests.[60] Berlioz's use of the term 'panorama' in the essay on imitation seems to conflate all three usages: the climber who sees the vista 'unrolled' invokes the first two meanings, while Berlioz is also talking about a panorama invoked purely through musical means, where the visualisation is necessarily internal.

In a similar fashion, the increasing metaphorical applications of 'Phantasmagoria' often carried psychological implications. Marina Warner suggests that the prevalence of supernatural or diabolical imagery in early phantasmagoria shows reveals how the phantasmagoria 'reproduces the mind's capacity to fabricate in the mind's eye what the faculty of sight

---

[59] Berlioz, *Lelio ou le Retour à la vie*, ed. Felix Weingartner, trans. John Bernhoff (Leipzig: Breitkopf & Härtel, n.d.), p. 8.
[60] 'Panorama' 1b, *Oxford English Dictionary*, www.oed.com, accessed 23 September 2013, emphasis added; Chateaubriand, *Mémoires d'Outre-tombe* (Paris: E. et V. Penaud frères, 1849–1850), ed. Pierre Clarac, 3 vols. (Paris: Libraire Générale Française, 1973), vol. III, p. 531.

cannot see.'[61] Eventually, the word itself became effectively dissociated from the displays of the popular entertainment. Not only are ghosts revealed to be manifestations of our thoughts rather than external projections, but thoughts themselves are understood to be ghostly in nature.[62] When 'phantasmagoria' began to be applied in a metaphorical sense, it was most commonly applied to illusory or obsessive thoughts.

While it is now commonly understood that the '*idée fixe*' concept originated in psychological discourse and literary invocations of psychology in the decade or so preceding *Symphonie fantastique*,[63] the ways in which this form of obsession interacted with conceptions of haunting and the supernatural are less widely appreciated. The understanding of psychology bordered closely on the supernatural in this era, and the concept of an '*idée fixe*' could suggest how the internalisation of the image of an absent beloved results in real people becoming more ghostly.[64] The physicality of vision itself was being rethought, as sight became extended to consideration of hallucinations and apparitions of the 'mind's eye'. Samuel Hibbert, for example, dismissed the possibility of spectral visions having any existence in reality by attributing them to projections of the 'inner eye' based on memories and recollections or deriving from distorted signals from the body resulting from alcohol, illness, or drugs. David Brewster (inventor of the kaleidoscope, considered later), similarly treated apparitions as distorted subjective perception based on external stimulus, suggesting that in fact both the actual eye and the mind's eye shared the use of the retina, which functioned as a kind of camera obscura for both types of image:[65]

[the eye] is thus a little camera obscura, thanks to which images of external objects paint themselves on the retina and are transmitted to the brain by means of which we are unaware. This astonishing organ can be considered like the sentry who guards the entrance between the worlds of matter and mind, and by which all their communications are exchanged.[66]

---

[61] Marina Warner, *Phantasmagoria: Spirit Visions, Metaphors and Media* (Oxford: Oxford University Press, 2006), p. 139.

[62] Terry Castle, 'Phantasmagoria: Spectral Technology and the Metaphorics of Modern Reverie', *Critical Inquiry* 15/1 (1988), 29.

[63] Francesca Brittan, 'Berlioz and the Pathological Fantastic: Melancholy, Monomania, and Romantic Autobiography', *19th-Century Music*, 29/3 (2006), 211–39.

[64] Terry Castle, *The Female Thermometer* (New York: Oxford University Press, 1995), pp. 136–7.

[65] David Brewster, *Letters on Natural Magic* (London: John Murray, 1838), ed. A. D. Vergnaud, *Nouveau manuel de magie naturelle et amusante* (Paris: Libraire Encyclopédie de Roret, 1839), p. 9; Charlesworth, *Landscape and Vision*, p. 43.

[66] Brewster, *Nouveau manuel*, p. 9.

The suggestions of psychosis and obsession in the programme of *Épisode de la vie d'un artiste* are fully in keeping with both the supernatural and psychological elements of the term 'phantasmagoria' during the period. Berlioz actually commented that he felt as if the ghost of Harriet Smithson (not dead, but recently relocated to London) haunted the streets of his Parisian neighbourhood – 'I seem to feel her around me', he wrote to a friend, as he struggled to commit his symphony to paper.[67] The opium-induced dreams of Berlioz's protagonist are certainly 'phantasmagoric', and indeed, Thomas de Quincey's *Confessions of an English Opium-Eater*, often identified as a direct influence on the symphony, offers an instance of the metaphorical use of the term, referring to the 'phantasmagoria' of the dreams of the opium eater.[68]

Berlioz's *Symphonie fantastique*, with its suggestions of psychosis and obsession, in which the beloved appears 'dans l'ésprit de l'artiste', plays powerfully upon the new metaphorical and psychological associations for the term 'phantasmagoria', but it does not abandon the original connection with the old ghost show. Indeed, by invoking themes that audiences may have experienced in the visual entertainments, but by withholding the images themselves, Berlioz heightens the sense of the internality of the ghostly visions. He stimulates in his listeners the *memory* of the event, causing each listener to experience it exclusively through his or her own thought rather than through the outer eyes.[69]

Colour and the kaleidoscope

During the same period in which the words panorama and phantasmagoria were taking on psychological implications, the camera obscura model was increasingly being challenged, as science began to demonstrate the mental aspects of vision itself. In 1810 Goethe published his widely influential treatise on colour theory, which provided a key example of this new understanding. As Crary points out, Goethe effectively closed the window of the camera obscura, observing how, if the aperture admitting the bright light

---

[67] *CG* I, p. 306.
[68] Thomas de Quincey, *Confessions of an English Opium-Eater* (London: Taylor and Hessey, 1823), p. 12; J.-G. Prod'homme, 'Berlioz, Musset, and Thomas De Quincey', *The Musical Quarterly* 32/1 (1946), 98–106.
[69] The intangibility of the images of the phantasmagoria has also been extended by Thomas Grey to a metaphor for the 'vaporous' nature of meaning in programme music more broadly (and in Mendelssohn's *Fingal's Cave* specifically): Grey, '*Fingal's Cave* and Ossian's Dream: Music, Image, and Phantasmagoric Audition', in Morton and Schmunk (eds.), *The Arts Entwined*, p. 92.

was obstructed, the viewer standing in a darkened room or with his or her eyes closed could still 'see' afterimages – ghostly traces, usually with the colours inverted. From these observations Goethe developed a theory of complementary colours, which was in turn taken up by artists. Goethe himself proposed extending his theory of complementarity to music, seeing the major and minor modes as the equivalent of light and darkness in the polarisation of light. His friend Zelter suggested that it was instead the difference between consonance and dissonance that replicated the polarisation.[70]

Berlioz often spoke of the importance of contrast in music.[71] But when Berlioz talks about colour his primary concern is usually with instrumental timbre: 'Instrumentation is to music precisely what colour is to painting', he states in his essay on 'The art of music', and the *Orchestration Treatise* offers a definition of instrumentation as 'the use of these various sonorities and their application [. . .] to colour the melody, harmony or rhythm'.[72] Similarly, Berlioz's reviews and descriptions of performances attribute colour to instrumental timbre, as in his response to Méhul's *Uthal*, whose instrumentation lends the work 'a melancholy colouring of the cloudy, Ossianic kind'.[73]

The conception of *instrumental* colour has become so deeply entrenched in relation to western art music that it may be difficult now to conceive that Berlioz's statements might have been in any way unusual at the time. Emily Dolan has traced the development of the association of colour with timbre in the late eighteenth and early nineteenth centuries as an important facet of the objectification of orchestral timbre.[74] But many writers of Berlioz's era continued to treat the musical analogy of colour as harmony. Thus E.T.A. Hoffmann's Kreisler is 'the little man in a coat the colour of C sharp minor with an E major coloured collar' (though Hoffmann elsewhere equated colour with orchestration).[75] Similarly, Louis Viardot compares melody with drawing, and harmony with colour.[76] During an era in which, as Dolan suggests, it was increasingly desirable to listen *through* orchestration to the

---

[70] Stephanie Campbell, 'Seeing Music: Visuality in the Friendship of Johann Wolfgang von Goethe and Carl Friedrich Zelter', in Morton and Schmunk (eds.), *The Arts Entwined*, pp. 47–62.
[71] Berlioz, 'On imitation in music', in Cone (ed.), *Norton Critical Scores*, pp. 45, 38.
[72] Berlioz, *The Art of Music*, p. 5; Macdonald, *Berlioz's Orchestration Treatise*, p. 6.
[73] Berlioz, *Evenings with the Orchestra*, pp. 352–3.
[74] Dolan, *The Orchestral Revolution*, pp. 24–52. [75] Ibid., p. 52.
[76] Marsha L. Morton, '"From the Other Side:": An Introduction', in Morton and Schmunk (eds.), *The Arts Entwined*, p. 14; Viardot, 'Ut pictura musica', *Gazette des Beaux Arts*, quoted in Philippe Junod, 'The New *Paragone*: Paradoxes and Contradictions of Pictorial Modernism', in Morton and Schmunk (eds.), *The Arts Entwined*, p. 29.

abstracted musical work 'beneath', Berlioz's insistence on the importance of orchestral colour is telling.

An extreme application of Berlioz's awareness of the polarity of timbre and instrumental colour might be seen in *Symphonie fantastique* in the way he distributes each consecutive note of a single melody in a different instrument or instrumental group, like an early form of *Klangfarbenmelodie* (Ex. 3.2).[77] The effect here is to render the principal march theme from the fourth movement into an appropriately uncanny nightmarish form, not unlike the spectral visions of the afterimage.

Afterimages broke down the camera obscura idea of vision as a direct and instantaneous transferral of a fixed external reality to the darkened mind of the viewer, for they demonstrated how the eye could see when there was no longer anything before it. The eye was not simply the window through which the light passed in order to project the image onto the mind, but could actually produce the image itself, given some form of initial stimulus.

We might in this context reconsider Berlioz's suggestion in the *Orchestration Treatise* that not only is orchestration like the colour applied to the preexisting 'drawing' of melody (such as the march theme), but the timbres of the orchestra might also exist *sui generis*. In identifying orchestral colour as an entity in its own right, Berlioz is suggestive of a particular technology of vision that focussed on patterns of abstract colour: the kaleidoscope, which was invented in 1815 as part of a scientific study of light before being popularised for domestic use. The kaleidoscope invited the viewer to look at an image in a darkened space, much like the camera obscura, but in the case of the kaleidoscope this image was not derived from anything in the 'real', external world but was instead abstracted and reflected, comprising symmetrical patterns of colour. The inventor of the device, David Brewster, saw the kaleidoscope as offering a new kind of industrial art. Critics of the kaleidoscope saw it as reflective of nothing but itself, violating the purpose of art to somehow exist in dialogue with the real world around it.[78]

Berlioz used the metaphor of the kaleidoscope to refer to instrumental colour. The average pianist composer, for example, was described by Berlioz as being heavily reliant on the kaleidoscope of colour facilitated by that instrument, but as often lacking any meaningful musical creativity when 'deprived of their musical kaleidoscope'.[79] The aesthetics of

---

[77] For further discussion of this passage, see Su Lian Tan, 'Hector Berlioz *Symphonie Fantastique*, Op. 14: An Exploration of Musical Timbre', unpublished PhD dissertation, Princeton University (1997), p. 58.

[78] Crary, *Techniques of the Observer*, pp. 113–4.   [79] Berlioz, *Mémoires*, p. 15.

Ex. 3.2 *Symphonie fantastique* IV 'Marche au supplice', bb. 109–13

Ex. 3.3 *Symphonie fantastique* V 'Songe d'une nuit de sabbat', bb. 456–87

Ex. 3.3 (cont.)

Ex. 3.3 (cont.)

the kaleidoscope might be seen in those passages of *Symphonie fantastique* which would, by Berlioz's own terms, be meaningless in piano reduction, where the sense comes almost entirely from the play of orchestral colour, and where Schumann, assessing the symphony with only Liszt's piano score to hand, was forced to internalise that colour to hear it in his head. The most obvious passages in this respect are found in the fifth movement, in the opening (with its wind glissandi, stopped horns, and muted divided strings), and later in the same movement where Berlioz makes use of the extended technique of *col legno* to form the first of an array of shifting blocks of sound from different instrumental groups – tremolo, trills, or drum rolls (Ex. 3.3). It was precisely such passages that challenged Berlioz's most hostile critics such as Fétis, who was as unwilling to relinquish the traditional demands of melody, harmony and rhythm as critics of the kaleidoscope were to sacrifice perspective and realism in their art.

Less directly, the play of colour and movement of the swirling dancers in a ballroom waltz, such as the one vividly evoked in Berlioz's second movement, has been likened to the kaleidoscope.[80] Indeed, symphonic music existed in a more symbiotic relationship with dance at this time than is generally acknowledged.[81] Berlioz's waltz, like those of Strauss and Lanner, emphasises how the spectacle of female beauty could be captured musically. At the first appearance of the *idée fixe*, the 'om-pa-pa' of the waltz accompaniment is momentarily suspended, giving way to tremolo chords that foreground the familiar melody. After two bars, the lower strings take up off-beat semiquavers that might recall the excited heart-beats in the same timbre and register which accompanied the *idée fixe* on its first appearance in the first movement, reminding us that the gaze we are drawn into is that of the protagonist. The waltz accompaniment soon resumes, and fragments of the primary waltz theme played by the strings swirl around the woodwind statements of the *idée fixe*, providing an almost synesthetic sympathy between the protagonist who gazes at his beloved through the swirling dances, and the audience who glimpse the woodwind through the flurry of bows (Ex. 3.4). McKee points out how Strauss and Lanner characteristically made use of metric disruption at moments where the spectator's gaze might be most forcibly directed. The *idée fixe* introduces one such moment (as was typical of 'feminine' themes, McKee suggests).[82] In bars 135 and 136 the alternating strong and weak bars of the hypermeter (indicated in

---

[80] McKee, *Decorum of the Minuet*, p. 99.
[81] J. Q. Davies, 'Dancing the Symphonic: Beethoven-Boscha's *Symphonie Pastorale*, 1829', *19th-Century Music* 27/1 (2003), 25–47.
[82] Ibid., p. 116.

Ex. 3.4 *Symphonie fantastique* II 'Un bal', bb. 120–39

Ex. 3.4 by the Arabic numbers) are interrupted by two implicitly strong bars (∗∗∗ marks the moment of disruption, reflected also in the irregularity of the metrical phrasing brackets at this point), as if to ensure that the gaze continues to be fixed on the woman and her melody at precisely the moment where the strings might begin to obscure it.

Hypermetric disruption was also characteristic of Strauss and Lanner's codas, particularly at the climax of a crescendo and at moments where an assertive or fanfare-type theme was succeeded by cadentially oriented music. Such clear breaks signalled to the dancers that the waltz was soon to conclude and that they might wish to begin to leave the dance floor, but McKee suggests that the musical rupture also directed the audience's gaze towards the band, and to the conductor, as the ultimate source of the disruption.[83] Berlioz reproduces this hypermetric disruption (among many other features characteristic of the waltz coda) when, in bars 287–8, two strong bars again appear in succession at the moment of cadential resolution (Ex. 3.5).

[83] Ibid., pp. 111–14.

Visions of Other worlds

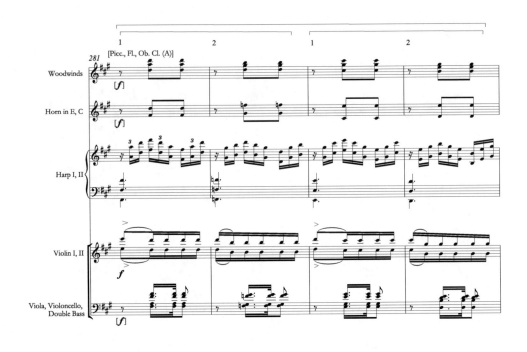

Ex. 3.5 *Symphonie fantastique* II 'Un bal', bb. 281–8

An even greater disruption occurs a few bars later and on a larger scale, when the *idée fixe* itself intrudes upon the coda. Perhaps we may imagine that enough dancers have taken their cue from the musicians and cleared the floor to allow the protagonist a much clearer view of his beloved. But the presentation of the theme in a tempo, dynamic, and orchestration so strongly differentiated from the surrounding coda material (which soon resumes once more) also suggests aspects of quotation or memory, as if the protagonist's vision has now moved inside his head (Ex. 3.6).[84]

The kaleidoscope provides a model of the symmetrical play of colours and focussed viewing characteristic of the waltz. However, we must turn to other visual technologies to find the most suggestive analogies for this kind of internalised vision.

Thaumatrope

The thaumatrope, invented in 1824, juxtaposed two distinctly different images on a piece of card. In one popular example, a bird and a cage were illustrated on the card, which, when spun rapidly, would appear to display the two illustrations fused into a single image in the mind of the viewer, the bird now appearing to be contained within the cage. Like the study of aftereffects, the thaumatrope broke down the relationship between a single fixed external reality and the image within the viewer's mind, for it revealed vision to be a temporal process and one in which the mind of the viewing subject is actually constructing the object, not simply receiving it. The most literal analogy in *Symphonie fantastique* of the thaumatrope would perhaps be those sections where Berlioz takes two quite different, self-contained melodic units and combines them simultaneously in such a way that each can be heard distinctly but with each now being part of a new combined whole. The so-called *réunion des thèmes* was a favourite thematic device for Berlioz. The technique had numerous precedents in opera, but Berlioz used it conspicuously in several nonstaged works and generally made more extensive and drastic use of this technique than perhaps any other composer of his time.[85] We have already encountered it in the Serenade of *Harold en Italie*, where we considered its demands on the coordination of the conductor. Here, let us instead consider the impact on the listener, who constructs a sonic world from two simultaneous scenes in the manner of

---

[84] Rosen gives a similar example from Schumann's *Carnaval*; *The Romantic Generation* (London: Harper Collins, 1996), pp. 97–8.

[85] Anselm Gerhard, *The Urbanization of Opera: Music Theater in Paris in the Nineteenth Centruy*, trans. Mary Whittall (Chicago and London: University of Chicago Press, 1998), pp. 202–6.

Ex. 3.6 *Symphonie fantastique* II 'Un bal', bb. 300–321

Ex. 3.7 *Symphonie fantastique* V 'Songe d'une nuit de sabbat', bb. 414–20

the thaumatrope. In the final movement of *Symphonie fantastique*, Berlioz signals the device to the listener or performer in the score. He labels both the *Dies irae* and the witches' round dance, before pointing out in both score and programme how he is combining the two (Ex. 3.7).

A similar mentality – perhaps even closer to the deeper significance of the thaumatrope – may be behind the way in which Berlioz absorbs his *idée fixe* into the various musical contexts of each movement. In these cases, the listener is forced straight into the mind of the protagonist. The image of the woman is distorted through his subjectivity as, like the caged bird of the thaumatrope, she is 'seen' in different settings such as the ball, countryside, or witches' Sabbath.

Stereoscope

If vision was being psychologised in the period of *Symphonie fantastique*, this was not at the expense of the physical body but quite the opposite. My final example of visual technology is the stereoscope – the device which Crary sees as most emblematic of the new visual paradigms which served to reembody vision at precisely the moment that it seemed to move furthest into the abstractions of the mind.[86] The stereoscope might be seen as the culmination of the process of the transformation of vision enacted by all the devices previously examined. Like the camera obscura, it involved the viewer looking at an image within a darkened chamber, but as in the panorama and diorama, this image was mediated – first painted and then, later in the century, photographed. As with the thaumatrope, the stereoscope employed two different images. However, in the stereoscope these images were not

[86] Crary, *Techniques of the Observer*, pp. 116–18.

contrasting but were instead almost identical depictions of the same scene, reproducing the slightly different perspectives of the two different eyes. When viewed together, the effect was of a single three-dimensional image. The stereoscope was popularised as a sort of toy in the later nineteenth century. However, in the 1820s and 1830s, when Berlioz was conceiving *Symphonie fantastique*, the stereoscope was new technology that built on serious science that reflected and shaped radical new thinking about vision. The three-dimensionality made the images of the stereoscope more realistic to the viewer than anything that had preceded it. Thus viewers felt as though they had really experienced the scenes and objects depicted. But rather than acting as a device to better enable the viewer to experience an external visual reality through an 'ideal eye', as the camera obscura as well as devices such as the telescope and microscope had already done, the stereoscope presented an image of something with no physical reality before them, and simulated the binocularity of the viewer's own body to do so.[87] Vision, in the stereoscope model, was thus both embodied *and* psychological.

The most obvious way in which Berlioz could be seen to evoke the mentality of the stereoscope is in his *stereophonic* treatment of the orchestra. He was acutely aware of the impact of spatiality on sound. An essay on 'The art of music' actually lists the placement of the sources of sound among the fundamental aspects of music (after melody, harmony, rhythm, expression, modulation, and instrumentation).[88] *Symphonie fantastique* makes conspicuous use of space in placing first the oboe of the third movement and then the bells of the final movement off-stage in a manner that was familiar in opera but highly unusual in a symphonic context. More subtly, Berlioz writes in such a way as to draw on the placement of the instruments *on* the stage, as with his treatment of the *idée fixe* in the second movement, where the clarinet, flute, and oboe are both visually and aurally 'glimpsed' through the swirling fragments of the strings' statements of the waltz theme (see Ex. 3.4, earlier).[89]

However, the most subtle and most interesting analogy between the new models of perception embodied in the stereoscope and Berlioz's *Symphonie fantastique* is to be found on a different level again. Hugh Macdonald has pointed to the way in which Berlioz divides a single melodic line between the two halves of each violin section.[90] The passage Macdonald refers to is

---

[87] Ibid., p. 129. [88] Berlioz, *The Art of Music*, p. 5.
[89] The second movement is also the one in which Kregor identifies the greatest element of gestural spectacle in Liszt's piano transcription: 'Collaboration and Content', 228.
[90] Macdonald, *Berlioz's Orchestration Treatise*, pp. xxx–xxxi.

Ex. 3.8 *Symphonie fantastique* I 'Rêveries – passions', bb. 410–15

given in Ex. 3.8,[91] where it lends 'depth' to the triumphal return of the *idée fixe* in the woodwind and cornets. An even more extreme example is heard in the final movement, where both groups of violins are divided in three and the violas are divided in two (Ex. 3.9).

Although Berlioz claims that such divisions facilitate performance, they can actually make the music slightly more difficult for the players than it would be if they each had the complete line.[92] The rapid tempo forces the players to spit out their fragments almost without listening to their peers who have the complementary notes – there is no time at this tempo for them to wait and respond to aural cues. Macdonald suggests that this represents a quite new approach to the orchestra for the time, evoking 'a great machine', and we might also imagine the divided (and disciplined) labour of new models of factory production. Such metaphors are in keeping with the emphasis Berlioz places on the composer-persona of the programme, whose creation takes precedence over the players' labour to provide the true 'unity' of the work. But viewing such passages through the lens of the stereoscope only adds resonance to both the mechanical and factory metaphors. The stereoscope has been described as objectifying reality, creating a world of seemingly tangible objects that the bourgeois consumer of factory goods needs to fill the inner void.[93] The eyes are fooled into perceiving a single consumable object in place of two intangible ones. Moreover, the

---

[91] See also from bar 431 of the same movement.
[92] Macdonald, *Berlioz's Orchestration Treatise*, pp. xxx–xxxi, 28.
[93] Crary, *Techniques of the Observer*, p. 125.

Ex. 3.9 *Symphonie fantastique* V 'Songe d'une nuit de sabbat', bb. 31–9

stereoscope makes the individual subject part of the machine – the vision is constructed through the machine itself, rather than the technology being a tool to facilitate the view of a 'real' object. In Berlioz's score the violins have similar but not identical figures that combine in the ears of the listener to create a single sound, but one in which the subtle differences resulting from the different players combine to give that sound complexity or depth.

Seeing the orchestra: The Wagnerian phantasmagoria

The fact that the audience member of Berlioz's time could actually *see* the different points of origin by watching the differing movements of the strings' bows in these examples may also be significant. Unlike later models, the earliest stereoscopes, which were developed shortly after the conception of *Épisode de la vie d'un artiste*, did not attempt to conceal the fact that there were two separate images as the source. The technology itself and the exposure of its 'magic' were part of the appeal.

What, then, of Berlioz's intention to conceal the orchestra behind a curtain? In 1855 in Weimar Berlioz was able, for the first time, to perform *Lélio* 'dramatically', with only the actor visible to the audience. His letters, however, imply that, although *Symphonie fantastique* was performed directly before *Lélio*, it was not subjected to this unusual staging.[94] Perhaps, in the absence of the actor, Berlioz wished the audience to locate the drama in both the sights and sounds of the orchestra, visible to the outer as well as inner eye. If that is the case, Berlioz occupies an interesting position in relation to the visibility of orchestral technology.

As Dolan points out, in the later nineteenth century increasing critical emphasis was placed on the metaphorical 'invisibility' of the orchestra. While it was considered necessary to *see* Liszt or Paganini, audiences for symphonic repertoire were meant to hear – or see – *through* the orchestra to 'the work itself',[95] to the extent that Liszt's piano transcription of *Symphonie fantastique* could be seen as, in Jonathan Kregor's words, a 'persistent tug-of-war between composer and performer' in which 'Berlioz's music and Liszt's spectacle' are often at odds.[96] As early as the late eighteenth century, some composers and critics began to articulate a desire to hide the orchestra, for what Hanslick described as 'the disturbing spectacle of the musicians' fiddling and puffing' was considered, in Choron's words, 'as shocking as the sight of the machines and the individuals employed as stage hands'.[97] However, J.Q. Davies has demonstrated how, earlier in the nineteenth century, there was a keen interest in viewing the orchestra and in interpreting their movements either literally or metaphorically through dance.[98]

Indeed, Berlioz did not express disdain for the sights of the orchestra. The sight as well as the sound of the harps in the ballroom of *Symphonie Fantastique* become significant – 'whenever I saw [a fine harp] I wanted to

---

[94] *CG* IV pp. 712–24.   [95] Dolan, *The Orchestral Revolution*, p. 210.
[96] Jonathan Kregor, 'Collaboration and Content in the *Symphonie fantastique* Transcription', 27.
[97] Lydia Goehr, *The Quest for Voice: Music, Politics, and the Limits of Philosophy* (Oxford: Oxford University Press, 1998), p. 163; Dolan, *The Orchestral Revolution*, p. 260.
[98] Davies, 'Dancing the Symphonic', 25–47.

go down on my knees and embrace it', he remarked in the *Memoirs*, and as he told Liszt, 'the look of the instrument has a great deal to do with it'.[99] Moreover, the appeal of 'glimpsing' the *idée fixe* in the woodwind through the waltzing strings in the second movement suggests a visuality that extends beyond the element of spectatorship inherent in the ballroom setting. The *idée fixe* is first presented to us by the strings of the first movement, before moving to the various clarinets – positioned at the very centre of Berlioz's orchestra – in all subsequent movements, directing the gaze of the attentive audience member into the interior of the orchestra itself.

Later in the century, the stereoscope would conceal its technology – the two separate images that together produce the illusion of three dimensions would be hidden within the casing of the apparatus. This occurred in precisely the period in which Wagner hid his orchestra in the sunken pit of Bayreuth and dimmed the lights, encouraging the audience to cross the so-called mystic abyss with their eyes and immerse themselves in the visions of his stage, and to avoid being made 'an unwilling witness of technical evolutions which should be almost as carefully concealed from him as the cords, ropes, laths and scaffoldings of the stage directions – which, seen from the wings, as everyone knows, destroy all vestige of illusion'.[100] Wagner's submersion of the orchestra at Bayreuth met with some resistance from the players themselves, who were cut off from the singers and struggled even to hear each other; they complained of feeling like machines rather than musicians.[101]

Wagner employed the terms of the phantasmagoria in relation to the ideal drama, where the concealed orchestra enables 'the full shapes of a dream-vision or the other world [to be] projected before us in a lifelike way as if by a magic lantern'.[102] Wagner's phantasmagoric approach would famously be critiqued by Adorno, who articulated discomfort over the way he conceals the technology – and labour – upon which this vision is

---

[99] Quoted in Macdonald, *Berlioz's Orchestration Treatise*, p. 79. Davies also notes how the harp was perceived as feminine because 'its mechanism was physical, seen, and never hidden'; 'Dancing the Symphonic', 26.

[100] Quoted Dolan, *The Orchestral Revolution*, p. 260. See also Edward A. Lippman, 'Wagner's Conception of the Dream', *Journal of Musicology* 8/1 (1990), 54–81. Direct analogies between Wagner's music and the stereoscope have been drawn by Lutz Koepnick, though the focus of this approach is on aspects of the staging and dramaturgy rather than on the role of the orchestra and its music. Lutz Koepnick, 'Stereoscopic Vision: Sight and Community in *Die Meistersinger*', in Nicholas Vazsonyi (ed.), *Wagner's Meistersinger: Performance, History, Representation* (Rochester, NY: University of Rochester Press, 2002).

[101] Quoted in Goehr, *The Quest for Voice*, p. 163; Frederic Spotts, *Bayreuth: A History of the Wagner Festival* (New Haven and London: Yale University Press, 1994), p. 12.

[102] Quoted in Goehr, *The Quest for Voice*, p. 158.

dependent.[103] However, rather than revisit Adorno's Wagnerian phantasmagoria, we may fruitfully take a closer look at Wagner's response to Berlioz's *Symphonie fantastique*, for here Wagner curiously anticipates Adorno's more critical use of the imagery of contemporaneous visual technologies. Wagner seems to evoke the phantasmagoria itself when he suggests that, in Berlioz's work, 'what we behold, are colossal clouds of smoke, parted and modelled into fleeting shapes by lightnings and tongues of fire.'[104] When Wagner writes that Berlioz's 'natural vision yielded to a purblind [...] *Vielsichtigkeit*'[105] – a neologism that literally means 'many-sighted-ness' – it is the science of the afterimage and the dizzying superimposition of the thaumatrope or stereoscope that are evoked. Finally, let us revisit Wagner's suggestion that Berlioz thus reached the point where he 'must sink as artist into mechanism, as supernatural, fantastic dreamer into an all-devouring materialism' until he is buried 'beneath the desert waste of his machines'. Here we might recall all the visual apparatus of the science and entertainment of sight available to Berlioz's audiences. But need it necessarily follow that an awareness of the technologies of vision in *Symphonie fantastique* is inherently a bad thing? Baudelaire, in his 'salon of 1859', wrote eloquently of his nostalgia for the explicit mechanism of the diorama: 'I long for the return of the dioramas whose enormous, crude magic subjects me to the spell of a useful illusion [...] Those things, so completely false, are for that very reason much closer to the truth, whereas the majority of our landscape painters are liars, precisely because they fail to lie.'[106]

Botstein speculates that it was not sound recording, as usually assumed, but sound *cinema* that led to the decline of concert attendance, arguing that it was the direct mapping of external image onto sound that undermined the familiar pleasures of listening for the *inner* eye.[107] Botstein's point overrides the increasingly pedantic distinctions between absolute and programme music in which Berlioz's symphony became entangled, and leaves aside questions of whether the composer overdetermined the programme. Instead, it is the process of internal visualisation itself which is seen as key to instrumental music, whether or not that music has a programmatic text specified by the composer. In situating Berlioz's symphony in relation to

---

[103] Adorno, *Versuch über Wagner* (Frankfurt: Suhrkamp Verlag, 1952), trans. Rodney Livingston, *In Search of Wagner* (London: Verso, 2005), pp. 74–85.
[104] Wagner, 'Letters from Paris (3)', 5 May, 1841, in *Richard Wagner's Prose Works*, trans. William Ashton Ellis, 8 vols. (New York: Broude, 1966), vol. VIII, p. 133.
[105] Wagner, *Opera and Drama*, in *Richard Wagner's Prose Works*, vol. II, p. 75.
[106] Quoted in Stephan Oettermann, *The Panorama*, p. 79.
[107] Botstein, 'Hearing Is Seeing', 585.

several contemporaneous technologies of vision, we may paradoxically be reawakened to the visual dimension of concert music that, in Botstein's view, has been silenced by cinema. And by uncovering some of the technologies of vision that surrounded *Épisode de la vie d'un artiste* we might better understand it within the context in which it arose, in which vision was being both internalised and reembodied, in which vision and hearing were being both autonomised and merged, and in which technology was a source of delight to be seen as well as concealed.

La nonne sanglante

Épisode de la vie d'un artiste achieves its effect precisely because it does not stage the supernatural. The magical orchestral technology bypasses the phantasmagoria's smoke and mirrors to appeal directly to our 'inner eye'; and while we see 'the artist' before us in *Lélio*, we do not see on the stage the ghosts of the 'Choeur d'ombres' that he imagines. In some senses, then, in turning now to Berlioz's operatic treatment of the supernatural in the duet of his incomplete setting of *La nonne sanglante*, we are stepping into more familiar territory, despite the fact the work itself is considerably less familiar than the symphony, having been left incomplete and having never actually been staged. However, even if we imagine that Berlioz's opera had reached the stage for which it was originally intended, *La nonne sanglante* raises related questions of materiality and vision.

The theme of Berlioz's *Nonne sanglante*, like some of the themes treated in *Épisode de la vie d'un artiste*, was popular in the phantasmagoria shows, but the story actually originated in Matthew Lewis's rabidly Gothic novel *The Monk* (1796), where it forms a self-contained subplot. *The Monk* spawned several adaptations, and details of the story vary significantly from one treatment to another, but the essential details, as presented in Scribe's libretto for Berlioz, are easily summarised: A young man (Rodolphe, in Scribe's version) seeks to elope with a young woman (Agnès) whose family oppose the union. To facilitate her escape, they agree that Agnès will pose as the ghost of the bleeding nun who has long haunted the house in which Agnès is being held. However, on the night of the escape, it is the 'real' ghost who elopes with the unwitting Rodolphe, and who haunts him until she can be laid to rest.

The popularity of the bleeding nun in France in the first decades of the nineteenth century was enhanced by post-Revolutionary French anticlericism. Robertson's phantasmagoria, which adapted the bleeding nun story, was for a period actually staged in a disused monastery. The tension between physical and metaphysical explanation also made the bleeding nun subject a particularly loaded one for the inherently 'irrational' genre of opera. Indeed, operatic treatments of the story were produced by Donizetti (*Maria de Rudenz,* which the librettist Cammarano based on an 1835 boulevard theatre play, *La nonne sanglante,* by Auguste Anicet-Bourgeois and Julien de Mallian) and Gounod (*La nonne sanglante,* based on Scribe's completion of the libretto initially provided to Berlioz).

Berlioz may have lost faith in *La nonne sanglante,* but resurrecting her in critical terms provides a telling counterbalance to the ways in which he explores supernatural worlds in *Épisode de la vie d'un artiste.* While the subject of the bleeding nun was itself closely connected to the phantasmagoria shows, the phantasmagoria was past its prime by the 1840s, and new frameworks for connecting with supernatural worlds were coming to the fore. As the Spiritualist movement first began to stir, it was the body of the medium or the subject of mesmerism that mediated between this world and the next. But the connection between technology and the supernatural only intensified. Similarly, while Berlioz's orchestra in *La nonne sanglante* may not literally occupy centre stage as it does in the symphony, and while the composer draws on specifically operatic conventions of the supernatural, *La nonne sanglante* represents another striking instance of how the orchestra was central to Berlioz's conception of Other worlds.

Meyerbeer and the orchestral supernatural

Surely one of the most visually spectacular evocations of the supernatural in the nineteenth century was the cloister scene from Meyerbeer's *Robert le diable,* which was premiered in Paris in 1831. The titular protagonist has met the sinister Bertram at midnight at an abandoned medieval cloister. Bertram persuades Robert to enter the cloister to seize a magic branch which will help him to win the love of the pure Isabel. As Robert enters, Bertram summons up the spirits of debauched nuns, who attempt to seduce Robert with alcohol, gambling, and sexual advances, which are enacted in an extended ballet.

The scene evokes all the visual spectacle of French grand opera – a genre which Meyerbeer's *Robert le diable* helped to define. Duponchel, the director of the Opéra, sent the set designer Ciceri to Arles in order to produce sketches of the cloister of St Trophime, upon which the set was based. The opera also introduced 'trappes anglaises' for the first time, rendering the nuns' appearances from beneath the stage novel and mysterious.[108] The heady mixture of scenic realism, Gothic mystery, and erotic female display was widely remarked upon by critics and evoked in numerous illustrations. Degas's famous painting, produced more than forty years after the opera's premiere, demonstrates the enduring appeal of the scene.

Berlioz was among the many who published a response to *Robert le diable*.[109] However, in his first column devoted to Meyerbeer's music, Berlioz offers not one word on the famous set, the costumes, or the choreography that had transfixed the gaze of critics and audiences generally. His response is titled 'On the *instrumentation* of *Robert le diable*'. In this most visually alluring of ghost scenes, it is what happens in the orchestra, rather than what is happening on the stage, that is Berlioz's primary concern. His response provides a form of template for understanding his own ghostly nun, and is worth considering in detail:

Everything is icy, dusty and leaden, as the marble tombs slowly open. The violins, violas, flutes, oboes and clarinets are silent. The horns, piston trumpets, ophicleide, timpani and tamtams alone groan out pianissimo chords, preceded by two strong pizzicato beats from the cellos and basses. After each of these horrible phrases, two solitary bassoons cluck out a more animated rhythm which already begins to anticipate the movement of the dances to which the half-resuscitated nuns will soon devote themselves. But it is so pale, so gloomy, so numb; the hand of death still weighs so heavily on these miserable creatures – it's as if you can hear the dull sound, the creaking of the galvanised cadavers, and see the hideous movements which are about to take place. Horrible! Horrible! Frightfully grotesque! These few pages are, in my opinion, the most prodigious inspiration of modern dramatic music. And yet, if you retain the rhythm, the nuances and the harmony, if you don't change a single note but you replace the brass instruments with woodwind and strings, or if you play the score at the piano, you will see how this sublime inspiration is ruined, no trace of it remains.[110]

Many reviewers commented on Meyerbeer's orchestration. But Berlioz takes this to new lengths. Certainly he refers to the scenario on the stage – to the ghosts of the nuns – but it is in the orchestral sound that Berlioz locates these movements: he suggests that we *hear* the creaking limbs in the bassoons. Moreover, in Berlioz's description the bassoons *anticipate* the movement of

---

[108] Marie-Antoinette Allevy, *La mise en scène en France dans la première moitié du dix-neuvième siècle* (Paris: Librairie E. Droz, 1938; repr. Geneva: Slatkine Reprints, 1976), p. 103.
[109] Berlioz, 'De l'instrumentation de *Robert le diable*' (*Gazette musicale de Paris* 12 July 1835), *CM* II, p. 214.
[110] Ibid., p. 214.

the nuns, almost as if the orchestra brings the nuns to life. He suggests the nuns' corpses are 'galvanized'.

The galvanism metaphor is a significant one. Indeed Berlioz had trialled it an earlier article on *Robert le diable* where, after commenting on the 'mortuary harmony' of the scene, he writes, 'in my opinion, nothing equals the horror caused by this grotesque bassoon solo appearing in the middle of the silent orchestra like a galvanised cadaver. It makes you tremble.'[111] This earlier reference reveals the origins of the galvanism concept in the scientific practice developed by Galvani whereby dead bodies or limbs were temporarily reanimated by electrical currents. In Berlioz's account, these nuns are thus very physical beings. They are corrupted bodies reanimated rather than intangible spirits. The galvanising electrical charge comes from the orchestra and, particularly, from the orchestral brass. Berlioz suggests that if we substitute wind or strings the effect will be lost. Berlioz had dissected corpses as part of his medical studies. He was 'strongly attracted by' Jean-Zuléma Amussat, an 'artist in anatomy' and a 'bold scientific explorer' with whom he kept in contact years after abandoning his medical classes, describing him as 'one of my dearest friends'.[112] Moreover, as a student Berlioz also attended physics lessons and classes in experimental electricity with Joseph Louis Gay-Lussac (a close friend of Humboldt).[113] It is thus very possible he had witnessed galvanism at first hand by the time he wrote his response to Meyerbeer's work.[114] In any case, he was doubtless aware when selecting his orchestral metaphor that the electrical current is most effectively relayed by metal (such as brass), not by wood or by strings of gut.

Berlioz's response to Meyerbeer's treatment of the supernatural provides a provocative framework for approaching his own staging of the supernatural in *La nonne sanglante*, encouraging us to direct our gaze into the pit. Moreover, his other accounts of the operatic supernatural reinforce the fact that, for him, it was in the orchestra, not in the visual presentation on the stage, that the true 'other-worldly' forces were located. For example, writing to his sister Nanci of one of his earliest operatic experiences in Paris, Berlioz describes the scene in Gluck's *Iphigénie en Tauride* in which Orestes dreams of having killed his mother:

---

[111] *CM* I p. 382.
[112] Berlioz, *Memoirs*, p. 20; Cairns, *Servitude and Greatness*, p. 604. In the same letter, cited by Cairns, Berlioz mentions another medical specialist, Dr Vidal, employed by the Opéra, whose passing he deeply regretted.
[113] Berlioz, *Memoirs*, pp. 20, 22.
[114] Harriet Smithson would later be galvanised as treatment for her physical ailments, and Berlioz himself, in 1859, was subjected to a course of electric therapy. *CG* IV, p. 216; *CG* VI, pp. 39–40, 43, 49–50, and 55.

you see the shadowy form of the mother whose throat he slit prowling around him with various ghosts who hold in their hands the torches of hell which they brandish around him. And the orchestra! All of that is in the orchestra. If you could hear how all the situations are painted by it, especially when Orestes appears calm.[115]

In this respect Berlioz provides an important supplement to contemporary approaches to the operatic supernatural, for while these offer insight into the role of the orchestra in both the physical and metaphysical realms of operatic works, they do not fully address the most distinctive aspects of Berlioz's approach.

Critical paradigms for numinous intruders in opera

Particularly influential in considerations of supernatural visitations in nineteenth-century opera has been Carolyn Abbate's paradigm of the so-called numinous intruder, in which she reveals how otherworldly characters (including Bertram in *Robert le diable*) create moments of narrative rupture in the orchestral fabric.[116] Such characters are described in a strophic stage song sung by another character, but these moments of self-contained narration in song collide with the narration of the opera as a whole. The ballads describe a supernatural character of the past who will soon appear on stage in person to disrupt the characters' own lives. The simplicity of the strophic repetition of the ballad form draws our attention to the narrating voice and makes us conscious of that text as narration. However, these moments in which operatic characters hear their own music *as* music threaten the distinction between the world the characters can perceive with their senses and the metaphysical world beyond. The repetition of strophic form seems to work against the forward momentum of the narrative heard in the text. But at the same time, that repetition echoes the ways in which the narration of past events is about to be reenacted in the drama onstage – the demon or ghost evoked in the historical ballad is, in each case, soon to become a disruptive force and an active generator of the plot of the opera itself. Extending Abbate's argument, Gary Tomlinson situates the 'numinous intruder' more directly within Kant's metaphysics, as showing an operatic striving for the intangible, 'noumenal' world beyond our understanding.[117]

---

[115] *CG* I, p. 37.
[116] Carolyn Abbate, *Unsung Voices: Opera and Musical Narrative in the Nineteenth Century* (Princeton, NJ: Princeton University Press, 1991), pp. 69–87.
[117] Gary Tomlinson, *Metaphysical Song : An Essay on Opera* (Princeton, NJ: Princeton University Press, 1999), 88–106.

In contrast with Abbate and Tomlinson, Melina Esse draws on Mary Ann Smart's study of musical gesture and calls for attention to the *physical* or 'embodied' aspects so characteristic of opera.[118] Esse points out how Tomlinson's approach essentially reinscribes a Germanic narrative of musical metaphysics onto Italian opera, and she examines the motivic gestures of the orchestra in Donizetti's *Maria de Rudenz* to show how certain musical figures evoke very directly the weeping, sighing, and trembling of the physical body of the character on the stage. In Donizetti's operas, Esse contends, 'bodily transcendence is achieved through gory corporeality and the metaphysical is approached via the blatantly physical'.[119]

Donizetti's text treats the same theme of the bleeding nun that Berlioz subsequently took up, but the immediate source of Donizetti's libretto was a boulevard play that differed radically both from Lewis's novel and from Scribe's libretto for Berlioz (and, later, Gounod).[120] In Donizetti's version, the ghost is not real – the heroine Maria, though stabbed by her lover, does not die from her wounds and is only pretending to be a ghost when she returns to seek revenge. As Esse points out, the bodily nature of the orchestral gestures of sighing, weeping, and trembling in Donizetti's music for Maria is thus particularly significant, for this supposed ghost possesses a living, suffering body, unlike the 'real' ghost of Scribe's libretto.

Abbate, Tomlinson, and Esse represent a familiar critical juxtaposition between metaphysics and embodiment, characteristic of opera and perhaps inherent in its appeal. The same juxtaposition is similarly characteristic of the supernatural more broadly, as we have already seen in relation to *Épisode de la vie d'un artiste*, where the artist's visions hover precariously in the liminal world between embodied sight and psychological construction. Indeed, Todorov suggests that this tension is crucial to the very nature of the fantasy genre: the fantastic requires the reader to 'hesitate between a natural and a supernatural explanation of the events described'.[121]

However, returning to Berlioz's response to Meyerbeer's nuns, we realise that the critical frameworks developed around the operatic supernatural do not in fact fully account for his approach. Abbate, Esse, and Tomlinson all

---

[118] Mary Ann Smart, *Mimomania: Music and Gesture in Nineteenth-Century Opera* (Berkeley: University of California Press, 2004); Melina Esse, 'Donizetti's Gothic Resurrections', *19th-Century Music* 33/2 (2009), 81–109.

[119] Esse, 'Donizetti's Gothic Resurrections', 84.

[120] Patrick Berthier, 'Un (mélo)drame exemplaire: *La nonne sanglante* (1835)', in Simone Bernard-Griffiths and Jean Sgard (eds.), *Mélodrames et romans noirs. 1750–1890* (Toulouse: Presses universitaires du Mirail, 2000), p. 371.

[121] Tzvetan Todorov, *The Fantastic: A Structural Approach to a Literary Genre*, trans. Richard Howard (Cleveland/London: The Press of Case Western Reserve University, 1973), p. 33.

put emphasis on the orchestra, whether they are primarily interested in the leitmotifs of German metaphysics or the gestures of Italian embodiment, but what they emphasise is the rhythm, nuances, harmony, or pitch – precisely the elements Berlioz says are irrelevant to the effect of Meyerbeer's orchestra.

A more closely corresponding paradigm might be found in Elizabeth Hudson's demonstration of how, in the duet of Verdi's *Macbeth*, the characters' relationship to the supernatural realm, their traversing of the boundary between phenomenal and noumenal, is enacted through their relationship to orchestral sound.[122] Sympathetic critical frameworks for Berlioz's supernatural orchestration can also be seen in writings that deal with unorthodox instruments or automata in the periods before and after Berlioz, which demonstrate how, in Dolan's words, '[t]hese instruments were not simply devices designed to harness the most perfect tone, but rather attempts to create portals through which humans could experience nature's sublime and ethereal voice.'[123] Yet none of these approaches fully articulates the distinctive aspects of Berlioz's perspective on Meyerbeer, which illustrates the crucial tenet of his *Orchestration Treatise*: orchestration may exist *sui generis*. Berlioz's interest in the orchestra as an end in itself represents a vitally different conception of dramatic meaning to those elucidated by opera scholars, who more typically discuss the orchestra in relation to its articulation of the libretto through the statement of motifs or the imitation of timbres associated with the supernatural. In understanding the implications of Berlioz's approach in relation to his own musical depictions of ghosts, we need to look for the ghost not in the form, harmony, or motif of the orchestra, but in instruments and instrumentation, situated in relation to nineteenth-century intersections between science, technology, and the supernatural. Even more than this, we need not only to consider instruments as 'portals' to other realms but also to consider instruments as objects within the physical entity of the orchestra, sounded by players' bodies and shaped by their subjectivity.

The body of the 'Légende'

Berlioz did not leave any music for the ghost of the bleeding nun herself to sing, but he did write and preserve a 'Légende' – a ballad enclosed within the lovers' duet, in which Agnès recounts the tale of the bleeding nun to her sceptical lover Rodolphe. The 'Légende' in many respects conforms to Abbate's discussion of the 'numinous intruder'. Agnès's story of the nun

---

[122] Elizabeth Hudson, '... qualche cosa d'incredibile...': Hearing the Invisible in "Macbeth", *Cambridge Opera Journal* 14 (2001): 11–29.

[123] Emily I. Dolan, 'E. T. A. Hoffmann and the Ethereal Technologies of "Nature Music"', *Eighteenth-Century Music* 5/1 (2008), 23; Carolyn Abbate, 'Outside Ravel's Tomb', 465–530.

is relayed in the strophic form characteristic of a narrative ballad, and it describes in a self-contained narration the ghostly figure who will soon take an active role in Agnès's and Rodolphe's own lives. Moreover, the 'Légende' literally intrudes upon the music of Agnès and Rodolphe, interrupting what was developing as a powerfully effective conventional duet: Rodolphe sings a verse ('Je meurs si vous m'êtes ravie'), Agnès sings a verse to the same music ('Je meurs si je vous suis ravie'), but before they can sing together, Agnès performs the 'Légende', introducing a dramatic change in the musical fabric.

Text and translation of the duet from *La nonne sanglante*

DUO

RODOLPHE
Je meurs si vous m'êtes ravie.
Agnès, décidez de mon sort!
D'un mot vous ranimez ma vie,
D'un mot vous me donnez la mort.

AGNÈS
Je meurs si je vous suis ravie.
Rodolphe, hélas! J'accepte mon sort.
Je dois accepter mon triste sort.
Pour moi notre hymen c'est la vie;
D'autres nœuds pour moi sont la mort.

RODOLPHE
Agnès, osez-vous y soustraire?

AGNÈS
Comment?

RODOLPHE
Tous deux fuyons ce soir!

AGNÈS
Braver l'autorité d'un père!

RODOLPHE
Tout est permis au désespoir...

Sous le rempart du nord, quand
  la nuit sera sombre,
Je vous attendrai !

AGNÈS
Non!

RODOLPHE
Agnès! à minuit!

AGNÈS
Ciel! à minuit!

DUO

RODOLPHE
I'll die if you are taken from me.
Agnès, decide my fate!
One word from you will give me new life,
One word from you will bring me death.

AGNÈS
I'll die if I am taken from you.
Rodolphe, alas! I accept my fate.
I must accept my sad fate.
For me our marriage means life;
All other nuptials are death for me.

RODOLPHE
Agnès, do you dare escape?

AGNÈS
How?

RODOLPHE
We will flee together tonight!

AGNÈS
To defy the authority of a father!

RODOLPHE
Everything is permitted to those who
  despair...
Beneath the northern battlements, when
  the night becomes dark,
I will wait for you!

AGNÈS
No!

RODOLPHE
Agnès! At midnight!

AGNÈS
Heavens! At midnight!

(cont.)

(cont.)

RODOLPHE Quoi ! vous frissonnez? . . .	**RODOLPHE** What? You tremble? . . .
AGNÈS Cette nuit Est celle où tous les ans son ombre Parcourt ces murs épouvantés.	**AGNES** This night Is the one on which every year her shade Walks the length of these terrified walls.
RODOLPHE Quelle ombre?	**RODOLPHE** What shade?
AGNÈS Écoutez ! écoutez! LÉGENDE Avant minuit les portes sont ouvertes Pour le fantôme en habits blancs ; La Nonne sanglante, à pas lents, Traîne ses pieds sur les dalles désertes. Dans l'ombre on la voit s'avancer ; La foudre gronde, l'air se glace ! Respectez la Nonne qui passe ! Vivants, laissez la mort passer !	**AGNES** Listen! Listen! LEGEND Before midnight the doors are opened For the phantom in a white habit; The bleeding nun, with slow steps Drags her feet across the deserted flagstones. In the shade one sees her approach; Lightning rumbles, the air turns icy! Respect the nun who passes! You who live, let death pass!
RODOLPHE Et vous croyez à cette fable ?	**RODOLPHE** And you believe this tale?
AGNÈS Rodolphe, en vain vous en doutez, On l'a vu, ce spectre effroyable !	**AGNES** Rodolphe, it is pointless to doubt it, People have seen it, this horrifying spectre!
RODOLPHE Erreur !	**RODOLPHE** Nonsense!
AGNÈS Écoutez ! Écoutez ! Sur ses habits, le sang tombe et ruisselle ; Son œil est fixe et sans regard : Sa main droite tient un poignard, Et dans la gauche une lampe étincelle. Livide on la voit s'avancer ; La foudre gronde, l'air se glace : Respectez la Nonne qui passe! Vivants, laissez la mort passer!	**AGNES** Listen! Listen! On her habit, the blood falls and gushes; Her gaze is fixed and without focus; Her right hand holds a dagger, And in her left a lamp twinkles. Deathly pale, you see her approaching; Lightning rumbles, the air turns icy: Respect the nun who passes! You who live, let death pass!
RODOLPHE Et vous croyez à cette fable?	**RODOLPHE** And you believe this story?
AGNÈS Rodolphe, nous y croyons tous; On l'a vu, ce spectre effroyable, on l'a vu! Que me répondrez-vous ?	**AGNES** Rodolophe, we all believe it. It's been seen, this frightful ghost, it's been seen! How can you answer me?

(cont.)

RODOLPHE	**RODOLPHE**
Je meurs si vous m'êtes ravie.	I'll die if you are taken from me.
Agnès décidez de mon sort!	Agnès, decide my fate!
Je meurs si vous m'êtes ravie.	I'll die if you are taken from me.
Agnès, décidez de mon sort !	Agnès, decide my fate!
AGNÈS	**AGNES**
Je meurs si je vous suis ravie.	I'll die, if I am taken from you.
Rodolphe, hélas! j'accepte mon sort.	Rodolphe, alas! I accept my fate.
Je dois accepter mon triste sort.	I must accept my sad fate.
RODOLPHE	**RODOLPHE**
D'un mot vous ranimez ma vie,	One word from you will give me new life,
D'un mot vous me donnez la mort.	One word from you will bring my death.
Si vous m'êtes ravie, je meurs!	If you are taken from me I shall die!
Agnès, décidez, décidez de mon sort!	Agnes, decide my fate!
AGNÈS	**AGNES**
Pour moi notre hymen c'est la vie,	For me our marriage is my life,
D'autres nœuds pour moi sont la mort.	Other nuptials will bring my death.
Si je vous suis ravie, je meurs.	If I am taken from you I shall die.
Et j'accepte mon sort.	I accept my fate.
RODOLPHE	**RODOLPHE**
La fable qui vous épouvante	The fable that terrifies you
Nous sauve, si vous consentez.	Will save us, if you consent.
AGNÈS	**AGNES**
Je devrais mon bonheur à la Nonne sanglante?	I would owe my happiness to the bleeding nun?
Non, non!	No, no!
RODOLPHE	**RODOLPHE**
Écoutez! Écoutez!	Listen! Listen!
RODOLPHE	**RODOLPHE**
Lorsqu'à minuit les portes sont ouvertes,	When at midnight the doors are opened
En habits blancs, l'œil sans regard,	In a white habit, with vacant gaze,
Tenant la lampe et le poignard,	Holding the lamp and the dagger,
Traînez vos pieds sur les dalles désertes!	Drag your feet across the deserted flagstones.
Quand ils la verront s'avancer,	When they see her approaching,
Fais, grand Dieu ! que l'effroi les glace;	Act, dear Lord, so that fear will chill them;
Grand Dieu ! c'est mon Agnès qui passe!	Dear Lord! It's my Agnes who passes!
Sous tes ailes fais-la passer!	Let her pass beneath your wings!
AGNÈS	**AGNES**
Braver le spectre au sortir de sa tombe!	To dare to meet the ghost as she emerges from her tomb!

(*cont.*)

(cont.)

Rodolphe	Rodolphe
Mais ce spectre n'existe pas!	But this ghost does not exist!
Agnès	Agnes
Je crois me sentir dans ses bras!	I feel as if I'm in her arms!
En y pensant, en y pensant de terreur je succombe...	Just thinking about it, I give in to terror!

Agnès prefaces both verses with the instruction 'écoutez' or 'listen'. This device, characteristic of the narrative ballad, enables the narrator to signal the moment at which the characters become aware of the audible nature of their own song. Also similarly to Abbate's examples, the strophic repetition of the 'Légende' allows listeners to focus on the narration itself, as Agnès effectively conjures the ghost into existence. However, in contrast to many such ballads, not much is revealed about the ghost's history (which is only disclosed later in the opera). Instead, Agnès describes the ghost's manifestations, using a present tense which seems to bring the ghost immediately before our eyes. Whereas, in Lewis's novel, Agnes has been sketching the ghost and explains her illustration to her lover, in Berlioz's setting of Scribe's libretto, it is for the orchestra to conjure the image.

Berlioz marks the tempo 'Moderato misterioso', and with its slow harmonic rhythm and the repeated diminuendi in the strings, which give the impression of long exhalations of breath, the music takes on a trancelike quality. Agnès functions almost like a spiritual medium here, channelling the ghost through her song. The Spiritualist movement of séances and mediums was only just beginning to take shape at the time Berlioz was working on *La nonne sanglante*. But Spiritualism was anticipated by a variety of other attempts to communicate via supernatural channels. The idea of a woman acting as a conduit for ghostly spirits from beyond was most strongly foreshadowed in the popular practice of mesmerism (or 'animal magnetism'), whereby subjects were sometimes put into a trancelike state through a form of hypnosis or through contact with hands or objects considered to be charged with special energy. Arising in the late eighteenth century, the practice was widespread by the time of *La nonne sanglante*, especially in France,[124] and the focus had moved from an original emphasis on physical cures to the idea of mesmerism as addressing the psyche and

---

[124] 'There is not a city in France that does not produce a good roster of magnetizers', Charles La Fontaine wrote in 1847: Heather Hadlock, *Mad Loves: Women and Music in Offenbach's Les contes d'Hoffmann* (Princeton, NJ: Princeton University Press, 2000), p. 52.

giving the subject an insight that bordered on the supernatural.[125] Some mesmerised subjects were believed to be able to communicate with Other worlds when in a trance state.[126]

The language of mesmerism evokes in literal ways the idea of a language that is beyond words, giving it sympathy with contemporaneous ideas of music. While this conception of communication through trance could be used to account for the composer's moments of inspiration, it is the performer – and particularly the singer – who provides the most potent analogy for this channelling of voice,[127] while the mesmeriser might be envisaged as the composer or conductor.[128] Operas that directly invoke mesmerism, somnambulism, or communication with the spirit realm lend weight to the metaphor. As Heather Hadlock has revealed, Offenbach's *Contes d'Hoffmann* invokes the practices of mesmerism through the characters of Giulietta (seduced by Dapertutto's diamond) and, particularly, Antonia, whose voice is both controlled from outside by Dr Miracle's violin, and conjured from within, and which channels her dead mother.[129] Hadlock points to the similarly mesmerised quality of Donizetti's Lucia and Wagner's Senta and Elsa.[130] And Sarah Hibberd studies the sensation of somnambulism in Paris in the late 1820s, as evoked in numerous musical works, revealing how mesmerism (or magnetism) came to represent Romantic conceptions of musical performance.[131]

Berlioz mentions magnetism several times in his writings. Sometimes he refers to the actual practice itself, as when recounting how, upon returning to Paris at the end of 1832, he discovered he was staying in an apartment vacated by Harriet Smithson just the night before: 'a believer in magnetic influences, secret affinities, and mysterious promptings would certainly find in all this a powerful argument in favour of his system.'[132] More interestingly, however, Berlioz also uses magnetism metaphorically, to

---

[125] Sarah Hibberd, '"Dormez donc, mes chers amours": Hérold's *La Somnambule* (1827) and dream phenomena on the Parisian lyric stage', *Cambridge Opera Journal*, 16/2 (2004), 116.

[126] Alison Winter, *Mesmerized: Powers of Mind in Victorian Britain* (Chicago: University of Chicago Press, 1998), p. 3.

[127] Tomlinson directly applies the metaphor of mediumship to singers generally. *Metaphysical Song*, p. 112.

[128] On the conductor as mesmeriser see Winter, *Mesmerized*, pp. 309–20, though her description of a caricature of Berlioz and Wagner as supposedly mesmerising each other with conductors' batons (Figure 75, p. 314) is a misinterpretation based on a poor-quality reproduction.

[129] Hadlock, *Mad Loves*, pp. 52–66.

[130] Ibid., pp. 60–61; Hadlock, 'Sonorous Bodies: Women and the Glass Harmonica', *Journal of the American Musicological Society* 53/5 (2000), 507–42.

[131] Hibberd, 'Dormez donc', 118–19.   [132] Berlioz, *Memoirs*, p. 189.

suggest the mysterious impact of a particular performer, such as the English harpist Elias Parish-Alvars, whom the composer encountered on his first German tour:

> [In Frankfurt] I again encounter Parish-Alvars, who magnetises me by playing his fantasy in harmonics on the chorus of the *Naïades* from *Oberon*. Undoubtedly this man is a sorcerer: his harp is a siren with a beautiful sloping neck, with long dishevelled hair, who breathes the fascinating sounds of an other world in the passionate embrace of his powerful arms.[133]

Parish-Alvars becomes the mesmeriser. Significantly, it is his harp (an instrument whose shape Berlioz elsewhere admired as feminine, as we have seen) which is personified as the typically female subject, bordering on transgression and madness and channeling the supernatural for the enraptured audience.[134]

Berlioz's Agnès is not explicitly a subject of mesmerism within the libretto, but she does evoke the conventions and the broader discourse identified by Hibberd. In Matthew Lewis's *The Monk*, Agnès is herself actually sceptical, responding to her lover's question about her own belief in the story: 'How can you ask such a question? No, no [. . .]! I have too much reason to lament superstition's influence to be its victim myself.'[135] In Berlioz's treatment the role of sceptic is transferred to Rodolphe, and Agnès is one of the believers, seeming to be haunted by the nun's voice in the same way Offenbach's Antonia responds to her dead mother, and terrified of encountering the ghost herself. That Agnès's ballad effectively generates the ghost through her song might be demonstrated by the fact that Rodolphe is subsequently able to see the ghost – indeed, he mistakes it for Agnès and elopes with it. The tension between reality and illusion necessary to sustain the fantasy genre is permitted by the possibility of a psychological interpretation of the narrative: mesmerised women were themselves often considered sexually transgressive, if unwittingly, and the bleeding nun can thus appear to be an extension of Agnès's own psyche.

Even if we accept the ghost as real, science is invoked. Both the Spiritualist movement of mediums and the practice of mesmerism were debated and articulated in scientific terms. In mesmerism it was the so-called animal magnetism stimulated by the mesmeriser that was subject to scientific enquiry. Several official commissions were charged with investigating the validity of the practice, with varying outcomes. While few disputed that

---

[133] Berlioz, *Mémoires*, p. 324.
[134] On the gendered associations of mesmerism and its association with transgression, see Winter, pp. 101, 204–5.
[135] Matthew Lewis, *The Monk: A Romance* (1796) (New York: Modern Library, 2002), p. 116.

mesmerism and magnetism had an effect on their subjects, opinions varied as to whether these effects were a result of physical causes situated in the body (such as the existence of 'magnetic fluid') or were primarily psychological.

Moreover, the mode in which ghosts supposedly manifested themselves in séances was closely intertwined with the technology of the time. Louis-Alphonse Cahagnet's account of his experiments in magnetism, which purported to put subjects in touch with the afterlife, was titled *Magnétisme: Arcanes de la vie future dévoilés* [Magnetism: Mysteries of the future life revealed] in its original French (1848–54), but was translated into English as *The Celestial Telegraph*. As with the phantasmagoria, the telegraph concept was becoming a metaphor, but just like the phantasmagoria, the technology of the telegraph was seen as literally giving access to the supernatural. The telegraph revolutionised the concept of communication, transforming the way space and time were conceived, and seeming to erase individual human bodies in favour of a large, collective electric current or nervous system.[136] This idea of disembodied communication easily supported the new Spiritualist practices. As the telegraph and Morse code took hold of the popular imagination, ghosts in séances began to signal to the living through rapping on tables, and sometimes this rapping employed Morse code. Indeed, some Spiritualists proposed that spirits had instructed the earthly pioneers of this technology to facilitate communication between worlds. Spiritual telegraphy was occasionally taken to extreme degrees of literalism: telegraphers in the afterlife were thought to 'materialise' a battery in the spirit world in order to operate their telegraphic system, and to recruit the spirits of dead telegraphers to operate it.[137] Another technological–supernatural crossover was manifested in the development of the phonautograph, which from the 1850s transformed aural phenomena into graphic form, thus providing an analogy for the practice of those mediums who would transcribe mysterious signals by hand, or who could channel the spirits of dead authors and composers and transcribe works supposedly by them.

Berlioz satirised this facet of the Spiritualist movement in his feuilleton 'Beethoven in the Rings of Saturn'. A medium summons Beethoven from his spiritual home, Saturn's rings, so that he might dictate a new sonata by causing the table to rise and fall a certain number of times for each note, in a form of telegraphic code. Berlioz invokes the terms of Spiritualism, of

---

[136] Marshall McLuhan, *Understanding Media: The Extensions of Man*, ed. W. Terrence Gordon (Corte Madera, CA: Gingko Press, 1964, new edition 2003), pp. 332–3.

[137] Steven Connor, 'The Machine in the Ghost: Spiritualism, Technology, and the Direct Voice', in Peter Buse and Andrew Stott (eds.), *Ghosts: Deconstruction, Psychoanalysis, History* (London: Macmillan Press Ltd., 1999), p. 212.

the concept of a state exactly between the physical and spiritual, with heavy irony:

Beethoven arrives and causes the feet of the table to say: 'Here I am!' The medium, delighted, nudges him in the ribs.

'Come now,' you will say, 'you are talking nonsense!'

'Not at all.'

'Yes, yes, and a moment ago you mentioned the brain in talking about a spirit. Spirits don't have bodies.'

'Perhaps not, but as you know very well, they have what might be called semibodies. It's all been thoroughly explained. Don't interrupt with pointless remarks; let me get on with my sad story.'

The medium, who is himself half spirit, half slaps Beethoven on the back and without further ado asks the demigod to dictate a new sonata.[138]

The resulting sonata is transcribed by the medium and then performed at the piano, to the dismay of the audience, who recognise it as 'not a half platitude, but a total platitude, an absurdity, sheer nonsense'.[139] For Berlioz, the story serves as confirmation of his long-held belief that there is no such thing as absolute beauty – there is no universal standard of musical beauty that can transcend culture and the spiritual realm.

Later, when the telephone was developed, many spirits abandoned rappings to communicate through disembodied voices which evoked the radical innovation of that new technology. However, at the same time, the Spiritualist movement also demonstrated how new technology was itself being received as ghostly. As the telegraph and telephone transformed common perceptions of space and sound, it sometimes felt as if there were, indeed, ghosts in the machine.[140]

Berlioz died before the creation of the telephone, but he was fascinated by electricity and the telegraph. He actually employed telegraphic technology in coordinating large orchestral forces, in the form of the electric metronome, as we will see in the following two chapters. However, in Berlioz's music, it is the orchestra itself that most compellingly represents the supernatural technology of the machine. Orchestral instruments become 'charged' objects, as if mesmerising Agnès as she sings. In his orchestration treatise, Berlioz describes how the individual players are like keys on a giant keyboard controlled by the conductor. Indeed, elsewhere in the treatise he suggests

---

[138] Berlioz, *The Art of Music*, p. 55.   [139] Ibid., p. 55.
[140] Connor, 'The Machine in the Ghost', pp. 211–12.

that the conductor animates the orchestra with an electrical charge. He writes, '[The conductor's] inner flame will warm [the players], his electricity will charge them, his drive will propel them. He will radiate the *vital spark* of music.'[141] Berlioz's language here suggests both the telegraph and the metaphor of galvanism: the conductor sends his electrical charge through the orchestra in order to bring life to a musical work. As we move to the second verse of Berlioz's 'Légende' from *La nonne sanglante*, it becomes clear that it is indeed in the orchestra that the ghostly forces are found, not only in the motivic writing of physical gesture or psychological motif, but also in the 'grain' of their timbres, and their own status between material presence and disembodied sound or spirit. In this respect Berlioz offers a powerful alternative to the usual focus in studies of the supernatural operatic vision on vocality and metaphysical sound.

Thematically and harmonically, the second verse of the 'Légende' is very similar to the first, except that Berlioz now introduces a dramatic bar of silence after the climax (compare Ex. 3.10a and Ex. 3.10b). It is as if he is forcing the listeners both on and off stage to hear the ghost in their minds; but perhaps we now also begin to listen more closely to the orchestra.

Berlioz was working on his *Orchestration Treatise* at precisely the same time that he developed his ghostly fable, and in that work he presents numerous examples of how the colours of particular instruments can be explored for supernatural effects, from the 'supernatural menace' of a double-bass pizzicato in the overture to *Der Freischütz* to the 'icily menacing' effects of the clarinet's low register as exploited by Weber. Most striking, perhaps, is Berlioz's description of the eerie disembodiment of the flute whereby Gluck suggests the 'thousand-fold sublime wailing of a suffering, despairing shade of the departed' in *Orphée*:

And Gluck's melody is conceived in such a way that the flute lends itself to all the vicissitudes of this eternal grief, still imprinted with the scars of passion from life on earth. At first it is a scarcely audible voice that seems afraid to be heard; then it begins to wail softly, rising to a reproach, then to profound grief, then to the cry of a heart rent by an incurable wound, and then falls back little by little to the lamentation, the wailing and the bitter sob of a soul resigned... What a poet![142]

Not surprisingly, in the second verse of Berlioz's 'Légende', as the ghost becomes more real to Agnès, it is the supernatural technology of his orchestra that Berlioz uses to conjure her. Here Berlioz follows Meyerbeer's approach in the numinous intruder ballad in *Robert le diable* ('Jadis régnait en Normandie'), each of whose three *couplets* is differently orchestrated to

---

[141] Macdonald, *Berlioz's Orchestration Treatise*, p. 337.   [142] Ibid., pp. 63, 124, 140–41.

Ex. 3.10a *La nonne sanglante* 'Légende', Climax of first verse, bb. 184–90

reflect the increasing awareness of the threat posed by the devilish suitor. In his article on the instrumentation of *Robert le diable*, Berlioz singled out for praise the orchestration of the third verse (where Meyerbeer transforms the original Harmonie-like texture by introducing measured tremolo in the strings and chromatic motion in the wind and brass).[143] In his own second verse, Berlioz similarly alters the orchestration. As the nun becomes more

[143] *CM* II, p. 211.

Ex. 3.10b *La nonne sanglante* 'Légende', Climax and continuation of second verse, bb. 217–25

182 Visions of Other worlds

Ex. 3.10b (cont.)

real to Agnès, the orchestra becomes more prominent. The rumblings of thunder are now evoked by the basses; moaning figures are introduced into the woodwind, and trembling in the strings. (See Ex. 3.10b earlier.) The moaning and trembling gestures function similarly to the physical gestures Esse finds in Donizetti's treatment of the related ghost story, where they suggest the embodied nature of the ghost and the fear it provokes in Agnès.

More unusually, Berlioz also makes extensive use in this second verse of four natural horns that employ crooks in A♭, E♭, G♭, and D♭ (Ex. 3.10b, earlier). The 'Légende' is based in A minor, and the notes Berlioz writes for these natural horns are not found in the ranges of their respective harmonic series. To produce the notes in Berlioz's score, each player must therefore stop the notes by inserting his or her hand into the instrument, thereby simultaneously distorting the timbre. The result is an eerie, literally 'unnatural' sound, as was obviously Berlioz's intention. Berlioz admired the use of low, stopped notes for fateful supernatural manifestations in Weber's *Freischütz* and Meyerbeer's *Robert le diable*. His review of *Robert le diable* draws particular attention to Meyerbeer's use of stopped notes as Robert approaches the ghostly nuns, and points out how these are contrasted with the open notes where Robert meets his honourable beloved; he remarks that 'this strange voice has certainly never before been heard at the Opéra'.[144] But it is an obscure opera by Méhul which Berlioz suggests provides the most vivid example of how stopped notes can be used simultaneously in several parts for 'scenes of silent horror'.[145] He describes Méhul's use of 'orchestral effects entirely new at the time, such as the use of four horns in their hollowest hand-stopped notes to accompany, like a sort of instrumental death-rattle, the voice of a dying man'.[146]

The stopped horn is an uncanny combination of the intangible and the physical – of man or nun poised between life and death – but also of the mechanical. The air of this 'strange voice', as Berlioz called it, passes not through the throat of a singer but through the metal of the instrument, before being confronted with the flesh of the hand inserted into the bell. Thus it must pass through both machine and body in order to sound. To the horn player, the sensation of 'stopping' the note suggests the entrapment of the air (or spirit?) within the instrument itself. The effect is similar to that of the 'Invisible Girl' popular in magic shows of the earlier nineteenth century, in which a copper sphere suspended in the air was supposed by spectators to contain a tiny invisible girl within it – a disembodied female spirit – who

---

[144] Ibid., p. 214.   [145] Macdonald, *Berlioz's Orchestration Treatise*, p. 170.
[146] Berlioz, *Evenings with the Orchestra*, p. 351.

would respond to questions posed by the audience into a speaking trumpet connected to the sphere (but also connected to an adjacent room where the real woman was concealed), and sing in a small, muffled voice.[147]

In the 'Légende' of *La nonne sanglante*, the players of the stopped horns themselves are forced into a sort of liminal world, stranded between the music they see and the music they hear, and Berlioz exaggerates this disorientation. Whereas Méhul writes for four horns in D, G, and F for chords of A♭ major, Berlioz takes the technique much further by forcing the players into obscure keys. Of course, horn players were inevitably accustomed to the disjunction between sound and sight in their transposing instruments. But how much more extreme is that disjunction when the key of their horn is a semitone or tritone removed from the key of the music? Berlioz elsewhere in the *Orchestration Treatise* implies that keys have a psychological impact on the performer – how else to account for the fact that a string player finds D♯ 'almost impracticable' while E♭ is 'easy'?[148]

This sort of 'out of body' experience of the horn players is anticipated in the first verse, shortly before the stopped horns are introduced. At the climax of the verse, Berlioz writes what is clearly *heard* as a chord of F minor, but the flutes, clarinets, and second violins see a G♯ rather than an A♭ in their score (Ex. 3.10a, earlier). Thus while their eyes tell them they have the leading note of A minor, the overall tonic, their ears hear the third of F minor. The players become physically stranded between the two primary tonal regions of the movement, caught between worlds like the ghost they are evoking. In his *Orchestration Treatise*, Berlioz comments on similar examples of enharmonic substitution for supernatural scenes in Gluck's *Orfeo* and in Weber's *Freischütz*. He suggests these enharmonic substitutions evoke 'majestic [and] deeply musical terror', and also states that they render the orchestra a 'large equal-tempered instrument [...] without the musician having any inkling at all'.[149] Berlioz thus turns his orchestral players into components of a machine – a machine that overrides their own sensory perceptions. However, unlike the music produced by the hidden 'mechanical' musicians at Bayreuth, in the case of Berlioz's music this mechanisation can be understood not as a byproduct of the work concept in question, but as contributing directly to the very horror that the scene evokes.

Turning now to another new element of the orchestration of the second verse of the 'Légende', we note that, beneath the sighing woodwind and uncanny horns, and immediately following the bar of suspenseful silence,

---

[147] Brewster, *Nouveau manuel*, pp. 124–6.
[148] Macdonald, *Berlioz's Orchestration Treatise*, p. 32.   [149] Ibid., p. 308.

Berlioz adds a solemn regular beat in the basses and drums. This could represent a slow heartbeat, or perhaps the heavy tread of a foot. The ambiguity is important to the fantasy genre: does a ghost's heart beat? Do the dragging footsteps of a ghostly nun make a sound? Is this ghost a sensual body, or is it a spirit, an idea? Is it seen with the eyes, or hallucinated with the inner eye? Some answers are provided by Gounod's treatment of Scribe's completed libretto. In Gounod's *Nonne sanglante*, the nun herself later appears and sings a duet with Rodolphe. Berlioz complained in his review of Gounod's setting that Rodolphe's duet with the nun (which he had not set himself) would have been more effective as a *solo* for Rodolphe. The problem, as Berlioz saw it, was that Gounod's nun sings too much like a living being; if she sang at all, Berlioz suggests, it should have been a 'strange, super-human' music. Indeed, it has been suggested that the corporality of Gounod's ghost – the fact that it sings, but is seen only by Rodolphe – was a factor in the failure of the work to secure a place in the repertoire.[150]

In Agnès's 'Légende', we do not hear the nun sing, but Berlioz finds a way to evoke her liminal status as a ghost, preserving the uncertainty of the fantasy genre, and indeed, heightening it, and he does so in terms suggestive of technology. He specifies that the basses should be divided and placed on opposite sides of the orchestra (Ex. 3.10b, earlier). The beat echoes backwards and forwards across the space of the orchestra itself. This device *embodies* the ghost, suggesting its movement in the physical space of the theatre; but it simultaneously *dis*embodies the ghost by implying it might be in two places at once, and thus not fully in either. Berlioz's divided basses affect the perfect realisation of the tension between physicality and transience typical of ghosts. They also seem to force the audience's vision of the ghost inward, for in order to *hear* the musical line as one, the audience must literally overlook the fact that their eyes are telling them there are two separate entities generating the sound.

Berlioz's splitting of the basses also evokes contemporary technology. As we have seen, he was fascinated by the telegraph, and by the near instantaneous communication across physical space that it permitted. In keeping with how Spiritualists saw the ghostly potential of the telegraph and Morse code for communicating with the dead, Berlioz here evokes the telegraph's ability to communicate between remote worlds, as Agnès's narration summons the ghostly nun from the world beyond. And perhaps, again, the visual and physical elements of the instruments themselves are significant.

---

[150] Ann Williams, 'Ghostly Voices: "Gothic Opera" and the Failure of Gounod's *La Nonne sanglante*', in Roberta Montemorra Marvin and Downing A. Thomas (eds.), *Operatic Migrations: Transforming Works and Crossing Boundaries* (Aldershot: Ashgate, 2006), p. 138.

The hand on the double bass string, sending and receiving sounds across space, recalls telegraphic communication in quite literal ways. For while the electric telegraph suggested on the one hand a communication that was disembodied, it was also dependent on electricity – a medium which is, as Marshall McLuhan writes, primarily 'tactile', being felt before it is seen or heard.[151]

If Agnès is positioned as a spiritual medium, Rodolphe remains a scientific sceptic, for at this point in the drama he has not yet *seen* the ghost. Immediately after her 'Légende' he restores order. He returns to the music that preceded the 'Légende' ('Je meurs si vous m'êtes ravie'), forcing the conclusion of the conventional duet that he had initiated before Agnès's narration. He insists that he will die if Agnès is taken from him, that she must decide his fate, and with one word she will either reanimate his life or give him death. Agnès joins him now, in the anticipated vocal union that her 'Légende' had interrupted. She, too, returns to her earlier words: 'I accept my fate. For me our marriage is my life. Other nuptials will bring my death.' But it is the next section of the duet that demonstrates the tension between rationality and the supernatural most powerfully. After the conclusion of the framing music, Rodolphe takes up the theme of Agnès's 'Légende', and effectively exorcises the ghost she had raised. (Refer to the text and translation of the duet from *La nonne sanglante*, earlier.) By comparing the text of this new verse ('Lorsqu'à minuit les portes sont ouvertes...') to the earlier verses of the 'Légende' ('Avant minuit les portes sont ouvertes...'), we see how Rodolphe twists Agnès's earlier words as he describes how they might turn her fable to their own advantage: Agnès herself will take the nun's place, he suggests. Rodolphe also twists Agnès's music: the tempo is now rapid, the key is a tone higher as he transforms the music of trance into music of physical action and excitement. More subtle, but equally significant, the stopped horns and telegraphic basses are absent. Their place is taken by *natural* horns and galloping strings and wind that suggest the urgency of Rodolphe's planned elopement (Ex. 3.11).

The most conspicuous supernatural element here comes not in the orchestra, but in Rodolphe's own violation of the strophic ballad form. After reaching the climax of the original ballad, Rodolphe breaks from the familiar melody to head into the stratosphere of his range, launching suddenly up to a high b'' at the words 'Dear Lord! It is my Agnès who passes', followed soon after by a high $d\#''$ (the highest pitch Berlioz wrote for tenor, and lying above the limits he himself gives for leading tenors of his

---

[151] Marshall McLuhan, *Understanding Media: The Extensions of Man (Critical Edition)* (Corte Madera, CA: Gingko Press, 1964, new edn. 2003), p. 334.

Ex. 3.11 *La nonne sanglante* Duet, bb. 319–37

generation, Nourrit, Duprez, and Hatzinger). It is, indeed, almost as if Rodolphe is channelling Agnès's own soprano voice (Ex. 3.12).

Agnès then begins what sounds like a strophic repetition of this new version of her 'Légende'. As she fearfully asks whether she 'Dare[s] to confront the spectre as it descends from her tomb!' the strings move to a Don-Giovanniesque swirl (perhaps an ironic reference to the fateful scepticism her lover shares with the earlier operatic hero). But Rodolphe cuts her off, insisting yet again that the nun does not exist. Had Berlioz completed the opera, we would have seen Rodolphe forcibly confront his error when he meets the nun in person and mistakes her for Agnès. As it stands, we can only imagine what music Berlioz might have given his nun in order to preserve the hesitation between scientific and supernatural explanation that is so effectively created in the duet.

Ex. 3.11 (*cont.*)

The haunting of Berlioz

Because Berlioz never completed *La nonne sanglante*, the music has little presence today, and has only been performed as a concert work. Thus, like *Symphonie fantastique*, *La nonne sanglante* relies on our imaginations to visualise the ghost conjured by its narrator and realised by Berlioz's

Ex. 3.12 *La nonne sanglante* Duet, bb. 350–70

orchestral technology. Some imagination is also required to render the musical fragments suitable for performance at all. Berlioz's manuscript for the duet between Agnès and Rodolphe breaks off abruptly, denying us the concluding cabaletta which the larger duet structure implies is imminent. Gounod's setting of *La nonne sanglante* reveals that Scribe did indeed provide further text for the scene. For a rare performance of Berlioz's opera in 2007, Hugh Macdonald supplied a conclusion by adapting music from Berlioz's much later opera, *Les Troyens,* to the text of the libretto as set by Gounod. Macdonald provides compelling evidence that he was in fact simply reinstating material Berlioz himself originally conceived for *La nonne sanglante*. The significance of the borrowing for *Les Troyens* will be examined in relation to that work in Chapter 5. For now, let us note that Berlioz's own process enhances the ghostly qualities of his fragmentary opera on a metatextual level: the opera lived the shadowy life of a revenant, haunting his later work.[152]

Berlioz's *Nonne sanglante* attracts little scholarly attention today. Given that the composer himself abandoned the work, the fact that it struggles to find responsive listeners is not surprising. Berlioz did, however, describe

[152] In this respect I also echo Esse, who examines Donizetti's reuse of material in the context of the ghostly ('Donizetti's Gothic Resurrections', 99, 108), and Hadlock, who notes how *Les contes d'Hoffmann* resides 'in a liminal condition of restless incompleteness' like the 'undead musical presences' it evokes (*Mad Loves*, p. 4).

the duet as among 'my best compositions',[153] and he carefully preserved this section when he destroyed most of the music he had composed for the opera. Perhaps there is a second reason that Berlioz's *Nonne* is overlooked: maybe we have lost the ability to understand its approach to Other worlds and, by extension, the supernatural realms of works such as *Épisode de la vie d'un artiste*. And as with *Symphonie fantastique,* it is critical approaches deriving from Wagnerian aesthetics which make it difficult for us to hear Berlioz's distinctive voice.

Resistance to Berlioz's supernatural evocations can again be traced back to Wagner himself, and to German aesthetics more generally. French ghost stories of the nineteenth century often lean more heavily on the rational, scientific, or materialistic side of the supernatural than do their German counterparts. Indeed, Berlioz's friend Théophile Gautier, who was himself the author of several ghost stories, commented on the ways in which French culture seemed antithetical to the German supernatural. According to Gautier, '[t]he Frenchman is not naturally disposed to fantasy, and in truth it is hardly easy to be so, in a land that has so many street lights and so many daily newspapers'.[154] It was this supposed French mentality that frustrated Wagner in Paris in the early 1840s, when he poured scorn on the rationality of the French audience, who were incapable of appreciating the supernatural mysteries of Weber's so thoroughly German *Der Freischütz*.[155] Wagner's famous criticism of Meyerbeer's operas as 'effects without causes' is in the same vein, and as we have seen, his condemnation of the 'machinery' of Berlioz's *Symphonie fantastique* would appear to tar Berlioz with the same brush.

Wagner's response to Berlioz's engagement with *Freischütz* is also telling. Berlioz had provided the recitatives for the staging of *Freischütz*, an opera which he adored. Earlier productions had been reworked, cut, and rewritten to the extent that they could scarcely be considered productions of Weber's opera at all. Berlioz detested what he described as 'mutilations' inflicted on masterworks – indeed, the 'Choeur d'ombres' of *Lélio* is followed by a diatribe on the subject of the fate of Shakespeare's plays at the hands of others. Berlioz referred to adaptations of works by Mozart, Weber, and so forth as being like galvanised corpses, artificially and unnaturally revived:

---

[153] Berlioz, *Memoirs*, p. 454.
[154] Théophile Gautier, preface to a French edition of writings of E.T.A. Hoffmann, quoted in *My Fantoms*, trans. Richard Holmes (New York: New York Review of Books, 1976), pp. 190–1.
[155] Wagner, 'Le Freischütz: Report to Germany', in William Ashton Wagner, '*Der Freischütz*', *Gazette musicale*, 23 and 30 May, 1840. Or Ellis (trans.), *Richard Wagner's Prose Works*, vol. VII (New York: Broude Brothers 1966), pp. 183–204.

'No, no, no; a hundred thousand times no. No man, be he who he may, has any right to compel any other man, be he who he may, to wear a mask not his own, to speak in tones not his own; to take a shape not of his own choosing; to become a puppet, subject to his will; or to be galvanised after he is dead.'[156] In Berlioz's recitatives for *Freischütz* – necessary if the work were to be staged at the Opéra – he endeavoured to be as faithful to Weber's style as possible. To Wagner, however, this was an additional flaw, for the result was boring and erased Berlioz's own individuality – better to be galvanised than a lifeless corpse, seems to have been his view. Indeed, the supernatural imagery has a particularly strong resonance for the afterlife of musical works. Berlioz's musical treatment of the supernatural, most explicitly articulated in the metanarrative of *Lélio*, dramatises the fate of his own music, which would get caught in the same space between historical corpse and critical galvanisation.

The very juxtaposition of historical and critical approaches might itself be broken down by supernatural imagery. Postmodernism has readily deployed the metaphor of the ghost, by necessity an entity that exists in the space between absolutes, between life and death, past and future, to challenge hegemonic discourse.[157] The half-life of the ghost, so shrewdly satirised in Berlioz's article on 'Beethoven in the rings of Saturn', carries a critical potency for his own supernatural compositions. Paradoxically, a postmodern approach to the supernatural can risk 'flattening out' history, as Bown, Burdett, and Thurschwell suggest, by overlooking how ghosts embodied (or disembodied?) different historical contexts. Their own collection of essays on the subject instead represents the 'turn to history'.[158] If we similarly navigate a careful path between history and criticism, if we understand Berlioz's approach to the supernatural as both historically contingent and critically engaging, we may begin to allow ourselves to be haunted by his works in pleasurable ways. This is not to say that the spectre of Wagner that haunts Berlioz's reception can be so easily exorcised, however. In the next chapter I will revisit the question of orchestral technology, this time in the context of gender, and in a work where the subjectivity of symphony and opera, illustrated in separate works in this chapter, come together in a dialectic of genre within a single work. In *La damnation de Faust* (whose generic title 'Légende dramatique' also recalls the 'Légende' of *La nonne*) Berlioz

---

[156] Berlioz, *Memoirs*, p. 63.   [157] Buse and Stott (eds.), *Ghosts*, pp. 10–11.
[158] Nicola Bown, Carolyn Burdett, and Pamela Thurschwell (eds.), 'Introduction' to *The Victorian Supernatural* (Cambridge: Cambridge University Press, 2004), p. 12.

succeeded in bringing to the stage – or concert platform – a work that occupies the liminal territory between the interiority of *Symphonie fantastique* and the spectacle of fully realised opera (territory occupied by *La nonne sanglante* by default rather than by design). Considering *La damnation de Faust* in relation to Berlioz's futuristic novella *Euphonia*, we will see how, like the ghosts of his supernatural realms, Berlioz engaged with a vision of and for the future, sometimes directly anticipating the Wagnerian metaphysics that awaited his own reception.

4 | Back to (the music of) the future

Aesthetics of technology in Berlioz's *Euphonia* and *Damnation de Faust*[1]

On his deathbed Berlioz is believed to have said, 'they are finally going to play my music.'[2] If the words have all the irony accumulated over a lifetime of perceived indifference towards his music, they are also prescient in their suggestion that Berlioz's works would find an enduring audience in the years after his death. Berlioz was famously described as 'a musician of the future' in a rather different sense during his lifetime when he became implicated in the debate over the Wagnerian aesthetics of *Zukunftsmusik*. However, there is a third, more literal, sense in which Berlioz could be seen to be a musician of the future. In several of his critical works, most famously in the novella *Euphonia*, Berlioz speculates about what form society might take in years – or centuries – to come. The futuristic worlds of Berlioz's writings present both a satirical critique of his own musical environment and an opportunity to express fantasies or fears about how the activities and art of musicians might eventually be transformed by new technologies. Berlioz's orchestral apparatus has already been considered, in the previous chapter, in relation to the scientific and technological aspects of magic and the supernatural. In this chapter we will revisit some of the same issues around the technological uncanny, but this time explore their significance for issues of temporality and the 'Other world' of the future – an exploration which also affords an opportunity to delve further into both the synchronicity and the tension between Berlioz's aesthetics and that of Wagner.

While Berlioz made plans for an oratorio set in a futuristic dystopia – the apocalyptic *Dernier jour du monde* – the project was abandoned, leaving us with no musical works by him that employ a literally futuristic setting (unless we consider the similarly apocalyptic *Dies irae* of the *Requiem*). We are thus denied an aural representation of Berlioz's conception of the future. However, when examined primarily in relation to technology, Berlioz's futuristic writings can provide, if not a crystal ball, then a lens that offers new perspectives on musical works regardless of the time of their setting.

---

[1] A version of this chapter was published as Inge van Rij, 'Back to (the Music of) the Future: Aesthetics of Technology in Berlioz's *Euphonia* and *Damnation de Faust*', *Cambridge Opera Journal* 22/3 (2012), 257–300.
[2] Cairns, *Servitude and Greatness*, p. 773.

Berlioz's *Euphonia* illustrates three technological tropes that also pertain to his music: the transformation of perceptions of time and space that resulted from the emerging technologies of Berlioz's world; the gendered discourse that positions men as technology and women as voice or body; and the questions that arise around agency – or who controls the machine. Berlioz's *La damnation de Faust* in particular benefits from being reexamined from this perspective. Completed in 1846, less than two years after the publication of *Euphonia*, *La damnation de Faust* was conceived some years before the Wagnerian discourse began to overrun Berlioz's reception, but that same discourse has proved inescapable in the subsequent interpretation and reception of Berlioz's work, to an even greater extent than is the case with *Symphonie fantastique*. Attempts to stage *La damnation de Faust* as an opera only compound the problem, for, paradoxically, these visually stimulating interpretations ultimately obscure the powerful ways in which Berlioz employs operatic idioms and conventions on a metadiegetic level. Viewing *La damnation de Faust* afresh through the lens of *Euphonia* enables us to uncover an aesthetics of technology, both visual and aural, that, after the fashion of futuristic fiction itself, both anticipates the (Wagnerian) future, and offers an alternative operatic vision which is no less persuasive for not having subsequently been realised in all its details.

Berlioz and the technological future

In *The Urbanization of Opera* Anselm Gerhard comments how Meyerbeer liked to compose on trains – something that was anathema to Rossini. Gerhard outlines thereby a new kind of modernity that infused Meyerbeer's music.[3] Cormack Newark similarly explores how metaphors of modernity framed the reception of Meyerbeer's operas in Berlioz's Paris, pointing in particular to the display in these works of instrumental technology, and connecting this to the interest in technological innovation evidenced by the increasingly popular industrial exhibitions.[4] Berlioz participated directly in industrial and international exhibitions. Like Meyerbeer, he would compose on trains, and while for Berlioz this practice may have been primarily a matter of necessity rather than a creative choice, his correspondence and criticism (including his own reception of Meyerbeer's music) reveal

---

[3] Anselm Gerhard, *The Urbanization of Opera*, trans. Mary Whittall (Chicago: University of Chicago Press, 1998), pp. 119–20.
[4] Newark, 'Metaphors for Meyerbeer', 23–43.

a mind attuned to the developing technologies of urbanisation. Indeed, Berlioz's upbringing, education, and employment all primed him to interact with the technological metaphors Newark identifies in Meyerbeer's music, sometimes in quite literal ways.

As a young medical student Berlioz recoiled from the grisly realities of the dissection room, and he ceased to attend Gay-Lussac's courses in experimental electricity after succumbing fully to the pleasures of the opera house. However, Berlioz's continuing fascination with electrical science is evident not only in references to galvanism, but also in numerous allusions in his writings and correspondence to other applications of electricity.[5] The performances of massive forces that Berlioz conducted at various civic events helped to build him a reputation for embracing the musical implications of industrialisation. In 1844 he coordinated 1,022 performers in a grand performance at the conclusion of the festival of industry, rehearsing the orchestra as the last of the industrial machines were being noisily towed away from the Palace of Industry.[6] And at the ceremony for the opening of the new railway line to Lille in 1846, Berlioz anticipated the confirmation of his reputation for excess when the local organisers pressed him to incorporate live cannons – though in the event the plan literally failed to ignite.[7]

Berlioz retained a general curiosity about technology throughout his life, writing in 1864 (five years before his death) how he admired modern civilisation, with its 'telegraphs, its steam, its electricity, slaves to human will, which allow thoughts to be transmitted so rapidly'.[8] His penultimate review, published in 1863, speculates upon where such innovations might lead. Berlioz imagines a world of the future where dirigible aircraft transport virtuosi around the world, and where geography is no barrier for the professional musician – though for Berlioz, in the ideal future (unlike the real one) the musical traffic is all in one direction:

What concerts we will organise! I can see myself giving orders to my orchestral assistant in the build-up to a big music festival: 'Where is Vieux-Temps? Where is Becker?' – 'Sir, they are in Sydney.' – 'Run and fetch them for me. And Sivori, and Bottesini and Piatti, where are they? I need them.' – 'Sir, they are in Canton, in Timor, and in Mindanao.' – 'Well then! Invite them while you're at it, it's on your way. Start up the locomotive, get to it, and don't spare the coal; I need these virtuosi in five days.'

---

[5] Berlioz, *Memoirs*, p. 22. Several examples of Berlioz's use of electrical metaphors can be found elsewhere in this chapter.
[6] Cairns, *Servitude and Greatness*, p. 303.
[7] Berlioz, *The Musical Madhouse*, pp. 184–8.   [8] *CG* VII, p. 150.

And then we will go to Asia and give concerts in Isfahan, in Tehran, in Nanking, in Nagasaki, to give a musical initiation to the Orientals who have never had any idea what music is, and at the final bar of Beethoven's Choral Symphony we will have speakers who turn towards the public, saying: '*This* is what it is, savages!'[9]

This imagined expansion of individual possibilities through the effective shrinking of the globe builds on the tendencies of Berlioz's own time. Berlioz travelled by steam train as far as Russia, but other musicians voyaged much further afield. In feuilletons of 1854 and 1855 Berlioz remarked wryly on the financial success of singers Rosine Stoltz (in Brazil) and Henriette Sontag (in Mexico), 'we can forgive you your millions and even praise you for having taken so much effort to earn them as to have sought them in Mexico, Rio, San Franciso, Sydney, Calcutta, and Nagasaki.'[10]

The futuristic fantasy of Berlioz's penultimate review suggests a bridging of cultural as well as geographical distance. Everyone speaks a common language – 'European (which is to say enriched French)' – and different cultures are experienced as exotic commodities readily available to the traveller.[11] The idea of a Francophone future is one of several elements of Berlioz's futuristic writings that may have originated in a science fiction novel of the period. In *Le roman de l'avenir*, Félix Bodin imagines that, in the salons of the late twentieth century, 'it is French that dominates; French, once the language of diplomacy in Europe, is today the language of intellectualism and industry for the universe.'[12]

The ostensible subject of this section of Berlioz's column – though he takes a long time coming to it – is the performance at the Opéra-Comique of Saint-Georges's *Les amours du diable* (with music by Albert Grisar). Berlioz's plot summary reveals that the opera had little discernable connection to the futuristic scenario that precedes it in his review.[13] As we have already seen, digressing on topics of no obvious relevance to the work at hand was a fairly typical ploy in Berlioz's columns: Tahiti or New Zealand provided an Other world and sanctuary for the imagination of the jaded opera critic, attractive precisely because of their distance from the banalities

---

[9] *Journal des débats*, 3 September 1863, 1.
[10] *Joural des débats*, 5 October 1854, 2. See also *Journal des débats*, 8 June 1855, 2.
[11] *Journal des débats*, 3 September 1863, 1.
[12] Félix Bodin, *Le roman de l'avenir* (Paris: Lecointe et Pougin 1834), p. 147.
[13] It may be incidental that Berlioz chose a futuristic setting for almost half of what was supposed to be a review of *Les amours du diable* – an opera set in Hungary and outlining a diabolic pact made between the hero and a devil in order to save a young woman. However, his choice does strengthen the analogy between the futuristic *Euphonia* and *La damnation de Faust* that this chapter will seek to establish, and in the review Berlioz himself points to similarities between *Les amours du diable* and the Faust story.

of yet another evening at the Opéra-Comique. In 1863, with the increasing ease of travel to previously remote countries, geography no longer always offered quite the same haven from the familiar. In his penultimate column Berlioz defines 'Otherness' temporally, but the intention is doubtless very similar: the future is another exotic locale. And if the familiar is ultimately inescapable, an exotic or futuristic setting has additional compensations, for it presents a convenient mask for satirical critique. While he does not tell us much about *Les amours du diable*, Berlioz's review nevertheless makes pointed comments about the tendencies of his own musical world.

Euphonia, or the Musical City

First published in instalments in the *Revue et gazette musicale* in 1844, *Euphonia* was subsequently republished, with minor alterations, as the twenty-fifth 'evening' in Berlioz's *Les soirées de l'orchestre* in 1852. But although it thus predates his penultimate review by two decades, *Euphonia* could be seen to articulate similar concerns. Again the story functions as a diversion from music Berlioz considered trivial. Like the critic who delays addressing the opera he has been assigned to review, the players of the imaginary orchestra listen to the story to avoid having to engage with the opera they are meant to be performing. However, *Euphonia* is both more famous and much more complex than the fantasy of Berlioz's later column, and it is in *Euphonia* that we find all three of our technological tropes articulated in a way that enhances our understanding of Berlioz's own musical practice. The story is set in the year 2344 – exactly five hundred years into the future for its initial readers. The selection of a remote future date that is chosen for its numerical connection to the time of publication alerts us to the fact that we are being offered Berlioz's satirical perspective on the musical scene in the Europe of his and his readers' present, as well as his hopes – and fears – for where such tendencies might lead.[14] The story is rich in detail that is germane to the argument of this chapter, and while nothing substitutes for reading the full novella in Berlioz's own words, I offer a summary of these details, as follows.

Berlioz opens his narrative as an epistolary novel with an exchange of letters between Xilef and Shetland, two musicians from the fictional German

---

[14] The practice is common in science fiction writing, as most famously seen in George Orwell's *1984* (first published in 1948).

city Euphonia.[15] Xilef has been posted to Italy to seek out good singers, but the Italy of 2344 is anathema to Xilef's conception of art, much as the Italy of 1831–2 had been anathema to Berlioz's musical sensibilities. Italian society is dominated by commerce, and music is completely debased. New operas are constructed out of rehashed bits of old ones and inspiration comes not from the music, nor from the libretto, but from the singers' choice of costumes. The audience pays the operas no regard in any case, for during the performances they eat, talk, play billiards, and even dance to the simultaneous music of a separate band. In such a place Xilef does not find any singers worthy of being taken to Euphonia. Xilef's frustration at being in Italy is intensified because it has forced him to leave behind in Paris his fiancée, Mina – a singer whom he loves desperately. Mina is not without her faults, however. Xilef confesses to Shetland that she 'prefers the florid style' and, worse still, 'thinks Beethoven's adagios are *too long*'. 'Oh, female of Homo sapiens!' Xilef writes in exasperation, seemingly attributing this grave deficiency to her gender.[16]

After two letters from Xilef to Shetland, Berlioz switches abruptly to a dramatic form, complete with stage directions. Now we encounter Mina herself in her drawing room in Paris. The fickle woman decides to abandon Xilef and travel to Euphonia. Mina's arrival is recounted by Shetland in a letter to Xilef. Out flying in his balloon, Shetland hears a woman singing the theme of his own First Symphony, which she ornaments extravagantly. When Mina, now going by the name Nadira, approaches Shetland the next day to seek a place in the Gluck festival, the composer dismisses her on account of the florid nature of her singing. At the festival itself, however, Nadira is humbled by the music. She removes the ornaments from her hair, 'flings them to the ground, tramples them underfoot (as a symbol of recantation)', and sings an aria from *Alceste*, winning over the audience and Shetland himself.[17] The two become lovers.

For some time Xilef and Shetland remain unaware that Xilef's Mina and Shetland's Nadira are one and the same. When Xilef finally discovers Mina in Euphonia he realises not only that she has betrayed him but also that she is betraying Shetland with other men. Xilef plots a vicious revenge. He persuades Shetland to purchase a massive keyboard, the so-called *piano-orchestre*, and an ornamental steel pavilion by the same 'celebrated

---

[15] Berlioz altered the names of some characters when he republished the story, as discussed further later. To be consistent with the most readily available English translation of the story, I am using the names as they appeared in *Les soirées de l'orchestre* in 1852.

[16] Berlioz, *Evenings with the Orchestra*, pp. 265–6.   [17] Ibid., p. 280.

mechanical genius'.[18] These contraptions provide the venue and the music for a ball in celebration of Nadira's (Mina's) birthday. Shetland, still ignorant of Nadira's deception, improvises dance music on the new instrument while, some distance away, couples waltz in the pavilion. Unbeknownst to all, Xilef has commissioned a distinctive feature in the pavilion. At the press of a button, it begins to contract, gradually crushing Nadira and her friends and lovers to a pulp in what is described in vivid detail by Berlioz as a 'smoking charnel-house in which human forms are no longer to be discerned'.[19] Shetland plays on, oblivious, but goes insane when he discovers what has happened. He dies a few days after Xilef, who has committed suicide upon the completion of his plan. Euphonia – the 'musical city' – is plunged into six months of mourning. Aghast at the fates of the two men, and 'the rest of the drama', the Euphonians take a vow of silence, broken only by the 'wail of horrified grief' from the town organ.[20]

What is missing from this account of the story *Euphonia* is the account of the city of Euphonia itself, which Berlioz provides, at the centre of his novella, in the form of a document Xilef supplies for the edification of the Italians. If the Italy of the future resembles, in exaggerated form, the Italy of Berlioz's own travels in that country, Euphonia is built on the foundations of Berlioz's experiences during his tour of Germany in 1842–3. It is in Euphonia that we see the fullest realisation of both the social and technological features of Berlioz's futuristic fantasy, as well as the disciplinary paradigms touched on in Chapter 2. Euphonia acts as a kind of conservatory for Germany, and as the site of the production of music for the nation. The whole city is devoted to music, which dominates the education of the citizens and determines every aspect of their lives.

Berlioz's Euphonia is part of a Germany ruled by a single Emperor – a prophecy that, while not realised in his own lifetime, would not have to wait until the third millennium to be fulfilled. But Berlioz is not concerned with political systems except insofar as they relate to music. The autocracy of Germany is echoed in microcosm in Euphonia's 'despotic regime' and the 'military fashion' of its government, which, he implies, is essential to the realisation of the aesthetic of high art.[21] When Mina expresses her intention to appeal to a higher authority for admission to the Gluck festival, Shetland reveals the extent to which authority is vested in the composer: 'the Minister of the Gluck Festival is my humble self; the Emperor of the Gluck Festival

---

[18] Ibid., p. 292.   [19] Ibid., p. 295.   [20] Ibid., p. 296.
[21] Berlioz, *Evenings with the Orchestra*, p. 283.

is likewise myself; the management of the ceremony is in my hands. I am absolute master, my word is law without appeal.'²²

Several aspects of Euphonia evoke the theories of Saint-Simonianism – a socialist movement that attracted a number of musicians in the early 1830s. Central to Saint-Simonian ideology was the concept of a strongly hierarchical meritocracy where society's leaders were taken from those who excelled in certain fields. In particular, the Saint-Simonians put their faith in industry and technology, for they saw these as the means of advancing society to a new productivity. In 1832 Charles Duveyrier, a prominent figure in Saint-Simonianism, published an article titled 'La ville nouvelle; ou, le Paris des Saint-Simoniens' ('The new city: or, the Paris of the Saint-Simonians'). The year before 'La ville nouvelle' was published, Berlioz had written to Duveyrier from Italy and revealed how he was taking an interest in the social philosophies of Saint-Simonianism, suggesting that he had 'eagerly read a wad of issues of [Saint-Simonian newspaper] *The Globe*'.²³ Recent issues of *The Globe* at the time of Berlioz's letter include articles about the subjugation of artists to 'les oisifs' (the idle rich), who crowd Paganini's performances decked out in the finery produced by the labour of the working classes, who are themselves unable to enter the concert hall. *The Globe* calls for artists to 'hasten towards a future where each works according to his tastes, following his inspiration, without putting himself in the service of an exploiter'.²⁴ Although Berlioz had strong reservations about Saint-Simonian notions of religion and spirituality, he praised their ideas on 'la réorganisation politique de la Société', and it is easy to see how he could have embraced the concept of a future in which the individual musician is both liberated and able to speak to a wider public. In this context, the socialist connotations of the planned concealment and eventual unveiling of the labour of the orchestra in *Épisode de la vie d'un artiste* (whose concluding 'mélologue' *Le retour à la vie* was conceived around the same time Berlioz was reading the *Globe*) are heightened. Indeed, Berlioz suggested that his few reservations about Saint-Simonianism should not prevent him 'uniting my hopes and efforts with your own', and he asked Duveyrier to consider how the Saint-Simonians might make use of him musically.²⁵

Berlioz's interest in Saint-Simonianism subsequently waned. Nevertheless, when constructing his own utopia, Euphonia, Berlioz may have been

---

²² Ibid., p. 279.   ²³ *CG* I, p. 476.
²⁴ See, for example *Globe*, No. 88 (29 March 1831), 336, and No. 111 (21 April 1831), 448.
²⁵ *CG* I, pp. 476–7. Berlioz's 'Chant des chemins de fer' anthem of 1846, though written more than a decade after this evidence of Berlioz's Saint-Simonian sympathies, comes strikingly close to embodying the ethos of that movement.

influenced by 'the new city' Duveyrier had envisaged, for in addition to references to balloon travel (a fairly popular futuristic trope at the time), Duveyrier's vision shares a number of elements with that of Berlioz.[26] In contrast to the Paris familiar to Duveyrier's readers, where, Duveyrier complains, different peoples and activities exist in a chaotic mixture within each district, in 'La ville nouvelle' Duveyrier imagined the ideal city laid out like a body, its limbs symbolising the different functions of the various districts, which are now physically separated – much like Berlioz's Euphonia, with its 'Soprano Street'. Thus, in Duveyrier's city, musicians assemble in a particular district and make music together every evening with 'a single voice',[27] a model of communal music-making perhaps recalled by Berlioz in Euphonia, where 'ten thousand voices burst out spontaneously on the chord of the diminished seventh followed by a magnificent cadence in C major', to express their approbation at the Gluck festival.[28] A more striking parallel between the two futuristic cities can be seen in the powerful organ Duveyrier places at the throat of his musical body, which unites the citizens in a manner similar to that of Berlioz's steam organ.[29] In Euphonia, there is a similar giant organ at the city's centre, used to regiment the lives of the citizens through the use of signals that communicate in what Berlioz describes as a form of 'aural telegraphy'.

Berlioz's 'visual telegraph', which helps his musicians to realise their parts, may also be anticipated by Duveyrier, though the 'immense machines which mark the time in space' in Duveyrier's Paris of the future do so for a music that is more blatantly industrial: 'sparks gush forth, and clouds of steam rise in the sky, which rings with the blows of the hammers and axes, the screeching of screws and saws, the whirling of mills, the rhythmic beat of the pumps and the songs of the workers.'[30]

Aesthetics of technology in *Euphonia*: Space and time, gender, agency

If Berlioz drew on Duveyrier's narrative in constructing *Euphonia*, he also incorporated technological innovations of his own world into his conception of the future. Hence the idea for the steam organ is attributed by

---

[26] Ralph P. Locke, *Music, Musicians, and the Saint-Simonians* (Chicago: University of Chicago Press, 1986), pp. 120 and 344 n. 101.
[27] Charles Duveyrier, 'La ville nouvelle, ou le Paris des Saint-Simoniens', *Paris ou Le livre des cent-et-un*, vol. 8 (Paris: Ladvocat, 1832), p. 325.
[28] Berlioz, *Evenings with the Orchestra*, pp. 280–81.
[29] Duveyrier, 'La ville nouvelle', p. 341.   [30] Ibid., p. 337.

Berlioz to Adolphe Sax, and the aural telegraph uses a musical language developed by Jean-François Sudre, originally designed for the purposes of military communication. The visual telegraph, too, could have been inspired by Sudre, who developed a translation of his 'langue musicale' into visual form, whereby the seven pitches were replaced by the segments of the fingers in the style of a Guidonian hand.[31] Another application of Sudre's system saw the pitches replaced with different coloured lights.[32]

However, while both Sudre and Duveyrier anticipate elements of Berlioz's visual telegraph, neither treats it as a device specifically for directing musicians. Bodin's *Roman de l'avenir* describes a similar type of technology that is used for coordinating large musical forces in his futuristic city; but Berlioz was either unaware of Bodin's work or unconscious of the similarity, for when an 'electric metronome' was developed a decade after *Euphonia* was published, he claimed the credit for having anticipated the concept.[33] In 1855 Berlioz commissioned one of the new devices from a Belgian manufacturer to help him control twelve hundred performers at that year's industrial exhibition. By tapping the finger of his left hand, while conducting with his right, Berlioz could communicate the beat to five subconductors by means of an electrical current.[34] The potential of the 'electric metronome' to enable him to transform physical space was satirised in a cartoon in *Charivari* in 1855 (Fig. 4.1). Berlioz uses his electric metronome literally to conduct a musical work instantaneously to remote lands. As with the global virtuosi of Berlioz's penultimate review, the cartoon implies that the only barrier to the creation of universal music is a physical one – one which the technology of the future will surmount.

The technological innovations of Berlioz's futuristic narratives – the aural and visual telegraphs, the electric metronome, and the dirigible aircraft – are all examples of what Wolfgang Schivelbusch has termed 'the industrialization of time and space' that was experienced by Berlioz's generation.[35]

---

[31] François Sudre, *Langue musicale universelle inventée par François Sudre, également inventeur de la Téléphonie* (Paris: G. Flaxland, 1866), n. p.

[32] Boleslas Gajewski, 'Sur la langue universelle de Sudre', *Bulletins de la Société d'Anthropologie de Paris* 8 (1885), 604.

[33] On this and other similarities between Bodin's novel and Berlioz's *Euphonia*, see Joël-Marie Fauquet, '*Euphonia* and the Utopia of the Orchestra as Society', in Bloom (ed.), *Berlioz: Scenes from the Life and Work* (Rochester, NY: University of Rochester Press, 2008), pp. 47–9. Fauquet also points to elements Berlioz's story shares with another futuristic narrative, Étienne Cabet's *Voyage en Icarie* (1840). On Berlioz and the electric metronome see Macdonald, *Berlioz's Orchestration Treatise*, p. 356.

[34] Berlioz, *Memoirs*, pp. 492–3.

[35] Wolfgang Schivelbusch, *The Railway Journey: The Industrialization of Time and Space in the 19th Century* (Berkeley: University of California Press, 1979).

Fig. 4.1 'Mr Berlioz takes advantage of his "electric baton" to conduct an orchestra which will have members in every region of the globe'. Illustration by 'Cham' for *Charivari*, 2 December 1855. Reproduction courtesy of Beinecke Rare Book and Manuscript Library, Yale University.

Schivelbusch's expression applies to several crucial innovations of the nineteenth century, including the telegraph and telephone. Moreover, the process had actually begun well before the nineteenth century, as the increasing uptake of mechanised timepieces transformed perceptions of time in the home and in the factory.[36] Berlioz's image of the steam organ regulating

---

[36] On the centrality of the mechanical clock to developing conceptions of modernity see Lewis Mumford, *Technics and Civilization* (New York: Harcourt, Brace and Company, 1934); E. P. Thompson, 'Time, Work-Discipline, and Industrial Capitalism', *Past and Present* 38/1 (1967), 56–97; Jacques Attali, 'Le temps des machines', *Histoires du Temp* (Paris: Fayard, 1982), pp. 192–228; David S. Landes, *Revolution in Time: Clocks and the Making of the Modern World* (Cambridge, MA: Harvard University Press, 1983).

the lives of the citizens of Euphonia certainly owes something to the industrial timekeeping of the factory whistle.[37] However, Schivelbusch's slightly different technological focus is equally interesting, for he employs the concept of the 'industrialization of time and space' with particular reference to one of the technological developments most emblematic of the experience of urbanisation of Berlioz's own era: the steam train.[38] To summarise Schivelbusch's argument, before the railway, overland travel meant close contact with organic life. Every aspect of the journey was determined by the contours of the land and the bodies of the animals that powered the vehicle. The railway, however, cut through the landscape, propelling passengers 'like a bullet', to use the metaphor frequently adopted by the travellers themselves. For many passengers the train almost seemed to defy space, plunging through mountains rather than following their contours. The railway also defied time. No longer was travel regulated by the demands of the animals, such as the need to stop to change or feed horses. Passengers frequently felt quite disconnected from the landscape and from humanity, for the new train stations were typically built on the outskirts of a city, not in the centre of the community like the old coach stations.[39]

The speed of travel, isolation, and separation from the land experienced by early train travellers may have left a mark on futuristic fantasies of air travel from the period, including Berlioz's *Euphonia*. In his desperate search for Mina, Xilef 'ate up space' in his balloon, driving it to 'the borderline of life' where 'the cold and dryness are such that the objects made of wood in the ship warped and cracked'.[40] More obviously influential in Berlioz's description of Xilef's extreme ascent, however, are the accounts of air pressure and high altitudes from the investigations of Gay-Lussac, who had himself used a hot air balloon to study the atmosphere at high altitudes in 1804, and Humboldt, who referred to his friend's experiments in relation to the rarefied atmosphere of Chimborazo.[41] The sublime terror of Xilef's

---

[37] Indeed, in the same year Berlioz conceived *Euphonia* (1844), a law was introduced in France decreeing that the beginning of the working day should be signalled (audibly) by a public clock. See Attali, *Histoires du Temp*, p. 218. See also p. 192, on the division of labour and its connection to transformations of time in 'the machine age'.

[38] Schivelbusch is not alone in identifying developments in the railway as altering common perceptions of the world and leading to a sense of the 'annihilation of space and time'. See, for example, Carlene Stephens, '"The Most Reliable Time:" William Bond, the New England Railroads, and Time Awareness in 19th-Century America', *Technology and Culture*, 30/1 (1989), 1–24.

[39] Schivelbusch, *The Railway Journey*.   [40] Berlioz, *Evenings with the Orchestra*, pp. 289–90.

[41] Humboldt, *Tableaux de la nature*, p. 386.

pursuit of Mina is thus a kind of unholy counterpoint to the transgressing of human physical limits by the Beethovenian condor.

The depiction in the opening of *Euphonia* of Etna as a crater lake created by massive volcanic upheaval evokes a natural rather than a technological transformation. Nevertheless, it contributes to the alteration in perceptions of time and space in the modern world. Berlioz followed the geological and paleontological discoveries of his contemporaries with interest. In 1866 he remarked upon the discovery of fossils in the Badlands area of Mississippi. This evidence of the erasure of entire species many years earlier put the pettiness of human existence into perspective – and Berlioz expressed the wish that humanity might now be similarly wiped out.[42] The pace of modern life seemed all the more frantic, the lifespan of man so much shorter, and the concerns of the masses so much more trivial, when confronted with the evidence of the gradual physical transformation of the planet.

In Berlioz's world, one thing might withstand both the rapid change brought about by industrialisation and the gradual change of the natural world: the musical masterwork. Etna may cave in, Germany may become an empire, and man may conquer the air, but Gluck's *operas* will still be the centrepiece of civilised society, capable of being transmitted across centuries of time just as they could be transmitted through space by the electric metronome. It is particularly significant that Berlioz should choose Gluck as his symbol of musical transcendence, for his writings on Gluck's operas, and on the preface to *Alceste*, illustrate the extent to which Gluck symbolised for him an operatic model that privileged the authority of the composer. In this familiar framework it is the degree of fixity enabled by a conception of the work that vests authority in the composer and his score that permits it to attain longevity, in contrast to the ephemeral transience of a tradition that locates authority in the performer. Berlioz describes how Gluck felt he needed to be present at the performances of his works. While Berlioz suggests this would not have been necessary had Gluck given more precise directions in the score, he nevertheless promotes a model for performance that situates supreme authority in a central figure who stands in for the composer. In writing of performances of Gluck's music in the 1850s, he goes so far as to plead for 'despotism in the theatre', in language even more extreme than the 'despotic regime' of Euphonia, where Shetland is 'Minister', 'Emperor', and 'absolute master' of the Gluck festival: 'Despotism is required; let it be supremely intelligent, by all means, but despotism it

[42] *CG* VII, p. 439.

must be, military despotism, the despotism of the commander-in-chief, the admiral of the fleet in time of war.'[43]

In Berlioz's conception of the very different musical practices of the Italians, the singers in opera dictate their demands to the so-called *operatore* who cobble together the music. The orchestra struggles to accommodate the singers' whims or forsakes ensemble altogether – opera is created by and for the singer's voice. Berlioz here positions himself in sympathy with Gluck who, he writes elsewhere, expressed strong dissatisfaction with the predominant Italian operatic models of his own time: 'According to this method, an opera was mainly a pretext for showing off singers who came on stage *to play their larynx*.'[44] In contrast, in Euphonia, everything is secondary to the composer's work, in accordance with the model Berlioz derived from Gluck: 'there are no leading singers, no property rights in title roles.' If a suitable singer cannot be found to do justice to Gluck's work, the entire festival will be cancelled altogether for that year.[45] The musical work thus outlasts any individual performance of it – as witnessed also by the staging of Gluck's operas in Euphonia, some six hundred years after their composition.[46]

Orchestral technology and the musical work in space and time

The position of technology in relation to this conception of musical transcendence is complex. On one hand, Berlioz implied that great music outlasts the innovations of technology. For example, when referring to his commission for a work to celebrate the opening of the new railway line from Paris to Lille in June 1846, Berlioz quipped that 'in pressing and *unexpected* circumstances like the inauguration of a railway, an artist shouldn't concern himself about whether forty centuries more or less will be familiar with his work'; the artist will instead content himself with 'a short-lived celebrity of a mere four or five thousand years', because 'at such times one's country has the right to demand absolute devotion from each of its children'.[47]

---

[43] Berlioz, 'The Revival of Gluck's *Alceste* at the Opéra' in *The Art of Music*, p. 147.
[44] Berlioz, 'The *Alceste* of Euripides' in *The Art of Music*, p. 97.
[45] Berlioz, *Evenings with the Orchestra*, p. 288.
[46] As Mark Everist points out, Berlioz's notion of the transcendence of Gluck's works, though a familiar critical stance to us today, was 'radical' at the time. See 'Gluck, Berlioz, and Castil-Blaze: The Poetics and Reception of French Opera', in Roger Parker and Mary Ann Smart (eds.), *Reading Critics Reading: Opera and Ballet Criticism in France from the Revolution to 1848* (Oxford: Oxford University Press, 2001), pp. 86–108.
[47] Berlioz, *Musical Madhouse*, p. 178.

Unlike the industrial future of the railway, Berlioz implies, the great art work is autonomous and will project much further into the future by transcending time altogether.

On the other hand, Berlioz was forced to grapple with the inevitable dependence of music on (instrumental) technology, itself in a situation of great flux during his lifetime. The role of technology raises ontological questions about the work itself. When the score is also transmitted across the centuries (as in the case of Gluck's works), are the specific instruments themselves to be considered essential to the work? We know Berlioz detested what he described as the 'trombonizing' and 'ophicleiding' of eighteenth-century works. He commented on a performance of *Le nozze di Figaro* in London (home of the industrial revolution, as he was very aware), that it was 'copper-bottomed like a ship of the line'.[48] In staging a revival of Gluck's *Orphée et Euridice* in 1859, Berlioz carefully removed the trombones that had been added to Gluck's score; and he substituted brass cornets for the wooden cornetto specified by Gluck only because players of the latter were by that time too difficult to find in Paris.[49]

Indeed, Berlioz was generally ambivalent about the use of new instruments. He writes favourably in *Euphonia* of the giant steam organ inspired by Adolphe Sax, 'harmonic cymbals', and a 'piano-orchestre' ('a huge piano whose variegated sound was so powerful that under the fingers of a single virtuoso it could hold its own with an orchestra of a hundred players').[50] But Berlioz does not suggest that such instruments are to be employed in performances of masterworks of the past, and he made only sparing use in his own music of the new instruments he cautiously described in his orchestration treatise as being potentially 'fatal to the art of music'.[51] The staves he allocated to saxophones in the *Epilogue* of *La damnation de Faust* remained blank.[52] In *Euphonia* Berlioz seems to vilify certain developments in instruments since Gluck's time. When describing the abominable Italian opera orchestra of the future Berlioz refers specifically to *keyed* bugles, *piston* trumpets, and *valve* trombones, which, when presented in the company of (among other things) three ophicleides (instruments he saw as 'monstrous' if their limitations were not respected),[53] would seem to frame the new

---

[48] Berlioz, *Evenings with the Orchestra*, p. 356.
[49] Joël-Marie Fauquet, 'Berlioz's Version of Gluck's *Orphée*', in Peter Bloom (ed.), *Berlioz Studies* (Cambridge: Cambridge University Press, 1992), p. 231.
[50] Berlioz, *Evenings with the Orchestra*, p. 292. The instrument is suggestive of the instruments being developed by Jacob and Edouard Alexandre (from whom Berlioz would later encourage Liszt to commission a 'piano-organ').
[51] Macdonald, *Berlioz's Orchestration Treatise*, p. 318.   [52] *NBE* vol. 8b, p. 459.
[53] Macdonald, *Berlioz's Orchestration Treatise*, p. 234.

technologies of chromatic brass as vulgar and antithetical to great art. In practice, however, Berlioz's attitude was inevitably more nuanced, and where he was persuaded that the advantages of the new technology did not come at the expense of beauty of sound, he would adopt them in his own music.[54]

If the temporal transmission of the musical work into the future establishes a potential tension between art and (instrumental) technology, the spatial transmission of the work of the future fuses art and technology by seeming to industrialise the players themselves. Here Berlioz would appear to embrace the technological metaphor. The electric metronome conveys essential elements of the work directly from the conductor (who in Euphonia is typically also the composer) to the players. The conductor becomes 'the absolute master of [the] huge intelligent instrument' of the orchestra itself, which is imagined as a keyboard with each player responding 'as do the hammers of a piano under the hand pressing the keys'.[55] The electric metronome functions as a literal extension of the conductor's own electricity, helping him to 'radiate the vital spark of music' and 'charge' the players.[56]

The suggestion that the orchestra is like a machine is similarly borne out in other writings, such as when Berlioz quantifies the strength of particular orchestras in terms of horsepower – the unit that was now being used to measure the power of steam engines.[57] And when the orchestra is a machine, the work is transmitted to the players rather than created by them, reinforcing the 'despotic' model of Euphonia that contrasts so strikingly with the Italian opera idiom.

Euphonia and Italy are also contrasted in terms of the position of the human body in performance, again reflecting fundamentally opposing conceptions of the musical work. Whereas in the Italy of the future, the audience may spontaneously begin to dance during operatic performances, in Euphonia the orchestra and choral singers alike are trained to suppress their own bodily responses, and to disguise the very breath that animates them:

[A]ll the breathing-places are decided on, and so arranged that never more than one fourth of the singers take a breath at the same time. In this way the vocal output of the entire mass never suffers any appreciable interruption.

The first rehearsals aim at literal exactitude; then come the broad nuances; lastly style and EXPRESSION. Any marking of the rhythm by bodily movements during the singing is strictly forbidden to the choristers.[58]

---

[54] See, for example, Macdonald's summary of Berlioz's changing attitudes towards chromatic horns: ibid., pp. 180–5.
[55] Berlioz, *Evenings with the Orchestra*, pp. 286–7.
[56] Macdonald, *Berlioz's Orchestration Treatise*, p. 338.   [57] *CG* IV, p. 417.
[58] Berlioz, *Evenings with the Orchestra*, p. 286.

Individual bodies are sacrificed to the body of Euphonia itself, which is dedicated to transmitting the masterwork. As Joël-Marie Fauquet and Katharine Kolb have both remarked, Berlioz's suppression of individual physicality is vaguely sinister.[59] The stillness of Berlioz's city is one way in which it differs markedly from its possible Saint-Simonian model. In Duveyrier's Paris of the future the body of the individual is celebrated – it is the microcosm of the city itself, and the city is alive with dance and song:

Come! Here the ground swells with man's desire for life; here the land gives to man, like a woman to her lover. The city the people inhabit is alive, adorned, resounding; she thinks, she works, she loves, she laughs, she dances. And the people will rush to the city, and they will know that they carry within themselves the forms and the map of my city; they will recognise her.[60]

'Mere woman after all': Gender and technology

The euphoric feminisation of the body of the city in Duveyrier's text ('And the temple is a woman!', Duveyrier proclaims of the building at its heart) is significant,[61] and is another element that signals Berlioz's departure from the Saint-Simonian model, for in *Euphonia*'s world of almost disembodied music, a marked tension arises around gender, particularly as embodied by Mina. However, before we consider the gendered implications of Berlioz's technological future, it is necessary to clarify the autobiographical context of *Euphonia*.

When Berlioz first published *Euphonia* in 1844, Shetland was named Rotceh – or 'Hector' spelled backwards – and Mina was named Ellimac, referring to Camille Moke (subsequently Camille Pleyel). The vivacious virtuoso pianist had been engaged to Berlioz, but she betrayed him shortly after his departure for Italy, and married the piano-manufacturer Pleyel instead. Berlioz was devastated. When his suspicions were first aroused he vented his anguish in terms suggestive of the manic balloon flight undertaken by Xilef: 'I am like a lost balloon, which must burst in the air, be engulfed in the waves, or come to a halt like Noah's ark.'[62] After Camille's betrayal had

---

[59] Fauquet, '*Euphonia* and the Utopia of the Orchestra as Society', pp. 58, 61–2; Katherine Reeve [Kolb], '*The Damnation of Faust*, or the Perils of Heroism in Music', in Bloom (ed.), *Berlioz Studies*, p. 166.
[60] Duveyrier, 'Paris', p. 333.
[61] Ibid., p. 339. A central preoccupation of the Saint-Simonian ideology was the faith in the coming of a female messiah, and the belief that the key to the enlightenment of man was the emancipation of woman.
[62] *CG* I, p. 424.

been confirmed, Berlioz plotted an elaborate revenge whereby, disguised as a maid, he would assassinate Camille, her lover, and her mother, before committing suicide himself.[63] In this context, *Euphonia* reads as an even more exaggerated and dramatic revenge fantasy.

The fact that Berlioz should transform the pianist Camille into the singer Ellimac/Mina is significant, for it positions Mina at one extreme of a familiar dialectical framework. As we have already seen, *Euphonia* juxtaposes a composer-centred art music based in Germany against sensational florid and improvised vocal display originating in an Italian tradition. The juxtaposition coincides in Berlioz's narrative with an opposition based on gender. Gender dichotomies that extend an opposition between male and female to one between mind/body, or culture/nature (to name only two of the many oppositional pairings associated with gender), have an ancient pedigree in western thought, but the advent of the industrial revolution saw the dichotomy reinforced in particular ways. Conceptions of a passive, female nature (in both senses) reflected and sustained the interests of a capitalist, bourgeois society whose advances were often dependent on the fruits of rational scientific enquiry and exploration (or exploitation) of nature's resources.[64] In this context, technology was typically configured as masculine – as the product of rational enquiry, as the implement of industrial control over nature, or, on a symbolic level, as either an extension of the phallus or as a particularly male (rational, enduring) creation that contrasts with the female creation of fragile human life.[65]

In musical terms, the gendered dichotomy can be articulated in two slightly different ways. The mind/body pairing can be extended to the contrast between a composer-centred tradition and one centred in performance, as famously articulated by Dahlhaus in his explication of the 'twin styles'.[66] But the mind/body gender dichotomy can also be manifested in the role of technology, in the contrast between the mechanics of musical

---

[63] Berlioz, *Memoirs*, pp. 125–9.
[64] Sherry B. Ortner, *Making Gender: The Politics and Erotics of Culture* (Boston: Beacon Press, 1996); Ludmilla Jordanova, *Sexual Visions: Images of Gender in Science and Medicine between the Eighteenth and Twentieth Centuries* (Hemel Hempstead: Harvester Wheatsheaf, 1989); Jan Zimmerman (ed.), *The Technological Woman: Interfacing with Tomorrow* (New York: Praeger, 1983); Sandra Harding, *The Science Question in Feminism* (Ithaca, NY: Cornell University Press, 1986).
[65] Ortner, 'Is Female to Male as Nature Is to Culture?' (1972), in *Making Gender*, p. 29; Joan Rothschild, Introduction to *Machina ex Dea: Feminist Perspectives on Technology* (New York: Pergamon Press, 1983).
[66] Carl Dahlhaus, *Nineteenth-Century Music*, trans. J. Bradford Robinson (Berkeley: University of California Press, 1989), pp. 8–15.

instruments (created and controlled by the intellect) and 'embodied' vocal performance.[67]

By making Mina a singer rather than a pianist, Berlioz enables these two variants of the gender dichotomy to merge. On the one side is the male-authored composition, which both is mind-based and involves a mastery of technology to realise its vision. Although the Euphonians certainly sing, the only music we hear of them composing is instrumental music. In Euphonia the (male) composer is also the conductor, controlling the orchestral technology and the lives of the citizens, and the keyboard is presented, literally or metaphorically, as the instrument through which this control is exerted. It is a steam organ that regulates the working day, the conductor controls the orchestra like a pianist at the keyboard, and Shetland's performance on the 'piano-orchestre' sends Mina and her friends dancing to their deaths.

On the other side of this gendered bifurcation is the female-authored composition that derives from the physicality of vocal performance originating inside the body, as represented in *Euphonia* by Mina. When Shetland first encounters Mina she is appropriating his own symphony to her quite different practice, ornamenting it at whim. Her body is literally ornamented, like her music. Here we see not 'woman as nature', but 'woman (and especially woman's voice) as artifice' – a particular manifestation of the gender dichotomy that Felicia Miller Frank has traced in nineteenth-century French literature, where it reveals 'an emerging anxiety about the implications of an inhuman modernity'.[68] Mina initially appears to cast off the superficial adornment or artifice of her body and voice. But rather than becoming a voice of 'nature' (in the more comfortable manifestation of femininity of the idealised gender dichotomy),[69] her body and gender are rendered more ambiguous. Both men fall prey to her charms when seeing her as disembodied – as air. Xilef nicknames her 'Ariel' after the ethereal spirit

---

[67] On the association of musical instruments with masculinity see, for example, Ellen Koskoff, 'When Women Play: The Relationship between Musical Instruments and Gender Style', *Intersections* 16/1 (1995), 114–27; Veronica Doubleday, 'Sounds of Power: An Overview of Musical Instruments and Gender', *Ethnomusicology Forum* 17/1 (2008), 3–39. On the technology of the orchestra as masculine, see also Ruth Solie, Introduction to *Musicology and Difference: Gender and Sexuality in Music Scholarship* (Berkeley: University of California Press, 1993), p. 12.

[68] Felicia Miller Frank, *The Mechanical Song: Women, Voice, and the Artificial in Nineteenth-Century French Narrative* (Stanford: Stanford University Press, 1995), p. 7. On the anxieties around artifice in female song, see also Hadlock, *Mad Loves*.

[69] For a manifestation of the idealised woman/nature relationship in nineteenth-century Italian opera, see Emanuele Senici, *Landscape and Gender in Italian Opera : The Alpine Virgin from Bellini to Puccini* (New York: Cambridge University Press, 2005).

of *The Tempest*, thus simultaneously also jeopardising Mina's gender, for Ariel is a male character, though typically played as a trouser role at this time.[70] 'There is no Nadira any more; it is I; no Shetland: it is she', Shetland proclaims rapturously after declaring his love.[71] However, this promise of the ultimate union of performer and composer is illusory. When Shetland proposes to his Nadira that they commit suicide together, to free their souls from their bodies and take their relationship beyond the physical world, Mina politely declines, to which Shetland responds, 'Oh, Nadira, you are a mere woman after all!'[72]

The one time Mina does seem to speak through an external instrument, the incident is marked as uncanny. When Shetland's first encounter with Mina and her music threatens to seduce him from his tranquillity, the composer exposes his Aeolian harp to the wind, perhaps hoping to hear music free of human agency that will erase Mina's voice from his consciousness. Instead, the harp produces the opening bars of his own symphony, which Mina had sung to him in the balloon, and when he opens his eyes he finds the woman herself standing before him, as if her seductive spirit has possessed the wind harp – normally the ultimate Romantic instrument because of its inherent erasure of human agency – and the harp's music in turn summons her body.[73]

Mina's voice is indeed hard to contain. The musical automata that were so popular in the late eighteenth century and in the first decades of the nineteenth century demonstrated how resistant the human voice was, in an age before sound recording, to being reproduced, imitated, or controlled by technology. While there were a number of popular keyboard automata, there were few automata that successfully captured the voice.[74] A rare exception was Joseph Faber's speaking automaton, exhibited in New York in 1844 – the same year Berlioz conceived *Euphonia*. The automaton went through several incarnations. One of these was a disembodied female head that appeared to

---

[70] 'Ariel' was also Berlioz's nickname for Camille at the height of their affair.
[71] Berlioz, *Evenings with the Orchestra*, p. 281.   [72] Ibid., p. 282.
[73] On the Romantic symbolism of the Aeolian harp, see Thomas L. Hankins and Robert J. Silverman, *Instruments and the Imagination* (Princeton, NJ: Princeton University Press, 1995), pp. 86–112.
[74] Joachim Gessinger, *Auge und Ohr: Studien zur Erforschung der Sprache am Menschen 1700–1850* (Berlin: Walter de Gruyter, 1994); Hankins and Silverman, *Instruments and the Imagination*, pp. 178–220; Steven Connor, *Dumbstruck: A Cultural History of Ventriloquism* (Oxford: Oxford University Press, 2000); Carolyn Abbate, *In Search of Opera* (Princeton, NJ: Princeton University Press, 2001), pp. 201–2; Jessica Riskin, 'Eighteenth-Century Wetware', *Representations* 83/1 (2003), 97–125.

Fig. 4.2 Faber's 'Euphonia' automaton. Reproduction courtesy of Circus World Museum, Baraboo, Wisconsin.

speak when operated by a keyboard (Fig. 4.2).[75] Faber's automaton captures some of the same ideal as Berlioz's *Euphonia*. The woman's body is erased, her voice produced and controlled by the 'composer' (male in this picture at least) operating the technology of the keyboard. When he took Faber's creation to London in 1846, P.T. Barnum actually named the automaton 'Euphonia' – a striking, if probably coincidental, token of the ideological resemblance the automaton shares with Berlioz's story.[76]

'This bedevilled mechanism': Agency and the machine

The 'Euphonia' automaton represents an ideal for Berlioz's futuristic city of the same name, but it is an ideal that Mina resists. Whereas the orchestra

[75] Hankins and Silverman, *Instruments and the Imagination*, pp. 214–19; Connor, *Dumbstruck*, pp. 354–6; Riskin 'Eighteenth-Century Wetware', pp. 107–8; Gessinger, *Auge und Ohr*, pp. 627–9.
[76] Did Berlioz know of Barnum's 'Euphonia' automaton? Certainly he was familiar with other acts promoted by Barnum, two of whom feature in stories in *Evenings with the Orchestra*: Tom Thumb (pp. 184–6); and Jenny Lind, the 'Swedish nightingale', whom Berlioz describes as having been caged for a few months by 'Mr Barnum, the clever bird-catcher' (p. 101).

players of Euphonia are members of a machine controlled by the composer/conductor, Mina does not cede control of her body to anyone. Mina ultimately refuses to allow others to speak or sing through her, driving Xilef to stifle her voice and absorb her body into the machine by force just when she is at her most physical in a dance with her lovers. The horrific excess of Berlioz's description of Mina's demise warns of the dangers that attend the Euphonians' suppression of individual agency and the sacrifice of human physicality.

Another story published in *Evenings with the Orchestra* enforces the sense of anxiety around loss of agency. In 'The piano possessed', thirty-one competitors in a piano competition play the same concerto (Mendelssohn's Concerto no. 1 in G minor op. 25) on the same piano, one after the other. The piano's mechanism gradually loosens as pianist after pianist beats out the work, until it is realised that the piano is actually playing the work unaided. Its keys have become so accustomed to the patterns of the concerto that they depress themselves, like those of an automaton. The human performer is erased, for the instrument has learnt 'the work', not one individual's interpretation of it. Again, there is something fearful in Berlioz's account of what might have seemed to be a composer's ideal:

> M. Erard arrives; but try as he will, the piano, which is out of its mind, has no intention of minding him either. He sends for holy water and sprinkles the keyboard with it – in vain: proof that it wasn't witchcraft, but the natural result of thirty performances of one concerto. They take the instrument and remove the keyboard, still moving up and down, and throw it into the middle of the courtyard next to the Warehouse. There M. Erard in a fury has it chopped up with an ax. You think that did it? It made matters worse: each piece danced, jumped, frisked about separately – on the paving stones, between our legs, against the wall, in all directions, until the locksmith of the Warehouse picked up this bedeviled mechanism in one armful and flung it into the fire of his forge to put an end to it. Poor M. Erard! Such a fine instrument! We were heartbroken, but what could we do? There was no other way to loose its grip. But after all, how can a piano hear a concerto thirty times in the same hall on the same day without contracting the habit of it? M. Mendelssohn won't be able to complain that his music isn't being played. But think of the damage![77]

Berlioz's narrative conveys the unease that was increasingly felt around mechanical automisation, musical automata and other sound-producing machines, in an age where admiration of the order and control brought about by the 'horological revolution', and symbolised by the image of God

---

[77] Berlioz, *Evenings with the Orchestra*, pp. 218–19.

as watchmaker, was typically replaced by a resistance to, or fear of, automisation, which was now frequently associated with the Devil.[78] As Carolyn Abbate points out, from the late eighteenth century onwards, the wonderment incited by musical automata became infused with anxiety around the question of human agency. If a machine might simulate human performance, the human performer could also appear machine-like, possessed by the composer's work; and in mechanisms such as the player piano (which Berlioz's story seems to anticipate),[79] the erasure of the human body and the fact that the work was somehow part of the mechanism itself were often felt to be uncanny.[80] Berlioz's *Euphonia* and his story of the piano possessed are similar in tone to those tales of E.T.A. Hoffmann which treat the subject of automata and musical performance. The measures taken to silence the demonic piano are also reminiscent of the apprentice's attempt to control his broom in Goethe's *Zauberlehrling*. In turning now to *La damnation de Faust*, we encounter another work by Goethe. However, here the machine is not found in the text but is the creation of Berlioz's music itself. In the previous chapter we encountered the anxiety arising from the uncanny disembodiment of technology which lay behind the supernatural applications of telegraph technology. In reexamining this anxiety here, our concern is with the implications not only for orchestral technology, but also for the body of the (female) singer.

La damnation de Faust

As Hugh Macdonald writes, Berlioz conceived *La damnation de Faust* to the 'rattling of iron wheels on iron rails'.[81] Berlioz himself tells us that he composed *Faust* 'where and when I could, in carriages, in trains, on steamboats'. Moreover, the composition of the work was interrupted so that Berlioz could fulfil the commission for the 'Chant des chemins de fer' written to celebrate the opening of the new train line to Lille. While the setting of *La damnation de Faust* can be assumed to be the sixteenth century of the

---

[78] Samuel L. Macey, 'The Clockwork Devil: A Romantic Reaction to Clockwork and Clockwork Automata', *Clocks and the Cosmos: Time in Western Life and Thought* (Hamden, CT: Archon Books, 1980), pp. 203–24.

[79] Indeed, later in the century, 'Euphonia' was the name of a brand of player pianos.

[80] Abbate, *In Search of Opera*, pp. 194–213. See also Jane Goodall, 'Transferred Agencies: Performance and the Fear of Automatism', *Theatre Journal* 49/4 (1997), 441–53; Connor, *Dumbstruck*, pp. 340–41; Miller Frank, *Mechanical Song*.

[81] Hugh Macdonald, 'Berlioz Takes the Train' in Matthias Brzoska, Hermann Hofer, and Nicole Strohmann (eds.), *Hector Berlioz: Ein Franzose in Deutschland* (Laaber: Laaber Verlag, 2005), p. 238.

story's origins, and thus far removed from the explicitly futuristic world of *Euphonia*, the 'rattle' of modernity that sounded around the conception of Berlioz's *Faust* resounds in this work also.

One movement known to have been at least partially noted down on a train is the 'Choeur d'étudiants et de soldats', the account of whose conception echoes several concepts from *Euphonia* as well as anticipating themes from *La damnation de Faust* as a whole. Suffering from ennui one Sunday in Paris, Berlioz decides to visit Heinrich Heine to shake his hand for his 'devil of a work', *Atta Troll*, though he fears thereby 'receiving an electric shock and injuring myself with [Heine's] iron grip'.[82] En route to Heine's residence, Berlioz encounters a military platoon, followed by a group of friars. Mentally replacing the friars with students, he finds his thoughts redirected to the 'espèce d'opéra' on *Faust* that he has been working on, and so preoccupied is he with pursuing the musical ideas that are now coming to him that he follows the crowd to the Gare du Nord and boards a train to Enghien. After arriving in Enghien, his music safely committed to paper, Berlioz witnesses an extravagant elopement by balloon – an 'enormous balloon of the power of thirty-seven horses' that flies away 'at a speed of fifteen leagues an hour'.[83] This and other less dramatic events fulfil all the elements of a prophecy for the year 1846 that had appeared in the popular Mathieu Laensberg almanac of predictions, thus supposedly instilling in Berlioz a new faith in this irrational art. The potent mixture in this one article of balloon travel and train travel, predictions of the future, devilish poems, and Faust suggests a nebulous sympathy between the concerns of *Euphonia* and *La damnation de Faust*.

The chorus that was the most direct musical outcome of the events Berlioz describes itself supports a reading of *La damnation* that is at least sensitive to the technology of urbanisation. The soldiers enter first, singing in B flat major, 6/8 time. They are followed by a Latin chorus from the students in an archaic monodic D minor in 2/4. As the two groups approach each other their musics similarly merge, resulting in a bitonal and bimetric though wholly consonant polyphony that is one of Berlioz's more extreme examples of his favourite 'réunion des thèmes' (Ex. 4.1.).

Various paradigms for this form of musical simultaneity have already been proposed, including the synchronised images of the thaumatrope. But was Berlioz also partly inspired by the railway that had witnessed the birth of the students' song? The simultaneous presentation of two quite different tonal and metrical worlds suggests something of the dual consciousness of

[82] *CM* VI, p. 220.   [83] Ibid., pp. 223–4.

'This bedevilled mechanism': Agency and the machine

Ex. 4.1 *La damnation de Faust,* 'Choeur d'étudiants et de soldats', bb. 132–49

the train journey (the worlds inside and outside the carriage), as well as the technology of the telegraph that enabled space to be erased and two remote spatial worlds to be experienced simultaneously. Stephen Kern has suggested that the experience of simultaneity, enabled by technology and

Ex. 4.1 (*cont.*)

characteristic of modernity more broadly, is reflected in bitonal or bimetric music of the turn of the twentieth century.[84] But Berlioz's music may enable us to trace this association between technology and simultaneity back several decades earlier. And while similar examples can be found in other works by Berlioz, such as *Harold en Italie* and *Symphonie fantastique*, in *La damnation de Faust* he himself, in his account of the work's conception, gives us grounds to connect the experience of simultaneity directly to the erasure of time and space characteristic of the railway – in this instance the train to Enghien that witnessed this music's birth:

> Still mumbling my *gaudeamus* I got into the train and it left. But as the movement of the locomotive beat out a rhythm quite different from the one that had been battering my brain a few minutes before, I could see that I was going to forget my song. I quickly wrote it down in my notebook, and after a difficult confinement I fell asleep.[85]

La damnation de Faust as a whole suggests the 'industrialization of time and space' characteristic both of early train travel and of the balloon travel and visual telegraph of *Euphonia*. Berlioz places his Faust in Hungary at the opening of the work, to give himself an excuse to incorporate his setting of the 'Rákóczy March' of that country. At least one German critic objected

---

[84] Stephen Kern, *The Culture of Time and Space 1880–1918* (Cambridge, MA: Harvard University Press, 1983), p. 75.
[85] Berlioz, 'Parc d'Enghien'. Translated in Macdonald, 'Berlioz Takes the Train', p. 239.

to this addition, which Berlioz justified on the grounds that 'the most eccentric travels may be attributed to such a personage as Faust without transgressing the bounds of possibility'.[86] Between the first and second parts Berlioz returns Faust to Germany at an anachronistically rapid speed – anachronistic, that is, for the historical Faust, but not necessarily for Berlioz, as the spreading tracks of the steam train facilitated rapid travel across increasing stretches of Europe.

Dialectics of genre

Berlioz's apparent disregard for geographical authenticity is made easier by his choice of genre, for his Faust is not bound to the operatic stage, with its attendant concerns for scenic realism and the practical difficulties arising from copious set changes.[87] Although eight numbers of *La damnation de Faust* originated in the late 1820s as a sort of independent incidental music, the completed work was never intended to be staged.[88] *La damnation de Faust* was written for concert performance. '[I]t is a grand opera without action, costumes or scenery', Berlioz wrote to Baron Taylor. Elsewhere he explained, 'it is not a symphony but a *légende dramatique* – a concert opera.'[89] The genre is ultimately ambiguous, freely mixing elements of opera with writing more suggestive of a dramatic symphony. While Berlioz's 'dramatic symphonies' themselves mix elements that could be loosely described as operatic with those more traditionally ascribed to the symphony, his employment of the operatic dimension in *La damnation de Faust* is more extensive. He at one time described the work as an 'espèce d'opéra', but he never referred to it as an 'espèce de symphonie', nor did he include it in his symphonic sequence. Moreover, it is significant that out of all of Berlioz's works written for concert performance, it is *La damnation de Faust* that has most frequently lent itself to visual realisation, through stagings that

---

[86] Berlioz, *Memoirs*, p. 419.
[87] Kolb Reeve comments on how both Goethe's *Faust* and Berlioz's treatment thereof 'go well beyond the norms of dramatic convention' and 'are problematic to stage, their free-wheeling use of time and space demanding imaginative leaps that a pre-cinematic *mise-en-scène* can only partially fulfil'. 'Perils of Heroism', p. 153. On the French desire to avoid scene changes within acts, see Rebecca Harris-Warrick, 'Lucia Goes to Paris: A Tale of Three Theatres', in Annegret Fauser and Mark Everist (eds.), *Music, Theater, and Cultural Transfer* (Chicago: University of Chicago Press, 2009), pp. 205–6 and n. 16.
[88] Berlioz provided the preceding and, in some cases, also the following lines from Goethe's play in his score.
[89] *CG* VIII, p. 265; *CG* V, p. 360.

inevitably evoke opera. In *La damnation de Faust*, more perhaps than in any other nonoperatic work, Berlioz sets up operatic expectations; but while these expectations are crucial to *La damnation*, it is partly through the way he *challenges* these expectations that the drama is realised, and it is here that a comparison with *Euphonia* is particularly illuminating.

The generic ambiguity of *La damnation de Faust* is strongly reminiscent of *Euphonia*, with its mixture of epistolary form, dramatic script, treatise, and novel. Moreover, the way in which Berlioz employs the different idioms in *La damnation de Faust* raises some of the same questions around gender and the body. Just as *Euphonia* builds towards the sacrifice of the female body and its excessive vocal display, *Faust*, as originally conceived, seems to erase the physical dimension of opera. There is dance music but no dancing, no costumes – in other words, all the things Berlioz describes as distracting the Italians from the music are removed from *La damnation de Faust*. This much is also true of *Roméo et Juliette*, for example, but in *La damnation de Faust* to a much greater extent than in the dramatic symphony, the central female character is set up as an operatic body, only to be erased. Marguerite, the only female character in Berlioz's pared-down text, is absent from two-thirds of *La damnation de Faust*, but when she does arrive she brings with her the most 'operatic' music in Berlioz's score.

The operatic nature of Marguerite's idiom needs to be seen in relation to the quite different idiom of Faust. Berlioz commented in his Foreword to *Roméo et Juliette* that he was trusting the parts of the eponymous lovers to the orchestra rather than singers because the work was a symphony and not an opera, because operatic lovers were numerous and he wished to be original, and because instrumental music allowed the greater freedom necessary to express this sublime love.[90] Faust, in contrast, is given a voice and text. However, his music is in many respects similarly 'symphonic'. Shunning the familiar forms of operatic set pieces, Faust's music unfolds in sections that are through-composed and lacking in the display of the typical tenor hero (ridiculed elsewhere by Berlioz in his account of 'How a tenor revolves around the public').[91] Faust is introduced to us as a voice within the orchestral polyphony (Ex. 4.2). He enters after just a few bars of introduction, effectively stating his place in what would usually be the orchestral prelude, and indeed, the orchestra takes over again shortly in a free-flowing development of the opening theme.[92]

[90] *NBE* vol. 18, p. 2. [91] Berlioz, *Evenings with the Orchestra*, pp. 64–74.
[92] Katharine Kolb Reeve offers a powerful analysis of this opening number and what it reveals of Faust's character in 'Perils of Heroism'. See also Gérard Condé, 'Commentaire musicale', *La Damnation de Faust, L'Avant Scène Opéra* vol. 22 (Paris : L'Avant Scène, 1995), p. 15.

Dialectics of genre 221

Ex. 4.2 *La damnation de Faust*, opening, bb. 1–22

In contrast with Faust's, Marguerite's idiom is more easily reconciled with opera, as has been noted by Rushton and Kolb, among others.[93] Marguerite's main numbers, inherited from the earlier *Huit scènes de Faust*, are closed forms. Moreover, she is introduced by that most operatic of idioms, a stage song: Marguerite's 'Le roi de Thulé' is framed as a diegetic song by

[93] Rushton, *The Music of Berlioz*, p. 309. Kolb Reeve, 'Perils of Heroism', p. 170.

Goethe. In placing it in *La damnation de Faust*, Berlioz further enhances the number's diegetic, dramatic, or performed nature by giving Marguerite an onstage audience, albeit one to whose existence she is oblivious. Whereas in Goethe's work both Faust and Mephistopheles leave the stage before Gretchen sings, Berlioz's stage directions have Faust conceal himself and listen to Marguerite's performance. Berlioz also marks the language of the song as performance by infusing it with altered scale degrees to suggest the foreignness of this 'Chanson gothique' to the prevalent musical idiom (Ex. 4.3).

Interestingly, the distinctive melody of 'Le roi de Thulé' is anticipated not only by the solo viola within the number itself, but also before Marguerite's appearance, in one of several instances in *La damnation de Faust* where Berlioz features recurring melodies. 'Je l'entends' ['I hear her'], Méphistophélès tells Faust in Scène X, as the melody of 'Le roi de Thulé' sounds in the clarinet. Marguerite may be the most operatic of the characters, but in this way she, too, emerges from the orchestra as sound rather than sight. The fact that the distinctive augmented fourth of 'Le roi de Thulé' is the tritone that characterises Méphistophélès, and that he here seems to conjure her forth, is also an ominous sign of things to come.

As Faust moves closer to consummating his relationship with Marguerite, he is drawn into her more operatic idiom in what Rushton calls the 'Italian formal solidity' of the duet and its 'egregiously operatic' trio.[94] The dialectic of genre is then resumed with Marguerite's final solo number, the 'Romance'; but the stylistic interplay is complicated and intensified. Though often set as a song, Goethe's 'Meine Ruh' ist hin' is, in the context of his play, more ambiguous as to whether it is a performed stage song or spoken reflection.[95] Berlioz leaves the question open. There is no onstage audience – the number is specifically designated 'Marguerite seule' – and Marguerite's impassioned expression shuns any question of conscious spectacle or performance. But even if not stage song, the relatively operatic nature of Marguerite's 'Romance' is apparent. The form is again a closed one, with several returns of the opening music forming a refrain separating three couplets.[96] In the third of these couplets, Berlioz makes us fully aware of

---

[94] Rushton, *The Music of Berlioz*, p. 310; 'Genre', *Cambridge Companion to Berlioz*, p. 50.

[95] Cyrus Hamlin suggests that '[d]espite frequent musical settings for Gretchen's monologue at the spinning wheel (notably by Schubert), she apparently speaks the lines of this scene.' Goethe, *Faust: A Tragedy; An Authoritative Translation*, trans. Walter Arndt, ed. Cyrus Hamlin (New York: Norton, 2001), p. 94 n. 1.

[96] See Condé for a detailed account of the form of the 'Romance': 'Commentaire musicale', in *La damnation de Faust*, p. 48.

Ex. 4.3 *La damnation de Faust*, 'Le roi de Thulé: Chanson gothique', bb. 9–26

Ex. 4.4 *La damnation de Faust*, Marguerite's 'Romance', bb. 87–95

Marguerite's physical body – an element of operatic spectacle – when he has the singer literally panting with her unfulfilled desire (Ex. 4.4). Marguerite's more operatic quality is again highlighted by comparison with Faust: his 'Nature immense', which immediately follows, is another free-flowing form and his line is once more part of the orchestral polyphony.[97]

Through his manipulation of form and idiom, Berlioz thus establishes pronounced differences between Marguerite and Faust. These differences are strongly suggestive of the play of genres in *Euphonia*. Where Xilef and Shetland are introduced in epistolary mode, communicating directly to each other (and to the reader), Mina is presented in a dramatic idiom, like a character in a play whom we watch from the audience. Mina's physicality, like that of Marguerite, is something to which Berlioz draws our attention – and something for which she will ultimately be punished.

To say that Marguerite's operatic idiom creates an analogy with Mina is certainly not to imply that Berlioz saw opera *per se* as antithetical to his ideals. His own stage works testify powerfully to the contrary, as does *Euphonia* itself, for the crowning event in the calendar of the 'musical city' is, after all, a festival that stages Gluck's operatic works. While Berlioz may have seen in Gluck a model for a composer-centred conception of opera, he nevertheless embraced the physical and visual aspects of the staging through which these works were realised. He may have looked at the score during many an operatic performance, but that is not to say that he did not also spare a glance for the stage and, indeed, in the same letter in which he tells Nanci of the orchestral evocation of the spirits that haunt Orestes (cited in the previous chapter), Berlioz also points out the powerful impact of the spectacle on the stage: 'The illusion is perfect', he writes of the visual realisation of the storm, later adding, 'you have to see it to believe it.'[98] Moreover, in identifying the qualities that constitute the ideal singer for Gluck's music, Berlioz repeatedly refers to the importance of physical gesture and expression.[99]

It might also be objected that Marguerite is altogether a far more sympathetic character than Mina, and our sympathy is none the weaker for the fact

---

[97] Ibid., p. 48. [98] *CG* I, p. 36.
[99] Thus, for example, he admired Alexandine Branchu, 'a tragic actress of the first rank', for 'the naturalness of her attitudes, the energetic truth of her gestures, and the fire in her eyes' – Berlioz, *Evenings with the Orchestra*, pp. 165, 144; and he praised Pauline Viardot's incarnation of Gluck's Orphée and Alceste in the 1850s: 'Her gestures are sober, as noble as they are true, and the expressive quality of her features, always powerful, is even more so in the mute scenes than when called on to heighten the nuances of the vocal part.' Berlioz, 'Gluck's *Orphée*', in *The Art of Music*, pp. 77–8.

that she is ultimately viewed by us through Faust's eyes. In fact, the operatic nature of Marguerite's idiom facilitates this sympathy. *La damnation de Faust* draws on *Euphonia*'s dichotomy between opera and symphony – a kind of 'rhetoric of meta-genre', to adapt Kallberg's expression – as an integral part of its narrative.[100] This narrative has other resemblances to *Euphonia*, but to understand this we must first examine the position of the third character, Méphistophélès, in the operatic–symphonic spectrum of Berlioz's *légende dramatique*.

Like Marguerite, Méphistophélès is characterised through prominent use of stage song, but whereas Marguerite's diegetic song frames her as powerfully emotive operatic spectacle for Faust (and for us), Méphistophélès's diegetic idioms have almost the opposite effect. Granted, his idiom, like that of Marguerite, could be described as 'operatic', and we might thus interpret the fundamental opposition of the work to be not one of gender, but rather, of a contrast between Faust, on one hand, and Marguerite and Méphistopheles, on the other. However, while Marguerite and Méphistopheles share an operatic idiom, their positions within the diegesis are also distinctly contrasted. In the language of film studies, whereas Marguerite typically receives 'the gaze', being the object we are encouraged to admire, Méphistopheles directs it, as a powerful masculine subject.[101] Aware of his music *as music*, Méphistophélès at times seems almost to step out of the diegesis and take on the role of conductor – a role associated with mesmeric control, particularly over vulnerable female subjects.[102] For example, in the bars before Méphistophélès's 'Sérénade', Berlioz leaves stage directions suggesting that the singer should make the gesture of playing a hurdy-gurdy as he tells the will-o-the-wisps and fiddlers to accompany him in a song to damn Marguerite. Many of Berlioz's stage directions appear to be for the benefit of the reader alone, but even if the singer does not follow Berlioz's instructions here, the *orchestra* embodies the same message. In the 'Sérénade' itself we see how Méphistophélès controls the strings, which are transformed, aurally and perhaps also visually, into guitars as Berlioz specifies that they should be strummed with the thumb. The extremely awkward arpeggios assigned to the second violins and violas force the strings – described by Berlioz as the 'faithful servants' of the orchestra, and often associated elsewhere in

---

[100] Jeffrey Kallberg, 'The Rhetoric of Genre: Chopin's Nocturne in G Minor', *19th Century Music* 11/3 (1988), 238–61.
[101] Laura Mulvey, 'Visual Pleasure and Narrative Cinema', *Screen* 16/3 (1975), 6–18.
[102] Winter, *Mesmerized*, pp. 101, 204–5, 309–20.

Ex. 4.5 *La damnation de Faust*, 'Sérénade de Méphistophélès', bb. 1–10

the score with Faust – into cruel distortions to do Méphistophélès's will (Ex. 4.5).[103]

Méphistophélès's control over the orchestral forces might also be seen in the earlier 'Évocation', where the devil first summons the

---

[103] Macdonald points to even more awkward arpeggios for the second violins later in this number. See *Berlioz's Orchestration Treatise*, p. 14.

Ex. 4.6 *La damnation de Faust*, 'Évocation', bb. 41–5

will-o'-the-wisps and then calls on them to perform a dance around Marguerite's house. Here (in Ex. 4.6) the first and second violin sections are at one point each divided to enable them to render a single line between them. This device, familiar from *Symphonie fantastique*, is suggestive not only of the stereoscope's binocularity, but also of the industrialisation of labour where players are forced to function as 'parts in a great machine, not as voices in a choir'.[104] It is the same division of labour also seen in Euphonia, and like the orchestral players of Euphonia, the musicians in *Damnation* can thus be compared to individual keys on the keyboard manipulated by the composer/conductor, who is the only one who can appreciate and control the whole.

'Évocation' is also interesting for its treatment of the brass instruments which characterise Méphistophélès throughout the work. The opening has been much remarked upon for its suggestions of atonality, but equally indicative of Méphistophélès's unnatural powers is the rough stopped d' of the natural horn (marked 'son bouché'). This was a note Berlioz suggested should only be used when a 'harsh, muffled, savage' sound was required.[105]

---

[104] Ibid., pp. xxx–xxxi.   [105] Ibid., p. 170.

Berlioz's employment of the stopped notes characteristic of the natural horn, at a time when the increasingly popular chromatic horns were rendering stopped notes unnecessary, could seem to indicate resistance to technology rather than mastery of it, and we might recall that in *Euphonia* it is the crass Italian orchestra that embraces chromatic brass. However, as with the stopped notes of *La nonne sanglante*, Berlioz's use in 'Évocation' of this most unpleasant note is doubtless wholly intentional, and the suggestion of a 'natural' instrument being forced to strain against its own limitations is entirely appropriate to the effect Méphistophélès has on those around him. An even greater distortion is demanded in the uncanny hunting horn calls that underpin Faust's and Méphistophélès's 'Récitatif et chasse', as Méphistophélès closes in on Faust's soul. In a rehearsal one of the horn players supposedly told Berlioz he had written a note 'which does not exist', describing it as 'a sort of sneeze like nothing on earth, an impossible din', to which Berlioz replied 'that is exactly what I wanted'.[106] Once again, player discomfort is scripted into the music – not simply overlooked in favour of the composer's vision, but an inherent part of the work.

'La course à l'abîme', which follows the recitative just mentioned, brings together the three strands of technology, driving them forward to a conclusion every bit as disturbing as the end of *Euphonia*. To save Marguerite from execution, Faust signs away his soul, promising to serve Méphistophélès tomorrow because, as he says, 'que me fait demain quand je souffre à cette heure?' ['What is tomorrow to me when I am suffering right now?'] Méphistophélès summons two demonic horses to hurtle them across time and space – for it is not to Marguerite's prison cell that they ride, but straight to hell. 'Tomorrow' seems to arrive almost instantly, the orchestral 'horsepower' driving the riders at a pace more like that of the steam train than any genuine equine transport. We are aware of the journey, but the pace feels frantic, perilous both to passengers and to those who stray across their tracks, as the travellers plough at a constant pace across (or through?) the 'mountains' specified in the scenic directions in Berlioz's score.

In Berlioz's time, train passengers were locked into their cabins as they were propelled at speeds that were initially considered dangerous to the human body, and occasionally they, too, were consigned to a fiery death. In 1842 France experienced a horrific train accident where more than fifty people – including Dumont d'Urville – lost their lives in a conflagration after a train travelling from Versailles to Paris left the tracks and caught fire. Berlioz was among those shaken by the news of the accident, and even

---

[106] Cited by Julian Rushton in *NBE*, vol. 8b, p. 459.

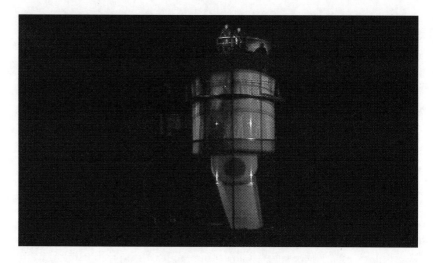

Fig. 4.3 Scene from 'Course à l'abîme', Salzburg Festspiel 1999, dir. Alex Olle and Carlos Padrissa. DVD available from Arthaus Musik.

four years later, when writing 'La course à l'abîme', his writings reveal that derailment was still a persistent fear.[107]

Did he draw on this fear in 'La course à l'abîme' itself? The relentless string ostinato that persists through most of the movement obviously suggests the pounding of the horses' hooves, but there is a mechanical aspect to its manically driving repetition as well. The bizarre growls from the brass instruments and screeches from the wind clearly evoke the hideous monsters and nighthawks of Berlioz's text. But might they also suggest the sounds of a steam train? (Ex. 4.7). Such an interpretation is doubtless too literal, but the scene does appear to carry a certain 'industrial' quality for at least some listeners. The directors of the 1999 Salzburg Festival production interpret the motion of 'La course à l'abîme' with technological allusions, projecting onto a massive cylinder images of automaton horses, multiplying like the dissected Erard piano of Berlioz's story, as well as images of a giant piston – a component not only of the developing technology of the orchestral brass, but also of the steam train (Fig. 4.3).

A staging of this scene almost *demands* an imaginative use of technology, as Berlioz himself acknowledged. In 1847 Berlioz sought to adapt *La damnation de Faust* as an opera for London. Aware that the spectacle of 'La course à l'abîme' would appear particularly difficult to realise

---

[107] *CG* III, p. 310; and Berlioz, *Musical Madhouse*, pp. 179–82.

literally, he assured Scribe, his intended librettist, 'The scene with the horses [...] won't scare the London stage hands [*machinistes*] and I believe they will be able to represent it in a very ingenious and dramatic fashion.'[108] Even without visual aids, an audience encountering the work in concert performance may still experience the fascinations and fears of technology. To obtain the wind and brass effects, Berlioz adopted recent developments in the manufacture of these instruments to push the bassoon, trombone, and ophicleide to the very bottom of their respective registers and produce colours that would have sounded unexpected or 'unworldly'.

Seeing the future: Genre and staging

In arguing that metaphors for modernity underpin Meyerbeer's operas, Newark points to the prominent visual display of instrumental technology on the stage. In *La damnation de Faust*, *all* instruments are effectively onstage instruments. In this context, instrumental technology could be foregrounded to such an extent that it might, paradoxically, become invisible, taken for granted or sublimated into the abstractions of the symphonic ideal. However, as my discussion of *Symphonie fantastique* has already demonstrated, being sensitive to the sights of Berlioz's instrumental music can yield interesting results. Rather than eschewing the visual dimension of opera and its instrumental technology, I would argue in *La damnation de Faust* Berlioz reworks that visual dimension into the experience of the work, and the fact that *La damnation de Faust* is not an opera intensifies rather than weakens the impact of the technological display.

When we watch a concert performance of Berlioz's work, as he intended, we are encouraged to *see* a mechanical quality to his nightmarish vision. The guitar hold for the strings in Méphistophélès's 'Sérénade' may be as much for visual effect as practical benefit, enabling an audience to see how Méphistophélès challenges the boundary between the diegetic and nondiegetic dimensions. And the galloping string figure of 'La course à l'abîme' forces the bows into a pistonlike motion. Berlioz was certainly capable of thinking in such terms, and some years earlier had written of Liszt's *staccato* that it sounded as if it was produced 'at the nut of the bow on a fine double bass *by a steam engine* – because I can imagine no human arm

[108] *CG* III, pp. 466–7.

[...] that would be capable of such incredible agility'.[109] Moreover, writing about the Festival de l'industrie in July 1844, Berlioz praised the strength of the string section of the Conservatoire orchestra, 'formed in the same school, having the same style, the same mechanism, in such a way that you could say that the violin, viola, cello and double bass parts are each played as if by a single artist who uses his powerful bow to set a gigantic instrument vibrating'. Strengthening the mechanical association of the strings, he then describes the concert he arranged to display Parisian orchestral forces in the 'salle des machines' at the exhibition.[110]

In watching a concert performance today, we are also particularly conscious of the suppression of Marguerite's voice, for the singer remains seated silently on the stage for more than twenty minutes after her final number.[111] There is no church or prison scene, as audiences familiar with Goethe's work might have expected, and as Gounod would later provide in his quintessentially operatic treatment. By the beginning of 'La course à l'abîme', Marguerite's voice has long since fallen silent; now it is replaced with a plaintive oboe melody (as seen in Exx. 4.7 and 4.8). Just as Mina's dramatic idiom in *Euphonia* gives way to the narrative of an omniscient narrator, Marguerite has moved from an independent operatic voice (albeit one that is itself anticipated by the orchestra when the clarinet sounds her 'Le roi de Thulé' melody) to one that emanates from within the orchestra. Of course, there is nothing inherently sinister or gendered in the notion of a character whose voice is embodied by the orchestra, as Berlioz's treatment of *Roméo et Juliette* attests. What distinguishes *La damnation de Faust* from that work, however, is the fact that Berlioz's Marguerite, unlike his Juliette (or Roméo), does have a physical presence, and her eventual instrumental idiom comes at the expense of the sacrifice both of that body, and of the operatic idiom with which it has been associated. In the final scene, in heaven, Marguerite is no more than a name intoned by an unspecified 'voice' as the chorus of 'celestial spirits' tell her to leave behind the earthly love that led her astray and put on

---

[109] Berlioz, *Journal des Débats* 12 June 1836; quoted and translated in Cécile Reynaud, 'Berlioz, Liszt, and the Question of Virtuosity', in Peter Bloom (ed.), *Berlioz: Past, Present, Future* (Rochester, NY: University of Rochester Press, 2003), p. 116.

[110] *CM* 5, p. 517.

[111] Whether the soloist in Berlioz's time would have remained on the stage after the conclusion of her part, as Anne Sofie von Otter does in her performance with the Chicago Symphony Orchestra and Chorus (cond. Solti, 1989), is difficult to establish. In his orchestration treatise Berlioz suggests that singers should clear the stage when they are no longer needed, in order not to interfere with the projection of the orchestra; but he is referring specifically to the chorus (which in *La damnation de Faust* is required until the end of the work), and Marguerite's body alone provides little acoustic obstacle for the orchestra. See Macdonald, *Berlioz's Orchestration Treatise*, p. 359.

Seeing the future: Genre and staging

Ex. 4.7 *La damnation de Faust*, 'La course à l'abîme', bb. 1–16

again the 'pristine beauty' which has been 'marred' by her error ('âme naïve que l'amour égara; Viens revêtir ta beauté primitive qu'une erreur altéra'). As Katharine Kolb points out, there is something uncomfortable about this conclusion, which, like the ending of *Euphonia*, positions women's physicality and sensuality as a problem, and offers instead the disembodied 'eternal feminine' as the ideal.[112] Marguerite, rather than Mina, seems to represent the erasure of body of Faber's Euphonia automaton. She is denied the physicality of opera and instead reduced to voice, confined to the orchestra, and then silenced altogether. Interestingly, the oboe melody that has been taken to represent Marguerite's voice fades away precisely when Méphistophélès starts spurring on the horses with a vigorous 'hop hop' that seems also to drive the orchestra itself (Ex. 4.8).

A notice appearing in *L'Illustration* before the first performance of *La damnation de Faust*, and thought to have been penned by Berlioz himself, suggests that the title – here given as 'opéra-légende' –'indicates a work destined to be read rather than performed'. Among other scenes, 'La course à l'abîme', with its 'frenetic gallop of two horses pursued by monstrous apparitions', is identified as one that it would be 'impossible to put on convincingly in the theatre'. *La damnation de Faust*, we are told, is addressed to 'the imagination rather than the eyes' – or, we might say in the terms of the previous chapter, to the inner eye of the mind rather than the physical eye of shared spectacle.[113] Katharine Kolb suggests that the numerous stage directions in the score confirm the notion that the work is to be read, and she argues persuasively on this basis for a closer examination of the text.[114] Does Berlioz in fact intend the work for the kind of listener who, like himself, attended performances with score in hand, who could read stage directions that would not actually be realised upon the stage?

Whatever Berlioz's intentions may have been regarding the listener's access to the score, we should not overlook the visual impact of a concert performance. Indeed, it is in the visual dimension of the concert performance that the originality of Berlioz's vision of the music of the future might be seen to be located. Berlioz did not request that the orchestra be hidden behind a curtain, as he had earlier done for much of *Épisode de la vie d'un artiste*, in which Lélio, like Méphistophélès, could be seen as a metaphorical on-stage conductor of sorts. In his *Orchestration Treatise* Berlioz describes a layout for the orchestra that uses steeply tiered risers, with the chorus placed in front of the orchestra on a temporary rigging slightly below the

---

[112] Kolb Reeve, 'The Perils of Heroism', p. 166. [113] Cited in *CG* III, p. 380.
[114] Kolb Reeve, 'The Perils of Heroism', p. 155.

Ex. 4.8 *La damnation de Faust*, 'La course à l'abîme', bb. 90–104

Ex. 4.8 (cont.)

level of the main stage. While designed to provide the optimal acoustic conditions for performance, this arrangement also has the effect of displaying every instrument (and singer) to the audience.[115] The vocal soloists are placed close to the conductor, and although Berlioz directs the conductor to face his orchestra, many conductors still faced the audience at this time.[116] Méphistophélès's status as a kind of stand-in for the conductor may thus have been enhanced visually for Berlioz's contemporary audience.

This layout, Berlioz tells us, is what he demands for his concerts in 'Paris, London, Berlin, Prague, Vienna and St Petersburg, whatever the dimensions of the stage'.[117] When mounting *Faust* in Dresden, however, he suggested that since the vocal part was so significant for this work (and for the other works to be performed in the same concert series, including *Roméo et Juliette*), the orchestra should be 'left below, in its usual position' – presumably in front of and below the stage, as for an opera.[118] Such an arrangement would have restricted the audience's visual connection with the orchestra, but the strengthening of the allusion to operatic performance would perhaps have heightened their awareness of the very ways in which Berlioz both draws on and subverts this idiom.

In performances that place the orchestra literally centre stage, we are encouraged to *watch* the technology of the orchestra in action as, driven forward by Méphistophélès, it threatens to usurp the position traditionally occupied by the body of the heroine in an operatic spectacle. Marguerite's body is not visibly crushed like that of Mina; it is not violently erased at the conclusion like those of the heroines of some of Berlioz's most familiar operatic contemporaries, such as Rachel, 'la juive', who leaps into the boiling cauldron, or Fenella, 'la muette', who throws herself into an active volcano. It is Faust who plunges into the flames in Berlioz's scenario, in a departure from Goethe's Part I. Berlioz's title – 'the *damnation* of Faust' – blatantly signals his intent; from the outset an audience is looking forward to Faust's future in a very literal sense. But Marguerite's fate is no less frightening for the fact that her body is spared the flames. Berlioz takes the familiar elements of opera – the spectacle of the female, the sensual enticement and threat to

---

[115] Macdonald, *Berlioz's Orchestration Treatise*, pp. 320–27. Donna M. di Grazia cites this, and a number of other writings by Berlioz and others, to reveal how the placement of the chorus in front of the orchestra was standard practice at the time, at least in Paris. See 'Rejected Traditions: Ensemble Placement in Nineteenth-Century Paris', *19th-Century Music* 22/2 (1998), 190–209. J.Q. Davies also discusses how orchestras were 'mounted' in ways that were 'visually appealing': 'Dancing the Symphonic', 34.

[116] Macdonald, *Berlioz's Orchestration Treatise*, p. 342; Agnès Terrier, *L'orchestre de l'Opéra de Paris de 1669 à nos jours* (Paris: Éditions de La Martinière, 2003), p. 140.

[117] Macdonald, *Berlioz's Orchestration Treatise*, p. 326.   [118] *CG* IV, p. 488.

rationality that the heroine presents, and the containment of this threat by her death – and transports them from the narrative to the metanarrative level. Paradoxically, it is only in a concert performance that we can be aware of this operatic metanarrative, as our gaze moves from Marguerite's silenced body to the orchestra, and as we hear her voice consumed by the powerful orchestral machine.

Performance as staged opera thus erases a vital dimension of the originality of Berlioz's *La damnation de Faust*. Indeed, when Berlioz thought he was going to have his *Faust* music staged in London, he undertook substantial revisions of the work. Méphistophélès would no longer appear as a diabolical conductor of an onstage orchestra, but as a sort of frustrated lover – an intriguing character, but a conventional operatic type none the less. Now Méphistophélès would sing a two-part aria in the conventional operatic plan, commencing with an Andante where he expresses his envy of Faust's mortal love ('Si je pouvais aimer! – Si je pouvais pleurer – Si je pouvais mourir!') and followed by an Allegro where Méphistophélès resolves instead to pursue his natural propensity for immortal rage and destruction.[119] As if in confirmation that full-fledged opera required greater concessions to singers, and evoking – if only very faintly – the Italian *operatore* in *Euphonia*, Berlioz acknowledges that this new aria was primarily designed to provide an opportunity to display to full effect the vocal qualities of Pischek, the singer who would take the role of Méphistophélès.[120]

In adapting *Faust* for the stage, Berlioz had less concern for his mezzo soprano (and still less for his Faust, who would acquire no new numbers); but now Marguerite would at least receive either her church scene or her garden scene. Concluding Marguerite's role with the church scene would potentially have enhanced the sense that she was trapped in a Euphonia-like torment. Goethe's Gretchen ('Marguerite' in the French translation by Nerval that was used by Berlioz) collapses as the organ, accompanying the choir who intone the *Dies irae*, 'stifles her breath': 'il me semble que cet orgue m'étouffe.' The cathedral itself seems to cave in upon Marguerite, just like the steel pavilion that crushes Mina to the tunes of the orchestra piano. Indeed, we must wonder if Berlioz had this passage in mind when he conceived *Euphonia*: 'Dans quelle angoisse je suis! Ces piliers me pressent, cette voûte m'écrase. – De l'air!'[121] ['What anguish I feel! These pillars are pressing upon me, this vault is crushing me. – Air!']

---

[119] *CG* III, pp. 484–5.   [120] *CG* III, pp. 474, 484–5.
[121] Goethe, *Faust* trans. Gérard Nerval (Paris: Dondey-Dupré, 1828), pp. 253–4.

Whereas Goethe has Gretchen return to the stage in the concluding prison scene, in Berlioz's operatic treatment the church scene would have marked Marguerite's final appearance, for there is no indication in his letters to Scribe that he wished to reinstate the prison scene. His comments about the conclusion relate primarily to the potential visual effects of the staging. Whether these visual effects would have incorporated a walk-on appearance from Marguerite (perhaps coinciding with the oboe part taken to represent her voice) we do not know. By withholding the prison scene, Berlioz resists a potent opportunity to relocate Marguerite securely within the *operatic* diegesis at her demise – an opportunity fully realised by Gounod. However, the truly radical nature of his treatment of the Faust story – which is infused with the same concerns about the industrialisation of space, the gender dichotomy, and the fear of loss of agency already seen in *Euphonia* – is best appreciated in the concert form of his original conception. Only when the orchestral machine is foregrounded can we *see* how Berlioz has dramatised the story through music.

Back to the 'music of the future'

Some fifteen years after *La damnation de Faust* and *Euphonia*, as Wagner prepared Paris for *Tannhäuser* with a series of concerts featuring orchestral and choral extracts from his operas, Berlioz published a response to 'the Richard Wagner concerts', which he subtitled 'The music of the future'.[122] In referring here not to Euphonian utopias but to the increasingly heated debate around Wagner's theories, Berlioz ostensibly treats the future in a rather different sense. *Euphonia* employs a futuristic setting to comment on the tendencies of Berlioz's own time, including the supposed disregard of the Italians for great music, and the German respect for Gluck and the symphonic tradition. In contrast, in 'The music of the future', Berlioz discusses the aesthetics of new music which 'is deemed to be diametrically opposed to the musical taste of the present day, and certain to find itself perfectly in harmony with the taste of a future time'.[123] In fact, upon closer inspection, the conceptions of the music of the future presented by *Euphonia* and 'The Richard Wagner concerts' are revealed to share a number of similar concerns.

---

[122] Berlioz, 'The Richard Wagner Concerts: The Music of the Future', in *The Art of Music*, pp. 202–9.
[123] Ibid., p. 206.

While Berlioz elsewhere expresses his estrangement from Parisian audiences and his hope (if increasingly merely ironic) that his music will endure to be appreciated by a future age, he did not see his own music as falling unambiguously into the school of 'the music of the future', as many of his contemporaries presumed. After discussing in some detail individual items performed in the Wagner concerts, Berlioz lays out two alternative ways of interpreting the so-called 'music of the future', one to which he is happy to subscribe, and one from which he feels wholly alienated. It is in this section of his article that concerns familiar from *Euphonia* resurface.

Berlioz is sympathetic to 'the music of the future' if the following conditions are met:

'Operas should not be composed for singers; on the contrary, the singers should be trained for the operas.

'Works composed for the sole purpose of showing off the talents of virtuosi can only be works of a secondary order, usually of little value.

'Performers are merely more or less intelligent instruments whose task is to bring out the form and inner meaning of the work; their despotic rule is over.

'The composer must remain the master; it is for him to command.

'Beauty of sound ranks below the idea; the idea ranks below feeling and passion.

'Lengthy and rapid vocal flourishes, ornaments, and trills, and many kinds of rhythms are all incompatible with the expression of most serious, noble, and deep feelings.'[124]

Here we might recognise the 'despotic regime' of Euphonia, where the singer serves the work of the composer and Mina's ornamentation is antithetical to genuine feeling. Well might a Gluck festival be the centrepiece of a musical city of the future, for, as Berlioz goes on to write, 'Gluck himself in one sense belonged to the school of the future', as he had already espoused these ideals.[125] Indeed, Berlioz's checklist here echoes that of the Preface to *Alceste*, which he discusses directly elsewhere in *À travers chant*.[126]

Berlioz next describes those potential attributes of the 'music of the future' with which he does not wish to be identified, concluding: 'If this is the new religion – very new indeed – I am very far from professing it; I

---

[124] Ibid., p. 207. [125] Ibid., p. 207.
[126] Compare, for example, Gluck's desire to divest opera 'of all those abuses, introduced either by the mistaken vanity of singers or by the too great complaisance of composers, which have so long disfigured the Italian opera'. 'Dedication for *Alceste* (1769)', in Leo Treitler (ed.), *Strunk's Source Readings in Music History* (New York: Norton, 1998), p. 933.

never have joined it, I do not join it now, and never shall. I raise my hand and swear: *Non credo.*'[127]

'We must concentrate only on the idea and ignore the senses altogether [...]

'Nor is the art of singing to be shown any consideration, nor should attention be paid to its nature or requirements.

'In opera we must do no more than set notes for declamation, to the point of using, if necessary, ugly, unsingable, outlandish intervals.

'No distinction need be made between music that is read by a musician sitting quietly in front of his stand and that which has to be sung from memory, on stage, by a performer who must also attend to his acting and that of others.

'We need not concern ourselves over what is possible or impossible in performance.'[128]

While the composer should be master, Berlioz is concerned that the singer's voice must nevertheless be respected. The music must reflect the physical realities of the stage and performance. The same tensions are anticipated in *Euphonia* and *La damnation de Faust*, where Mina and Marguerite are sacrificed to the technology of the orchestra (or to the 'piano-orchestre'). Berlioz may write for Faust as a voice in the orchestral polyphony, but he does not thereby sacrifice vocally idiomatic writing, and, in any case, his singers are less obviously required 'to attend to [their] acting'. Similarly, while Berlioz's use of anticipatory motifs invites comparison with Wagner's leitmotifs, such a comparison serves only to highlight the differences in their practice. When Berlioz anticipates the melody of 'Le roi de Thulé' before Marguerite's appearance, he creates not the union of orchestra and drama of the ideal *Gesamtkunstwerk*, where ultimately the orchestra's goal is 'of *not being heard at all*' in its 'mechanical' capacity.[129] Rather, he creates a palpable *tension* between symphony and opera, between the machinery of the orchestra and embodied performance that is central to Marguerite's plight. Two variants of the gender dichotomy here merge: Marguerite, as woman and as body, is set up against a masculine paradigm that combines both mind (or compositional authority) and technology (or instrumental materiality); the combination proves too powerful for Marguerite, who is 'synthesised' into the composer's orchestral machinery.

'The Richard Wagner concerts' was published in Berlioz's final authorised collection of essays, *À travers chant*, which Kolb suggests functions as

---

[127] Berlioz, 'The Richard Wagner Concerts', p. 209.   [128] Ibid., p. 208.
[129] Wagner, *Opera and Drama* in *Richard Wagner's Prose Works*, vol. II, p. 371.

a kind of treatise that outlines Berlioz's answer to Wagner's own theoretical works.[130] One of those works is *Oper und Drama*, where, as we saw in the previous chapter, Wagner critiques *Symphonie fantastique* for making of the orchestra 'a huge array of the most complicated machines', reaching a point at which 'he needs must sink as artist into mechanism'.[131] *Symphonie fantastique* was closely connected to the Faust story. Nerval's French translation introduced Berlioz to Goethe's play in 1828, feeding his initial ideas for a 'dramatic symphony' and perhaps leaving traces in the fifth movement. The *Dies irae* recalls Marguerite's church scene, while the witches' Sabbath of the same movement evokes the *Walpurgisnacht* of Goethe's text. The sinister quality of the orchestral machine which Wagner detects in *Symphonie fantastique* might equally be seen in *La damnation de Faust*. And again, if in the latter work the artist is buried by the machine, the battle between embodied music and the technology of the orchestra is part of a larger narrative that Wagner's comments would seem to ignore.

It has been suggested that where Wagner built Bayreuth to encapsulate his musical ideal, Berlioz constructed *Euphonia*.[132] But we have already seen many indications that *Euphonia* is not entirely ideal, and Berlioz's response to Wagner's music similarly intimates fears of the negative implications of his own utopian construction. Mina ironically denies the eager Shetland the opportunity to enact a kind of 'Liebestod' when she refuses to leap from the balloon with him at the height of their love. Mina's superficiality and sexual excess may warrant retribution, but the complete erasure of her body comes at a cost that is unreasonable on Berlioz's own terms when her death renders Euphonia, 'the musical city', silent. Creating the music of the future can be a dangerous enterprise if the potential and risks of technology are not negotiated with the utmost care. Though it is Jules Verne's more optimistic works that achieved lasting popularity, the majority of nineteenth-century French science fiction was characterised by an increasing technophobia, reflecting fears that the utopian world initially promised by industrial innovations was threatened by the negative ends to which such technology might be employed.[133] While Berlioz generally followed the technological developments of his age with admiration and

---

[130] Katherine Kolb, 'Flying Leaves: Between Berlioz and Wagner', *19th-Century Music* 33/1 (2009), 25–61.
[131] Wagner, *Opera and Drama*, p. 76.
[132] Christophe Deshoulières, 'Mises en scène', Pierre Citron, Cécile Reynaud eds., *Dictionnaire Berlioz* (Paris: Fayard, 2003), p. 353.
[133] Paul K. Alkon, *Science Fiction before 1900: Imagination Discovers Technology* (New York: Twayne Publishers, 1994).

awe, some of this technophobia is translated into musical terms in a world where pianos play themselves and singers are crushed, where physical space is erased altogether, and everything is sacrificed to the composer's work.

To say that Berlioz was sometimes fearful of the future is not to say that his own music is regressive, as his description of Gluck as a musician of the future, or his refusal to follow the Wagnerian path might have encouraged some to believe. *La damnation de Faust* is a forward-looking work. Fauquet suggests that in *Euphonia* Berlioz shows us that '*how* one listens is what in a way creates the musical space – a notion over which the twentieth century's avant-garde has spilt a great deal of ink'.[134] The same can be said of *La damnation de Faust*. But in order fully to appreciate the innovative aspects of *La damnation de Faust* we need to reconsider just how Berlioz creates this musical space in his own works.

Today Berlioz's *légende dramatique* is performed around the globe, in Tel Aviv, Mexico, Buenos Aires, Melbourne, and Shanghai, simultaneously fulfilling two of the composer's prophecies.[135] Ever since Raoul Gunsbourg staged the work for the first time in Monte Carlo in 1893 (perhaps not coincidentally at the height of Wagnerism), it has often been staged performances that have attracted the most attention. Productions such as that at the Salzburg Festival and the recent spectacular staging by Robert Lepage have employed all the technological resources of their day and ours to bring Berlioz's work into the future in ways even he may not have been able to imagine when forecasting from his deathbed that his music would now be played.

However, when Berlioz's work is transformed into a kind of Wagnerian *Gesamtkunstwerk*, we literally lose sight of some of the ways in which Berlioz was most innovative.[136] Berlioz did not conceive *La damnation de Faust* as we know it for the hidden pit of Bayreuth, nor did he conceal any part of it with a curtain. His orchestra is not separated from his singers by a 'mystical abyss', but is displayed as an integral element of the visual dimension of the work. This is not opera, or Wagnerian 'music drama', but *opéra de concert*, to use Berlioz's own expression. The sacrifice of Marguerite's body to Faust's restless striving beyond the physically attainable is enacted in the dialectic between opera and symphony. Opera and concert are fused, the orchestra

---

[134] Fauquet, '*Euphonia* and the Utopia of the Orchestra as Society', p. 48.
[135] The recent performance history of *La damnation de Faust* can be traced through www.hberlioz.com/Archive/index.htm (accessed 19 January 2011).
[136] An affinity between Wagnerian opera-drama and Berlioz's *Damnation de Faust* is perhaps also reinforced for the contemporary listener by the fact that Robert Lepage cut his Met teeth on Berlioz's work before undertaking the *Ring* cycle.

becoming spectacle just as the singers become part of the orchestra. The attendant anxieties of such a fusion are germane to the narrative of the work, and also to its place within a wider discourse about music's path into the future. It is when we watch that great orchestral machine in action that we become most acutely aware of how Berlioz dramatised through music the opportunities and anxieties of the technology of the emerging modern age, of a future world that bears the attractions and uncertainty of the Other. In this way, reading *La damnation de Faust* afresh through the lens of *Euphonia* helps us to appreciate Berlioz as a musician of the future on his own terms.

Berlioz would go back to the future in *Les Troyens* – a work whose dramatic fabric explicitly invokes prophecy just as its music draws on a dialectic of technology. Indeed, Berlioz's grand opera would provide an even more direct realisation of his deathbed prophecy, 'finally they are going to perform my music', for the work awaited the future beyond his grave for its full realisation in performance. But, as we shall see in the final chapter, while *Les Troyens* extends the Other world of the future, it also casts its gaze over the past, not only that represented by its classical source, but also that of the composer, as the Other worlds of Berlioz's earlier works are reimagined.

5 | Exhibiting Other worlds

Les Troyens, museum culture, and human zoos

> DIDON
>
> Énée,
> Ah! daignez achever
> Le récit commencé
> De votre long voyage
> Et des malheurs de Troie.
> > [DIDO: Aeneas, Ah! Deign to complete the tale already begun
> > of your long voyage and the misfortune of Troy.][1]

With *Les Troyens* Berlioz might be seen to be completing his own tale of the long voyage of his career. The *Memoirs* open with the inspirations of his youth – travel writing and the *Aeneid* – and their closing chapters contain accounts of the conception and partial performance of the massive opera that has been described as the 'culminating work of Berlioz's career' and as a 'conscious summing up' of the tendencies of Berlioz's creative life.[2] In terms of the themes examined in this book, *Les Troyens* brings together not only travel writing and Virgil, but also Italy and military imperialism, supernatural visions and visitations, the call of the past and the fearful anticipation of the future, instrumental technology on the stage and in the pit, and operatic women silenced within what Berlioz many times referred to as his 'great machine'.[3]

In this chapter I focus exclusively on *Les Troyens*, using it to revisit those core themes. Begun a decade after *La damnation de Faust*, and conceived in the different climate of the Second Empire, *Les Troyens* configures many of the themes explored in his earlier works in new ways. Moreover, the opera also invokes distinctive contexts of its own, centred on museum culture and

---

[1] Berlioz, *Les Troyens* ed. Hugh Macdonald, *NBE* vol. 2b, p. 553.
[2] Rushton, 'Genre' in Bloom (ed.), *The Cambridge Companion to Berlioz*, p. 51; Cairns, *Servitude and Greatness*, p. 598.
[3] *CG* V, pp. 286, 388, *CG* VI, pp. 403, 455.

exhibitions – contexts which will be used to shape this chapter as a whole and to provide the direct focus of its second half.[4]

Museums, exhibitions, human zoos

Berlioz himself points to the significant influence of one particular museum on his opera. As Didon reclines on her day bed to listen to Énée tell of the fate of Andromache, Berlioz gives detailed stage directions:

Didon has her left arm resting on the shoulder of Ascagne, her hand draped over the child's chest; the child smilingly removes Sichée's ring from the finger of the queen.[5]

To his sister Adèle, Berlioz made clear what many critics attending the first performances noted for themselves. The scene is derived from a painting by Pierre-Narcisse Guérin ('Idée empruntée au tableau de Guérin', as Berlioz put it), which still hangs in the Louvre today.[6] (See cover image.) That Berlioz's representation of the *Aeneid* should be influenced by another artist's depiction is unremarkable. More interesting is the fact that the tableau quality of the scene extends to the Carthaginian acts as a whole, as one early reviewer pointed out: 'Mr Berlioz has arranged [the opera] in tableaux rather than in acts in the strictest sense.'[7] Indeed, *Les Troyens* invokes a distinctive form of museum culture on multiple levels.

It was not only Guérin's painting in which Berlioz could have found inspiration at the Louvre, nor even other illustrations of scenes from the *Aeneid*, but also the spoils of empire and artefacts of the past – objects signifying Other worlds. And among the objects Berlioz encountered in museums were musical instruments. The antique cymbals used in *Les Troyens* (and earlier, in *Roméo et Juliette*) were inspired by similar instruments seen in the Pompeii museum in Naples in 1831, while the Louvre itself acquired an ancient sistrum in 1852.[8] Aspects of this form of museum ideology, in which foreign cultures are objectified (in both senses) for a western European visitor, were adopted in the International Exhibitions of London (the 'Great Exhibition'

---

[4] Exhibition culture can encompass the library and art gallery as well as the museum. Indeed, French does not distinguish as clearly as English does between the public art gallery and the museum (both are *musée*).

[5] *NBE* vol. 2b, p. 559.   [6] *CG* V, pp. 437–8.

[7] Quoted in Frank Heidlberger (ed.), *Hector Berlioz: Les Troyens à Carthage. Dossier de presse parisienne (1863)* (Bietigheim: Musik-Edition Lucie Galland, 1995), p. 19; See also Violaine Anger, 'Le représenté et le ressenti', in Georges Zaragoza (ed.), *Berlioz, homme de lettres* (Neuilly-lès-Dijon: Éditions du Murmure, 2006), pp. 269–71.

[8] Ian Kemp, *Berlioz: Les Troyens* (Cambridge : Cambridge University Press, 1988), p. 205.

of 1851) and Paris (the 'Exposition universelle' of 1855), in which, in the years immediately preceding the creation of *Les Troyens*, Berlioz acted as a judge of musical instruments. Berlioz also experienced the legacy of the Great Exhibition when he visited the restored Crystal Palace at Sydenham, which he described as 'one of the marvels of the world', adding: 'I thought I'd seen Aladdin's palace, the Gardens of Semiramis... it's like a dream!'[9] Indeed, the Great Exhibition and its successors developed new mechanisms of display and spectatorship which exerted a profound and enduring influence on the practice of museums and other institutions dedicated to the exhibition of objects.[10]

The position of European art music in this developing exhibition culture is complex. Musicologists now routinely explore and deconstruct the 'imaginary museum of musical *works*',[11] but the most obvious musical items to be subjected to exhibition in a literal sense are musical instruments, and although museology and organology have tended to be separated from ontological enquiries about the work concept, consideration of music's place in the physical museum actually enhances appreciation of its metaphysical achievements during Berlioz's era. Berlioz was directly involved in the exhibition of instruments through his role as curator of the music instrument collection of the Paris Conservatoire from 1866 until his death. During his tenure the collection comprised primarily European instruments from the Renaissance to the present. The fifteen non-European instruments, as well as the earlier specimens in the collection at this time, were valued chiefly for their decorative status rather than for their function as sounding bodies.[12] Similarly, at the international exhibitions, non-European musical instruments were seen but not heard. They were included among the objects displayed in the sections devoted to Europe's colonies. But whereas European instruments were assessed against each other in numerous specialised categories in a fierce competition for industrial supremacy, instruments from the colonies were displayed as objects of ethnic Otherness. One commentator at the Paris exhibition in 1855 complained that the various Indian

---

[9] *CG* V, p. 113.
[10] Tony Bennett, *The Birth of the Museum: History, Theory, Politics* (London: Routledge, 1995), p. 61.
[11] In addition to Goehr's volume of the same name, and of particular relevance to the context of Berlioz and his orchestra, see Katharine Ellis, *Interpreting the Musical Past: Early Music in Nineteenth-Century France* (Oxford: Oxford University Press, 2005), and J. Peter Burkholder, 'The Twentieth Century and the Orchestra as Museum', in Joan Peyser (ed.), *The Orchestra: Origins and Transformations* (New York: Billboard Books, 2000), pp. 409–32.
[12] Jann Pasler, 'The Utility of Musical Instruments in the Racial and Colonial Agendas of Late Nineteenth-Century France', *Journal of the Royal Musical Association*, 129/1 (2004), 33.

instruments, for example, were jumbled up with baskets, knives, and fruit, as well as instruments that were not Indian at all, and that they were mostly in a state of disrepair.[13] Berlioz himself described the Indian and 'Oriental' instruments displayed at the exhibition as 'primitive', 'crude', 'clumsy' or 'ridiculous', surmising largely on this basis that '[t]he Orientals [...] give the name of music to what we should call a din.'[14]

Only later would exhibitions incorporate staged performances of foreign identity within the exhibition buildings themselves. In that context, instruments could be experienced as sounding bodies, contextualised in relation to cultural practices of their regions of origin – albeit these practices were heavily mediated. But while the international exhibitions in which Berlioz participated did not include live performance by non-western musicians, he did not have to look far to encounter 'exotic' music in performance. For some years before the international exhibitions, Paris and London had hosted foreign performers who staged cultural displays for the curiosity of European audiences. Moreover, the Great Exhibition stimulated an increase in 'ethnic' performances which endured for decades to come.[15] Outside the Crystal Palace, visitors to London in 1851 could see Syrians performing instrumental music as part of a Holy Land panorama at the Egyptian Hall, and an Algerian family performing at Vauxhall.[16] The Great Exhibition of 1851 also attracted a large number of foreign visitors to the city, who themselves became objects of spectacle: 'the whole world is on our streets', the *Times* commented,[17] and Berlioz remarked upon the popular performances of the 'Small-footed Lady' and the Chinese musicians who entertained visitors on a junk moored on the Thames, as well as Scottish and Indian street musicians and English musicians performing in blackface.[18]

Moreover, the significance of the presence of foreign peoples within the halls of the first international exhibitions is often underestimated. While the 1867 Paris Exposition universelle is credited as being the first to incorporate foreigners as part of the exhibition itself, the practice of treating

---

[13] Adrien de La Fage, *Quinze visites musicales à l'exposition universelle de 1855*, (Paris: Tardif, 1857), p. 22.
[14] Berlioz, *Memoirs*, pp. 251–2.
[15] Nadja Durbach, 'London, Capital of Exotic Exhibitions from 1830 to 1860', in Nicolas Bancel, Pascal Blanchard, Gilles Boëtsch, Eric Deroo, and Sandrine Lamaire (eds.), *Human Zoos: Science and Spectacle in the Age of Colonial Empires* (Liverpool: Liverpool University Press, 2008), pp. 81–8; Sadiah Qureshi, *Peoples on Parade: Exhibitions, Empire, and Anthropology in Nineteenth-Century Britain* (Chicago: University of Chicago Press, 2011), p. 3.
[16] Edward Ziter, *The Orient on the Victorian Stage* (Cambridge: Cambridge University Press, 2003), pp. 112–14.
[17] Quoted in Ziter, *The Orient on the Victorian Stage*, p. 103.
[18] Berlioz, *Evenings with the Orchestra*, pp. 246–51.

foreign peoples almost as living displays within the exhibition hall was anticipated at the Crystal Palace in 1851.[19] Berlioz commented at length on the activities of a solitary Chinese attendant, alone at dawn in the Crystal Palace,[20] and though Berlioz did not remark upon it, the section of the Great Exhibition dedicated to Tunisia included an 'extremely picturesque and obliging native *custodien*' who was admired by the visitors, and whose presence helped to frame the exhibited objects as props in an ethnographic display, rather than as mere bric-a-brac.[21] In these ways, foreign visitors and attendants, as well as the foreign performers in popular venues outside the exhibitions, could themselves be framed as museum exhibits. Indeed, in the age that invented the so-called human zoo, live performance was no safeguard against objectification.[22] With its display of instruments and staging of Otherness – including the setting of Tunisia's ancient city of Carthage – *Les Troyens* can thus be situated in relation to a museum culture broadly defined to encompass an interrelated cluster of institutions that framed objects – and peoples – for display: the exhibition, the museum, and the human zoo.

Later in this chapter I will explore how Berlioz drew directly on one particular performance of staged Otherness when conceiving *Les Troyens*. And through its onstage display of instruments new, old, and exotic, as well as its overt interactions with colonisation and imperialism, *Les Troyens* evokes the museum aspect of the exhibitions quite directly. However, considering *Les Troyens* in the context of museum and exhibition culture also raises more far-reaching questions. Tension between material objects or artefacts and embodied performance was present both in the displaying of 'exotic' instruments and peoples, and in the treatment of European music at the exhibitions, for while European instruments were played and judged, European *music* was similarly reduced to its most conspicuously material 'objects'. At the exhibitions it was instruments, rather than scores, which were displayed, despite the fact that the latter were increasingly accepted as representing 'works' to be studied independent of performance – a function they fulfilled in libraries.[23]

---

[19] Sadiah Qureshi, *Peoples on Parade: Exhibitions, Empire, and Anthropology in Nineteenth-Century Britain* (Chicago: University of Chicago Press, 2011), p. 249.
[20] Berlioz, *Evenings with the Orchestra*, pp. 236–7.
[21] Ziter, *The Orient on the Victorian Stage*, p. 108.
[22] This use of the term 'human zoo' can be attributed to Blanchard et al., *Zoos humains: de la Vénus hottentote aux reality shows* (2002); see Charles Forsdick, 'Postface: Situating *Human Zoos*', in the English edition: Blanchard et al., *Human Zoos: Science and Spectacle*, p. 385.
[23] In his capacity as librarian of the Paris conservatoire, Berlioz noted that the library, at least, was an appropriate venue in which to acknowledge a concept of the musical work located in the

At the Great Exhibition in 1851, musical instruments were displayed in Class X, 'Philosophical, Musical, Horological, and Surgical Instruments' – objects loosely associated with the notion of precision.[24] Berlioz was on the jury responsible for awarding medals not only to instruments, but also to all the other objects with which they were classed. As he commented ironically, lives could be lost if he made the wrong decision about the latest developments in surgical tools.[25] The Paris exhibition of 1855 introduced a separate competition for 'Beaux Arts', playing to the strength of the host nation.[26] Music was again classed with the products of industry, displayed through instruments. But musical instruments were now separated from tools of precision and placed in Class XXVII of the Seventh Group: 'Furniture and decoration, millinery, industrial drawing, printing and music' – objects that could be admired aesthetically as well as in terms of the industrial prowess or technological innovation demonstrated by their manufacturers. Nevertheless, two decades after Liszt had called for 'the foundation of a musical museum' centred on works, while painting, engraving, carving and architecture could all now be considered on aesthetic grounds, there was still no assessment of musical compositions within the exhibition halls.[27]

The same paradox can be approached from another angle. The status of instruments-as-objects has increasingly been problematised by organology, while the 'new museology' reveals the manifold ways in which the meaning of objects is contingent, and constructed by those exhibiting and beholding them, often in pronounced contradiction to indigenous attitudes.[28] Thus, even when they were framed exclusively by European agendas, objects including musical instruments were themselves pulled between the

---

score: 'A music library must [. . .] be a collection of musical works which one can study and which, consequently, one *can read.*' *CG* VII, p. 234.

[24] John R. Davis, *The Great Exhibition* (Thrupp, Stroud, Gloucestershire: Sutton Publishing Ltd, 1999), p. 148.

[25] Berlioz, *Musical Madhouse*, p. 30.

[26] There was a 'fine arts' display at the London exhibition, but Davis suggests 'it should be noted that this meant art *as applied to industry.* Few of the objects were displayed solely on aesthetic grounds but were instead exhibited to show how new techniques, materials or machinery could be used to produce art or, conversely, how art could be used to improve industrial goods.' *The Great Exhibition*, p. 159.

[27] Goehr, *The Imaginary Museum of Musical Works*, p. 205. On musical museums of works, see also Ellis, *Interpreting the Musical Past*, pp. 4–7.

[28] On the agency of instruments, see Eliot Bates, 'The Social Life of Musical Instruments', *Ethnomusicology* 56/3 (2012), 363–95. On new museology, see Peter Vergo, ed. *The New Museology* (London: Reaktion Books, 1989). See also Tim Barringer and Tom Flynn (eds.), *Colonialism and the Object: Empire, Material Culture and the Museum* (London: Routledge, 1998), including Eilean Hooper-Greenhill, 'Perspectives on Hinemihi: A Maori Meeting House', which articulates conflicting Māori and British attitudes towards the agency of objects.

competing claims of aesthetics, industrialism, and the sociocultural status of the artefact.

In considering *Les Troyens* this chapter joins in imaginary sympathy with Berlioz who, like Énée, can be seen to 'complete the long tale' begun in his earlier works. A closer look at the objects displayed with musical instruments in Class X of the Paris 1855 exhibition offers a fascinating snapshot – or daguerreotype – of mid nineteenth-century industry, and it also invites us to revisit almost all the frameworks invoked by Berlioz's works in previous chapters. Among the objects with which musical instruments were categorised were the surgical tools Berlioz imagined saving the lives of soldiers in the Crimea; the latest developments in dissolving views, magic lanterns and daguerreotypes; 'electro-galvanic machines' and an '[a]pparatus for restoring suspended animation in persons apparently dead'; a massive mechanical man and uncanny artificial limbs; and telegraph technology, railway technology and 'aerial machines' – including one with 'two revolving wheels for propelling, and a rudder at each end to steer the machine'.[29]

Just as the exhibitions displayed all the paraphernalia of military communication, supernatural entertainments, and the transformations of time and space of the technologically driven future, so does *Les Troyens* revisit the rooms of Berlioz's imaginary exhibition. Visitors could delight in the uncanny implications or Otherness of some of this technology. But the exhibitions also staged control over technology as a particular feat of western Europe, and especially the host nations, Britain and France. Mastery of technology was an attribute that enabled those countries to rule over the regions designated their colonies at the exhibitions, where the Other was defined in racial terms. This more problematic ideology, too, is present in *Les Troyens*, as we shall see.

Acknowledging the classification of instruments at the international exhibitions, this chapter traces, through an initial series of relatively discrete 'tableaux' or 'exhibits', the ways in which the Otherness of travel writing, military imperialism, supernatural visions and the future culminate in *Les Troyens*. I will also explore in more depth Berlioz's response to a racial Other when encountered, not through objects, but through living people. Viewing *Les Troyens* through the lens of a variety of museum cultures thus presents us with an opportunity to consider again the material and

---

[29] *Official Catalogue of the Great Exhibition of the Works of Industry of All Nations* (London: Spicer Brothers, 1851), pp. 66–75; the description of the balloon is quoted in Davis, *The Great Exhibition*, p. 148.

performative aspects of Berlioz's music. This is particularly pertinent when dealing with an age in which a famous soprano such as Jenny Lind could be toured and exhibited as a curiosity under the aegis of the indomitable P.T. Barnum, positioned somewhere amidst mechanical curiosities on the one hand and the 'Feejee mermaid' on the other. While Berlioz was sceptical of the blatant exhibitionism of some performers (and he satirises Lind's American tour in *Evenings with the Orchestra*),[30] a consideration of his opera in relation to the literal context of the exhibition nevertheless provides a direct challenge to the '*imaginary* museum of musical *works*', inviting us to behold the objects and peoples upon whom that music was dependent.[31]

Exhibit 1: Instruments of travel

Berlioz referred to *Les Troyens* itself in terms of travel writing, describing his opera as that 'sea of music', or 'Robinson's canoe'.[32] More literally, Didon's request that Énée continue 'the tale already begun of your long voyage' reminds us that Virgil's *Aeneid* could itself be construed as a form of travel writing. The travel narrated in Virgil's text, in the scene depicted in Guérin's painting, is not actually enacted on Berlioz's stage, but is instead implied in and impelled by the cries of 'Italie!' that intrude at crucial moments, as well as in the way Berlioz evokes some of the ideology and techniques of travel writing in his presentation of the worlds of ancient Troy and Carthage.

Berlioz loved Virgil and his protagonists as if he knew them personally: 'It feels as if I knew Virgil and Shakespeare, as if I see them',[33] he wrote, elsewhere enthusing, 'Would you believe I have fallen *in love*, completely in love, with my Carthaginian Queen?'[34] However, he was also aware that the worlds they inhabited were very foreign to his own, with customs that his contemporaries would not comprehend. Berlioz therefore added a number of editorial comments and footnotes to his score, treating it as an object to be viewed, and as a form of travel writing in which the scholarly author or editor cites his sources or explains details that would be obscure to his audience.[35]

---

[30] Berlioz, *Evenings with the Orchestra*, pp. 99–105.

[31] Ronald Radano and Philip V. Bohlman have similarly pointed to the ways in which race was forcibly erased by the European construction of music as a 'free-floating essentialized object'. 'Introduction: Music and Race, Their Past, Their Presence', in Radano and Bohlman (eds.), *Music and the Racial Imagination*, p. 43.

[32] *CG* V, pp. 332, 517, 549.   [33] *CG* VIII, p. 425.   [34] *CG* V, p. 338.

[35] Thus, for example, in Act V, when the stage directions instruct that Didon, abandoned by Énée, should come on stage with one foot bared, Berlioz adds a footnote citing Virgil, Ovid

Berlioz did not travel to Carthage himself, but he did draw on the research Flaubert undertook in Carthage for the novel *Salammbô*, whose 'science archéologique' he greatly admired.[36] *Salammbô* is actually set some five centuries after Dido's time, but the potential anachronism does not appear to have bothered Berlioz, for he sought Flaubert's advice on the costumes for his opera. *Les Troyens* was subsequently praised by *La Presse* for capturing 'la science d'un archéologue' in a fashion that Flaubert would recognise.[37] Indeed, opera, like the realistic illusions of the panorama and diorama, could present the audience with a kind of virtual travel to remote destinations. Opera thus interacted with aspects of museum and exhibition culture in the ways it represented the Other worlds of travel through the careful assemblage and creation of objects, costumes and sets, as well as in its cultivation and regulation of particular forms of spectatorship, and in sheer expense.[38] Moreover, museum culture (broadly defined) was itself heavily shaped by travel writing, and when living humans were included in exhibitions it became possible to claim, as did the *Illustrated Magazine of Art* in 1853, that 'man, now-a-days, need not encounter the perils of the sea and the dangers of the land to make himself acquainted with the varieties of the human race.'[39]

One of the most important ways in which Berlioz's opera evokes the intersections between travel writing and museum or exhibition culture is through the use of archaic or exotic instruments. Such instruments feature in various numbers throughout the opera. The stage directions for the opening chorus of Act I mention three 'doubles flûtes antiques ou trois hautbois' played atop Achilles's tomb; the chorus of the Trojan march (No. 11) refers to 'la trompette phrygienne' and 'la lyre troyenne'; the sacred processional 'Marche et hymne' (No. 4) features 'sistres antiques sur la scène'; in the Act II finale the Trojan women sing themselves to their deaths to the accompaniment of lyres (No. 16); the 'Pas d'esclaves nubiennes' (No. 33c) has parts for 'cymbales antiques' and a 'tarbuka', which is to be played from the stage; and Iopas performs to the accompaniment of an onstage 'harpiste thébain' wearing 'le costume religieux égyptien' (No. 34).

---

and Horace (in Latin), before noting, 'This was part of the ceremony in sacrifices to the gods of the underworld.' *NBE* vol. 2b, p. 713.

[36] *CG* VI, p. 373.   [37] Heidlberger (ed.), *Dossier de presse*, p. 127.
[38] Vergo, 'The Reticent Object', in Vergo (ed.), *The New Museology*, p. 43; on spectator behaviour in museums see Carol Duncan, 'Art Museums and the Ritual of Citizenship', in Ian Karp and Steven D. Lavine (eds.), *Exhibiting Cultures: The Poetics and Politics of Museum Display* (Washington and London: Smithsonian Institution, 1991), pp. 88–103.
[39] Quoted in Durbach, 'London, Capital of Exotic Exhibitions', in Blanchard et al. (eds.), *Human Zoos*, p. 82.

In addition to the instruments he encountered in museums, Berlioz may have drawn not only on orchestration treatises but also on travel writing for inspiration. The closest models identified for the 'tarbuka' are found in Gérard de Nerval's *Voyage en Orient* and in Edward Lane's *An Account of the Manners and Customs of the Modern Egyptians*.[40]

The antique cymbals produced their own sound, and the tarbuka, though doubled by a tambourine in the pit, may also have sounded from the stage. However, for the most part, where Berlioz evokes an instrument that was foreign to the orchestra, belonging either to a distant time or place, that instrument is given voice by conventional orchestral instruments from the pit. The 'doubles flûtes antiques' are sounded by oboes, the Phrygian trumpet by saxhorns, the sistra by triangles, and lyres by harps.[41] The archaic instruments on the stage are thus objects for display. Like the instruments encountered in museums and exhibitions in Berlioz's time, their own voices are largely silent, and the idiom they voice is heavily mediated by Berlioz's aesthetic ideals and those of his audience. Indeed, they occupy a space, characteristic of contemporaneous exhibitions, between scientific or ethnological realism on the one hand, and spectacle on the other.[42]

Berlioz's approach to musical exoticism in his use of instruments in *Les Troyens* largely follows the recommendations of Anton Reicha, one of his former teachers at the Conservatoire. In writing of 'couleur locale' in opera, Reicha suggested that while the set and costume designers, poet, and actors should endeavour to replicate the setting and customs of the places depicted, it was not the job of the composer to attempt to imitate in any authentic way the music of that region:

As for the composer, he should generally write his music as if it is destined for his own country. Indeed, for a piece set in China is it necessary to write Chinese music? Or for a work in which the action takes place in Africa, should he imitate the music of the Ethiopians or Egyptians or the Negros [Nègres]? We advise against this.[43]

Reicha goes on to suggest that it is sufficient for the purposes of exoticism for the composer to employ, within his own idiom, a national air, or to evoke an instrument characteristic of the country in question:

He employs the harp to accompany Ossianic songs; he imitates the mandolin in Italy, the guitar in Spain and the bagpipe in Scotland. The guitar, mandolin and often

---

[40] Kemp, *Les Troyens*, p. 207.   [41] Ibid., pp. 204–12.
[42] Sylviane Leprun, *Le théâtre des colonies: Scénographie, acteurs et discours de l'imaginaire dans les expositions 1855–1937* (Paris: Harmattan, 1986), p. 17.
[43] Antoine Reicha, *Art du compositeur dramatique, ou cours complet de composition vocale* (Paris: A. Farrenc, 1833), p. 96.

also the harp are imitated in the orchestra by string instruments playing pizzicato; the bagpipe or the pipe by the oboe.[44]

Berlioz's use of the 'doubles flûtes', Phrygian trumpets and so forth could be seen to fall squarely within the tradition outlined by Reicha, albeit the Other worlds Berlioz is invoking are defined in temporal as much as geographical terms. The practice was anticipated in a range of works before those of Berlioz. For example, in Auber's *L'enfant prodigue* (reviewed by Berlioz in 1850, and a significant work in relation to *Les Troyens*, as we shall see), costume designs include images of an Egyptian woman and a priestess carrying sistrums, while one of the dances has a continuous triangle part which may have been intended to produce the equivalent sound.[45] More extravagantly, Le Sueur's *Alexandre à Babylone* called for sixteen 'trompettes macédoniennes' to play on stage in the final chorus, and 'a crowd of people of both sexes, dancing to the sound of a great number of antique instruments' in an earlier scene.[46] Berlioz noted that Lesueur's work was never performed, but in any case the 'instruments antiques' are not assigned any music in the score.[47] Like Lesueur's references to antique modes supposedly used in the harmony (but aurally indistinguishable from major and minor keys), these archaising touches appear to have been predominantly aimed at the eyes rather than the ears.[48]

The museum-like aspect of the display of instruments-as-objects in *Les Troyens* is echoed in the fact that several of Berlioz's on-stage instruments are employed in scenes that are static in terms of the larger dramatic narrative. The instruments thus participate in music that is itself objectified within diegetic numbers to be listened to – and looked at. For example, the sistrums accompany a procession, and the tarbuka and antique cymbals in the dance of the Nubian slaves function in similar ways to the objects paraded by the labourers before Didon earlier in the opera.

The on-stage saxhorns of the Trojan march function rather differently. They sound their own voice, which is associated with the music of action, and they are more closely connected to the industrial progress glorified

---

[44] Ibid., p. 97.
[45] Daniel François Esprit Auber, *L'enfant prodigue* (Paris: Brandus, 1850), pp. 262–5. Illustrations of the costume designs by Paul Lormier are available through Gallica (http://gallica.bnf.fr), Bibliothèque nationale de France, département Bibliothèque-musée de l'opéra, D216–16.
[46] Commodore John Keith Jr., 'The Operas of Jean-François Le Sueur', unpublished Doctor of Philosophy dissertation, University of Cincinnati (1981), p. 269.
[47] Berlioz, 'Lesueur', *Revue et gazette musicale* 15 October, 1837; *CM* III, p. 298.
[48] Jean Mongrédien, *Jean-François Le Sueur: Contribution à l'étude d'un demi-siècle de musique française (1780–1830)* (Berne: Peter Lang, 1980), p. 783.

in the international exhibitions than to the exotic repose of the colonies represented by many other unusual instruments staged with *Les Troyens*. However, when the saxhorns appear in the 'Chasse royale et orage' they move offstage into a liminal realm. They signal the hunting horns of Énée's and Didon's troupe, but these horns sound in a sublime landscape inhabited by mythical creatures, heralding the consummation of the relationship of Didon and Énée amidst a fierce storm, in a scene which draws on pantomime and all the stage machinery and orchestral power Berlioz could conceive. Berlioz's setting evokes an anthropomorphisation of nature obviously suggestive both of his Virgilian source and of Beethoven's Pastoral Symphony. But Berlioz's treatment is also evocative of the sublime landscapes of Humboldt. Indeed, the 'Chasse royale et orage' recalls Berlioz's own ideal orchestra, whose 'mysterious sounds of virgin forests' were described in Humboldtian terms at the original conclusion of the *Orchestration Treatise*. The ideal nature of the orchestra for the 'Chasse royale et orage' is suggested by Berlioz in a note in the score, laden with what we might assume to be weary resignation 'In order to execute this scene effectively it is also necessary to have an orchestra of a power rarely found in theatres.'[49]

At the climax of the 'Chasse royale et orage', Berlioz deploys this powerful orchestra at full force in a passage that realises the vision of the *Orchestration Treatise:* 'the most rebellious beings would tremble to watch its crescendo swell and roar like an enormous, sublime conflagration!'[50] (Ex. 5.1.) The 'conflagration' of the 'Chasse royale et orage' is reinforced through intense metrical dissonance. Thus, two saxhorns sound a hunting call in 6/8 against the other two saxhorns in 3/4, while the trombones sound a different hunting call in 4/4; the woodwinds are in 4/4 but are heavily syncopated. The bassoons, cellos, and basses imply 3/4 through their articulation (though they are still barred in 4/4); and the upper strings imply 2/2. At the same time, the off-stage timpani sound at irregular intervals, echoed a beat later by the bass drum in the pit. All eyes are likely to be directed at the stage at this moment, as nymphs and fawns flee in anxiety, satyrs and sylvans cavort in the shadows, streams of water form on the rock, and finally lightning strikes a tree. Nevertheless, this is a crucial moment for the navigating prowess of the conductor in the pit, since the multiple isolated subjectivities of the metrically clashing orchestral lines are held together by the only individual with oversight of the whole. Coming at the peak of a crescendo

---

[49] Quoted in Gérard Condé, 'Commentaire musicale et littéraire', *Les Troyens, L'Avant Scène Opéra*, vol. 128/129 (Paris: L'Avant Scène, 1990), p. 93.
[50] Macdonald, *Berlioz's Orchestration Treatise*, p. 335.

Ex. 5.1 *Les Troyens*, No. 29 'Chasse royale et orage', bb. 242–63

Ex. 5.1 (cont.)

Ex. 5.1 (cont.)

in terms of orchestration as well as dynamics, this is also the moment where Berlioz adds voices in the form of an offstage chorus, intoning just one word amidst their vocalisations: 'Italie!' Ostensibly the voices sound a warning that Énée is getting pulled off-course, in this moment when his relationship with Didon is consummated. But 'Italie' also emerges from the turmoil like the creation of a sublime new world from chaos – a world which straddles the real and imagined landscapes of Berlioz's own travels.

Exhibit 2: Instruments of war and empire

'I sing of arms and of a man'[51]

The opening words of Virgil's *Aeneid* foreground the centrality of military concerns to the epic narrative in which the foundations of the Roman Empire of Virgil's day are shown to have been laid through battle. Berlioz's operatic treatment of Virgil's work was in turn framed by an acute consciousness of the imperial and military frameworks of his own era. He pointed out to his uncle Félix Marmion, the former soldier of the grande armée, that he began work on the libretto on 5 May (1856) – a 'date épique', for it was the anniversary of Napoleon's death.[52] And *Les Troyens* reflects Berlioz's hopes that Napoleon III would realise his uncle's legacy. At one time Berlioz even intended the opera to conclude with reference to France's recent victories in North Africa.[53] Although Berlioz revised the ending, *Les Troyens* continues to 'sing of arms' and of Empire in ways that spoke directly to his audience in the Second Empire; and those same messages of imperial power were manifested through the spectacle and friendly rivalry of the first international exhibitions.

Berlioz's opera opens with the Trojans celebrating over the detritus of arms left, as they think, by the fleeing Greeks, and closes with Didon prostrate on the pyre beside Énée's weapons. Within this frame, *Les Troyens* rings with the sounds of war, from the Trojan war itself, to the calls to arms that presage the battle with Didon's Numidian enemy Iarbas, and the calls of the reveille with which Énée stirs his men to depart Carthage. Most significantly, Didon's death is followed by the 'Trojan march', which punctuates the entire opera, and in which Nation and then Empire are formed through the fusion of arms and of men (Ex. 5.2).

---

[51] Virgil, *The Aeneid*, trans. Allen Mandelbaum (Berkeley: University of California Press, 1971), p. 1.
[52] *CG* V, p. 328.   [53] *CG* V, p. 401.

Ex. 5.2 *Les Troyens* No. 11 'Marche Troyenne', bb. 1–32

Ex. 5.2 (cont.)

The Trojan march is not initially presented as serving an explicitly military purpose, except in the sense that it might suggest the civic procession of a military band in peacetime. In Act I Cassandre describes the sound of the approaching march at its first appearance as 'the sacred choruses of Ilion'

Ex. 5.2 (*cont.*)

['les choeurs sacrés d'Ilion']. And the march fulfils Priam's order to appease the goddess Pallas Athena (whom the Trojans believe responsible for the grim fate of Laocoon) by introducing the massive horse into Troy with appropriate 'solennité'.

It is in subsequent acts that the military aspects of the march become more explicit, though the process is a gradual one. Dissociated from its text and rendered in a doleful B flat minor ('dans le Mode Triste', Berlioz signals in the title), the march accompanies the Trojans' arrival in Carthage. When the Carthaginians and Trojans unite to fight the African armies of Iarbas, they sing their battle cry to new music (No. 28). However, as Énée readies himself to leave Carthage in Act V, it is the Trojan march, newly restored to the major mode, that invigorates him, and when Didon hears her fate

Ex. 5.2 (cont.)

in its offstage strains, she refers to it explicitly as a battle song ('ce chant de triomphe'). When the march appears at the time of Didon's death, it accompanies a premonition of the future glory of Rome, symbolised by a procession of legions before the Emperor. Berlioz notes in the score: 'In the distance is heard the Trojan march, passed down to the Romans by tradition and become their victory song.'[54]

For the audience, too, the march becomes (military) tradition through its repetition within the work. But its eventual nature as a popular triumphal song is facilitated by the fact that, from its first appearance, it invokes the idioms of military and festive music familiar to Berlioz's audience. While the only words sung to the Trojan march in the opera are defensive rather than aggressive in nature, the resounding repetitions of this national anthem recall in general terms the idioms and functions of the *Marseillaise*, which was similarly employed as a signifier of national identity in Berlioz's Paris.[55] The *Marseillaise* was widely seen as a formidable incitement to arms. Indeed, Kastner cited the *Marseillaise* in his manual on military music as being one of the most powerful pieces in its genre, capable of overcoming men's natural fears in battle and transforming them into a powerful force.[56] On the other hand, in peacetime the overt aggression of the *Marseillaise* could almost appear distasteful. Jules Janin commented that the *Marseillaise* expressed the 'furies des discordes civiles'.[57] And while Berlioz provided his own settings of the *Marseillaise* twice, in 1830 and in 1848, in 1851 he, too, criticised the *Marseillaise* and other revolutionary songs as 'nothing but hymns of wrath and vengeance'.[58] He also complained that France had no national anthem to equal those of Austria, Russia and England. For the performance of national identity to be staged at the Great Exhibition in London he suggested instead that his own 'Hymne à la France' would be better suited to the occasion.[59] Indeed, the international exhibitions were promoted as manifestations of peaceful relations between nations, even if they masked imperial rivalry and colonial conquest.[60]

Both Janin and Berlioz contrasted the *Marseillaise* with Britain's *God Save the Queen*, which could be heard at numerous official functions in London

---

[54] Berlioz, *Les Troyens*, NBE vol. 2b, p. 743.
[55] Marianne Macdonald proposes a direct relationship between the two marches: *Sing Sorrow: Classics, History, and Heroines in Opera* (Westport, CT: Greenwood Press, 2001), p. 105.
[56] Kastner, *Manuel général de musique militaire*, p. 167.
[57] Jules Janin, *Le mois de mai à Londre et l'exposition de 1851* (Paris: Michel Levy Frères, 1851), p. 140.
[58] *CG* IV, p. 71. [59] Ibid., p. 71.
[60] Paul Greenhalgh, *Ephemeral Vistas: The Expositions Universelles, Great Exhibitions and World's Fairs, 1851–1939* (Manchester: Manchester University Press, 1988), pp. 64–5.

Ex. 5.3 *Les Troyens* No. 18 'Chant national: Gloire à Didon', bb. 7–14

at the time of the Great Exhibition.[61] Berlioz planned to write a composition of his own on the theme of the British anthem. The piece did not eventuate, but his tribute to *God Save the Queen* eventually bore fruit in *Les Troyens*.[62] The Carthaginian hymn 'Gloire à Didon', which is sung by Didon's people in Act III (Ex. 5.3), clearly recalls the British anthem in its words, musical idiom, and purpose. Indeed, Berlioz acknowledged as much to his sister Adèle: 'C'est le *God save the Queen* de Carthage.'[63]

The first performance of the Carthaginian hymn in *Les Troyens* might also recall contexts in which Berlioz heard *God Save the Queen* in London. 'Gloire à Didon' introduces ceremonies in which Didon awards prizes to her builders (a silver set square and axe), sailors (a rudder and oar) and labourers (a golden sickle). Finally, with a crown of flowers in her hand, she proclaims the labourers to be the supreme winners of this veritable exhibition of colonial industry. The scene evokes aspects of the royal presence at exhibition ceremonies, as one critic noted with disapproval in 1863 (finding it a 'too

[61] Janin, *Le mois de mai*, p. 140.　[62] Cairns, *Servitude and Greatness*, p. 395.
[63] *CG* V, p. 471.

Museums, exhibitions, human zoos

Ex. 5.3 (cont.)

modern reference for such an ancient subject').[64] At the opening ceremony for the 1851 Great Exhibition, as the Queen and royal family entered the Crystal Palace, *God Save the Queen* was sung by a massed choir. After Victoria had mounted a throne, and the event was introduced by Prince Albert and blessed by the Archbishop of Canterbury, the Queen joined a procession that surveyed the exhibits, accompanied by music from a military band and four organs, signifying her ownership of the exhibition, while she moved amongst her subjects in a manner that was unprecedented.[65] Promotional material for subsequent exhibitions would reinforce this image of the white woman benevolently surveying her colonial possessions.

'Gloire à Didon' provides a telling foil for the 'Marche troyenne' in this subtle imperial battle. Although the words of the initial presentation of the 'Marche troyenne' strip away the bloodthirsty aggression of France's 'hymn of vengeance', the music nevertheless retains a discrete association with the characteristic French theme, and with revolutionary and military idioms more broadly. From its first appearance the 'Marche troyenne' propels performers and listeners forward with its repeated anacruses, dotted rhythms, fanfare-like leaps onto strong beats and vigorous marching metre – not exactly easy to sing along to, but almost demanding the muscular bonding typical of a march. Its idiom is thus greatly contrasted with that of 'Gloire à Didon', which preserves the heavily symmetrical four-bar phrasing, the frequent repetition, and the triple time (antithetical to marching) which are found in *God Save the Queen*. In other words, 'Gloire à Didon', like its British counterpart, bears the traits of a hymn to be learnt and sung by a 'peaceful people'. Together Berlioz's two anthems presage the respective fates of the Carthaginians (so ill-prepared for war against Iarbas that many can only arm themselves with scythes, axes, and slings, and who will eventually fall with their Queen) and the Trojans (who will press forward to victory at the expense of others).

Reinforcing the connection between the Trojan march and contemporaneous ideas of military pageantry is its orchestration – most notably the presence of troops of saxhorns. The saxhorns might be intended to stand in for the 'Phrygian trumpets' mentioned in the libretto; however, these instruments also bore strong associations with modern military music for an audience of Berlioz's time. Cormac Newark has pointed out how Meyerbeer's famous display of up to eighteen saxhorns in *Le prophète* in 1849

---

[64] Paul de Saint-Victor, quoted in Heidlberger, *Dossier de presse*, p. 121.
[65] Davis, *The Great Exhibition*, p. 127; Pieter van Wesemael, *Architecture of Instruction and Delight: A Socio-historical Analysis of World Exhibitions as a Didactic Phenomenon (1798–1851–1970)* (Rotterdam: Uitgeverij 010, 2001), pp. 199–200.

speaks to a sense of modernity and 'ostentatious novelty' in which audiences could enjoy the explicit employment of technology.[66] Newark also remarks how the associations that critics sometimes drew between musical instruments and weapons in Meyerbeer's work might have been encouraged by the fact that saxhorns were employed by military bands.[67] Indeed, Sax and his instruments were central to the reforms of military music that had taken place in 1845. Berlioz wrote at length in the *Journal des débats* supporting the reforms, which saw a full complement of saxhorns of different ranges replace bassoons, oboes, and horns.[68] His preference was primarily based on the timbre of the saxhorns, which he saw as providing consistency of tone across a wide range, and as capable of projecting well in open-air settings. But the saxhorns were also well suited to military employment for physical reasons, since with their compact size and upright playing position, they could easily be carried by cavalry musicians and by soldiers marching in closed ranks.[69]

In 1848 the revolution saw the reversal of the governmental decree that had promoted Sax's instruments. It was only in 1852 that Napoleon III returned Sax and his instruments to a position of prominence in military music. By 1856, when Berlioz wrote saxhorn parts in the 'Trojan march', the instrument would thus have established itself firmly in the audience's minds as a military instrument and, perhaps, one associated with the imperial authority of Napoleon III.

In the years immediately preceding the composition of *Les Troyens*, the propagation of Sax's instruments through the 1851 and 1855 international exhibitions (the latter of which was initiated by Napoleon III in response to the earlier British event) served only to strengthen the associations of the saxhorn with the power of the French empire. Berlioz made it clear in a letter to the French Minister for Agriculture and Commerce that his brief for the 1851 London exhibition was 'to defend the French exhibiters, insofar as the interests of art and the justness of their cause permits me'.[70] Sax, though Belgian by birth, was seen as representing the Parisian instrument industry – Berlioz reported to d'Ortigue: 'It is France which is far and away the winner over the whole of Europe. Erard, Sax and Vuillaume.'[71] In fact, the international exhibitions saw musical instruments became weapons in the staging of a kind of virtual warfare between the two greatest European imperial powers of the age, emphasised by the fact that the first international exhibitions – and all of those in Berlioz's

---

[66] Newark, 'Metaphors for Meyerbeer', 30–2.   [67] Ibid., p. 33.   [68] *CM* VI, pp. 19–26.
[69] Kemp, *Les Troyens*, p. 208.   [70] *CG* IV, p. 55.   [71] Ibid., p. 73.

lifetime – simply alternated back and forth between Paris and London: 'The two countries share[d] domination of the world', as Yvonne Brunhammer has suggested.[72]

In the international exhibitions, national identity was staged in ways that highlighted these imperial rivalries. To some in France, the London exhibition of 1851 seemed to appropriate an exhibition concept that belonged to the French: 'it appeared that England, invading our ground, wrested from us our national glory, just as she took our colonies when we had rendered them productive.'[73] Exhibits from the colonised lands themselves augmented the 'territory' occupied at exhibition grounds by the two rival imperial powers. One French commentator suggested that the visitor to the 1855 exhibition might admire how 'the two great sovereigns seem to say, without even speaking: Queen, the Indies are yours; Emperor, Africa is yours to be civilised!'[74] Objects and raw materials from the lands of imperial conquest were displayed not merely as curiosities, but to reinforce the British or French sense that these distant lands were 'theirs', and thereby to justify the expansion of imperialist policies.[75]

The French were forced to concede that Britain had the upper hand in the technology of the industrial age. It was thus partly in the interests of national pride that the 1855 exhibition emphasised the importance of 'beaux arts', where France could be seen to have the advantage,[76] and through the fine arts, France was considered to promote a 'civilizing' force.[77] But musical instruments were an area in which France was able to compete on terms that were industrial as well as aesthetic. Moreover, when those instruments were military instruments actively employed by troops in battle, the imperial connotations become even more direct. In *Les Troyens* the actual battles all take place offstage – everyone who dies on stage does so at their own hands. As was the case at the exhibitions, imperial strength is instead manifested through the display of the objects of industry – and of war. While the

---

[72] Yvonne Brunhammer, 'Comment fait-on l'exposition des expositions universelles?' in Yvonne Brunhammer, François Mathey, Daniel Janicot, and Robert Bordaz (eds.), *Le livre des expositions universelles 1851–1989* (Paris: Union Centrale des Arts Décoratifs, 1983), p. 12.

[73] Baron Charles Dupin, 'Comparison of the Industry of Paris and London', translated and reprinted in Dionysius Lardner, *The Great Exhibition and London in 1851* (London: Longman, Brown, Green, and Longmans, 1852), p. 444. See also Patricia Mainardi, *Art and Politics of the Second Empire: The Universal Expositions of 1855 and 1867* (New Haven and London: Yale University Press, 1987), p. 22.

[74] J.-J. Arnoux, 'Le travail universel. Revue complète des œuvres de l'art et de l'industrie exposées à Paris en 1855', quoted in Brunhammer et al. (eds.), *Le livre des expositions universelles*, p. 38.

[75] Greenhalgh, *Ephemeral Vistas*, pp. 53–4.

[76] Mainardi, *Art and Politics of the Second Empire*, p. 30.

[77] Greenhalgh, *Ephemeral Vistas*, pp. 115–6.

saxhorns symbolise the military strength of the imperial power, the 'tarbuka' and antique cymbals of the 'Pas d'esclaves nubiennes' become in effect the spoils of colonial conquest, laid out before two rival colonial forces for their entertainment.

Berlioz does not depict actual battle on the stage, but he does further solidify the nexus between technology and military prowess in the 'Marche troyenne' through the way he first establishes, and then effectively 'conquers', physical space. The saxhorns form part of two separate bands which approach from offstage to convey the movement of the Trojan procession, while a third band comprising harps and oboes is also placed offstage, albeit closer to the audience. Like the climax of the 'Chasse royale et orage', the coordination of these three separate off-stage groups as well as the musicians in the pit was a feat that required militarily inspired tactics on behalf of the conductor. Berlioz here puts his 'electric metronome' to good use, stipulating its employment in the score. (See Ex. 5.2, earlier.) The device, already trialled for the chorus of invisible (offstage) angels in *L'enfance du Christ*, in this new context evokes some of the militaristic uses of the early telegraph technology to coordinate distant battalions, as well as the industrial prowess celebrated in the exhibitions.[78]

Like the pilgrims' march of *Harold en Italie*, the Trojan march approaches and recedes in essentially a large dynamic hairpin, though the effect is this time enhanced by the actual physical approach and retreat of the various groups of instrumentalists and singers. Where in *Harold en Italie* we imagined the march through the subjectivity of Harold, whose viola persona (and *idée fixe*) provided the constant point of reference, the 'Marche troyenne' gives us Cassandre, present on stage throughout, and responding in distress to what she and we, the audience, know is a fateful moment.

The effect of the first presentation of the 'Marche troyenne' is further strenthened because earlier militarily inflected music in Berlioz's opera takes the form of staged displays in which the audience maintains more distance, as witnesses of spectacle. For example, the 'Pas des lutteurs' (No. 5) is positioned as an injection of couleur locale, recalling the Pyrrhic dances of ancient Greece. The flurry of movement in the piccolo and rapid tempo are consistent with the features of the ancient war dance, which Kastner suggested was performed by young men to the accompaniment of a flute, and with a first section characterised by rapid footwork.[79] Berlioz ensures

---

[78] Indeed, the inventor Verbrugghe was involved in setting up the electric metronome for the massive concerts associated with the 1855 Exposition Universelle, in which Berlioz conducted with five subconductors.

[79] Kastner, *Manuel général de musique militaire*, p. 10 fn. 2.

that the audience will remain distanced from the dance as spectacle when, in the contrasting section, he ventures into 5/8 time – a metre incompatible with the Parisian ballroom or the march of the streets. When we then get a march redolent of the *Marseillaise* we can easily imagine a quite different reaction of familiarity and physical identification. However, this is precisely what Berlioz initially thwarts through Cassandre's presence. During the approach of the march the orchestra in the pit largely supports Cassandre with sustained notes that mirror her recitative, thus creating a division between the music of her mind and the music of the approaching masses. But as the procession draws nearer, the orchestra gradually becomes more and more committed to the march, even simulating a walking rhythm in pizzicato strings (from b. 93, at 'Au son des flûtes de Dindyme'). In this way the audience gets pulled into the communal idiom, and at the same time we see that Cassandre's vision and the Trojan reality are drawing closer to each other as the moment of crisis approaches.

The 'Pas des lutteurs' presents the audience with a display of dance. In contrast, in the first statement of the Trojan march we are for a long time denied the element of spectacle – a spectacle that, like the glint of arms in the pageantry of Grand Opera, the sights of the International Exhibitions, and the military parades on the streets of Paris, could be construed as a vital component of audience gratification that simultaneously helped to build national spirit. Significantly, when the saxhorns finally appear on the stage they arrive at precisely the same moment as the horse – the ultimate symbol of military technology, which is likened in the libretto to a 'machine'. At the same moment, the orchestra and bands unite for a *forte* statement of the march theme. Cassandre is veritably overwhelmed by the orchestral technology. 'L'énorme machine roulante s'avance!' [The enormous wheeled machine is nearing!] she exclaims shortly before the saxhorns and chorus enter the stage. 'La voici!' ['Here it is!']. She then falls out of the texture altogether as the Trojan march resounds, and she is not heard again until the military brass and horse have left the stage.

The fearsome nature of the Trojan horse is due to the fact that it literally conceals human agency, making it the most potent form of weapon. The relationship between horse-as-weapon and orchestral technology is dramatically exposed at the moment when the march is briefly interrupted by the clatter of Greek weapons from within. Berlioz simulates the sound by a timpani roll in the pit, culminating in a clash of cymbals offstage. The sound is produced just seconds after the saxhorns, too, have left the stage, and in this brief rupture of the musical fabric there is a moment in which the clatter of saxhorns in the wings and the clatter of the weapons imagined to be within the horse become one. Similar ruptures are found elsewhere in the opera, as at the end of Act IV, when the god Mercury strikes his caduceus against Énée's shield, in which a gong is concealed. Mercury thereby breaks the spell of the sublime duet of Didon and Énée with a reminder that 'Italie' beckons. More subtly, the sounds of musical weaponry breach the division between diegetic and nondiegetic sound when Énée is awoken from his troubled sleep in the midst of the siege of Troy by what Berlioz describes as 'Un bruit d'écroulement' [a rumble of destruction] sounded by a fortissimo tutti chord and rolling bass drum and cymbals. While opera frequently plays off this relationship between the realms of diegetic music heard by the characters and nondiegetic music heard only by the audience, in Berlioz's *Les Troyens* the world of military music repeatedly collides with the noumenal world of the characters in a way that seems particularly fraught – or indeed, militant. In this 'song of arms and of a man', the song and arms are united in musical instruments which themselves act almost as 'numinous intruders'. These moments in which instruments voice weapons not only jolt the characters out of their reverie, but also invite the audience to question the role of music, and of the opera itself, in their own imperial context.

Exhibit 3: Instruments of supernatural vision

When he was in Italy in the early 1830s, Berlioz seemed to see the spirits of Aeneas and the victims of the siege of Latium materialising before his eyes, as the Subiacco region stirred his memories of the *Aeneid*: 'the funniest part of it was that my grief was so real.'[80] Two decades later, *Les Troyens* could be seen to give life to his spiritual vision. Unlike the duet of *La nonne sanglante*, *Les Troyens* also presents its ghosts directly to the characters and to the audience rather than evoking them obliquely through narrative ballads that appeal to the inner eye. The manifestations of *Troyens*' ghosts are described in detail in Berlioz's stage directions. However, Berlioz also returns to elements of the idiom of the unseen ghost of *La nonne sanglante*, with the supernatural scenes of the later opera revealing a similar focus on orchestral sonority. And Berlioz's *Troyens* reenacts in musical terms the characteristic tension between corporeality and fantasy that is essential to the ghost's nature. That tension between, on one hand, material objects

---

[80] Berlioz, *Memoirs*, p. 146.

visible to the eye, and, on the other, worlds 'beyond', which are accessible only to those capable of seeing 'through' those objects, is charged with significance for the discourse surrounding Romantic music, as we have seen elsewhere. Significantly for the framework of this chapter, that same tension was also inherent in the developments in museum culture and exhibitions in the nineteenth century.[81] Drawing those two contexts together, we can see how musical instruments might evoke the supernatural through both their physical properties and their ability to produce ephemeral sound. In looking at the ghost scenes of *Les Troyens* we are made particularly aware of the dual status of Berlioz's musical instruments.

The first spectral apparition in *Les Troyens* is the ghost of Hector, who appears to Énée to send him on his mission during the destruction of Troy. However, Hector's ghost is foreshadowed by Cassandre, who prophesises the fall of Troy and describes her vision of the spirit of the Trojan prince (still living at this point). Cassandre's prediction of the ghost recalls aspects of the narrative ballade, for it emphasises the way in which ghosts disrupt the temporal fabric of the tangible world. In this case the disruption is extreme: Hector's ghost as glimpsed by Cassandre is not simply an apparition from the past, speaking to the present of the future. Rather, it is a vision of a spirit belonging to a person still living, for in Cassandre's world, those around her are already ghosts.

As in the 'Légende', for Cassandre's premonition of Hector's ghost Berlioz employs the distinctive sonority of stopped horns: a single horn stops the second note of each pair in a repeated timbral diminuendo. Stopped horns also accompany the subsequent appearance of the actual ghost to Énée. Although valve horns were prevalent by this time, Berlioz asks for two of the four horns to be natural horns and directs all four to play the notes stopped. His stage directions and music together preserve all the eerie ambiguity between corporeality and metaphysics typical of the operatic supernatural: Hector's ghost, when it appears to Énée, is bloody, his beard and hair disordered – an image Berlioz draws from Virgil's text, which reminds us that that ghosts are not pure spirit, for they bleed (as the very title of the ghost opera *La nonne sanglante* suggests). Moreover, Berlioz indicates that Hector's ghost should approach Énée from a dark corner of the stage, walking slowly 'sur le rhythme de l'orchestre' in a clear case of orchestrally embodied gesture. The ghost is here completely one with the orchestral sound (Ex. 5.4). The sound that awakens Énée and

---

[81] Bennett, *The Birth of the Museum*, p. 35.

Ex. 5.4 *Les Troyens* No. 12 Scène et récitatif, bb. 75–94

Ex. 5.4 (cont.)

ruptures the divide between worlds utilises the release of open notes in the horns. But when Hector's ghost addresses Énée, the horns return to the stopped notes so characteristic of Berlioz's ghosts, as breath – or spirit – is trapped by flesh. Finally, in Hector's long-drawn-out chromatic descent

Ex. 5.4 (*cont.*)

we hear the physical weakening of an *almost* lifeless body, which Berlioz directs should recede into the distance, becoming more and more indistinct (Ex. 5.5).

When Hector's ghost returns in the second half of *Les Troyens* to urge Énée to resume his quest, it is accompanied by the ghosts of Cassandre and King Priam (Ex. 5.6). Each ghost sings briefly, confined to a wholly

Ex. 5.5 *Les Troyens* No. 12 Scène et récitatif, bb. 108–42

static prolongation of a single pitch. Again it is the orchestral sonority that draws our attention – though not the sonority of stopped horns this time, but a play of contrasting timbres that emphasises the disorientation of the diminished-seventh harmonies which dominate the movement. A low *D* (written as *C*) sounds in the horns (the lowest note Berlioz wrote for this instrument) and bassoons, as well as in the double basses – who must tune their lowest string down a tone to reach this pitch. A chorus of ten 'invisible' basses emerge from the orchestral shadows to intone Énée's name on the same pitch. Next it is the turn of the rest of the woodwinds (the oboe replaced by cor anglais and the second clarinet replaced by bass clarinet for a more veiled sound), who sustain a diminished seventh chord. This is

Ex. 5.5 (cont.)

succeeded by an arpeggiated diminished seventh arising from the depths of the strings and leading to a stratospheric chord of harmonics played by four solo violins, heralding the arrival of Priam's ghost. These three basic timbral blocks are repeated, with variation, for each of the ghosts as it renders itself visible and speaks to Énée.

The high string harmonics were earlier used by Berlioz in *Reine Mab* and in *Roméo et Juliette* for a suitably delicate, otherworldly sound, as well as in 'Au cimetière' in *Les nuits d'été* at the moment when the narrator imagines a veiled female figure, half ghost, half memory, passing by the grave. Indeed, string harmonics were evocative of the ghostly technology of Berlioz's time. They could suggest the sonority of the glass harmonica, which was a favourite instrument to accompany ghosts in the

Ex. 5.5 (cont.)

phantasmagoria shows and mesmerism.[82] String harmonics also suggest the equally supernatural sounds of the Aeolian harp – the ultimate instrument of disembodied voice. In a study devoted to the Aeolian harp, Kastner suggested that the most effective way to imitate the instrument was through simultaneous string harmonics – an observation Kastner claims to have shared with Berlioz.[83] The Aeolian harp was in turn associated with the telegraph, and with all the fascinations of disembodied or spiritual communication that accompanied the new technology. Kastner relates how many in Paris had been enchanted and disturbed by the sound of the wind in

---

[82] Hadlock, 'Sonorous Bodies: Women and the Glass Harmonica', *Journal of the American Musicological Society* 53/3 (2000), 529.

[83] Georges Kastner, *La harpe d'éole et la musique cosmique: Études sur les rapports de phénomènes sonores de la nature avec la science et l'art* (Paris: Brandus, 1856), p. XII.

Ex. 5.5 (*cont.*)

the telegraph wires, which 'made those wires vibrate and drew from them harmonious sounds that exactly recalled those of ancient Aeolian harps'. Kastner adds, 'By moonlight, in the still of the night, this noise mixed with the murmur of the river, making a deep impression on the observer and peopling his mind with uncanny memories. It was like attending the scene of a melodrama, and one could very nearly see phantoms on the quays.'[84]

Les Troyens draws on the industrial ambitions of the international exhibitions as well as museum culture to give voice to instruments from 'Other worlds'. As we have seen, Berlioz had encountered at least some of the exotic and archaic instruments he brings onto the stage of *Les Troyens* in museums

---

[84] *L'Assemblée nationale*, 19 December 1850, quoted in Kastner, *La harpe d'éole*, p. 105.

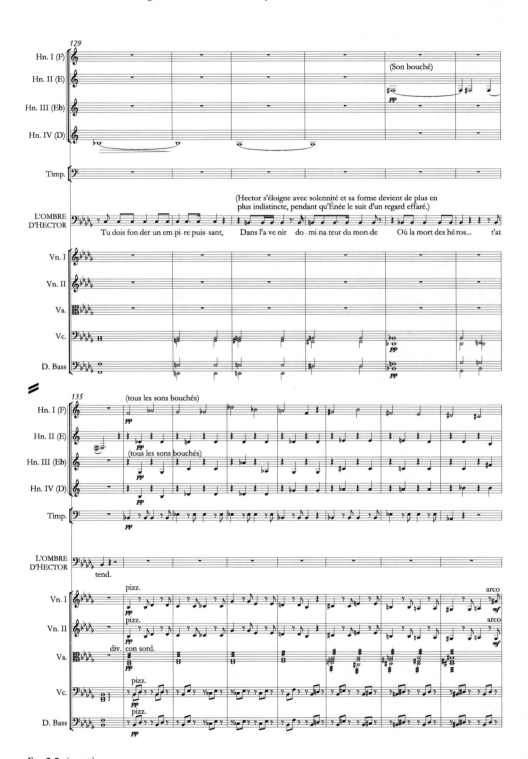

Ex. 5.5 (cont.)

Ex. 5.6 *Les Troyens* No. 42 Scène, bb. 1–15

and at international exhibitions – exhibitions whose display could itself be described in the terms of the potency of mesmerism to, as Charlotte Brontë expressed it, 'rule and subdue by some invisible influence'.[85] Often it was

---

[85] Quoted in Winter, *Mesmerized*, p. 27.

Ex. 5.6 (*cont.*)

the objects themselves, rather than the visitors to exhibitions, who might be construed as mesmerised subjects. Objects like the antique cymbals, which Berlioz had viewed at the Herculaneum museum amidst artefacts unearthed at Pompeii, were sometimes perceived as possessing a kind of

Ex. 5.6 (*cont.*)

ghostly agency, as if they were arisen from the grave of the past.[86] When visiting the archaeological sites of the cities buried by the eruption of Vesuvius, Berlioz commented on the uncanny quality of these historic settings: 'Who has not lingered sadly among the skeleton remains of desolate

[86] Macdonald, *Berlioz's Orchestration Treatise*, p. 279. Berlioz used the cymbals in *Roméo et Juliette*; unlike other ancient instruments evoked in *Les Troyens*, these do sound and do not require an orchestral double.

Ex. 5.6 (*cont.*)

Pompeii, or stood waiting, a solitary spectator, on the steps of the amphitheatre, for the curtain to rise on a tragedy of Euripides or Sophocles, for which the stage seems all prepared?'[87] Like the archaic or exotic instruments of museums and exhibitions of Berlioz's time, his double flute, antique cymbals, sistrum, and tarbuka either do not sound or have their sound reinforced from the orchestra pit. The tactic is suggestive of a common trick in magic shows of the time, in which the sound of an on-stage instrument or singer was produced by another musician offstage in an act of fake ventriloquism.

[87] Berlioz, *Memoirs*, p. 165.

But it also recalls the ghostly spirits channelled by a medium or a mesmerist. For example, under the spell of Dr Miracle, Antonia in Offenbach's *Les contes d'Hoffmann* 'sings' with the voice of a clarinet, representing quite literally mesmerism's tendency to treat its human subjects as instruments animated by external forces.[88]

In *Les Troyens* it is Cassandre who channels supernatural visions, not through mesmerism but through the power of prophecy, which enables her to see and listen to the ghosts of the future. Berlioz radically increases Cassandre's role relative to her presence in Virgil's *Aeneid*, and indeed Cassandre's dilemma resonated not only on a personal emotional level for Berlioz, but also in terms of the broader context during a period in which clairvoyance was an increasingly controversial topic, subject to competing claims on behalf of psychology and science.[89] Cassandre's ability to hear the stopped horns of Hector's ghost before he has even died encapsulates that dilemma, but she seems also to channel an instrumental voice in her subsequent duet with Chorèbe. The fraught statements of her distress in the lower strings ebb away, though a restless oboe remains, and when Chorèbe tries to reassure her with a lyrically seductive cantabile section, the oboe line constantly interjects at irregular intervals with reminders of Cassandre's anxiety (Ex. 5.7). The effect is similar not only to that of Antonia's clarinet, but to the instrumental embodiment of illusion or madness in, for example, Lucia di Lammermoor's mad scene (doubled by flute) or Lady Macbeth's sleepwalking (punctuated by oboe appoggiaturas), to take examples of nineteenth-century operatic heroines whose visions of things invisible to their audiences instead manifest themselves aurally.

If Cassandre invokes aspects of mesmerism and technologically infused clairvoyance in her instrumental interjections to Chorèbe, at the conclusion of their duet the idea of haunting seems to be taken to the level of operatic metanarrative. The stretta of the duet is, Macdonald persuasively suggests, lifted directly from the conclusion of the duet between Agnès and Rodolphe in *La nonne sanglante*, which breaks off at precisely this point.[90] If we compare this text to Scribe's libretto for *La nonne*, we see the pronounced similarities that support Macdonald's claim. Some phrases reappear almost word for word, as in each duet one lover pleads with the other to flee before

---

[88] Winter, *Mesmerized*, pp. 63, 309.
[89] Louise Henson, 'Investigations and Fictions: Charles Dickens and Ghosts', in Bown, Burdett, and Thurschwell (eds.), *The Victorian Supernatural*, p. 59.
[90] The autograph manuscript of fragments of the abandoned *Nonne sanglante* specifically states in Berlioz's handwriting that the work is 'à consulter', but also 'à brûler après mon mort'. *NBE* vol. 4, p. 322.

Ex. 5.7 *Les Troyens* No. 3 Duo, bb. 165–94

Ex. 5.7 (cont.)

dawn. Only minimal alteration to the music is required to enable the *Troyens* duet to fit the text of *La nonne sanglante*.

Comparison of the text of the duets from Scribe's *La nonne sanglante* (as set by Gounod) and *Les Troyens* No. 3

RODOLFE	CASSANDRE
Ô toi que j'adore !	Quitte-nous dès ce soir,
Ô toi que j'implore !	Entends-moi, je t'implore,
Bien avant l'aurore	Dans nos murs que l'aurore
Il faut fuir tous deux !	Ne puisse te revoir !
L'amour, qui m'inspire,	D'épouvante j'expire
Saura nous conduire.	Et mon cœur se déchire !
Consens, ou j'expire	Et mon cœur se déchire !
D'amour à tes yeux !	Pars ce soir, pars ce soir !
AGNÈS	**CHORÈBE**
Mon cœur, qui t'adore,	Te quitter, dès ce soir !

(cont.)

(cont.)

Te prie et t'implore !	Cassandre ! et je t'adore !
Quand viendra l'aurore	Sauve-moi, je t'implore,
Fuis seul de ces lieux !	D'un affreux désespoir.
Tu vas me maudire...	Tu veux donc que j'expire ?
Et dans mon délire	Sans pitié peux-tu dire :
Je t'aime !... et j'expire	Sans pitié peux-tu dire :
De crainte à tes yeux	Pars ce soir, pars ce soir !
[Rodolfe: O you whom I love, O you whom I implore, well before dawn we must flee together! Love, which inspires me will be our guide. Consent, or I will die of love before your eyes!	[Cassandre: Leave us tonight. Hear me, I implore you! Within our walls dawn must not see you here! I am dying of terror and my heart is breaking! And my heart is breaking! Leave tonight, leave tonight!
Agnès: My heart, which loves you, pleas and implores you: when dawn comes flee alone from this place! You are going to curse me, and in my madness I love you!... and I will die of fear before your eyes!]	Chorèbe: Leave you tonight? Cassandra! I adore you! Save me, I implore you, from awful despair. Do you want me to die? Without pity, you say: leave tonight! Leave tonight!]

Moreover, Berlioz renders the music of the stretta uncanny through the way he introduces it into *Les Troyens*. The first phrase of the melody is actually foreshadowed earlier in the duet (in the interlude between Chorèbe's first two verses in the Cavatine), but in grossly distorted form, in a sequence in which Berlioz ventures further towards atonality than he was generally comfortable with. Indeed, the 'ugly' dissonance of this section suggests the negative attributes Berlioz later ascribed to the 'music of the future', and it accompanies a particularly intense vision of the grisly fate of the Trojans that Cassandre desperately tries to communicate to Chorèbe (Ex. 5.8). When the lovers are united in the stretta at the end of the duet, the transformed theme suggests a more optimistic view of the future – but one whose optimism we have good reason to doubt, retaining as it does the music of Cassandre's despair.

Berlioz quite often reused music, finding new homes for material from works that he had abandoned and which he did not expect to be performed again. The fact that now, thanks to the work of editors and recordings, the abandoned works, too, can be made accessible means that contemporary audiences may draw on a richer web of intertextual allusion, leading to a situation where one work can be seen to haunt the other. The insertion – or reinsertion – of material into Berlioz's Trojan opera effectively 'galvanises'

Museums, exhibitions, human zoos 291

Ex. 5.8 *Les Troyens* No. 3 Duo, bb. 101–64

Ex. 5.8 (*cont.*)

the limbs of the fragmentary *Nun*, permitting it to be brought back to life for a modern audience, while also bearing uncanny traces of the later opera from which this material is more likely to be familiar. For *Les Troyens*, an allusion to the earlier opera about ghosts might encourage us to realise the extent to which the mature work is itself haunted by 'numinous intruders': Cassandre, like Agnès, sees ghosts in visions her lover is unable to share until too late. The ultimate irony, of course, is that Cassandre herself would remain only a ghostly vision for Berlioz, who was unable to have the first two acts of the opera staged in his lifetime. The preservation of *Les Troyens* as an integral work would depend on its own place in the imaginary museum, from which it was revived in different times and places after Berlioz's death.

Exhibit 4: Instruments of the future

In May 1851 Gounod's *Sapho* was drawing to the end of its brief first season in Paris while in London the first international exhibition got underway.

Berlioz attended both events, departing Paris for London on 9 May to take up his duties as judge. In the years that followed, he drew inspiration for *Les Troyens* from a lifetime of events and experiences. However, singling out these two events from the period immediately anticipating *Les Troyens* reveals a provocative dialectic.

The Great Exhibition was feted as a eulogy to progress, which, like the implicit narratives of many museums, emphasised the benefits of industry, 'fetishized the machine', and placed western man as the telos of an evolutionary trajectory which projected constantly forwards.[91] European instruments were thus positioned as objects of industrial progress, while instruments from other countries and especially those from colonial possessions such as India were situated outside that narrative. Those instruments were often displayed among raw materials, and by implication relegated to an earlier stage of the evolutionary model, or were depicted as existing outside temporal considerations altogether. However, the industrialism of the exhibition, and of the treatment of music within it, was not always viewed positively. Paul Greenhalgh claims that the Great Exhibition shifted the emphasis from the consumption of products to the process of their fabrication, to encourage and validate the labour upon which the products were dependent and to foster a good work ethic among the British population. However, Tony Bennett suggests that emphasis inevitably fell on the marvels of the products themselves, and that subsequent exhibitions increasingly had the effect of 'stupefying' the worker and effectively alienating him or her from his or her own labour.[92] In terms of the display of musical instruments, the emphasis on manufactured products over the labour of performers might have been seen to reinforce a similar ethos. Berlioz related the 'abominable chore' of listening to the hundreds of mostly bad wind and brass instruments, which he described as 'nasty machines' which made him 'lose his head' ('la tête me part à écouter ces centaines de vilaines machines').[93] In 1852, in response to a revival of *Sapho*, he wrote of 'our time of mechanisation, mannequinism (and neologism), and industrialism disguised to a greater or lesser extent under the pretext of art'.[94]

In contrast to the modernist anxieties of the instrumental presence at the exhibitions, Berlioz presents Gounod's opera as an antidote to the industrialism of the age, and praises the work's 'good artistic sense, poetic nature,

---

[91] Greenhalgh, *Ephemeral Vistas*, p. 13.
[92] Paul Greenhalgh, 'Education, Entertainment and Politics: Lessons from the Great International Exhibitions', in Vergo, *The New Museology*, p. 87; Bennett, *The Birth of the Museum*, p. 81.
[93] *CG* IV, p. 69.
[94] *Journal des débats*, 7 January 1852, 1. See also Cairns, *Servitude and Greatness*, p. 592.

simple truth, modest grandeur and power without brutality'.[95] In writing his own classically oriented opera, he might be expected to have aspired to the same qualities he identified in Gounod's work, and to have eschewed the industrial mechanism of the exhibition. If this was his aspiration, to many critics he would appear to have failed. Berlioz's reputation for noisy orchestration was still with him when the Carthaginian acts of Les Troyens were premiered in 1863, and reviewers had no difficulty in finding evidence of his continued misdemeanours in this regard. Paul de Saint-Victor in La Presse suggested, for example, that in places the orchestra 'takes the stage and the voices are stifled by this formidable apparatus of wood and brass';[96] and Auguste Durand in L'esprit publique claimed that the suppression of the 'Chasse royale et orage' after the first performance was not the fault of Carvalho's stage machinery (there had been a forty-five minute delay in preparing the set for the subsequent scene), but of the music – 'cette inconcevable production instrumentale' – which had left the public cold.[97]

In fact, Berlioz himself referred to Les Troyens itself as a 'machine' numerous times. Such a use of the word 'machine' was not particularly unusual, for it suggested the multiple components (including stage machinery) that went into a massive operatic work of this kind. But Berlioz's ready adoption of the mechanical metaphor might encourage us at least to reconsider the concept of mechanism within Les Troyens. Indeed, such a reconsideration reveals in Les Troyens a concern with technology closely aligned with a sense of futurism more explicit than that of La damnation de Faust. Moreover, as in the earlier 'légende dramatique' and Euphonia, the anxiety that attends the conspicuous presence of orchestral technology in Les Troyens may be considered part of the dramatic fabric of the work itself. The low trombones and horn that snarl from the pit when Énée, at his first appearance, describes the serpent that killed Laocoon and his sons are a conspicuously mechanistic portent of Troy's fate (recalling the similarly 'ugly' brass of Méphistophélès's 'Évocation'). Furthermore, each half of the work concludes with fatalistic visions of the future, which overwhelm first Cassandre and then Didon. When Cassandre's orchestral support becomes engulfed in the music of the onstage band at the appearance of the horse, and when both she and Didon die surrounded by the weaponry of men, we hear echoes of the fate of Emillac. That the women of Troyens take their own lives distinguishes them profoundly from the unfortunate antagonist of Euphonia, but again it should be noted that in Les Troyens the only 'onstage' deaths are

---

[95] Ibid., 1.   [96] Paul de Saint-Victor, in Heidlberger, Dossier de presse, p. 127.
[97] Quoted in Heidlberger, Dossier de presse, p. 29.

of women, whose fate is sealed by the technology of concealed masculine agency. Furthermore, when the Trojan march sounds at Didon's demise, it not only anticipates the Roman Empire to come but also recalls the horse that accompanied its first entrance and precipitated the Trojans' quest.

As Didon lies on her deathbed, she narrates her own ghostly predictions, foreseeing the future greatness of the Roman Empire and the fate of her African realm. The conclusion transports the listener instantly across centuries in a manner Anselm Gerhard likened to that of the telegraph:

[T]he combination of two scenes separated by several hundred years in historical reality as well as several hundred miles in distance has a breathtaking modernity about it which it is almost impossible to overstate. Like the only recently invented electric telegraph, it transports the audience 'into a world of simultaneity and instancy that went beyond human experience'.[98]

Though Gerhard bases his technological analogy on the scenario rather than the music, we might also note that another of Berlioz's favourite 'réunions des thèmes' accompanies this moment: the Carthaginians' swearing of future vengeance is superimposed over a final appearance of the Trojan march. It is an instance of the 'synchronization of an ever greater number of processes' which was, as we have seen, typical of the disciplines and technologies of the self-consciously modern age.[99]

Thus if critics rehashed favourite complaints about Berlioz's noise or sonic materialism, *Les Troyens* might actually be seen to work the fear of industrialisation into the relentless drive towards the future that underpins its very dramatic structure. In fact, the critics also found plenty to praise in Berlioz's orchestration, at least in certain areas of the opera. Durand, for example, juxtaposed the 'full orchestral din' of the 'Chasse royale' against the ballet music of the same act, which was 'full of freshness and melody', and several other critics similarly singled out the orchestration of the Act IV ballets for praise, for here the conspicuous employment of the orchestra was seen to be positive.[100] A closer examination of the Act IV ballets reveals ways in which orchestral technology frames an othering based in gender and ethnicity that, while perhaps more palatable to Durand than the noisy mechanism he saw in the 'Chasse royale', nevertheless partakes in the same

---

[98] Gerhard, *The Urbanization of Opera*, p. 206.
[99] Rudolf Wendorff, cited in ibid., p. 206. It is surprising that Gerhard does not note the musical device in *Les Troyens*, since the superimposition of different themes (including in Berlioz's instrumental works) is the subject that he discusses immediately prior to this passage (ibid., pp. 205–6).
[100] Heidlberger, *Dossier de presse*, pp. 114, 160.

aesthetics of the future. But to understand this, we need first to explore the background to Berlioz's conception of the ballet, and to step beyond the halls of the 1851 and 1855 exhibitions and into the territory of the 'human zoos'.

Exhibit 5: Bayadères in the human zoo[101]

In February 1857, when Berlioz was fully immersed in the composition of *Les Troyens*, he wrote to his sister Adèle about ideas for the ballet that entertains Didon and Énée and their respective entourages at the Carthaginian court in Act IV:

> I want to have a *pas d'almées* with the music and dancing exactly like the Bayadères' ballet which I saw here sixteen or seventeen years ago. My colleague Casimirski, of the *Débats*, is going to give me some verses by Hafiz, the Persian poet, which I will have sung in Persian by the singing almas, as the Indian women used to do. There is no anachronism, I have gone into it; Dido could easily have had Egyptian dancers at her court who had earlier come from India.[102]

What were Indian dancing girls doing at Didon's court? In denying the anachronism Berlioz inevitably draws our attention to it. His term 'bayadère', which in the original Portuguese simply denotes a female dancer ('bailadeira'), was typically used to refer to Indian temple dancers or *devadasis*, but in introducing bayadères into Didon's court Berlioz was anticipating their existence by at least thirteen hundred years. Berlioz may have found sources that connected bayadères to Virgil's time, at least.[103] Other texts posit general connections between the musical traditions of India and Egypt.[104]

---

[101] This section draws significantly on material published in Inge van Rij, '"There is no anachronism:" Indian Dancing Girls in Ancient Carthage in Berlioz's Les Troyens', *19th-Century Music* 33/1 (2009), 3–24.

[102] *CG* V, p. 433. This translation is from Hugh Macdonald, 'Composition', in Kemp (ed.), *Les Troyens*, p. 55.

[103] The ballet *Sacountala*, which was set to music by Reyer and performed two years after Berlioz's comments to his sister, features bayadères, and in his scenario for the work Théophile Gautier claims that the Indian author of the original story was a 'contemporain de Virgile' – though Kalidasa was in fact active at least four centuries later.

[104] For example, Lichtenthal's musical dictionary (the French edition of which Berlioz reviewed favorably in 1839) points out in the entry on India, 'There is such a great resemblance between the musical and astronomical system of India and those of the Egyptians and the Chinese that one could logically attribute to them a common origin, or believe that these sciences passed by tradition from one of the peoples to the two others.' Pietro Lichtenthal, *Dizionario e bibliografia della musica* (Milan: A. Fontana, 1826); translated and augmented by Dominique Mondo as *Dictionnaire de Musique* (Paris: Troupenas et Compagnie, 1839), vol. 1, p. 508. Berlioz's review of the French edition appears in the *Journal des débats*, 18 October 1839 (*CM* IV, pp. 189–91.)

Various other authors make similar connections between Indian and Egyptian music and dance.[105] However, none go quite so far as to place bayadères in the Carthage of Didon's time. If Berlioz really wanted to avoid anachronism, he should, to use his own words, have 'étudié la question' and 'gone into it' further. But authenticity was presumably not his primary objective. In conceiving the ballets to be performed in Didon's Carthage he surely did not begin with historical accounts of the ancient world, or the presumed authenticity of the museum, for his first impulse was to emulate the bayadères he had seen in Paris sixteen or seventeen years earlier.

In examining Berlioz's more contemporary models, we enter a different kind of museum culture, where live bodies and practices were exhibited in a manner anticipating in many respects the so-called human zoo: peoples of other cultures performed or were displayed to western viewers for the purposes of entertainment and/or science.[106] Such acts could be situated in a variety of contexts, from performances in theatres (as in the case of Berlioz's bayadères) or as living props in panoramas, to acts within international exhibitions or zoological gardens such as the Jardin d'Acclimatation (which first introduced human exhibits in 1877). Human zoos thus acted as a provocative nexus between more familiar forms of performance and the display of inanimate objects in museums and exhibitions, with each mode drawing from and impacting on the other. Though foreigners were objects of curiosity in Europe for centuries, the practice of 'human zoos' really took hold in the nineteenth century as a result of a confluence of three interrelated factors: the European construction of the Other; scientific thinking on racial hierarchy; and the expansion of colonial empire.[107] Berlioz's bayadères, though a relatively early instance of the human-zoo mentality, engage with all three strands.

Berlioz may have encountered a variety of markedly Other performers in Paris and London. For example, he left accounts of his impressions of Chinese musicians in London at the time of the Great Exhibition, and the disdain he expressed for the Botocudo people of Brazil when ironically

---

[105] See, for example, Augustus Bournonville, *My Theater Life*, trans. Patricia N. McAndrew (Middletown, Conn.: Wesleyan University Press, 1979), pp. 8–9.

[106] At the time of writing, human zoos are again in the news, as Norway stages a re-enactment of the 'Kongolandsbyen zoo' of the 1914 Oslo World Fair – an exercise designed to expose historical racism, but which threatens instead to perpetuate it. Bwesigye bwa Mwesigire, 'Norway to Restage 1914 "Human Zoo" That Exhibited Africans as Inmates', *Guardian Africa Network*, 29 April 2014, www.theguardian.com/world/2014/apr/29/norway-human-zoo-africans-as-inmates; accessed 2 June 2014.

[107] Blanchard, Bancel, and Lemaire, 'From Scientific Racism to Popular and Colonial Racism in France and the West', in Blanchard et al. (eds.), *Human Zoos*, p. 105.

praising the representation of the inauthentic 'beautiful savages' in Félicien David's *Perle du Brésil* may indicate that he witnessed the sensational display of a Botoduo man and woman in Paris in 1844.[108] However, this chapter will focus on the Indian bayadères of 1838, as they provide a unique instance where Berlioz not only witnessed the 'human zoo' and its imitation in European staged works, but also contemplated imitating it himself.

Acknowledging the ways in which Berlioz drew on living performers rather than historical evidence does nothing to detract from questions around authenticity and anachronism, for these are effectively the twin bogies of exoticism, and in negotiating the gap between Indian temple and French theatre, between historical artefact and human zoo, between ancient Carthage and contemporary Europe, or, more broadly, between historical or anthropological veracity and operatic convention, Berlioz engaged in a discourse very familiar in the nineteenth century. As recent studies of musical exoticism have ably demonstrated, this discourse typically tended to privilege the second party in each of the above pairings – i.e., nineteenth-century European operatic convention – for exoticism inevitably reflects the host culture more than the culture supposedly being depicted.[109] More broadly, the New Museology has exposed similar agendas in museum practice, and the literature on human zoos has tended to focus on how foreign performers were framed and constructed by their western managers and audiences, while acknowledging the importance of considering the performers' perspectives in the relatively rare cases where those are available.[110] In this context, Berlioz's bayadères – both the originals and their imitations – could be seen as an almost textbook case of exoticism. The distinction between the two sides of the traditional oppositional pairings is heightened, for we have an instance of real bayadères encountered in the flesh by a composer who persistently proved resistant to the charms of music from cultures remote from his own.[111] Berlioz's

---

[108] '[...] those frightful Botocudos of Brazil, chubby, paunchy, heads shaved like monks, and with their lower lips, eight inches long [...], and containing a disc of wood.' *Journal des débats*, 27 November 1851, 1.

[109] Locke, 'Constructing the Oriental "Other"', 261–302; 'A Broader View of Musical Exoticism', *Journal of Musicology* 24/4 (2007), 477–521; and *Musical Exoticism*.

[110] Vergo, *The New Museology*, pp. 1–5; Forsdick, 'Postface: Situating Human Zoos', pp. 377–92; Qureshi, *Peoples on Parade*, pp. 9, 127.

[111] Indeed, Berlioz's disdain may have been infamous: in surveying the Indian instruments at the Great Exhibition, Gautier assumed that Berlioz 'would critique them bitterly', though Gautier himself was of the opinion that 'even if they have little appeal to the ear they are at least charming to the eye'. Gautier, *Caprices et Zigzags* (Paris: Victor Legou, 1852), p. 257.

own musical exoticism has been memorably described as 'nugatory' – with the potent but rare exception of the Act IV ballet itself.[112] But rather than simply dismissing Berlioz's ballet as mere exoticism, we should explore the tension of this dialectic, for such an exploration enriches our understanding of *Les Troyens* and informs our responses to modern productions of his opera – productions whose aesthetics reconfigure in interesting ways the issues of authenticity and anachronism, as we shall see.

Little attention has been given to Berlioz's comments on the origins of the Act IV ballet in *Les Troyens*. Julian Rushton quotes Berlioz's letter to his sister and suggests in a footnote that the bayadère performance was 'possibly danced by real Indian dancers, possibly only at the Opéra'.[113] In fact, other references to the bayadères in Berlioz's writings reveal them to have been very real. In a review of Auber's *L'enfant prodigue* in 1850 Berlioz mentions the 'Indian bayadères who appeared around ten years ago at the Théâtre des Variétés'.[114] While the Théâtre des Variétés was well accustomed to visits from exotic Spanish dancers, the Otherness represented by the bayadères was much more sensational, for this may have been 'the first professional Indian dance troupe to perform in Europe'.[115] The four female dancers, three musicians, and one child were brought to Europe from a Hindu temple in Thiruvendipuram (a small town not far from Pondicherry) by the French impresario E.C. Tardivel. According to one of numerous articles about the group that appeared in the *Courrier des théâtres* before and during their Paris season, Tardivel 'was forced to charm an entire college of Brahminees' to obtain the release of the bayadères from their temple.[116] As was fairly common practice in the performances of 'human zoos', whose managers were keen to dispel any sense of unfair treatment, the *Courrier des théâtres* also published Tardivel's contract with the group.[117] This provides the ages of the dancers (thirty, eighteen, fourteen and thirteen years respectively) and reveals that, in exchange for a set salary and costs, the dancers and musicians

---

[112] Rushton, *The Music of Berlioz*, p. 143.
[113] Ibid., p. 145, n. 38. The editors of the *Correspondance générale* suggest that Berlioz may have been inspired by a revival of Auber's *Le dieu et la bayadère* in 1841, but also mention the visit to Paris of the genuine bayadères in 1838 (*CG* V, p. 433, n. 1).
[114] *Journal des débats*, 9 December 1850, 2.
[115] Joep Bor, 'Mamia, Ammani and other *Bayadères*: Europe's Portrayal of India's Temple Dancers', in Bennet Zon and Martin Clayton (eds.), *Music and Orientalism in the British Empire 1780s–1940s* (Aldershot: Ashgate, 2007), p. 39. See also Binita Mehta, *Widows, Pariahs, and Bayadères: India as Spectacle* (London: Associated University Press, 2002).
[116] *Courrier des théâtres*, 7171 (10 August 1838), 3.
[117] Qureshi, *Peoples on Parade*, p. 136.

agreed to accompany Tardivel wherever he wished to take them in Europe, to perform 'customary dances and music' in theatres of his choosing, and to execute any of Tardivel's commands concerning their exposure to the public.[118]

These are surely the performers referred to by Berlioz.[119] Reports of the 'véritables bayadères' started to reach Paris from Bordeaux, the first stop on Tardivel's itinerary, in late July of 1838. No fewer than eight articles were devoted to the bayadères in the *Courrier des théâtres* in the three weeks preceding their first performance at the Théâtre des Variétés on 22 August. This advance publicity paid off. A journalist in *Le Figaro* commented that the box office takings for the bayadères set a record high. The entire theatre was sold out days in advance for each performance, and the season was extended.[120]

Some idea of the expectations of the Parisian audience can be gained from the play performed as a prologue to the bayadères' first appearance at the Théâtre des Variétés. The manuscript of *Le Corridor des Baignoires* (held in the archives of the Théâtre des Variétés at the Archives Nationales in Paris) is dated 22 August 1838 on its cover – the date of the bayadères' Paris premiere. As the title states, this excessively self-reflexive play is set in the corridors of the ground-floor boxes of the Théâtre des Variétés itself. A representative sample of those likely to be in attendance – the usher, a regular attendee of the theatre, a little female dancer, a young lawyer, and a 'dandy from the provinces, a ridiculous tourist' – discuss what they have heard of the bayadères, and what they expect to see, while they find their seats and wait for the curtain to go up.[121] *Le Corridor des Baignoires* thus both reflects and constructs the audience's response, providing a frame not dissimilar to the curatorial commentary of a museum or exhibition. The author, Philippe Dumanoir (the director of the Théâtre des Variétés), presumably drew on accounts of the bayadères' performances in Bordeaux – indeed these are referred to within the play. By putting the previous responses of critics into the mouths of characters representing the Paris audience he ensures a certain continuity of reception. The prologue play is thus a prime example of how the bayadères were objectified and exoticised for Parisian audiences. Instead

---

[118] 'Les Bayadères: Leur traité avec M. Tardivel', *Courrier des théâtres*, 7207 (15 September 1838), 2–3.

[119] He is two years out in his estimation (in 1850) that he saw the Indian dancers ten years previously, but there are similar instances of chronological confusion in his *Memoirs* and other writings.

[120] 'Les Bayadères', *Le Figaro*, 312 (27 August 1838), 1–2.

[121] Philippe Dumanoir, *Le Corridor des Baignoires*, unpublished manuscript, Archives nationales, Paris, F^{18} 784, No. 1793.

Fig. 5.1 'Costumes des bayadères, Th. des Variétés', printed by Maison Martinet, No. 1223 of '1637 estampes coloriées représentant des acteurs en costumes de scène (1796–1843)'. Reproduction courtesy of the Bibliothèque nationale de France.

of being allowed to encounter the bayadères directly, to immerse themselves in the bayadères' world, and to form original, personal responses, the members of the audience are instead confronted with themselves as spectators, are forced to think about the bayadères in relation to the culture of the Théâtre des Variétés, and are fed particular frameworks for their reactions. The bayadères become living museum exhibits and members of a 'human zoo'.

While Berlioz himself did not review the bayadères' performance, accounts by his colleagues, Théophile Gautier and Jules Janin, further reveal some of the attractions and challenges of the bayadères' Parisian appearances. The desire of audience members to interact with performers, in their own home environment as well as in the theatre, was common in the case of foreign performers, and it was in this tradition that Gautier was one of a very small group of Frenchmen to be allowed to visit the bayadères in their temporary Parisian home, where he struck up a 'touchingly paternal relationship' with one particular young woman, named 'Amany'.[122]

As Gautier catalogues Amany's charms for his Parisian readers, we can feel his gaze trailing slowly across her body. In a disturbing, if common, mixture of quasi-ethnographical objectivity and erotic subjectivity Gautier acknowledges points where European and eastern ideals of beauty diverge, though clearly it does not require much effort for Gautier to reconcile himself to the differences: 'And again, quite contrary to our ideas of elegance, the left nostril has been pierced, together with the nasal septum, to allow a silver ring, encrusted with precious stones, to pass through it and rest on the upper lip. At first this ornament seems barbaric in taste, but one quickly becomes accustomed to it and finally discovers a depraved and piquant grace in it.'[123] As Binita Mehta writes,

> Gautier's erotic, purely physical description of Amani as a combination of savagery and grace totally objectifies her. He describes her not on her own terms, but in relation to European women. He conflates the terms 'asiatique' and 'sauvage' while discussing her, thus adding a racial element to the description. Different parts of her body, her skin, her eyes, and her teeth are depicted as animal-like. Gautier perceives Amani not as a living, breathing human being, but as a sum of body parts.[124]

Gautier's description also suggests the objectification of the museum exhibit. In *Le Corridor des Baignoires* the bayadères are similarly objectified under the guise of science, during a period in which aesthetic racism was laying the groundwork for the scientific racism of early ethnology.[125] Ribaud, the elderly theatre regular, 'penetrates' the dancers' dressing room at the Théâtre des Variétés ('j'ai penetré, malgré la portière!') and describes rubbing their skin, supposedly to verify that it is genuinely black. The justification for such behavior is as much a reflection of Parisian theatre culture and its objectification of the female dancer in general as it is proof of anthropological curiosity about a foreign Other. In the early 1830s the director of the Paris Opéra, Louis Véron, had instituted reforms that had far-reaching implications for female dancers both on and off the stage. While cutting the salaries of the young women of the corps de ballet, he effectively set up an alternative source of income for them by granting a number of the faithful

---

[122] Qureshi, *Peoples on Parade*, pp. 160, 162. On Gautier's visit, see Guest, *Gautier on Dance*, p. xxv.
[123] Guest, *Gautier on Dance*, p. 42.   [124] Mehta, *Widows, Pariahs, and Bayadères*, p. 158.
[125] Nanette Jacomijn Snoep, 'Savage Imagery', in Blanchard et al. (eds.), *The Invention of the Savage*, p. 121; Qureshi, *Peoples on Parade*, Chapter 6, pp. 185–221.

male subscribers backstage access to the foyer of the Paris Opéra and to the dancers who congregated there. It was customary for the Ribauds of Paris to exploit this privilege.

Gautier relates how, at the performance in the Théâtre des Variétés, the audience was initially 'taken aback rather than charmed' – though the attractions of Amany soon won them over.[126] The bayadères were received by at least some members of the audience with suspicion: was Amany simply 'a shopgirl who had dyed her skin with liquorice juice'?[127] In *Le Corridor des Baignoires* Ribaud shares these reservations about the bayadères' authenticity, claiming he never believes the 'phénomènes' that are presented in Paris: 'the giraffe was a ruse/And the Osages... came from Savoy.'[128] The giraffe is presumably the animal that was brought to Paris as a gift from Muhammad Ali in 1827 (it was the first giraffe in France), while the 'Osages' must refer to the group of six Osages who came to Paris from Missouri, also in 1827 (and who, indeed, were taken to see the giraffe as well as visiting the Opéra and having an audience with the King).[129] Seen in this context the bayadères' role is clear. They, too, are exotic spectacle, imported for the entertainment of the Parisian audience. The Théâtre des Variétés is set up as a venue for spectacular or bizarre display: 'What is it to be today, then?' asks Ribaud, the regular theatre-goer, as he arrives; 'is the Arc de Triomphe going to dance the cachucha with the Madeleine?'[130]

While some apparently expressed skepticism about the origins of the bayadères, the Indian group was occasionally also criticised for being *too* authentic. Six years after the bayadères appeared in Paris, Gautier noted regretfully that the French public ultimately preferred the Parisian bayadère imitations to the real bayadères themselves.[131] For their part, the bayadères were apparently not favorably impressed by French music and dance. With an irony that cannot have been unintentional, they were taken to a performance of Auber's *Le dieu et la bayadère*. The French audience crowded forward to glimpse the 'véritables bayadères' while the bayadères themselves watched the French representing bayadères on the stage, affording what would become an element of self-critique (albeit here still ironically intended) common to 'human zoos'.[132] According to the *Courrier de*

---

[126] Gautier, 'Th. des Variétés: Début of the Bayaderes', *La Presse*, 27 August 1838, 1–2; Guest, *Gautier on Dance*, p. 48.
[127] Guest, *Gautier on Dance*, p. 48.   [128] Dumanoir, *Le Corridor des Baignoires*, p. 8.
[129] Snoep, 'Savage Imagery', p. 107.   [130] Dumanoir, *Le Corridor des Baignoires*, p. 5.
[131] Guest, *Gautier on Dance*, p. 135.
[132] Barbara Kirshenblatt-Gimblett, 'Objects of Ethnography', in Karp and Lavine (eds.), *Exhibiting Cultures*, p. 410.

Bordeaux, as reported in *The Times*, '[t]he French dancing they look upon as being licentious; and as to a *pirouette*, they cannot bear it!'[133]

Some of the same ambivalence is expressed by Jules Janin in his review of the bayadères for the *Journal des débats*. Unlike Gautier, Janin did not visit the bayadères in their home before the performance. This is a significant difference, for Janin concludes that proper appreciation of the bayadères is dependent on viewing their dance in the intimate context for which it was presumably conceived. He imagines the viewer – inevitably male – enjoying the performance in an Indian temple, as a 'dreamer transported by tobacco, by poetry, or by opium': 'And while the women spin around you, and they are yours alone and you are theirs alone, your head and your heart turn with them, and they burn you with a limpid gaze not seen in the theatre, and brush you with the edge of their floating scarf.'[134] Janin suggests that in the Parisian theatre, viewed from a distance, the bayadères astonish the audience with their novelty but leave the Parisians emotionally cold. He compares their effect to that of a circus act – an important arena for the displays of the 'human zoo', which, as exemplified in the case of P.T. Barnum's famous shows, interacted with carnivals as well as the more highbrow institutions of exhibitions and museums. Janin suggests that the juxtaposition between these temple dancers and their new Parisian context is a violent one. He concludes: 'Of all the poetic anachronisms of the last ten years, I'm aware of none more improbable than this.'[135]

Perhaps it was the perceived anachronism of the presence of authentic bayadères on the Parisian stage that ultimately led to the preference in Paris for representations of bayadères over the bayadères themselves. Both Gautier and Janin refer to Marie Taglioni, as does Albert in *Le Corridor des Baignoires*. Taglioni performed the mute role of a bayadère in Auber's *Le dieu et la bayadère*, and she actually came to see the bayadères perform in Paris, just as they attended the performance of *Le dieu et la bayadère* in Bordeaux. Ironically, Auber wrote his opera before the visit of the real bayadères to Paris. Indeed, it was the popularity in Europe of the *idea* of the bayadère, as embodied in works such as Auber's opera, on which Tardivel was doubtless cashing in when he undertook to bring the troupe from India. *Le dieu et la bayadère* was revived several times after the Indian *devadasis* visited in 1838, while bayadères also featured in numerous other new theatrical works such as Gautier's own *Sacountala* (1858) and Auber's opera *Le premier jour de bonheur* (libretto by d'Ennery and Cormon, 1868). There was even to be a

---

[133] Quoted in Bor, 'Mamia, Ammani and other *Bayadères*,' p. 58.
[134] Jules Janin, 'Théâtre des Variétés: *Les Bayadères*,' *Journal des débats*, 24 August 1838, 2.
[135] Ibid., 2.

bayadère amongst the wilis in Gautier's original conception for that whitest of *ballets blancs*, *Giselle*.¹³⁶

Auber also appears to have revisited the bayadère concept in his music for Scribe's *L'enfant prodigue* in 1850, drawing directly on his experience of the 1838 Indian dancers. At least, such was Berlioz's impression. Although the scenario is based on the Biblical narrative, Scribe spiced things up by adding dancing girls to the temptations encountered by the prodigal son in his wanderings in Egypt. Berlioz's response to Auber's ballet sequence highlights what he took to be its inspiration:

I don't know if you still remember the peculiar music that accompanied the movements of the Indian bayadères who appeared, around ten years ago, at the Théâtre des Variétés? It consisted of some weak murmuring sounds from a bass voice and sustained by those of the bayadères who weren't dancing; chanting that wavered exclusively on the minor third, around a single tone, continuously sustained by a fife into which an Indian blew, while the rhythm of the dance was marked with the fingers of his right hand on a small drum. Mr. Auber hasn't tried to reproduce the poverty of this primitive instrumentation, but he has skillfully recalled the main traits. The air itself has a distinctive physiognomy [. . .] and the accompaniment of the sustained droning of the cor anglais beneath the melody, sometimes in the major mode, produces an entirely new and striking effect. If we add that the dance designed by the choreographer to accompany this charming music is, similarly, a poetically conceived imitation of the dance of the daggers that was executed with so much audacious verve by the Indian bayadères, you will understand the enthusiasm this piece has excited.¹³⁷

Berlioz's review of Auber's opera tells us more about the music of the original Indian bayadères than either Gautier or Janin in their reviews of the performances themselves. But Berlioz shares the other reviewers' ambivalence with regard to the music and, while he appreciated the energy of the original dagger dance, he was obviously less impressed by its orchestration.

In another review, this time of Halévy's *Prométhée enchaîné*, Berlioz criticises the bayadères' music more explicitly, describing it as

something resembling rhythmical noise, accompanying the dance of the Indian bayadères that we saw in Paris some years ago [. . .]

---

¹³⁶ See Lisa C. Arkin and Marian Smith, 'National Dance in the Romantic Ballet', in Lynn Garafola (ed.), *Rethinking the Sylph: New Perspectives on the Romantic Ballet* (Hanover, New Hampshire: University Press of New England, 1997), p. 48. Ziter offers other examples of anachronistic or inauthentic appearances of 'bayadères' and 'almées' in stage works. See *Orient on the Victorian Stage*, pp. 143, 156–7.
¹³⁷ *Journal des débats*, 9 December 1850, 1.

If someone had told us that the flute of the Indian musician only produced a single note that was prolonged indefinitely like the buzzing of a wasp, and that his drum only produced a feeble and muted sound, comparable to that obtained by lightly hitting the fingers against the body of a hat; that the bayadères, in the supposed *song* that accompanies their dance, contented themselves by murmuring every now and then, in an undertone, some words on the note prolonged by the flute of their musician, while embellishing only *as required* this note by means of two other sounds that form with the main sound the interval of a second or minor third, like *la la la – ti do, la la – do ti do la*, and continued in this way for an hour, most likely we wouldn't have wanted to believe it. And yet this is the case; and this isn't without character; and it is this very character of some sounds grouped by chance, or according to a vague natural human instinct, that has incorrectly allowed the title of *music* to be given to these puerilities and which lets them be taken for a form of art. Thus, while accepting that the *orchestras* of Lahore or Delhi might very well be superior to those that the bayadères had us listen to in Paris, arguably we have only an approximate idea of the *music* of India.[138]

In this review Berlioz uses the bayadères to illustrate the dangers of generalising about unfamiliar music on the basis of a few examples. To him the bayadères' music is simply primitive. The sense of remoteness that Halévy, in *Prométhée enchaîné*, conveys through the use of quarter-tones is redefined by Berlioz in geographical rather than temporal terms. The evidence of the narrowness of Berlioz's tastes is in itself not particularly interesting, and the effortless equation of exoticism and classicism is also quite typical of his time, in which cultural and racial difference was either projected onto an evolutionary trajectory with western man as its apogee, or removed from temporal development altogether. Jones's *Music of India* offers a particularly pertinent example of the familiar mentality behind Berlioz's idea, speaking of 'the similitude between the music of the classical nations and that of India'.[139] That Berlioz connects Indian exoticism and classical antiquity is significant, however, given that he was to consider imitating the same Indian dancers in his own 'classical' opera a decade later. Moreover, *Les Troyens* has as its telos the founding of Rome and of western civilisation – the civilisation that, for Berlioz, is nothing less than 'the culmination of history', as Paul Robinson suggests.[140] Rather than simply damning Berlioz's insensitivity, we would more appropriately respond to his critique of the

---

[138] *Revue et gazette musicale*, 25 March 1849, 94. Berlioz's response here is in keeping with his accounts of genuine Indian music he heard in London when acting as a judge of instruments at the Great Exhibition in 1851. *Evenings in the Orchestra*, p. 252.

[139] William Jones and N. Augustus Willard, *Music of India* (Calcutta: Nabajiban Press, 1962), p. 2.

[140] Paul Robinson, *Opera and Ideas: From Mozart to Strauss* (New York: Harper & Row, 1985), p. 110.

bayadères' music if we first ascertained which elements of the Indian performance Berlioz intended to introduce into his own opera, and second delved more deeply into the reasons that a composer so hostile to Indian music would wish to imitate it in an opera on which he staked so much. *This* is the anachronism we must confront, and it is here, too, that the question of instrumental technology begins to surface.

The task of establishing the elements of the bayadères' performance that Berlioz introduced into *Troyens* is complicated by the fact that he is generally thought to have abandoned his intention to imitate the Indian music explicitly. A sketch survives for a 'Negro dance air with a simple accompaniment for muffled drum (tarbuka) following the rhythm of the melody' ('Air de danse de Nègres avec un simple accompagnement de tambour sourd (tarbuka) suivant le rythme de la mélodie'). The 5/4 time and erratic chromaticism were presumably intended to convey the savage barbarism of the 'Nègres', whose African origin is more readily plausible in the context of *Les Troyens* than the Indian ancestry of the bayadères.[141] This sketch was in turn abandoned, but the third of the ballets in Act IV of *Les Troyens* (No. 33c) preserves the conspicuous use of the 'tarbuka' drum (thought to be a darabukka – common in North Africa and Turkey),[142] while it replaces the 5/4 time and chromaticism with pentatonic and Phrygian inflections and a drone (see Ex. 5.9). (5/8 time is instead employed in the 'Pas de lutteurs', as we have seen.)

Rushton describes the result as 'Eurovision Orientalism' and suggests that, while 'no ethnomusicologist would accept [the music] as North African [. . .] such is the working of musical semantics that no listener can doubt what is signified'.[143] Berlioz seems himself to spell out exactly what is signified by entitling the ballet 'Pas d'esclaves nubiennes'. This, then, is Africa, not India. Or is it both? Earlier in the nineteenth century, Nubia had been absorbed into Egypt by Muhammad Ali, and we might recall that Berlioz told his sister that his Indian dancers were to have come to Carthage via Egypt. The note repeatedly stressed in the 'Pas d'esclaves nubiennes' is the minor third (of a Phrygian scale), and it is the minor third that Berlioz remembers the Indian musicians emphasising in the bayadères' performance. The 'tarbuka' may not be of Indian origin, but it is employed in a fashion similar to the drum of the bayadères as described in Berlioz's review of *Prométhée enchaîné*. The tarbuka is specifically to be played on the stage, as part of

---

[141] The sketch is reproduced in *Collection musicale André Meyer: Catalogue 1973* (Abbeville: Imprimerie F. Paillart, 1973), vol. 3, plate 5. For a transcription, see *NBE* vol. 2c, p. 938.
[142] See Kemp, *Les Troyens*, pp. 205–7.   [143] Rushton, *The Music of Berlioz*, p. 147.

Ex. 5.9 *Les Troyens* No. 33c 'Pas d'esclaves nubiennes', bb. 1–12

the ballet, though its sound is reinforced in the pit by the tambourine, with which it shares a stave. We have already seen Berlioz's critique of the 'primitive instrumentation' of the bayadères and his praise for Auber's repackaging of their idiom. Like the dancers it accompanies, Berlioz's tarbuka is perhaps intended primarily for the eyes, another museum exhibit brought to life but framed for its audience, thus evoking the common interaction between foreign peoples and objects in the carefully staged and mediated performances of the 'human zoos'.[144]

Berlioz does not specify *who* is to play the tarbuka. Images and accounts of the 1838 bayadères suggest that the instruments were played by men while the women danced, and a bifurcation aligning women with body and men with technology was certainly not confined to Berlioz's Paris. Interesting in this respect, however, is the way Berlioz handles the juxtaposition of the 'primitive' instrument onstage with those in his orchestra. As the dance continues, the violins escape from their brief ornamented echoes of the pitch given by the singers to break into rapid unison figurations with changing patterns of articulation which require some precision in their execution. It is a passage that conspicuously challenges the 'Eurovision exoticism' of the opening of the movement. The moment was remarked upon by Joseph d'Ortigue in his review of the opera, and d'Ortigue also commented on a similarly disruptive moment for the strings in the opening ballet of the group (the 'Pas des almées'):

[144] Qureshi, *Peoples on Parade*, pp. 116–18.

Then come two decidedly pretty 'airs de ballet';[145] nevertheless, in the case of the one in G I would reproach Mr Berlioz for having made the violins climb up to a very high trill on *a*, producing a kind of indistinct quivering; next comes the dance of the Nubian slaves in E minor without a sharp in the clef, in other words in a mode which isn't without resemblance to the third plainchant mode; the piece is delicious and bizarre at the same time. Tired of staying immobile on the little *grupetti* the violins devote themselves suddenly to the frolics of a mad farandole, as if they wanted to spin like goblins through the steps and rhythms of the dancers.[146]

D'Ortigue's description is interesting for the way in which it assigns (or implies that Berlioz assigns) a degree of agency to the string players, or rather, to their music.[147] He emphasises their physicality in a way that suggests that they, too, are part of the display of dancers on the stage; if we hear the violin line as the music of dancing goblins it suggests an additional layer of supernatural Othering through which our experience of the bayadères is filtered, recalling the 'féerique' mode of 'La Reine Mab'. But we also get the sense from d'Ortigue that the violins resist the world of the bayadères. They become exasperated by their role simulating what Berlioz himself referred to as 'primitive orchestration' and break free to assert their own physicality and virtuosity. Indeed, this redirection of attention to the orchestral voice brings the lengthy dances to an end, as if Didon is no longer able to sustain the illusion that the exoticism of her slave dancers is entirely contained by the stage.

The language sung in Berlioz's ballet is assumed to have been invented by Berlioz himself, so again it does not bind the dance decisively to a particular country, but perhaps we can also see here the traces of his original Indian conception: Berlioz intended his bayadère imitation to be accompanied by the singing of text in a foreign language, albeit a real language (Persian) that could conceivably have been comprehended by the occasional audience member. His colleague at the *Journal des débats* was more than up to the task he supposedly planned to set him: 'Casimirski' was Albin de Kazimirski Biberstein (1808–1887) – a French orientalist who translated the Koran and authored a book of French/Persian dialogues. Whether Berlioz actually approached Kazimirski Biberstein is not recorded, but if he had stuck with

---

[145] The second of Berlioz's three dances (the 'Danse des esclaves') was omitted in 1863, which can only have solidified the sense that the ballets present a display of the female form. (The 'Danse des esclaves' is assumed to have been intended for male dancers – Condé, 'Commentaire musicale et litteraire', *Les Troyens*, *L'Avant Scène Opéra*, p. 95.)

[146] Heidlberger, *Dossier de presse*, p. 71.

[147] D'Ortigue was not alone in remarking upon the orchestration of the ballets. See for example the review in *Le Pays* on 9 November 1863: Heidlberger, *Dossier de presse*, p. 114.

Ex. 5.10a Auber, *L'enfant prodigue* Air de ballet No 1, 'Pas de séduction', bb. 1–7

Ex. 5.10b *Les Troyens* No. 33a, 'Pas des almées', bb. 1–7

this plan of having the Carthaginian entertainment performed to words by Hafiz, it would only have heightened the sense of anachronism, given that Hafiz was active in the fourteenth century CE.

The title of the first dance of the Act IV ballet (No. 33a), 'Pas des almées', also raises interesting questions about Berlioz's sources. 'Almée' was a term applied to Egyptian dancing girls, and it has been suggested that he may have taken the title of his dance from Félicien David's popular ode-symphonie *Le désert*, which contains a similarly named '*Danse* des almées'.[148] Certainly Berlioz admired David's work, but it is more likely his model for the title of this dance came not from David, but from Auber. The ballet sequence of *L'enfant prodigue* – the very same sequence, set in Egypt, which Berlioz suggested was inspired by the 1838 bayadères – contains an identically titled 'Pas des almées'. Again, we should remind ourselves that Berlioz tells his sister that his Indians came to Carthage via Egypt. What he omits is the fact that the dancers might have come to Carthage via *Auber's* Egypt. Not only the title ('Pas des almées') but also the music of Berlioz's first dance would suggest that this is the case. Auber's ballet sequence in *L'enfant prodigue* opens with a 'Pas de séduction' in which the women seduce the prodigal son with a *piano* G-major melodic line underpinned by a sinewy chromatic descent D-C♯-C-B in 6/8 time and with a lilting accompaniment in the lower strings (Ex. 5.10a). Compare this to Berlioz's 'Pas des almées' (Ex. 5.10b).

[148] Rushton, *The Music of Berlioz*, p. 145, n. 38.

Auber's librettist, Scribe, 'went into it', to use Berlioz's expression, and consulted a number of historical sources.[149] The costumes were by Paul Lormier, a 'champion of local color and historical exactitude' who had designed the costumes for Berlioz's *Benvenuto Cellini* as well as numerous other works.[150] Both the costumes and the set of *L'enfant prodigue* were admired for their authenticity – the authenticity of a museum exhibit: 'Picture to yourself the Charles X Museum and the Egyptian room of the Louvre come to life', wrote Gautier, adding that the production was 'très beau et très exact'.[151] Whether the sources drawn from by the creators of *L'enfant prodigue* included references to Indian dancing girls in ancient Egypt is not clear. Nor do we know if the Indian element Berlioz perceived in *L'enfant prodigue* originated with Scribe, Lormier, the choreographer (Arthur Saint-Léon), or Auber himself. It is also hard to know whether Berlioz's 'Pas des almées' resembles Auber's ballet because both were inspired by the same bayadère performance, or whether Auber's work was an independent influence in its own right. The latter seems quite likely, and we may see certain similarities between the plots of the two works: Énée is, in effect, the prodigal son who is being steered from his rightful course by the seductions of North Africa, but who will soon repent and fulfill his duty to his homeland.

Why bayadères?

The second main question arising around Berlioz's reference to the bayadères is one of motivation. Given his antipathy for the musical idiom of the original, why did Berlioz consider introducing Indian dancers in his ancient Carthage? The ballet sequence of *Les Troyens*, like that of Auber's *L'enfant prodigue*, represents an exotic distraction from the hero's true path. To some extent, any ballet would perform this function. Gautier comments of dance in general that it is 'essentially pagan, materialistic and sensual',[152] and it is widely known that male audience members appreciated the 'sensuality' of their favorite Parisian dancers off the stage as well as on it, particularly after Véron's reforms were introduced at the Opéra. But how much more

---

[149] Herbert Schneider, 'Scribe and Auber: Constructing Grand Opera', in David Charlton (ed.), *The Cambridge Companion to Grand Opera* (Cambridge: Cambridge University Press, 2002), pp. 187–9.
[150] Nicole Wild, *Décors et costumes du XIXe siècle* (Paris: Bibliothèque Nationale, 1993), p. 328.
[151] Gautier, 'Opéra–*L'enfant prodigue*...', *La Presse*, 9 December 1850, 1. See also Nicole Wild, *Décors et costumes du XIXe siècle: collections de la Bibliothèque-Musée de l'Opéra*, vol. 1 (Paris: Bibliothèque Nationale, 1987), p. 89.
[152] Guest, *Gautier on Dance*, p. 29.

sensual was the evocation of these eastern women, upon whom could be projected erotic longings beyond those it was proper to express within a European context, even with dancers of questionable social status. Many audience members believed that *devadasis* were, from a western perspective, akin to prostitutes. Indeed, Gautier uses the word 'harem' to describe their abode.[153] *Devadasis* underwent a ritual marriage to the god, consummated by a male member of the temple, and were expected to be sexually available to select visitors thereafter. Again, the situation is not so remote from the lives of many Parisian dancers, and some newspapers were at pains to point out that, with regard to morals, the bayadères were actually 'infinitely superior to the ladies of the *corps de ballet* at home'.[154] Nevertheless, the element of sacred prostitution was addressed quite explicitly as an exotic curiosity in the press. Cullivier-Fleury, for example, states in the *Journal des débats*, 'As for civil marriage, they [the bayadères] are prohibited by law. They choose a Brahma and live with him until satiety separates them; for no legal ties bind them to each other. It's a completely sensual cohabitation that their god tolerates.'[155]

The Act IV ballet of *Les Troyens* could thus be interpreted as an extension of the feminine charms of Didon, who has given herself to the son of the goddess of love and who has in turn seduced Énée from his true path. Indeed, a review of the 1838 bayadères even suggested that one part of Amany's performance evoked the abandoning of Dido: 'Amany is now going to mime an amorous dance. She leaves, softly lifting her eyes and lids [...] She is doubtless trying in vain to seduce some heart of stone. Bitter disappointment overcomes her; [...] then an amorous curse is hurled at his head. It is Ariadne abandoned, it's Dido, it's Medea!'[156]

The exotic origins of Didon's dancers carry an additional interpretative burden. Berlioz describes the dancers of the third ballet not only as Nubians, but as Nubian *slaves*. The sensuality of their dance is contained – they have been captured by the coloniser and are now exhibited in a show of imperial power. As Rushton writes, 'the fact that these three ballets form an entertainment at Dido's court develops the political framework of the opera; Dido was a colonist, Aeneas intends to become one.'[157] It is perhaps

---

[153] Ibid., p. 49.
[154] 'The Bayaderes', *Era*, 4 October 1838, quoted in Bor, 'Mamia, Ammani and other *Bayadères*', p. 70.
[155] 'Les Bayadères aux Tuileries', *Journal des débats*, 20 August 1838, 3.
[156] 'Les Bayadères à Bordeaux', reprinted from *Le Courrier de Bordeaux*, *Journal des débats*, 3 August 1838, 1.
[157] Rushton, *The Music of Berlioz*, pp. 147–8.

no coincidence that both northern Africa and India – the two regions that Berlioz thought to evoke in the ballet sequence – were the objects of French imperial ambitions in Berlioz's time. The 1838 bayadères came from a village near Pondicherry, which was one of France's few remaining Indian possessions – goods from Pondicherry had been proudly displayed in this capacity at the 1844 Paris industrial exhibition.[158] Thiruvendipuram itself, however, was described in many journals, and in the bayadères' contract, as being in 'territoire anglais'.[159] In advertising the fact that they had managed to uproot the bayadères from British soil, were the French perhaps celebrating a minor victory over their greatest imperialist rival? Whatever the case, we come closer to understanding how Berlioz could condemn Indian music as primitive and savage, and then turn around and seek to imitate it in the opera that was otherwise conceived as the highest expression of his artistic ideals. In the context of *Les Troyens*, this primitivism is deliberate. It demonstrates the superiority of the culture of the coloniser, who can capture and frame the music of exotic peoples as an evening's entertainment.

Tardivel took the bayadères to perform before both French and British audiences. The fact that they were subjected to the gaze of these two competing colonial powers becomes particularly apposite when we watch their exotic sisters perform before the combined Trojans and Carthaginians in *Les Troyens*. The same ethos was more subtly present at the international exhibitions, where the spoils of imperial conquest could be admired as objects arranged in tableaux, with India forming a particularly potent centerpiece of the 1851 Great Exhibition. Indeed, India even supplied the grand chair upon which Didon's symbolic descendent, Queen Victoria, surveyed her subjects and their wares at the opening ceremony.[160]

The association frequently suggested in the nineteenth century between the female body and exotic lands – both objects to be conquered by the white European male – is now all too familiar. It was reenacted in countless opera plots and other theatrical entertainments, and the same associations were sometimes continued off stage. Two of the most celebrated Parisian courtesans of the 1840s were renamed after French conquests abroad: Céleste Venard was known as Mogador after that Moroccan city (now Essaouira)

---

[158] Greenhalgh, *Ephemeral Vistas*, p. 64.
[159] 'Les Bayadères: Leur traité avec M. Tardivel', *Courrier des théâtres* 7207 (15 September 1838). See also, for example, Cullivier Fleury, 'Les Bayadères aux Tuileries', *Journal des débats*, 19 August 1838. In *Les soirées de l'orchestre*, however, Berlioz suggests that the bayadères were from Calcutta: *Evenings with the Orchestra*, p. 251.
[160] Michael Leapman, *The World for a Shilling: How the Great Exhibition of 1851 Shaped a Nation* (London: Headline Books, 2001), p. 116.

fell to France in 1844; and Mogador's rival and friend, Elise Sergent, went by the name La Reine Pomaré, after the Queen of Tahiti, as we have seen. The two courtesans illustrate again the close affiliations in public consciousness between dance, exotic appearance, and sexual availability. The women earned their reputations – and attracted their clients – as dancers, albeit at public balls and variety theatres rather than in the Opéra ballet. Mogador even performed in the same Parisian theatre that had housed the bayadères in 1838. In fact, the boundaries between 'social and theatrical dance' were fluid at this time and, as Lisa C. Arkin and Marian Smith point out, 'staged scenes of national dances entertaining onstage characters [...] actually mirrored the events of a real-life public ball'.[161] Like Mogador and Pomaré, the bayadères were seen as foreign territory to be conquered by the French male – by force if necessary. Gautier presents a similar perspective when he comments that there had been several attempts to break into the bayadères' Parisian residence and kidnap them.[162]

It is no wonder, then, that Didon seems a little disturbed at the end of the ballet sequence, suddenly rising from her seat and proclaiming 'enough, my sister: I can scarcely bear these tiresome festivities.'[163] She requests a more wholesome poem of the fields 'sur un mode simple et doux' – seemingly the antithesis of the dancers' exoticism and all it implies. However, not even Iopas's song can sooth her 'inquiétude extreme'. Didon is herself a coloniser in Carthage and the entertainments she has just staged for Énée are presumably intended to embody her own imperial power before her noble guest (and now lover), in the manner of numerous opera ballets. However, by associating *female* sexuality with foreign lands to be conquered, Didon has simultaneously subverted her own power as queen and placed herself in the position of the one to be controlled. It is a short step from here to her abandonment by Énée, and the devastation of her new civilisation in Carthage.

If Berlioz's Didon identifies the dancers as bayadères, she has further cause to be disturbed by their presence and to recognise in their performance an anticipation of her fate. Nineteenth-century western literature about India tends to conflate the quite separate roles of bayadère and

---

[161] Lisa C. Arkin and Marian Smith, 'National Dance in the Romantic Ballet', in Lynn Garafola (ed.), *Rethinking the Sylph: New Perspectives on the Romantic Ballet* (Hanover and London: Wesleyan University Press, 1997), p. 20.
[162] Guest, *Gautier on Dance*, p. 40.
[163] 'Assez, ma soeur, je ne souffre qu'à peine cette fête importune.' 'Importune' here is usually translated as 'tiresome' but can also mean 'ill-chosen' – and thus approaches the sense of 'anachronistic'.

Sati – the widow who commits ritual suicide on her husband's funeral pyre. Many popular treatments of bayadères (including Goethe's *Der Gott und die Bajadere* – the inspiration for Scribe's libretto for Auber's *Le dieu et la bayadère*) depict a *devadasi* prepared to hurl herself onto the flames for her lover. Although Didon will stab herself before her body is committed to the flames, and Énée is only metaphorically dead to her (it is his toga, helmet, sword and bust rather than his body that she follows onto the pyre), the coincidence is certainly not a happy one for the Carthaginian queen.

In many respects, Berlioz's approach to the Act IV ballet of *Les Troyens* is typical of exoticism. He conflates various racial types (Indian bayadères, Egyptian almées, Nubian slaves – singing in Persian or in a wholly invented language whose only criteria is that it is Other), and he maintains a veneer of questionable authenticity while simultaneously expressing his distaste for genuine exotic music and his preference instead for a repertoire of exotic signifiers. Although the invented language and the uprising of the strings from the pit suggests particular ways in which Berlioz might nuance or even challenge this Othering, in broad terms his approach is common to many of his contemporaries, and Berlioz's choices as readily lend themselves to a postcolonial reading as those of Verdi, Saint-Saëns, and other more typical subjects of studies of nineteenth-century musical exoticism.

Interpreting bayadères

Indeed, politically sensitive, revisionist productions of *Les Troyens* abound. The Greek soldiers may be depicted as United States marines en route for Iraq, or the Trojan horse interpreted as halfway between 'a panzer and Big Bertha'.[164] However, despite the political potential of the Act IV ballet, there is a tendency for many modern productions to omit this section – the most obvious outlet of *Les Troyens*' exoticism – along with other danced numbers. The booklet notes of the 2000 Salzburg Festival production explain the omission as being due to the director's 'lack of interest in that which is purely illustrative,' continuing, 'In this way Wernicke opposes the representative

---

[164] See Jean-Luc Macia's reviews of the Châtelet and Opéra national du Rhin productions in *La Croix* (16 October 2003 and 30 October 2006 respectively). The production team of the latter was aiming to evoke Verdun in 1917 in the Trojan acts, while the United States this time supplied the inspiration for Carthage's 'situation d'agonie et de décadence'. See Andreas Baesler, Hermann Feuchter, and Gabriele Heimann, 'Tout le monde a dans son cœur un billet pour Rome' [interview], in *Berlioz: Les Troyens* [programme booklet], Strasbourg: Opéra National du Rhin, 2006, p. 36.

spirit of grand opéra, yet at the same time succeeds in bringing out of the action an eternal, mythical level of interpretation – the feminine spirit which affirms love, life and peace is subordinated to the destructive male spirit of discovery and conquest.'[165]

Sylvain Cambreling, conductor of both the Salzburg Festival production and its revival at Opéra Bastille in 2006, defends the decision to omit the ballets, including those of Act IV, which he terms the 'act of boredom'. The production team had been tempted to retain the 'Pas d'esclaves nubiennes', Cambreling reveals, on account of its exoticism; but they also felt that this exoticism was incongruous within *Les Troyens* as a whole and the dance too brief to enable them to 'deal in some way with the question of racism'.[166]

In fact, the question of racism arises elsewhere in *Les Troyens* and *needs* to be dealt with: 'exterminate the black army' ('exterminez/exterminons la noire armée') is the cry that unites Didon and Énée and their peoples as they prepare to wage war against the Numidians. This is another remnant of what Berlioz elsewhere described as 'a pure chauvinist puerility' ('une pure puérilité chauvinique') – and which he accordingly suppressed. In December 1856 Berlioz informed Princess Carolyne Sayn-Wittgenstein that he had altered Didon's closing monologue in which she was to refer to 'la domination française en Afrique'.[167] Instead Didon calls on Hannibal to avenge the Carthaginians, only to be granted a dying vision of the ultimate downfall of her people and the triumph of 'Rome immortelle!' But when, just two months later, Berlioz wrote to his sister of his intention to evoke bayadères in what would later become the dances of African slaves, we get the sense that the 'chauvinist puerility' of imperial France is still embedded in the conception of the work. Certainly this is the view of Edward Said, who suggests that 'Berlioz's daring theatrical imagination used *Les Troyens* as an artistic vehicle for paralleling in music the contemporary expansion of the French empire in North Africa.'[168]

The other reason Cambreling provides for the omission of the ballets is ostensibly less problematic: they are 'pieces which Berlioz wrote to obey

---

[165] Alexandra-Maria Dielitz, booklet for *Hector Berlioz: Les Troyens*, Salzburger Festspiele 2000, Arthaus Musik 100 350, p. 19.

[166] Sylvain Cambreling, in an interview with Gunther Braam, 28 July 2000. See www.hberlioz.com/others/reviews.htm#Interview, accessed 10 April 2014. And see Sylvain Cambreling, in an interview with Pierre-René Serna, 31 May and 2 June 2006, www.hberlioz.com/others/PRSerna-6.htm, accessed 10 April 2014. This interview was also published in the programme for the 2006 Opéra Bastille performance.

[167] *CG* V, p. 401.

[168] Edward Said, 'Les Troyens', originally published in *The Nation* 258/25 (27 June 1994); reprinted in *Music at the Limits* (London: Bloomsbury, 2008), p. 183.

the conventions of the *Opéra* in [the] Paris of his time'.[169] As such, the ballets are supposedly a 'purely decorative' interruption to the action that was introduced merely to satisfy the nineteenth-century public, 'who liked to enjoy little female dancers'.[170] But isn't this the point? Or rather, couldn't we say that, far from simply pandering to the basest desires of the Jockey Club, Berlioz is here drawing on the potent associations between dance, the exotic woman, sexual conquest, and imperial domination to make a complex statement about the situation of his central protagonists? Indeed, the ballet sequence vividly embodies the very opposition between the female spirit of love and the male spirit of conquest that Wernicke highlights as crucial to *Troyens* as a whole? The fact that Berlioz conveys this message through 'the conventions [...] of his time' is hardly reason to omit the ballets. Following that logic we would never perform any of the opera – or much else, for that matter. Admittedly, a full understanding of the implications of these ballets is enhanced by an historical understanding of the context in which they arose. But not every audience member must 'étudier la question' or 'go into it' in order to understand the basic message of this exoticism in the context of *Les Troyens*. The unusual musical language and the invented sung language of the 'Pas d'esclaves nubiennes,' the onstage use of unusual instruments, and even the fact that the section is danced, highlight the Otherness of the ballets. The very stagedness of the ballets helps to frame this message. Just as the audience of the 1838 bayadères had their responses fed to them by their onstage reflections *Le Corridor des Baignoires*, in *Les Troyens* we watch Didon and Énée watching the dancers perform. In this way we are encouraged to identify with the colonising protagonists, but also, perhaps, to share with Didon her anxiety that the space that safely separates us from them may be collapsed.

'Il n'y a pas d'anachronisme', Berlioz said of his intention to include bayadères in ancient Carthage. Whatever traces remain of the bayadères in *Les Troyens*, there can be little doubt that our experience of the 1838 *devadasis* through this work is a highly inauthentic one. Despite Berlioz's claims, the notion of Indian dancing girls at Didon's court is almost certainly anachronistic. However, rather than dismiss the anachronism, might we not embrace it? If anachronism is the presence of something before its proper time, it could be seen to be a crucial principle in *Les Troyens* as a whole, for the opera is characterised by a relentless drive forwards into our history.

---

[169] Cambreling/Braam interview, www.hberlioz.com/others/reviews99-02.htm#LesTroyens1. www.hberlioz.com/others/reviews.htm#Interview. Accessed 10 April 2014.

[170] 'qui se régalait de petites danseuses.' (Cambreling/Serna interview, www.hberlioz.com/others/PRSerna-6.htm. Accessed 10 April 2014.)

This anachronism is most obviously embodied in the recurring concept of prophecy, from Cassandre's fateful visions in the first two acts of a future others refuse to accept, to the Trojans' repeated cries of 'Italie!' – a country that in the world of the opera does not yet exist – to the dying Didon's evocation by name of Hannibal a thousand years before his birth.[171] Act IV and its ballet are frequently treated as a point of stasis in the trajectory of the opera – the antithesis to the Trojan thesis, and the pausing of time *en route* to the Roman synthesis in the dialectic of the whole, which Paul Robinson suggests embodies Hegelian concepts of history prevalent in Berlioz's era (those same concepts which, as we have already seen, position Europe's Others as less evolved). According to Robinson, in the 'romantic lethargy' of the ballet, Didon and Énée are 'robbed of all responsible sense of time'.[172] In fact, by evoking the 1838 bayadères – through the anachronism itself – Berlioz reminds us that this stasis is temporary, that the clock is still ticking, as we glimpse forward into both the legacy of European colonialism and the more immediate and personal sacrifice of Didon that this necessitates. The Nubian slaves, and their bayadère sisters, could be added to Robinson's other 'victims of history', 'Andromache, Hylas, the sentries,' who 'all, in a sense, pave the way for Dido'.[173] It is the very anachronism of the bayadères – the fact that they are transported into ancient Carthage from imperial France – that makes their existence at this point in the opera seem authentic, that is, an authentic expression of the ethos of the work. The presence of Indian dancing girls in ancient Carthage is anachronistic, but the presence of bayadères in *Les Troyens*, as performed in Berlioz's France, is an entirely appropriate reflection of the topical subtext of the work as a whole.

The bayadères take their place within the narratives of imperial and military conquest, ghosts, and the perils of the technological future that compose the Other worlds of *Les Troyens*, and Berlioz's works more generally. Berlioz's music, like the instruments and other objects he encountered in museums or international exhibitions, benefits from being understood in the context that shaped it. Indeed, audiences today must consider the possibility that to experience his music invokes a kind of cultural framing not dissimilar to the play that shaped Parisian audiences' responses to the bayadères. Berlioz's world may well be an Other world to 'us', his opera and other music itself an 'anachronism' in performance today, albeit an appealing one. If there is a constant, however, and a way in to Berlioz's

---

[171] As Robinson points out, this is Berlioz's doing, not Virgil's – the latter does not go so far as to name Hannibal. *Opera and Ideas*, p. 149.
[172] Ibid., p. 138. [173] Ibid., p. 146.

world, it is surely to be found in the performance itself, and particularly in the orchestra that dramatises its own voyage. For while Berlioz's framing of Other peoples is beholden to all the ideological baggage of his time, we might at least appreciate how Berlioz's music embraces – even as it problematises – the spectacle of performance in the orchestra as well as on the stage. In this way, when contemplating Berlioz's orchestral musicians and their instruments, we are permitted to recover some of the marvel of the museum, exhibition, or human zoo.

Epilogue

In writing in 1852 of Vincent Wallace's adventures in New Zealand, the year after experiencing the imperial display of the Great Exhibition, Berlioz depicts Wallace as a conflicted but ultimately loyal colonist:

On deck I could not endure it any longer; I turned round and was on the point of leaping into the water, swimming ashore, and embracing all three of them [the Māori women, including Tatea], to flee with them into the forest, letting the frigate sail away loaded with my curses, when the commander, guessing my rash impulse, made a sign to the regimental musicians on board. 'Rule, Britannia' rang out, a supreme, heart-breaking upheaval shook me and, three-fourths insane, I rushed into the saloon, where I remained till evening, stretched out on the floor like a living corpse.[1]

Four years later in *Les Troyens*, Énée steps into a similar role, as Berlioz injects the fanfares of modernity into the imperialism of Virgil's epic to strengthen his hero's resolve.

ÉNÉE	ÉNÉE
Je vous aime, Didon: grâce! l'ordre divin Pouvait seul emporter la cruelle victoire. (*On entend la fanfare de la marche troyenne.*)	I love you, Didon: mercy! Only the divine command could take this cruel victory. (*The fanfare of the Trojan march is heard.*)
DIDON	DIDON
A ce chant de triomphe où rayonne ta gloire, Je te vois tressaillir! Tu pars?	At the sound of this song of triumph where your glory shines, I see you tremble! You are leaving?
ÉNÉE	ÉNÉE
Je dois partir...	I must leave...

Vincent Wallace and Énée are, quite literally, worlds apart, both temporally and geographically; and yet their fates coalesce at the moment when each man forsakes the pleasure of the exotic land in which he has enjoyed

---

[1] Berlioz, *Evenings with the Orchestra*, p. 375.

sensual enchantments, in order to answer the call of duty and board his ship. For Vincent Wallace and for Énée, it is the sounds of instruments that break through their reverie and incite them to resume action, and to return to – or establish – 'civilization'.[2] The men must leave behind the seductions of Tatea's song, or of Didon and her dancing slaves.

The imperial plot archetype evoked by both works is a familiar one. The masculine idiom of the march, associated with military solidarity and the imperial strength of the reader's or audience member's own (presumed) world is juxtaposed against the Other, which is embodied as enticingly feminine, in music that flirts with a delicious incomprehensibility. The similarities in the manner in which Berlioz presents the fates of Tatea and Didon, and Wallace and Énée, also remind us of the way Dumont d'Urville and his contemporaries drew analogies between Māori and Classical antiquity. While the contemporary imperial analogy could be seen to bring Berlioz's opera to life, giving it topical resonance for his audience, for the real Tatea and her kin classicising analogies risked having the opposite effect, confining a living culture to a distant past.

Berlioz ostensibly encourages us be at least a little uncomfortable at the cost of the imperial mission, through the sympathy he offers for Tatea's plight and, of course, for that of Didon; but all the while he – and we, his intended audience or readers – overtly or surreptitiously indulge in the increasingly guilty pleasures of exoticism. Today we can conveniently attribute the more problematic aspects of such narratives to history: Berlioz's views are reflective of his time, and thus Other to us. Alternatively, in a postcolonial world a director may either soften the message of works such as *Les Troyens* by omitting more problematic numbers altogether, or directly confront the implications of such narratives in contemporary terms.

A turn to history offers another way to acknowledge and to question the imperial subtext of the musical museum. Musical works have helped to normalise and propagate the ideology they embodied, not only in performances in Europe but also in Europe's colonies. In this book I have been concerned with revealing Berlioz's diverse approaches to problematising and negotiating with Otherness, including ways in which the orchestra itself enacts the role of Other, and I have considered the reception of his music only insofar as it relates to European audiences. But what if, instead of listening

---

[2] Énée's hesitation was even more evident in earlier versions of the work. Berlioz originally had a stage direction signalling that it was the Trojan march that spurred him back into action: 'Énée, resté un instant immobile, semble se ranimer à ces clameurs guerières.' *NBE* 2c (Commentary), p. 778.

to and implicitly identifying with Berlioz's authorial persona as he recounts Wallace's story, we attempt to listen more closely to the voice of Tatea? – or, since that is virtually impossible, what if we look at the 'adventures' of Vincent Wallace and his peers in New Zealand from within that country more broadly, and from the 'Other' side? Louis Berlioz (the composer's son) wrote in some amazement to his father how, as far away as India, he still encountered people (such as the Indian wife of the French consul in Bombay), who knew his father's music: 'after a crossing of 128 days I still find myself in a land where you are known!'[3] European performers were touring North Africa, as Berlioz knew.[4] Indeed, in 1845 following Leopold de Meyer's performance in Constantinople, Berlioz speculated that pianists would now be able to rake in money in Carthage itself:

To Carthage! To Carthage! To Algeria! To Morocco! Share out amongst yourselves the Mediterranean coast! You will see grateful peoples chasing your heels! And why not carry the benefits of musical art into the interior of these lands? Have you forgotten that Constantine is ours? – that you will find French people there, brothers, happy to hear and applaud you? Moreover music isn't just made for the French, and I don't see what right you have to deprive the black populations of these distant countries, who are said to be so sensitive to melody. Depart! Depart soon![5]

Conversely, Berlioz satirised the possibility of 'pianistes [. . .] australiens, tasmaniens, taïtiens, nouka-hiviens, carolins, vitiens, de Vanikoro, de Mallicolo, des îles de Java et de Sumatra' touring Paris, and he envisaged a 'Conservatoire of New Zealand' where the inferior singers of a performance at the Opéra must have received their training.[6] But however ridiculous it was to Berlioz to conceive of art music being created in New Zealand (or however convenient it was as a device for him to preserve that country as a paradise free from European 'civilisation'), there, too, the 'natives' could hear his music.

In this epilogue I focus on three brief historical vignettes of music in New Zealand, representing respectively the period of Wallace's own trip (1838); the time Berlioz published *Evenings with the Orchestra*, when his own music was playing a role in the establishment of townships (in the early 1850s);

---

[3] *CG* VIII, p. 442.   [4] *CM* VI, pp. 58–9.   [5] Ibid., p. 2.
[6] *Journal des débats* 17 March 1853, pp. 2–3; 30 September 1851. Berlioz failed accurately to envisage the future on this occasion: New Zealand-trained opera singers, including some, such as Simon O'Neill or Madeleine Pierard, who trained at the New Zealand School of Music and its predecessors (the Victoria University and Massey University music schools), thrive on the stages of international opera houses today.

and finally the year immediately following the premier of *Les Troyens*, when New Zealand experienced its first season of fully staged opera (1864). I may thereby appear to present a retreat into history (and a highly selective one at that), and to a geographical context that still remains relatively unfamiliar to many Anglo-American or European readers. However, an appreciation of the ways in which the assumptions of art music – assumptions Berlioz himself promotes – were instilled in this former colony, and at what cost, is not only relevant to a broader historical understanding of the music and writing of Berlioz or Wallace, but also reveals both the problems posed and potential solutions offered by the legacy of this tradition today.

1838. Jigs, fugues and 'queer song': Wallace's musical encounters

While Berlioz relays (or more likely invents) a description of Tatea's song, we need to look elsewhere for an account of Wallace's own music-making in New Zealand. Such is provided in the unpublished biography written by Wallace's niece, Annie de Meurant Mulligan, and supposedly based in large part on interviews with his son.[7] In this version of the story, Wallace settles briefly in a small whaling community in New Zealand – a community comprising both Māori and Europeans. In these very early days of settlement, and particularly in the largely transient whaling and sealing population, there was little call for 'art music', and Wallace is presented as having entered the community not as a musician but as an adventurer. When he picks up his violin in front of the locals it is to entertain, not to enlighten. The contrast is implied by Mulligan herself. In the tavern Wallace is depicted playing 'rollicking Irish jigs' and improvising to tunes provided by the sailors.[8] However, when alone in his cabin and contemplating what role New Zealand might play on the world stage in future, Wallace plays 'snatches of sonata's [*sic*], fugues',[9] as if it is only this very different idiom that is capable of supporting serious reflection and transcending the immediacies of time and place.

There is no cannibalism or amorous relationship in Mulligan's version of Wallace's story, though again attention is focussed on an individual Māori girl, here named Waiata. When he hears Waiata approaching, Wallace abandons his fugues and starts up 'a rollicking Irish Tune',[10] seemingly excluding

---

[7] Mulligan, 'In Happy Moments'. [8] Ibid., p. 32. [9] Ibid., p. 33. [10] Ibid., p. 33.

Māori from participation in his vision of musical and national transcendence. Vanessa Agnew has pointed out how early European explorers of the Pacific would use Highland music to try to communicate with the locals as this was seen as being at a level similarly 'rudimentary' to their own traditions.[11] And Matthew Gelbart has demonstrated how, within Europe, Scottish music became essentialised as 'folk' in opposition to 'art music' during the period in which the very terms themselves were being constructed. The Highlanders in particular were the first to be construed as 'a primitive Other that was in fact a stratum within European society'.[12] Wallace's move to an Irish tune for Waiata can be seen in the same light, all the more ironic since the composer was himself Irish:

Then he finished his solitary meal, he sat in the doorway of his hut amusing himself, playing snatches of sonata's [sic], fugues [...] It is said, that William [Vincent Wallace] oftentimes wished that he had the vision of New Zealand a century later, as he predicted great things. He played as he mused.

What was that...?

He listened. Solitary footsteps were approaching.

He knew the Maori's [sic] were passionately fond of music, so he began a rollicking Irish Tune.

Then he caught sight of a bushy head, big brown eyes, peeping round the corner of the hut.[13]

Likening Waiata to a child, Wallace allows her to hold the instrument with his assistance, but when she overcomes her initial fear and is eager to produce sounds on her own he tells her the instrument is getting tired and wishes to sleep, before placing it out of her reach. In anthropomorphising his instrument, Wallace creates a fiction in order to protect a valuable object from an Other he considers incompatible with its technology. However, by attributing agency to the instrument in this way, Wallace simultaneously invokes and unexpectedly draws together the two world views his ruse would seem designed to keep apart: on the one hand, Māori themselves attributed agency to instruments, which were seen to have individual voices, created or inhabited by gods, and sometimes carved with faces;[14] on the other hand, as

---

[11] Vanessa Agnew, *Enlightenment Orpheus*, p. 88.
[12] Matthew Gelbart, *The Invention of 'Folk Music' and 'Art Music'* (Cambridge: Cambridge University Press, 2007), p. 11.
[13] Mulligan, 'In Happy Moments', p. 33.
[14] Brian Flintoff, *Taonga Pūoro: Singing Treasures; The Musical Instruments of the Māori* (Nelson: Craig Potton, 2004), pp. 14, 16, 120.

Berlioz's *Orchestration Treatise* emphasises repeatedly, the personification of instruments at the expense of their performers could be a facet of the composer's control over the musical work.

The distinction between Māori and European musical idioms is reinstated through the description of Waiata's own music, which is juxtaposed against that of Wallace and shown as emanating from a body rather than instrument. Indeed, 'Waiata' is the Māori term for 'song' (though this is not stated in Mulligan's text). Moreover, Waiata's body is Other in terms of gender, race, and perhaps even the supernatural. Mulligan first describes how the girl sang Wallace a love song: 'Waiata immediately began to sing a soft crooning melody...the Maori way of expressing their feelings in music.'[15] Later Wallace succumbs to a mysterious illness, which other whalers imply might be the 'bewitching' effect of his exchange with the woman he describes as his 'fairy'. In these circumstances he turns to his violin, 'his only pleasure', for solace, attempting to find physiological restitution through 'a favourite Sonata'. But '[e]ven this soon wearied him'. Now Waiata sings again: 'Waiata squatted down on the floor, certain that it would work and began chanting a queer song. This had the effect of soothing the sick man...when the day dawned, William felt quite himself again. The pain had gone, and the throbbing...ceased.'[16]

Waiata's 'queer song' forms part of a ceremony that appears to cure Wallace, and he is able to make his own music again.

> William [Vincent Wallace] did not feel equal for work that day, so decided to rest and practice some of his own compositions. And it is assumed that it was during his stay in New Zealand that he composed the overture of the opera *Lurline*, which he shelved for years, producing it as his third opera, at Covent Garden, London in 1860, nearly twenty two years after.[17]

Mulligan's suggestion that it was at this time Wallace conceived the overture for his opera *Lurline* is intriguing. *Lurline* is a treatment of the German Lorelei myth. The titular character is the mysterious sirenlike maiden who lures sailors to their doom through her song. However, in Wallace's operatic treatment Lurline falls in love with and rescues a mortal man from a watery death. All other evidence would suggest that Wallace actually wrote *Lurline* some nine years later (in 1847), but by connecting *Lurline* directly to New Zealand, Mulligan would seem to draw an implicit connection between the Māori girl and the Germanic siren of the folk tale. Hence exotic Otherness becomes European folk legend, and is thereby absorbed into European

---

[15] Mulligan, 'In Happy Moments', p. 34.   [16] Ibid., pp. 34, 35.   [17] Ibid., p. 35.

Ex. 6.1 Vincent Wallace, *Lurline* No. 3, 'The Naiad's Spell'

art. Where we might expect a professional musician such as Wallace to have transcribed Waiata's song and preserved at least a sense of her original voice, in this version of his narrative Wallace appropriates Otherness to prop up his own conception of art. In Wallace's opera, Lurline's music bears no obvious traces of anything we might now identify as a Māori influence, but instead draws on idioms familiar from Wallace's European operatic models. Lurline's Romance opens with a charmingly lyrical melody that also appears in the overture supposedly conceived in New Zealand. After the chorus warns that the water nymph's music spells death to mortal men, this melody gives way to the wordless vocalisations characteristic of numerous other operatic women whose otherworldly sexuality or irrationality threatens to seduce or bewitch the male hero (Ex. 6.1).

In Mulligan's version of Wallace's time in New Zealand, his art music is juxtaposed against the entertainment of the lower classes and against the natural – or supernatural – powers of Waiata's song. It is Wallace's sonatas and fugues that promise a future for New Zealand, and in this future the only place for Waiata's song is to be reconfigured for exoticising pleasure. Is Mulligan's version of Wallace's adventures in New Zealand close to what Berlioz heard from Wallace in London? Are there elements that provided the base from which Berlioz constructed his own fantasy? While Berlioz may not have Wallace play his violin in his version of the story, the premise is the same (though he perhaps would not have chosen fugues as his indicator of supreme musical transcendence). Whatever the 'authentic' origins of the Māori text, in the context of Berlioz's narrative Tatea's song is an exotic fantasy, juxtaposed against the music of the 'old world' and appropriated for an evening's entertainment at the opera.

1852/3. A 'noble mode of civilisation': Regimental band performances of the music of Berlioz and Wallace

Just two years after Wallace's visit to New Zealand, the country was officially made part of the British Empire when in 1840 representatives of Queen Victoria and various Māori rangatira (chiefs) signed the Treaty of Waitangi that promised the Māori British protection in exchange for a degree of governance over their lands.[18] European colonisation now began in earnest, and in the fledgling towns music played an increasingly vital role in creating a sense of community amongst the new settlers, and in maintaining their connection to the remote lands they still considered 'home'. One of the earliest forms of public performance by the colonists took the form of recitals from the regimental bands. In the early 1850s in Wellington the band of the 65th Regiment of Foot of the British Army performed open-air concerts, whose programmes were announced in advance in local newspapers. Berlioz's *Waverley* overture made several appearances in the band's repertoire, along with much more frequent performances of arrangements of Wallace's music (particularly items from his opera *Maritana*). Charlotte Godley, the wife of an important British colonist and a prolific letter writer, heard one such performance within her first few days in Wellington. Her account stresses the proficiency of the band, its connection to the homeland, and the way in which the performance was a gathering point for the

---

[18] The English and Māori versions of the Treaty differed significantly, and the interpretation and implementation of the Treaty continues to be contested.

settlers. However, perhaps the most interesting aspect is her reference to the presence of Māori:

> It is a very tolerable band, and they play a great number of very pretty things, and altogether reminded me almost *too much* of home. There we met everyone, walking or sitting about in summer dresses, bonnets with feathers and flowers, etc., and two or three parties of natives, rolled in their blankets and *squatted* just behind the great drum.[19]

Thus while Berlioz and Wallace were sharing a bowl of punch in London, and while Berlioz was constructing his story of Wallace and Tatea, the real Tateas and Waiatas were listening to the music of the two men on the other side of the world. Indeed, Berlioz's own music was now actively taking part in the 'civilising' of Tatea and the colonising of her land. In 1846 and again in the 1860s the 65th Regiment participated in the land wars that forcibly suppressed Māori dissatisfaction with European settlement. While it is unlikely Berlioz's *Waverley* overture sounded on the battlefield, its performance before Māori in Wellington reflects a subtler version of the same colonising impulse. We have seen how Berlioz worked with military bands in France, employing the characteristic muscular bonding and visual display to create communal and national identity in his *Symphonie funèbre et triomphale,* and subtly subverting and absorbing the militaristic aspects in *Harold en Italie.* In his treatise on military music, published four years before Godley's account, Kastner described how the powerful features of regimental bands could be effectively deployed in the (French) colonies to create this same sense of community among local populations:

> Judging by a report which appeared in the papers of 1846, the state of music in the French settlements of Oceania has rapidly changed in appearance. In fact, at the request of the governor and the officials commanding the different islands under our rule, a regiment of military musicians must accompany the reinforcements who, during this time, depart for this region. Besides, since the beginning, European music has had the most positive effects on their inhabitants. In the main places occupied by our troops, someone had the fortunate idea of instituting military concerts. These concerts which take place in the evening, attract a crowd of natives: everyone comes and attends with their women and children, after the day's work, and demonstrates unambiguously their pleasure and satisfaction. These musical festivals have produced such good results that it has been deemed useful to increase this most noble mode of civilisation.[20]

---

[19] John R. Godley (ed.), *Letters from Early New Zealand by Charlotte Godley 1850–1853* (Christchurch: Whitcombe & Tombs Limited, 1951), p. 35. Emphasis in the original.
[20] Kastner, *Manuel général de musique militaire*, pp. 161–2.

In the colonies, as in parades at home, the military bands presented 'music for the eyes': Godley later comments how 'the soldiers [of the regimental band] look like home, and like civilization'.[21] Kastner stresses the importance of the visual dimension for the presence of bands abroad also, but interestingly, when Kastner suggests that the citizens of Cairo literally fell into line with their French conquerors through the power of the military bands, it is the musical instruments themselves that are shown to exert the most powerful attraction:

What better influence could there be, for example, on the populations to be ruled over and subdued, than the impressive and sumptuous display of a military procession? Those thousands of dazzling colours that shimmer before you, that jingling of shining weapons that catch the eye, that warlike music that seizes the senses and, in its manly expression, seems to defy the enemy and sing of victory – all of this, is it not designed to dazzle, to captivate? When our army made its entry into Cairo, to the noise of fanfares, it attracted in its wake a crowd of the inhabitants, who, seized with astonishment and admiration at the look of the soldiers, and encouraged moreover by their welcoming expression and physiognomy, came to examine with curiosity their weapons, clothing, cannons, and *especially the musical instruments* of these new masters who seemed to have been sent from heaven, in its clemency, in place of the turbulent and fierce hordes under the yoke of whom they had for so long been suffering.[22]

Similarly, Godley's account suggests that it is the instruments that attract the Māori – they have positioned themselves near the bass drum. However, already there is a sense from Godley and others within the colony that something is being lost. Godley describes a 'kind of mock war-dance' (haka) but suggests the performers seemed embarrassed, and a colonel who was present recalled seeing a much more powerful expression of the haka years earlier, with a revealing use of the past tense: 'They seem to have been very formidable enemies.'[23] Māori would actually prove themselves 'formidable enemies' again in the land wars of the 1860s. However, Godley instead paints a picture of two peoples coming together through music – Berlioz's and Wallace's music – but purely on the terms of one group only. Tatea's song was already beginning to fade at the time Berlioz put it in writing, suppressed by missionaries and losing the contexts and practices that gave it meaning, while new idioms introduced by the colonists, including military

---

[21] Godley, *Letters from Early New Zealand*, p. 87.
[22] Kastner, *Manuel général de musique militaire*, p. 185. Emphasis added.
[23] Godley, *Letters from Early New Zealand*, pp. 48–9.

bands, provided powerful alternatives.[24] By understanding it in its fuller context, we see the full irony of Berlioz's Wallace narrative, which idolises an imagined tradition as the antithesis of Europe at precisely the same time that his own music was part of the mission that, whether by accident or design, was reconfiguring the reality of that music in its native land.

1864. 'Local hits' and 'high class music': The first opera season

By 1864, the year after Berlioz's *Les Troyens* (or half of it) was premiered in Paris, the main cities of New Zealand had communities big enough to sustain their first season of fully staged opera, and the company of Irishman William Saurin Lyster crossed the Tasman Sea from Australia. Not surprisingly, given the difficulties Berlioz had getting *Les Troyens* staged, not to mention the hostile reception of *Benvenuto Cellini* in London, Berlioz's operas played no role in this season. But Wallace's operas were performed – indeed, his *Maritana* was the most popular work on the tour, which also included *Lurline* as well as operas by Verdi, Donizetti, Mozart, Meyerbeer, and Gounod. The newspapers were abuzz with accounts of the opera season, and a brief survey of these reveals the ways in which performances of Wallace's music played into negotiations over culture and identity in New Zealand, illustrating in the process the role of the Other worlds of the colonies in European musical aesthetics more generally.

That New Zealand inherited some of the broader debates around opera from Europe is not surprising. The opera season was seen as connecting the settlers with 'the homeland', generally assumed to be Britain. Thus one local critic talked about how the operas allowed the audience 'to recall vividly old impressions, now alas, growing somewhat faint, and which we never thought to have had revived on these so lately uninhabited shores'.[25] The journalist's comment needs to be treated highly critically from the outset, for the shores of New Zealand had, in fact, been inhabited by Māori for more than five centuries. The remark is symptomatic of the unspoken assumptions behind almost every account of the opera season. Culture in New Zealand meant European culture, and to establish it effectively meant acting as if Māori did not exist. The first opera season also coincided with one of the most heated periods in the land wars between Māori and the settlers, in which Māori were being aggressively forced off land by both British soldiers and local settler militia, who believed (or chose to believe) that land deals done under the Treaty gave them ownership rights.

---

[24] McLean, *Maori Music*, pp. 270–2, 274, 276–8.   [25] *The Press* 6/606, 8 October 1864, 2.

Lyster's opera company directly acknowledged this context in a Burlesque they performed during their New Zealand season: Irish-American John Brougham's *Po-ca-hon-tas; or The Gentle Savage*. Brougham's play was a hit in mid nineteenth-century America. In New Zealand Lyster's company loaded the work with what the newspapers recognised as 'local hits'. For example, settler women were depicted as forming an inept local militia (presumably to do battle against Māori), and when the soldiers threaten to leave, the settlers exclaim 'Oh, dear, what shall we do if the troops go away? We shall all be tattooed!'[26]

According to the newspaper critics, *Po-ca-hon-tas* was a great success with New Zealand audiences, but we must wonder whether the satire missed its original mark in more ways than one. In America Brougham's play provocatively satirised and critiqued a number of specific works, including Wallace's *Maritana*. However, it also took aim at the grand theatrical tradition that had been propagating the myth of the Indian Noble Savage, so useful in creating a sense of American heritage and identity while simultaneously confining Indian cultures to the past. Moreover, *Po-ca-hon-tas* spoke directly to a predominantly lower class audience ready to mock the pretensions of earlier theatrical presentations of the story.[27] But in New Zealand, while the ideology of the Noble Savage was certainly being applied to Māori, the serious theatrical traditions embalming it were yet to be generated. In other words, the satire of *Po-ca-hon-tas* risked being perceived as directed against Māori themselves, rather than against those who were exploiting them through theatrical representation.

Furthermore, in New Zealand the audience for *Po-ca-hon-tas* saw the work immediately after a performance of *La Traviata* and in the context of an opera season targeted not at a lower class audience frustrated with the pretensions of those above them, but at a broad audience actively adopting the rituals they associated with high art and, indeed, the upper classes. As Lawrence W. Levine has demonstrated, opera in the United States was capable of straddling the 'high brow/low brow' divide; but in New Zealand – a colony whose residents of European descent typically still actively identified with a European homeland rather than asserting their independence – that divide was often configured in different ways, particularly around issues such as class.[28] A brief examination of the 1864 season thus reveals how even operas such as Wallace's *Maritana* and *Lurline* with no overt 'local hits'

---

[26] *Daily Southern Cross*, 20/ 2311, 16 December 1864, 4.
[27] Zoe Detsi-Diamanti, 'Burlesquing "Otherness" in Nineteenth-Century American Theatre: The Image of the Indian in John Brougham's *Met-a-mora; or, The Last of the Pollywogs* (1847) and *Po-Ca-Hon-Tas; or, The Gentle Savage* (1855)', *American Studies* 48/3 (2007), 101–24.
[28] Levine, *Highbrow/Lowbrow*, pp. 83–104.

might do the work of cultural imperialism through their status as events. It also shows elements of conceptual imperialism in relation to opera as a genre.

The local papers in New Zealand reprinted stories that emphasised the class associations of different forms of opera in Europe – the 'aristocratic place of recreation' of the Italian opera was contrasted with the 'more numerous class of lovers of sweet sounds' who attended Covent Garden.[29] But in New Zealand the opera season by necessity brought together those separate audiences in what was usually the only theatre in town: 'Every class of the community has been represented in the crowded audiences which have nightly assembled at the Princess Theatre', reported a journalist in Dunedin.[30] Moreover, one newspaper referred to the fact that only a single theatre entrance would be available to the public. (In Australia, Lyster's company had performed to a theatre where the classes could enter their respective areas without mingling.)[31] However, there was also a sense that the opera represented something at the upper end of the class spectrum. Newspaper accounts reveal that the theatres usually underwent a major overhaul in preparation – not merely to facilitate the performance, but also to give them the requisite level of grandeur.[32] They advertised opera dresses and fine jewellery that could be purchased in advance, and readers were advised that it was to be 'full dress' in the stalls and boxes.[33] One reviewer commented that the class of people attending the operas was quite different to the usual theatre crowd: 'The contrast [in Dunedin's Princess Theatre] between its present light and airy appearance, and the dinginess which preceded it, is however nothing to the contrast between the present nightly occupants of the dress circle and the usual audience secured by the dramatic company, when it was a dress circle only in name.'[34] However, there were also repeated calls to make ticket prices affordable to a greater cross-section of the community. Indeed, the opera season was perceived as a crucial event in forming that community. One reviewer described it as a significant event 'in the history of a young colony' and suggested that it 'marks a new era in our social history'.[35]

It was important to the success of the season that opera was perceived not as 'mere entertainment' or simply as an excuse to display a new dress. Many reviewers noted that the opera season saw the arrival of 'high Art in music',

---

[29] 'Extracts from Our London Correspondent's Letter', *Colonist* 7/646, 5 January 1864, 3.
[30] *Otago Daily Times* 845, 6 September 1864, 4; Adrienne Simpson, *Opera's Farthest Frontier: A History of Professional Opera in New Zealand* (Auckland: Reed, 1996), p. 68.
[31] *Otago Daily Times* 827, 15 August 1864, 4.   [32] *Timaru Herald* 1/16, 24 September 1864, 4.
[33] Ibid., 4.   [34] *North Otago Times* 2/30, 15 September 1864, 3.
[35] *Otago Witness* 665, 27 August 1864, 13.

'high-class music', or 'the best music of the day'.[36] There was an automatic sense of an operatic canon – of the 'compositions of the best masters'[37] or the 'standard musical compositions'[38] – being instilled in the colony, for in the absence of any local composers (or, indeed, a sufficient body of suitably trained local performers), opera in New Zealand was necessarily a set body of works whose merits and success had been determined earlier and elsewhere.

However, a closer look at the reviews also reveals the constant negotiations taking place within the repertoire, as well as an inability completely to subdue questions about opera's status as high art. New Zealand newspapers reproduced condemnations of opera's dependency on libretti that were seen as ridiculous or, in the case of *La Traviata*, downright immoral.[39] Perhaps it was partly for this reason that one local critic could identify Meyerbeer's *Huguenots* as the greatest opera in existence.[40] With its representation of powerful community and religious solidarity in the face of violent oppression, its appeal to settlers trying to build a new community around the church is understandable. The same critic also repeatedly stresses that what the community really needed was a strong choral society, so that the opera could inspire locals through showing them what was possible with high standards of vocal performance; but, he continues,

> Depend upon it in the voluptuous enjoyment of operatic music great transient delight will be experienced, but no sound school of musical taste will be evoked. It is in the hard labor, the sacrifice of time, the steady discipline required to deliver the choruses of the greater masters, that the solid foundations of a sound musical judgment will be laid, and in the constant performance of these great works that a true classical taste in music will grow in our rising community.[41]

In other words, it was choral singing that would instil in colonists the values they needed to build their colony – hard labour, time, and discipline, as well as 'a perfect subordination of every voice to the whole, an utter abnegation of self'. Elsewhere an article was devoted to national pastimes.[42] Although it was conceded that the cultivation of music had beneficial effects for a community, opera was seen as emblematic of the 'luxurious' Italians,

---

[36] *Otago Witness* 668, 17 September 1864, 13; *Daily Southern Cross* 20/2236, 20 September 1864, 4; *Daily Southern Cross* 20/2272, 1 November 1864, 4.
[37] *Daily Southern Cross*, 220/2272, 1 November 1864, 4.
[38] *Nelson Examiner and New Zealand Chronicle*, 23/132, 1 November 1864, 2.
[39] 'The moral aspect of operas', *The Press* [Canterbury], 6/616, 20 October 1864, 20.
[40] *The Press* [Canterbury], 6/608, 11 October 1864, 2; and 6/616, 20 October 1864, 2.
[41] 'The amateur concert', *The Press* [Canterbury], 4/ 442, 31 March 1864, 2.
[42] 'Colonial amusements', *Nelson Examiner and New Zealand Chronicle*, 23/24, 25 February 1864, 3.

and it was instead sport that characterised solid English values and outdoorsy prowess – qualities inevitably considered desirable in the colonists also.

Of course, this mentality was itself imported, but it plays out particularly strongly, and perhaps with higher stakes for those concerned, in opera's 'farthest frontier'.[43] Indeed, this is where we might see the most dangerous aspects of Berlioz's Vincent Wallace narrative, for Berlioz's *Evenings with the Orchestra* conflates an aesthetic of great-opera-as-culture with a wilful refusal to listen to the culture of the Other: we hear about Tatea only because the opera that particular 'evening' fails to satisfy the orchestral musicians' standards, and then Tatea is packaged into an exotic opera plot. Moreover, within New Zealand these dialogues over the nature and benefits of opera all took place amongst the colonists themselves, or between the colonists and the 'homeland'. It seems unlikely that Māori attended the performances.[44] The success of opera was dependent on not interacting with Tatea except to transform her into the universal Other of Lurline's vocalise, or a Pocahontas-type noble savage.

Wallace's *Maritana* indeed does some of the work of the Pocahontas type, for the plot centres on the relationship of the exotic gypsy Maritana (a street-singer), and a soldier; the marriage of the two characters ultimately manages to save not only the soldier but also the King (and, by implication, Maritana herself, who is brought within the fold of 'civilised' culture through her union to the soldier). The gentle exoticism of Maritana's strophic ballades is contrasted against the tenor hero's 'Let me like a soldier fall'. While we may be missing the chorus of belligerent natives, we are again not too far from the exotic plot archetype of Wallace's own narrative, as told by Berlioz – a plot archetype of particular potency when we remember the land wars raging not far outside the opera house, and when we recall that many of the numbers of *Maritana* had been widely popularised in New Zealand through arrangements for military bands of the same regiments that were engaging in battle with Māori. Add to this the fact that Wallace's operas were by a composer the audience could identify as British,[45] and his success in the colony is not difficult to understand.

---

[43] Simpson, *Opera's Farthest Frontier*.
[44] I have found no reference to Māori audience members in the numerous accounts of the opera season. In contrast, when a group of Aboriginals were taken to hear Lyster's troop in Melbourne in 1862 this was noted in the press: Harold Love, *The Golden Age of Australian Opera: W. S. Lyster and His Companies 1861–1880* (Sydney: Currency Press, 1981), p. 137.
[45] In a later column Berlioz reveals he thought of Wallace as an Englishman born in Ireland. *Journal des débats* 20 March 1863, p. 2.

However, though a source of pride to the British, Wallace's operas were also criticised in the European press for sounding by turns Italian, German, or French and thus failing convincingly to embody a national voice of his own.[46] Maybe the extent of Wallace's initial success in New Zealand was a consequence of the even more marginal status of that country. In this context the 'double bind' of nationalism could actually work in Wallace's favour.[47] Rather than marking him as either exotic or parochial, any perceived Britishness in Wallace's operas could give the settlers a sense of cultural connectedness that transcended the 12,000 miles separating them from the 'old country'. Conversely, what to an audience in Europe might have sounded derivative of the Italian, German, or French operatic idioms could, to the settlers, sound simply like European 'Art'. Indeed, in 1902, one British critic condescendingly described *Maritana* as 'one of the most popular operas for half a century in the suburbs, the provinces, and the Colonies'.[48] Europe and Britain herself had been discreetly dropping Wallace from the repertoire. Perhaps that process had already begun in Berlioz's Wallace narrative, for in the context of *Les soirées de l'orchestre*, his refusal to say anything about Wallace as a musician reads like his critiques of so many other operas he classed as second-rate and thus barely discussed at all. Moreover, in New Zealand, too, Wallace's works would eventually lose their privileged place in the repertoire. As more operas were imported, as more touring companies came, and as local performers formed orchestras and opera companies of their own, the need to identify with a British homeland was surpassed by a sense that national strength might better be served by music whose value is deemed 'universal'.

Postscript – Or 'Second Epilogue'

In the twenty-first century it is Berlioz's music, not Wallace's, that is played in New Zealand, but it takes its place in a diverse soundscape in which musicians engage with a variety of ways of defining their national identity. A successful European tour not merely of a pianist or two but of the entire national orchestra of New Zealand is no longer the satirical improbability

---

[46] Arthur Pougin, *William-Vincent Wallace: Etude Biographique et Critique* (Paris: Alfred Ikelmer & Compagnie, 1866).
[47] Richard Taruskin, 'Nationalism', *Grove Music Online. Oxford Music Online*, Oxford University Press, www.oxfordmusiconline.com/subscriber/article/grove/music/50846, accessed 10 April 2014.
[48] www.musicwithease.com/wallace-maritana.html; accessed 19 September 2013.

Berlioz construed it to be, and the New Zealand Symphony Orchestra's performances of his own *Symphonie fantastique* received particular acclaim in Germany, Slovenia, and Switzerland in 2010.[49]

However, in New Zealand, Berlioz's music inevitably takes its place in a diverse soundscape in which the aesthetic outlook it represents is just one voice among many, and a voice whose privilege is highly contested. While in the twentieth century New Zealand composers within the European instrumental tradition increasingly explored new ways of articulating their national identity in orchestral repertoire and opera,[50] Māori sustained, revived, or reinvented their own traditional musical practices.[51] Moreover, the metaphorical descendants of Wallace and of Tatea (or Waiata) no longer always part ways as 'Self' and 'Other'. Performers of Māori descent have international careers as interpreters of European works, while a leading figure in the revival of Māori musical instruments is a New Zealander of European descent. And other musicians explore ways in which Pakeha (European New Zealander) and Māori performance traditions might coalesce within single works or events.[52]

Read from within this context of a postcolonial, bicultural, or multicultural New Zealand, Berlioz's Wallace narrative thus risks turning the polarities he himself establishes on their head. It is Berlioz who can appear 'Other', his exoticising account of Tatea and her European lover appearing as, at best, an historical curiosity. At worst, the story might expose

---

[49] Report from the New Zealand Symphony Orchestra's 2010 international tour; www.nzso.co.nz/wp-content/uploads/2011/09/NZSO˙IntTourReport˙LR.pdf pp. 8–9; accessed 22 September 2013.

[50] Douglas Lilburn, 'A Search for Tradition' (1946), in *A Search for Tradition: A Search for a Language* (Wellington: Lilburn Trust, 2011), pp. 17–47.

[51] Peter Beatson, 'Richard Nunns: The Renaissance of Traditional Maori Instruments', *Music in the Air: Song & Spirituality* 16 (2003), 17–33.

[52] Ian Whalley, 'Traditional New Zealand Māori Instruments, Composition and Digital Technology: Some Recent Collaborations and Processes', *Organised Sound: An International Journal of Music Technology*, 10/1 (2005), 57–65. See also Jenny McLeod, *Hōhepa: A Chamber Opera*. McLeod is a Pakeha composer (of European descent), but she worked extensively with Māori to tell the story of Hohepa Te Umuroa, who died in Australia in the 1840s after having been unjustly exiled from New Zealand for supposedly posing a threat to settlers. McLeod incorporates Māori performance practices, including a traditional funeral call and haka (or war dance), as well as working Māori idioms into the operatic texture. The first performance of the work was attended by many of the Māori whose ancestral story was being told on the stage, and they responded with a traditional call of their own at the end of the performance: www.youtube.com/watch?v=RL2Dq4wRUEw and http://youtube.com/watch?v=9iRTFvnmDRg; accessed 3 October, 2013. There are also less happy instances where Māori traditions have been perceived as being appropriated by Pakeha. See, for example, the contested uses of the haka: Jay Scherer and Steve Jackson, 'From *Ka Mate* to *Kapa o Pango*: Haka as Contested Terrain', in *Globalization, Sport and Corporate Nationalism* (New York: Peter Lang, 2010), pp. 139–66.

an ideology that is latent in Berlioz's music, revealing some of the cost incurred when European art music, including Berlioz's own works, asserted its presence in Europe's colonies by means which I have touched on in this epilogue.

The dilemma as to whether such music is valued in 'historical or aesthetic' terms is highly familiar in musicological discourse.[53] When confined to musical works in the abstract, and particularly when the Otherness embodied is of a type unlikely to carry direct personal implications for many modern listeners – such as historical attitudes towards the supernatural or technology – the debate might seem primarily of academic interest. However, when that Otherness is assigned to groups with which people continue to identify (Māori or women, for example), and when we consider music not simply as text but as an event in which concepts of Otherness are enacted and enforced through performance, it becomes more difficult to ignore their force and consequences.

Does this mean we must either look the other way when listening to Berlioz's music, or subject Berlioz's mentality to the same interrogation that has confronted Wagner's anti-Semitism? Perhaps; but if it is in performance that negative stereotypes of Otherness might be actively propagated, it is also through performance that we might see identity being renegotiated. Moreover, as I have argued throughout this book, Berlioz directly dramatises and problematises the very act of performance and the way in which performance can incorporate Otherness. It is not simply a matter of encouraging Tatea's descendants to master European idioms and play Berlioz's music. Rather, within his works Berlioz explores the ways in which performers themselves, regardless of gender, race, or other markers of identity, negotiate the divide between Self and Other through the very act of performance. In the *Orchestration Treatise* Berlioz depicts performers both as the explorers of Other worlds and as the Others to be conquered by the composer's work. *Symphonie funèbre et triomphale* and *Harold en Italie* explore, in different ways, not only how military discipline might contain the collective orchestral Other, but also how individual subjectivity might contest that collective identity. In *Symphonie fantastique* and *La nonne sanglante* Berlioz's orchestral performers are positioned on the margins between this world and the Other world of the supernatural, alternately concealed as noumenal essence or revealed as visible bodies much like the supernatural beings evoked by the works themselves. In *La damnation de Faust* and *Euphonia* it is gender that

---

[53] Carl Dahlhaus, trans. J. B. Robinson, *Foundations of Music History* (Cambridge: Cambridge University Press, 1983), pp. 19–32.

is marginalised, but again Berlioz problematises the process through the way he plays with the physicality of his performers, drawing on the generic ambiguity of the media in question. Finally, with *Les Troyens* the 'puerile chauvinism' that remained in Berlioz's libretto is offset (if not excused) by the fact that the Otherness of the military discipline, the supernatural, the future, and of instrumental technology itself are all recalled as part of the dramatic fabric of the music itself.

Looking at the Other worlds of Berlioz's musical works and writings allows us to see the very process by which the problematic notion of musical transcendence became enacted during his lifetime. If Berlioz was, on one hand, a strong advocate for music's supreme power and for compositional authority, he was also, in each of the cases examined in this book, crucially sensitive to the attendant tensions created for the composer's Others, the performers. In particular, Berlioz positions the orchestra as the bridge between worlds, alternately visible and invisible, technology or body, collective or individual, exotic or industrial. Thus while audiences today might wish to distance themselves from aspects of the mentality of Berlioz and his age, and might define Otherness in very different terms, through Berlioz's orchestra they might still confront and delight in the exploration of Other worlds. And perhaps, as Berlioz himself says at the end of *Evenings with the Orchestra*, 'That's epilogue enough.'

Select bibliography

Works by Berlioz

CG: *Correspondence générale*, general ed. Pierre Citron, Paris: Flammarion, 1972–2003
I: 1803–32, ed. Pierre Citron (1972)
II: 1832–42, ed. Frédéric Robert (1975)
III: 1842–50, ed. Pierre Citron (1978)
IV: 1851–5, ed. Pierre Citron, Yves Gérard, and Hugh Macdonald (1983)
V: 1855–9, ed. Hugh Macdonald and François Lesure (1988)
VI: 1859–63, ed. Hugh Macdonald and François Lesure (1995)
VII: 1864–9, ed. Hugh Macdonald (2001)
VIII: Supplements, ed. Hugh Macdonald (2003)

CM: *Critique musicale*, general ed. Yves Gérard, Paris: Buchet/Chastel, 1996–
I: 1823–34, ed. H. Robert Cohen and Yves Gérard (1996)
II: 1835–6, ed. Anne Bongrain and Marie-Hélène Coudroy-Saghaï (1998)
III: 1837–8, ed. Anne Bongrain and Marie-Hélène Coudroy-Saghaï (2001)
IV: 1839–41, ed. Anne Bongrain and Marie-Hélène Coudroy-Saghaï (2003)
V: 1842–4, ed. Anne Bongrain and Marie-Hélène Coudroy-Saghaï (2004)
VI: 1845–8, ed. Anne Bongrain and Marie-Hélène Coudroy-Saghaï (2008)

NBE: *New Berlioz Edition*, general ed. Hugh Macdonald, Kassel: Bärenreiter, 1967–2006. Volumes cited:
2a–c. *Les Troyens*, ed. Hugh Macdonald (1969–70)
4. *Incomplete Operas*, eds. Ric Graebner and Paul Banks (2002)
7. *Lélio ou Le retour à la vie*, ed. Peter Bloom (1992)
8a–b. *La damnation de Faust*, ed. Julian Rushton (1979–86)
13. *Songs for Solo Voice and Orchestra*, ed. Ian Kemp (1975)
15. *Songs for One, Two or Three Voices and Keyboard*, eds. Ian Kemp and Ian Rumbold (2005)
16. *Symphonie fantastique*, ed. Nicholas Temperley (1972)
17. *Harold en Italie*, eds. Paul Banks and Hugh Macdonald (2001)
18. *Roméo et Juliette*, ed. Kern D. Holoman (1990)
19. *Grand symphonie funèbre et triomphale*, ed. Hugh Macdonald (1967)
24. *Grand traité d'instrumentation et d'orchestration modernes*, ed. Peter Bloom (2003)

26. *Portraits of Hector Berlioz*, eds. Gunther Braam, Richard Macnutt, and John Warrack (2003)

Grand traité d'instrumentation et d'orchestration modernes, Paris: Schonenberger, 1844; revised and expanded 1855.
Macdonald, Hugh (ed., trans.), *Berlioz's Orchestration Treatise: A Translation and Commentary*, Cambridge: Cambridge University Press, 2002.

Les soirées de l'orchestre, Paris: Michel Lévy frères, 1852.
Guichard, Léon (ed.), Paris: Gründ, 1968.
Barzun, Jacques (ed., trans.), *Evenings with the Orchestra*, Chicago: Chicago University Press, 1956, 1973. Reprint, with foreword by Peter Bloom, 1999.

Les grotesques de la musique, Paris: Librairie Nouvelle A. Bourdilliet et Cie, 1859.
Bruce, Alastair (trans.), Hugh Macdonald (Introduction), *The Musical Madhouse*, Rochester, NY: University of Rochester Press, 2003.

À travers chants, Paris: Calmann Lévy, 1862.
Csicsery-Rónary, Elizabeth (ed., trans.), *The Art of Music and Other Essays*, Bloomington and Indianapolis: Indiana University Press, 1994.

Mémoires de Hector Berlioz, Paris: Michel Lévy frères, 1870; reprinted Farnborough: Gregg International Publishers, 1969.
Newman, Ernest, *Memoirs of Hector Berlioz*, New York: Knopf, 1932; reprinted New York: Dover, 1966.

General

Abbate, Carolyn, *Unsung Voices: Opera and Musical Narrative in the Nineteenth Century*, Princeton, NJ: Princeton University Press, 1991.
'Opera; or, the Envoicing of Women', in Ruth A. Solie (ed.), *Musicology and Difference*, Berkeley: University of California Press, 1993, pp. 225–58.
'Outside Ravel's Tomb', *Journal of the American Musicological Society* 52/3 (1999), 465–530.
In Search of Opera, Princeton, NJ: Princeton University Press, 2001.
Adorno, Theodor W., *In Search of Wagner*, London: Verso, 2005.
Agnew, Vanessa, *Enlightenment Orpheus: The Power of Music in Other Worlds*, Oxford: Oxford University Press, 2008.
Albright, Daniel, *Berlioz's Semi-operas*, Rochester, NY: University of Rochester Press, 2001.
Allevy, Marie-Antoinette, *La mise en scène en France dans la première moitié du dix-neuvième siècle*, Paris: Libraire E. Droz, 1938; repr. Geneva Slatkine Reprints, 1976.
Anger, Violaine, 'Hector Berlioz et l'Orient', in Chantal Spillemaecker and Antoine Troncy (eds.), *Berlioz et Hugo, fantasmes d'orient*, La côte-Saint-André, Isère: Musée Hector-Berlioz, 2004.

Attali, Jacques, *Histoires de Temp*, Paris: Fayard, 1982.

Auber, Daniel François Esprit, *L'enfant prodigue*, Paris: Brandus, 1850.

Bainbridge, Simon, *Napoleon and English Romanticism*, Cambridge: Cambridge University Press, 1995.

Banks, Paul, 'Harold, de Byron à Berlioz', in Christian Wasselin and Pierre-René Serna (eds.), *Hector Berlioz*, Paris: Éditions de l'Herne, 2003, pp. 152–61.

Bannister, Roland, 'How Are We to Write Our History? Perspectives on the Historiography of Military Music', *Musicology Australia* 25 (2002), 1–17.

Barringer, Tim and Tom Flynn (eds.), *Colonialism and the Object: Empire, Material Culture and the Museum*, London: Routledge, 1998.

Barzun, Jacques, *New Letters of Berlioz 1803–1868*, New York: Columbia University Press, 1954.

Bates, Eliot, 'The Social Life of Musical Instruments', *Ethnomusicology* 56/3 (2012), 363–95.

Bennett, Tony, *The Birth of the Museum: History, Theory, Politics*, London: Routledge, 1995.

Blanchard, Pascal, Nicolas Bancel, Gilles Boëtsch, Eric Deroo, Sandrine Lemaire, and Chalres Forsdick (eds.), *Human Zoos: Science and Spectacle in the Age of Colonial Empires*, Liverpool: Liverpool University Press, 2008.

Bloom, Peter, 'A Return to Berlioz's "Retour à la Vie"', *The Musical Quarterly* 64/3 (1978), 354–85.

  'La mission de Berlioz en Allemagne: Un document inédit', *Revue de Musicologie* 66/1 (1980), 70–85.

  The Life of Berlioz, Cambridge: Cambridge University Press, 1998.

  (ed.), *The Cambridge Companion to Berlioz*, Cambridge: Cambridge University Press, 2000.

Bodin, Félix, *Le roman de l'avenir*, Paris: Lecointe et Pougin, 1834.

Bonds, Mark Evan, 'Sinfonia Anti-eroica: Berlioz's Harold en Italie and the Anxiety of Beethoven's Influence', *The Journal of Musicology* 10/4 (1992), 417–63.

Bor, Joep, 'Mamia, Ammani and Other Bayadères: Europe's Portrayal of India's Temple Dancers', in Bennet Zon and Martin Clayton (eds.), *Music and Orientalism in the British Empire, 1780s–1940s*, Aldershot: Ashgate, 2007, pp. 39–70.

Born, Georgina (ed.), *Western Music and Its Others*, Berkeley: University of California Press, 2000.

Botstein, Leon, 'Hearing Is Seeing: Thoughts on the History of Music and the Imagination', *Musical Quarterly* 79/4 (1995), 581–9.

Bowen, José Antonio (ed.), *The Cambridge Companion to Conducting*, Cambridge: Cambridge University Press, 2003.

Braam, Gunther and Arnold Jacobshagen (eds.), *Hector Berlioz in Deutschland: Texte und Dokumente zur deutschen Berlioz-Rezeption (1829–1843)*, Gottingen: Hainholz, 2002.

Brittan, Francesca, 'Berlioz and the Pathological Fantastic: Melancholy, Monomania, and Romantic Autobiography', *19th-Century Music* 29/3 (2006), 211–39.

Brown, Nicola, Carolyn Burdett, and Pamela Thurschwell (eds.), *The Victorian Supernatural*, Cambridge: Cambridge University Press, 2004.

Brunhammer, Yvonne, François Mathey, Daniel Janicot, and Robert Bordaz (eds.), *Le livre des expositions universelles 1851–1989*, Paris: Union Centrale des Arts Décoratifs, 1983.

Byron, Lord George Gordon, 'Childe Harold's Pilgrimage', in Jerome McGann (ed.), *Lord Byron: The Major Works*, Oxford: Oxford University Press, 2000, pp. 19–206.

Cairns, David, *Berlioz: The Making of an Artist 1803–1832*, London: Penguin Books, 2000.

   Berlioz: Servitude and Greatness 1832–1869, London: Penguin Books, 2000.

   'Berlioz: Autobiography, Biography', in Peter Bloom (ed.), *Berlioz: Scenes from the Life and Work*, Rochester, NY: Rochester University Press, 2008, pp. 221–34.

Campagnoni, Donata Pesenti and Paolo Tortonese (eds.), *Les arts de l'hallucination*, Paris: Presses de la Sorbonne Nouvelle, 2001.

Campbell, I. C. *"Gone Native" in Polynesia: Captivity Narratives and Experiences from the South Pacific*, Westport, CT: Greenwood Press, 1998.

Cardwell, Richard A. (ed.), *The Reception of Byron in Europe*, London: Thoemmes Continuum, 2004.

Carse, Adam, *The Orchestra from Beethoven to Berlioz: A History of the Orchestra in the First Half of the 19th Century, and of the Development of Orchestral Baton-Conducting*, Cambridge: W. Heffer & Sons Ltd., 1948.

Cary, Jonathan, *Techniques of the Observer*, Cambridge, MA.: MIT Press, 1990.

Castle, Terry, 'Phantasmagoria: Spectral Technology and the Metaphorics of Modern Reverie', *Critical Enquiry* 15/1 (1988), 26–61.

   The Female Thermometer: Eighteenth-Century Culture and the Invention of the Uncanny, New York: Oxford University Press, 1995.

Chard, Chloe, *Pleasure and Guilt on the Grand Tour: Travel Writing and Imaginative Geography 1600–1830*, Manchester: Manchester University Press, 1999.

Charlesworth, Michael, *Landscape and Vision in Nineteenth-Century Britain and France*, Aldershot: Ashgate, 2008.

Charlton, David (ed.), *The Cambridge Companion to Grand Opera*, New York: Cambridge University Press, 2002.

Claviez, Thomas, 'Done and Over With – Finally? Otherness, Metonymy, and the Ethics of Comparison', *PMLA* 128/3 (2013), 608–14.

Condé, Gérard, *Les Troyens, L'Avant Scène Opéra* vol. 128–9. Paris: L'Avant Scène, 1990.

   La damnation de Faust, L'Avant Scène Opéra, vol. 22, Paris: L'Avant Scène, 1995.

Cone, Edward T. (ed.), *Norton Critical Scores: Berlioz Fantastic Symphony*, New York: Norton, 1971.

Connor, Steven, 'The Machine in the Ghost: Spiritualism, Technology, and the Direct Voice', in Peter Buse and Andrew Stott (eds.), *Ghosts: Deconstruction, Psychoanalysis, History*, London: MacMillan Press Ltd., 1999, pp. 203–25.

Dumbstruck: A Cultural History of Ventriloquism, Oxford: Oxford University Press, 2000.

Craik, George L., *The New Zealanders*, London: Charles Knight, 1830.

Crary, Jonathan, *Techniques of the Observer: On Vision and Modernity in the Nineteenth Century*, Cambridge, MA: MIT Press, 1990.

Davies, J. Q., 'Dancing the Symphonic: Beethoven-Boscha's *Symphonie Pastorale*, 1829', *19th-Century Music* 27/1 (2003), 25–47.

Davis, John R., *The Great Exhibition*, Thrupp, Stroud, Gloucestershire: Sutton Publishing Ltd, 1999.

Deaville, James, 'The Politics of Liszt's Virtuosity: New Light on the Dialectics of a Cultural Phenomenon', in Michael Saffle and Rossana Dalmonte (eds.), *Liszt and the Birth of Modern Europe: Music as a Mirror of Religious, Political, Cultural, and Aesthetic Transformations. Proceedings of the International Conference Held at the Villa Serbelloni, Bellagio (Como) 14–18 December 1998*, Hillsdale, NY: Pendragon Press, 2003, pp. 115–42.

di Grazia, Donna M., 'Rejected Traditions: Ensemble Placement in Nineteenth-Century Paris', *19th-Century Music* 22/2 (1998), 190–209.

Dolan, Emily I., 'E. T. A. Hoffmann and the Ethereal Technologies of "Nature Music"', *Eighteenth-Century Music* 5/1 (2008), 7–25.

The Orchestral Revolution: Haydn and the Technologies of Timbre, Cambridge: Cambridge University Press, 2013.

Dolan, Emily I., and John Tresch, 'A Sublime Invasion: Meyerbeer, Balzac, and the Opera Machine', *The Opera Quarterly* 27/1 (2011), 4–31.

Dumanoir, Philippe, 'Le Corridor des Bagnoires', F18 784, No. 1793, Archives Nationales, Paris.

Dumont d'Urville, J.S.C., *Voyage de découvertes autour du monde et à la recherche de la Pérouse*, Five volumes in ten, Paris: Librairie Encyclopédique de Roret, 1832.

Voyage de la corvette l'Astrolabe; Exécuté pendant les années 1826–1827–1828–1829 sous le commandement de Jules Dumont d'Urville, capitaine de vaisseau; atlas, Paris: Tastu, 1833.

Dusen, Robert van, *The Literary Ambitions and Achievements of Alexander von Humbolt*, Bern: Herbert Lang, 1971.

Duveyrier, Charles, 'La ville nouvelle, ou le Paris des Saint-Simoniens', in *Paris ou Le livre des cent-et-un*, Paris: Ladvocat, 1832.

Edmond, Rod, *Representing the South Pacific: Colonial Discourse from Cook to Gauguin*, Cambridge: Cambridge University Press, 1997.

Ellis, Geoffrey, *The Napoleonic Empire*, Basingstoke: Palgrave Macmillan, 2003.

Ellis, Katharine, *Interpreting the Musical Past: Early Music in Nineteenth-Century France*, Oxford: Oxford University Press, 2005.

Esse, Melina, 'Donizetti's Gothic Resurrections', *19th-Century Music* 33/2 (2009), 81–109.

Fauquet, Joël-Marie, 'Berlioz's Version of Gluck's Orphée', in Peter Bloom (ed.), *Berlioz Studies*, Cambridge: Cambridge University Press, 1992, pp. 189–253.

'Euphonia and the Utopia of the Orchestra as Society', in Peter Bloom (ed.), *Berlioz: Scenes from the Life and Work*, Rochester, NY: University of Rochester Press, 2008, pp. 47–63.

Foucault, Michel, *Discipline and Punish: The Birth of the Prison*, trans. Alan Sheridan, London: Penguin, 1977, repr. 1991.

Galkin, Elliot W., *A History of Orchestral Conducting in Theory and Practice*, New York: Pendragon Press, 1988.

Garafola, Lynn (ed.), *Rethinking the Sylph: New Perspectives on the Romantic Ballet*, Hanover and London: Wesleyan University Press, 1997.

Gautier, Théophile, *Gautier on Dance*, ed. Ivor Guest, London: Dance Books Ltd, 1986.

Gelbart, Matthew, *The Invention of 'Folk Music' and 'Art Music'*, Cambridge: Cambridge University Press, 2007.

Gerhard, Anselm, *The Urbanization of Opera: Music Theater in Paris in the Nineteenth Century*, trans. Mary Whittall, Chicago and London: University of Chicago Press, 1998.

Gernsheim, Helmut and Alison Gernsheim, *L.J.M. Daguerre: The History of the Diorama and the Daguerreotype*, London: Secker & Warburg, 1956.

Gessinger, Joachim, *Auge & Ohr: Studien zur Erforschung der Sprache am Menschen 1700–1850*, Berlin, New York: Walter de Gruyter, 1994.

Goehr, Lydia, *The Imaginary Museum of Musical Works*, Oxford: Oxford University Press, 1991, rev. 2007.

The Quest for Voice: Music, Politics, and the Limits of Philosophy, Oxford: Oxford University Press, 1998.

Goethe, *Faust*, trans. Gérard Nerval, Paris: Dondey-Dupré, 1828.

Gooley, Dana, 'Warhorses: Liszt, Weber's "Konzertstück", and the Cult of Napoléon', *19th-Century Music* 24/1 (2000), 62–88.

'The Battle against Instrumental Virtuosity in the Early Nineteenth Century', in Christopher H. Gibbs and Dana Gooley (eds.), *Franz Liszt and His World*, Princeton, NJ: Princeton University Press, 2006, pp. 75–112.

Greenhalgh, Paul, *Ephemeral Vistas: The Expositions Universelles, Great Exhibitions and World's Fairs, 1851–1939*, Manchester: Manchester University Press, 1988.

Hadlock, Heather, *Mad Loves: Women and Music in Offenbach's Les contes d'Hoffmann*, Princeton, NJ: Princeton University Press, 2000.

'Sonorous Bodies: Women and the Glass Harmonica', *Journal of the American Musicological Society* 53 (2000), 507–42.

Hankins, Thomas L. and Robert J. Silverman, *Instruments and the Imagination*, Princeton, NJ: Princeton University Press, 1995.

Heidlberger, Frank (ed.), *Hector Berlioz: Les Troyens à Carthage. Dossier de presse parisienne (1863)*, Bietigheim: Musik-Edition Lucie Galland, 1995.

Hibberd, Sarah, '"Dormez donc, mes chers amours": Hérold's *La Somnambule* (1827) and Dream Phenomena on the Parisian Lyric Stage', *Cambridge Opera Journal* 16/2 (2004), 107–32.

Holoman, D. Kern, 'The Berlioz Sketchbook Recovered', *19th-Century Music* 7/3 (1984), 282–317.
 Catalogue of the Works of Hector Berlioz, Kassel: Bärenreiter, 1987.
 Berlioz, Cambridge, MA: Harvard University Press, 1989.
Hudson, Elizabeth, "'... qualche cosa d'incredibile...'": Hearing the Invisible in "Macbeth"', *Cambridge Opera Journal* 14/1 (2001), 11–29.
Humboldt, Alexander von, *Cosmos: Sketch of a Physical Description of the Universe*, Edward Sabine, four volumes in five, London: Longman, Brown, Green, and Longmans, 1847–58.
 Ansichten der Natur, trans. E. C. Otté and Henry G. Bohn, *Views of Nature: Or Contemplations on the Sublime Phenomena of Creation*, London: Henry G. Bohn, 1850; trans. Charles Galuski, *Tableaux de la nature*, Nouvelle édition, Paris: Théodore Morgand, 1865.
Hunter, Mary, '"To Play as If from the Soul of the Composer": The Idea of the Performer in Early Romantic Aesthetics', *Journal of the American Musicological Society* 58/2 (2005), 357–98.
Irving, David R. M., *Colonial Counterpoint: Music in Early Modern Manila*, Oxford: Oxford University Press, 2010.
Jay, Martin, *Downcast Eyes: The Denigration of Vision in Twentieth-Century French Thought*, Berkeley: University of California Press, 1993.
Johnson, James H., *Listening in Paris: A Cultural History*, Berkeley: University of California Press, 1995.
Kallberg, Jeffrey, 'Chopin's Music Box', in Artur Szklener (ed.), *Chopin's Musical Worlds: The 1840s*, Warsaw: Narodowy Instytut Fryderyka Chopina, 2008, 189–202.
Karp, Ivan and Steven D. Lavine (eds.), *Exhibiting Cultures: The Poetics and Politics of Museum Display*, Washington and London: Smithsonian Institution, 1991.
Kartomi, Margaret J., *On Concepts and Classifications of Musical Instruments*, Chicago: University of Chicago Press, 1990.
Kastner, Georges., *Traité général d'instrumentation* (1837) and *Supplément au Traité général d'instrumentation* ..., Paris: Minier, c. 1840.
 Cours d'instrumentation (1839) and *Supplément*, Paris: A. Meissonnier & J. H. Heugel, 1844.
 Manuel général de musique militaire à l'usage des armées françaises, Geneva: Minkoff Reprint, 1848, 1973.
 La Harpe d'Éole et la musique cosmique: Études sur les rapports de phénomènes sonores de la nature avec la science et l'art; Suivies de Stéphen ou La harpe d'Éole – Grand monologue lyrique avec chœurs, Paris: Brandus, 1856.
Kawabata, Maiko, 'Virtuoso Codes of Violin Performance: Power, Military Heroism, and Gender', *19th-Century Music* 28/2 (2004), 100–103.
 'The Concerto That Wasn't: Paganini, Urhan and Harold in Italy', *Nineteenth-Century Music Review* 1/1 (2004), 67–114.

'Virtuosity, the Violin, the Devil... What Really Made Paganini "Demonic"?', *Current Musicology* 83 (2007), 85–108.

Paganini: The 'Demonic' Virtuoso, Woodbridge, Suffolk/Rochester, NY: The Boydell Press, 2013.

Kemp, Ian (ed.), *Berlioz: Les Troyens*, Cambridge: Cambridge University Press, 1988.

Kendall, Thomas and Samuel Lee, *A Grammar and Vocabulary of the Language of New Zealand*, London: R. Watts, 1820.

Koepnick, Lutz, 'Stereoscopic Vision: Sight and Community in Die Meistersinger', in Nicholas Vazsonyi (ed.), *Wagner's Meistersinger: Performance, History, Representation*, Rochester, NY: University of Rochester Press, 2002, pp. 73–97.

Kolb [Reeve], Katherine, 'The Poetics of the Orchestra in the Writings of Hector Berlioz', unpublished Doctor of Philosophy thesis, Yale University (1978).

The Damnation of Faust, or the Perils of Heroism in Music', in Peter Bloom (ed.), *Berlioz Studies*, Cambridge: Cambridge University Press, 1992, pp. 148–88.

'Flying Leaves: Between Berlioz and Wagner', *19th-Century Music* 33/1 (2009), 25–61.

Kramer, Lawrence, *Musical Meaning: Toward a Critical History*, Berkeley: University of California Press, 2002.

Kregor, Jonathan, 'Collaboration and Content in the *Symphonie Fantastique* Transcription', *The Journal of Musicology* 24/2 (2007), 195–236.

Lamb, Andrew, *William Vincent Wallace: Composer, Virtuoso and Adventurer*, West Byfleet: Fullers Wood Press, 2012.

Le Guin, Elizabeth, *Boccherini's Body: An Essay in Carnal Musicology*, Berkeley: University of California Press, 2005.

Le Men, Ségolène *La Cathédrale illustrée de Hugo à Monet: Regard romantique et modernité*, Paris: CNRS Éditions, 1998.

Leask, Nigel, *Curiosity and the Aesthetics of Travel Writing, 1770–1840*, Oxford: Oxford University Press, 2002.

Leppert, Richard, *The Sight of Sound: Music, Representation, and the History of the Body*, Berkeley: University of California Press, 1993.

Lesson, M.-R.-P., *Notice historique sur l'Amiral Dumont d'Urville*, Rochefort: Henry Loustau et Cie., 1846.

Levine, Lawrence W., *Highbrow/Lowbrow: The Emergence of Cultural Hierarchy in America*, Cambridge, MA: Harvard University Press, 1988.

Lewis, Matthew, *The Monk: A Romance* (1796), New York: Modern Library, 2002.

Lichtenthal, Pierre, *Dictionnaire de Musique*, Dominique Mondo, two volumes in one, Paris: Troupenas et Ce., 1839.

Liszt, Franz, 'Berlioz und seine "Harold Symphonie"', in L. Ramann (ed.), *Gesammelte Schriften von Franz Liszt*, 6 vols., Leipzig: Breitkopf und Härtel, 1882, vol. IV, pp. 1–102.

Locke, Ralph P., *Music, Musicians, and the Saint-Simonians*, Chicago: University of Chicago Press, 1986.

'Constructing the Oriental "Other": Saint-Saëns's *Samson et Dalila*', *Cambridge Opera Journal* 3/3 (1991), 261–302.

'A Broader View of Musical Exoticism', *Journal of Musicology* 24/4 (2007), 477–521.

Musical Exoticism: Images and Reflections, Cambridge: Cambridge University Press, 2009.

Macdonald, Hugh, *Berlioz's Orchestration Treatise: A Translation and Commentary*, Cambridge: Cambridge University Press, 2002.

'Berlioz Takes the Train', in Matthias Brzoska, Hermann Hofer and Nicole Strohmann (eds.), *Hector Berlioz: Ein Franzose in Deutschland*, Laaber: Verlag, 2005, pp. 237–41.

Macey, Samuel L., *Clocks and the Cosmos: Time in Western Life and Thought*, Hamden, CT: Archon Books, 1980.

Mainardi, Patricia, *Art and Politics of the Second Empire: The Universal Expositions of 1855 and 1867*, New Haven and London: Yale University Press, 1987.

McKee, Eric, *Decorum of the Minuet, Delirium of the Waltz: A Study of Dance–Music Relations in 3/4 Time*, Bloomington: Indiana University Press, 2012.

McLean, Mervyn, *Maori Music*, Auckland: Auckland University Press, 1996.

McLuhan, Marshall, ed. W. Terrence Gordon, *Understanding Media: The Extensions of Man (Critical Edition)*, Corte Madera, CA: Gingko Press, 1964, new edn. 2003.

McNeill, William H., *Keeping Together in Time: Dance and Drill in Human History*, Cambridge, MA: Harvard University Press, 1995.

Mehta, Binita, *Widows, Pariahs, and Bayadères: India as Spectacle*, London: Associated University Press, 2002.

Miller Frank, Felicia, *The Mechanical Song: Women, Voice, and the Artificial in Nineteenth-Century French Narrative*, Stanford, CA: Stanford University Press, 1995.

Montagu, Jeremy et al., 'Military Music', *Grove Music Online. Oxford Music Online*, Oxford University Press, www.oxfordmusiconline.com/subscriber/article/grove/music/44139, accessed 10 April 2014.

Morton, Marsha L. and Peter L. Schmunk (eds.), *The Arts Entwined: Music and Painting in the Nineteenth Century*, New York and London: Garland, 2000.

Mulligan, Annie de Meurant, 'In Happy Moments', A1336 Item 19660, National Archives of Australia, Canberra, 1930.

Newark, Cormac, 'Metaphors for Meyerbeer', *Journal of the Royal Musical Association* 127/1 (2002), 32.

Newcomb, Anthony, 'New light(s) on Weber's Wolf's Glen Scene', in Thomas Bauman and Marita Petzoldt McClymonds (eds.), *Opera and the Enlightenment*, Cambridge: Cambridge University Press, 1995, pp. 61–90.

Oettermann, Stephan, *The Panorama: History of a Mass Medium*, trans. Deborah Lucas Schneider, New York: Zone Books, 1997.

Official catalogue of the Great Exhibition of the Works of Industry of all Nations, London: Spicer Brothers, 1851.

Ortner, Sherry B., *Making Gender: The Politics and Erotics of Culture*, Boston: Beacon Press, 1996.

Pascall, Robert, 'Those Grand Heroics Acted as a Spell: Aspects of Byron's Influence on Music in Nineteenth-Century Europe', *Renaissance and Modern Studies* 32 (1988), 128–35.

Pasler, Jann, 'The Utility of Musical Instruments in the Racial and Colonial Agendas of Late Nineteenth-Century France', *Journal of the Royal Musical Association* 129/1 (2004), 24–76.

Porter, Dennis, *Haunted Journeys: Desire and Transgression in European Travel Writing*, Princeton, NJ: Princeton University Press, 1991.

Pratt, Mary Louise, *Imperial Eyes: Travel Writing and Transculturation*, London: Routledge, 1992, 2008 (2nd edn.).

Qureshi, Sadiah, *Peoples on Parade: Exhibitions, Empire, and Anthropology in Nineteenth-Century Britain*, Chicago: University of Chicago Press, 2011.

Radano, Ronald and Philip V. Bohlman (eds.), *Music and the Racial Imagination*, Chicago and London: University of Chicago Press, 2000.

Reicha, Antoine, *Art du compositeur dramatique; Ou cours complet de composition vocale*, Paris: A. Farrenc, 1833.

Reynaud, Cécile, 'Berlioz, Liszt, and the Question of Virtuosity', in Peter Bloom (ed.), *Berlioz: Past, Present, Future*, Rochester, NY: University of Rochester Press 2003, 105–22.

  'Berlioz et l'Europe', in Alban Ramaut (ed.), *Hector Berlioz: Regards sur un dauphinois fantastique*, Saint-Étienne: Université de Saint-Étienne, 2005, pp. 167–78.

Robertson, E. G., *Mémoires récréatifs, scientifiques et anecdotiques d'un physicien-aéronaute*, Langres: Cafe Clima Editeur, 1985.

Robinson, Paul, *Opera and Ideas: From Mozart to Strauss*, New York: Harper & Row, 1985.

Rushton, Julian, *Berlioz: Roméo et Juliette*, Cambridge: Cambridge University Press, 1994.

  The Music of Berlioz, Oxford: Oxford University Press, 2001.

Said, Edward, *Culture and Imperialism*, New York: Random House, 1993.

Samson, Jim, *Virtuosity and the Musical Work: The* Transcendental Studies *of Liszt*, Cambridge: Cambridge University Press, 2003.

Schivelbusch, Wolfgang, *The Railway Journey: The Industrialization of Time and Space in the 19th Century*, Berkeley: University of California Press, 1986.

Simpson, Adrienne, *Opera's Farthest Frontier: A History of Professional Opera in New Zealand*, Auckland: Reed, 1996.

Smart, Mary Ann, *Mimomania: Music and Gesture in Nineteenth-Century Opera*, Berkeley: University of California Press, 2004.

Smith, Bernard, *Imagining the Pacific: In the Wake of the Cook Voyages*, Hong Kong: Melbourne University Press, 1992.

Snoep, Nanette Jacomijn, 'Savage Imagery', in Pascal Blanchard, Gilles Boëtsch and Nanette Jacomijn Snoep (eds.), *The Invention of the Savage: Human Zoos*, Paris: Musée du Quai Branly, 2011, pp. 20–53.

Solie, Ruth (ed.), *Musicology and Difference: Gender and Sexuality in Music Scholarship*, Berkeley: University of California Press, 1993.

Spitzer, John, 'Metaphors of the Orchestra – The Orchestra as Metaphor', *The Musical Quarterly* 80/2 (1996), 242–5.

Spitzer, John and Neal Zaslaw, *The Birth of the Orchestra: History of an Institution, 1650–1815*, Oxford: Oxford University Press, 2004.

Stabler, Jane, 'Byron's Digressive Journey', in Amanda Gilroy (ed.), *Romantic Geographies: Discourses of Travel 1775–1844*, Manchester: Manchester University Press, 2000, pp. 223–39.

Sterne, Jonathan, *Audible Past: Cultural Origins of Sound Reproduction*, Durham, NC: Duke University Press, 2003.

Tan, Su Lian, 'Hector Berlioz *Symphonie Fantastique*, Op. 14: An Exploration of Musical Timbre', unpublished Doctor of Philosophy thesis, Princeton University (1997).

Temperley, Nicholas, 'Wallace, Vincent', *Grove Music Online. Oxford Music Online*, Oxford University Press, www.oxfordmusiconline.com/subscriber/article/grove/music/29838, accessed 10 April 2014.

Terrier, Agnès, *L'orchestre de l'Opéra de Paris de 1669 à nos jours*, Paris: Éditions de la Martinière; Opéra National de Paris, 2003.

Todorov, Tzvetan, *The Fantastic: A Structural Approach to a Literary Genre*, Richard Howard, Cleveland: The Press of Case Western Reserve University, 1973.

Tomlinson, Gary, *Music in Renaissance Magic: Toward a Historiography of Others*, Chicago: Chicago University Press, 1993.

Metaphysical Song: An Essay on Opera, Princeton, NJ: Princeton University Press, 1999.

Tovey, Donald Francis, 'Berlioz: "Harold in Italy", Symphony with Viola Obbligato, Op. 16', in *Essays in Musical Analysis*, 7 vols., London: Oxford University Press, 1936, vol. IV, pp. 74–82.

van Rij, Inge, '"There Is No Anachronism:" Indian Dancing Girls in Ancient Carthage in Berlioz's *Les Troyens*', *19th-Century Music* 33/1 (2009), 3–24.

'Back to (the Music of) the Future: Aesthetics of Technology in Berlioz's *Euphonia* and *Damnation de Faust*', *Cambridge Opera Journal* 22/3 (2012), 257–300.

van Wesemael, Pieter, *Architecture of Instruction and Delight: A socio-historical analysis of world exhibitions as a didactic phenomenon (1798–1851–1970)*, Rotterdam: 010 Uitgeverij, 2001.

Vergo, Peter (ed.), *The New Museology*, London: Reaktion Books, 1989.

Virgil, *The Aeneid*, trans. Allen Mandelbaum, Berkeley: University of California Press, 1971.

Vivier, E., *De la Madeleine à la Bastille et, de là, chez Tom-Pouce*, Nice: J. Ventre, n.d.

Wagner, Richard, *Richard Wagner Prose Works* ed. William Ashton Ellis, 8 vols., New York: Broude Brothers, 1966.
Warner, Marina, *Phantasmagoria: Spirit Visions, Metaphors and Media*, Oxford: Oxford University Press, 2006.
Wevers, Lydia, *Country of Writing: Travel Writing and New Zealand 1809–1900*, Auckland: Auckland University Press, 2002.
Wild, Nicole, *Décor et costumes du XIXe siècle*, Paris: Bibliothèque Nationale, 1993.
Williams, Ann, 'Ghostly Voices: 'Gothic Opera' and the Failure of Gounod's La Nonne sanglante', in Roberta Montemorra and Downing A. Thomas Marvin (eds.), *Operatic Migrations: Transforming Works and Crossing Boundaries*, Aldershot: Ashgate, 2006, pp. 125–44.
Winter, Alison, *Mesmerized: Powers of Mind in Victorian Britain*, Chicago: University of Chicago Press, 1998.
Woodward, Patricia Jovanna, 'Jean-Georges Kastner's Traité général d'instrumentation: A Translation and Commentary', unpublished Master of Music thesis, University of Texas (2003).
Young, Robert J. C., *Colonial Desire: Hybridity in Theory, Culture and Race*, London: Routledge, 1995.
Ziter, Edward, *The Orient on the Victorian Stage*, Cambridge: Cambridge University Press, 2003.

Index

Abbate, Carolyn, 168, 169, 170, 174, 215
Adorno, Theodor, 162–63
Aeolian harp, 33, 65, 212, 280–81
Agnew, Vanessa, 6, 324
Alexandre, Edouard, 58, 207
Alexandre, Jacob, 58, 207
Ali, Muhammad, 303, 307
almées, 310
Amussat, Jean-Zuléma, 167
anachronism, 253, 296–97, 298, 304, 307, 310, 317–18
antihero, 11, 99, 104, 105, 106, 108, 111, 112, 121
Auber, Daniel François Esprit
    Le dieu et la bayadère, 299, 303, 304, 315
    L'enfant prodigue, 255, 299, 305, 310–11
    La muette de Portici, 237
    Le premier jour de bonheur, 304
automata, 170, 212–13, 214–15, 234

barbarism. *See* civilisation and barbarism
Barnum, P. T., 213, 252, 304
bass drum, Berlioz's views on the, 55–56
Baudelaire, Charles, 163
bayadères, 13, 296–97, 298–308, 310, 311–13, 314–15, 318
Bayreuth, 162, 184, 242, 243
beachcombers, 19, 24, 39
Beethoven, Ludwig van, 44, 46, 65, 72, 92, 110, 125, 128, 177, 191
    Symphony No. 6, 256
    Symphony No. 9, 79, 110, 132, 196
Bellini, Vincenzo, 102
Bennett, Tony, 293
Berlioz, Hector. *See also* conducting, Berlioz as conductor; works by Berlioz
    travels of, 15, 39
        in German lands, 42–44, 54, 70, 76, 91, 93, 98, 122–25, 199
        in Italy, 38–40, 99, 100–02, 103, 199, 273
Berlioz, Louis (son of the composer), 16, 25, 26, 322
Bernardin de Saint-Pierre, Jacques-Henri, 66

Bodin, Félix
    Le roman de l'avenir, 196, 202
Bohrer, Antoine, 43, 44, 46, 47, 65
Bohrer, Sophie, 43, 47
Botstein, Leon, 133, 163, 164
Branchu, Alexandrine, 225
Brewster, David, 144, 147
Brougham, John
    Po-ca-hon-tas, 331
Byron, Lord, 11, 103–11, 126
    Childe Harold's Pilgrimage, 103–04, 105, 106, 107–09

Cabet, Étienne
    Voyage en Icarie, 202
Cairns, David, 44
Cambreling, Sylvain, 316
camera lucida, 135
camera obscura, 135–36, 138, 144, 145, 157, 158
Carvalho, Léon, 294
Cécille, Admiral Jean Baptiste Thomas Medée, 25–26
Chateaubriand, François-René de, 66, 143
China
    music of, 296
    musicians of, in London, 248, 297
civilisation and barbarism, 15, 28–30, 37, 42, 58
clarinet, as described by Berlioz and Kastner, 62–65
class, 331–33
classical antiquity, 39, 58, 306
    as analogy for Māori, 28, 321
classical music, ideology of. *See* western art music, ideology of
classification of instruments, 60–61, 250
colonialism, 6, 11, 27, 28, 46, 318, 327, 328–29, 333
colour, 145–47
conducting, 91–95, 175, 208, 226, 237, 256, 271
    Berlioz as conductor, 8, 11, 70, 73, 91, 92–94, 111, 118–22, 124, 202

351

conducting (*cont.*)
   military associations of, 11, 70, 91–92, 93–94
   with baton, 93–95
   with bow, 91–92, 93
Cook, Captain James, 6, 27, 68
Cooper, James Fenimore, 66
couleur locale, 58, 102, 254–55, 271
Craik, George L.
   The New Zealanders, 24
Crary, Jonathan, 134, 136, 145, 157

Daguerre, Louis, 138, 140
daguerreotype, 136, 138, 251
Dahlhaus, Carl, 210
dance, 130, 152–55, 161, 272, 302–03, 304, 311, 312, 314, 316–17. *See also* bayadères
David, Félicien
   Le désert, 310
   La perle du Brésil, 298
Degas, Edgar, 166
Delacroix, Eugène, 130
devadasis. *See* bayadères
Diderot, Denis, 28
   'Supplément au voyage de Bougainville', 28
diorama, 128, 130, 133, 134, 138–40, 157, 163, 253
discipline, Foucault's concept of, 11, 72, 77, 88, 337
division of labour, 68, 159, 204, 228
Dolan, Emily I., 9, 10, 73, 146, 161, 170
Donizetti, Gaetano, 330
   Lucia di Lammermoor, 175, 287
   Maria de Rudenz, 165, 169, 183
d'Ortigue, Joseph, 87, 129, 133, 308–09
Dumanoir, Philippe
   Le Corridor des Baignoires, 300–01, 303, 304, 317
Dumont d'Urville, Jules Sébastien César, 15, 22–25, 26, 28, 32–33, 38, 43, 44, 45, 48, 58, 60, 67, 69, 107, 321
   Voyage de la corvette l'Astrolabe, 22, 24, 27, 55, 67–68
Duveyrier, Charles, 200
   'La ville nouvelle', 200–01, 209

Egypt, 137, 248, 254, 296, 305, 307, 310, 311, 329
electric metronome, 178, 202, 208, 271
Erard, Sébastien, 214
Esse, Melina, 169, 183
exhibitions, 12, 194, 246

Industrial exhibition, Paris 1844, 195, 232, 321
international exhibitions, 247–51, 256, 260, 269–71, 272, 281–84, 297, 313, 318
   Exposition universelle, Paris 1855, 13, 37–38, 202, 247–48, 250, 251, 271, 322
   Exposition universelle, Paris 1867, 248, 325
   Great Exhibition, London 1851, 13, 247, 248–49, 250, 265–68, 292, 293, 297, 306, 313, 320–21
exoticism, 5, 17, 28, 51, 102, 197, 254–55, 298–99, 306, 315, 321, 325, 334

Faber, Joseph, 212, 234
fantasy, 169
Fauquet, Joël-Marie, 47, 209, 243
Fétis, François-Joseph, 53, 152
Flaubert, Gustave
   Salammbô, 253
Foucault, Michel, 72, 137. *See also* discipline
France
   musical aesthetics of, 90, 128, 131
Fresne, Marion du, 27
future, 7, 12, 13, 193, 195–97, 204, 208, 239, 242, 244, 245, 251, 295, 296, 318, 338. *See also* works by Berlioz, *Evenings with the Orchestra*, *Euphonia*

galvanism, 167, 179, 190–91, 195, 251
Gautier, Théophile, 34, 35, 190, 298, 301–02, 303, 304, 305, 311, 312, 314
   Giselle, 305
   Sacountala, 296, 304
Gay-Lussac, Joseph Louis, 64, 167, 195, 204
gender, 7, 12, 13, 24, 176, 191, 194, 210–12, 226, 241, 295, 308, 321, 325, 337
genre, 12, 109, 191, 219–26
Gerhard, Anselm, 194, 295
Germany, 39
   musical aesthetics of, 5, 7, 12, 44, 47, 93, 123, 125, 126, 127–28, 169, 190
Girard, Narcisse, 43, 119
glass harmonica, 279
Gluck, Christoph Willibald Ritter von, 198, 205, 206, 225, 239, 240, 243
   Alceste, 65, 198, 205, 240
   Iphigénie en Tauride, 167–68
   Orfeo, 184, 207
God Save the Queen, 265–66, 268
Godley, Charlotte, 327–28, 329
Goehr, Lydia, 5, 6, 8, 72, 125
Goethe, Johann Wolfgang von

on colour, 145–46
Faust, 130, 222, 232, 237, 238, 239, 242
Der Gott und die Bajadere, 315
Der Zauberlehrling, 215
Gooley, Dana, 81, 113, 114, 115, 124
Gounod, Charles, 330
  Faust, 232, 239
  La nonne sanglante, 165, 169, 185, 188
  Sapho, 292, 293
Grand Tour, 39, 42, 58
grande armée, 71, 91, 260
Guérin, Pierre-Narcisse, 246, 252
guitar, Berlioz's views on the, 53–54
Gunsbourg, Raoul, 243

Habeneck, François, 92, 123
Hafiz, 310
Halévy, Fromental
  La juive, 237
  Prométhée enchaîné, 305–06, 307
Hanslick, Eduard, 161
Hauptmann, Moritz, 94–96
Haydn, Franz Joseph, 9
Heine, Heinrich, 73, 113, 114, 216
Hibbert, Samuel, 144
Hoffmann, E.T.A., 146, 215
  Les contes d'Hoffmann, 287
Hugo, Victor
  Le dernier jour d'un condamné, 140
  Les Orientales, 40
human zoo, 13, 249, 296, 297–98, 301, 303, 304, 308
Humboldt, Alexander von, 15, 44–46, 48, 61, 62, 66, 68, 167, 204, 256
  Cosmos, 17, 44, 53, 59, 138
  Tableaux de la Nature, 44, 45–46, 64–65, 107

imperialism, 6, 11, 13, 27, 245, 251, 260, 265, 269–71, 312–13, 314, 316, 321, 332
India, 137, 293, 314, 322
  dancers of. *See* bayadères
  music of, 296, 305–06, 313
  musical instruments of, 247–48, 306
  musicians of, in London, 248
instrumentation. *See* orchestration
instruments, musical, 58, 246, 247, 253–55, 281–86, 307–08. *See also* Aeolian harp; clarinet; classification of instruments; glass harmonica; India, musical instruments of; guitar; saxhorn;
  stopped notes on horn; violin, military associations of the ancient or exotic
  newly invented, 59
'Invisible girl', 183–84
Italy, 39, 47, 58, 100–02, 333. *See also* Berlioz, Hector: travels of: in Italy
  opera of, 7, 8, 12, 39–40, 102, 111, 169, 206, 208
  'wild Italy', 40, 103

Janin, Jules, 135, 265, 301, 304, 305
Joachim, Joseph, 61, 118

kaleidoscope, 144, 147–52, 155
Kastner, Georges, 280–81
  Manuel général de musique militaire à l'usage des armées françaises, 77, 78, 119, 265, 271, 328–29
  orchestration treatises of, 48, 52–53, 54, 57, 59, 60, 61, 62, 63
Kawabata, Maiko, 90, 107, 112
Kazimirski Biberstein, Albin de, 309
Kendall, Thomas, 22, 31–32, 33
  A Grammar and Vocabulary of New Zealand, 22, 32
Kolb [Reeve], Katherine, 98, 209, 221, 234
Kramer, Lawrence, 114, 115

La Marseillaise, 76, 265, 272
Lane, Edward
  An Account of the Manners and Customs of the Modern Egyptians, 254
Lanner, Joseph, 152, 153
Le Guin, Elisabeth, 7, 8, 117, 128
Le Sueur, Jean-François
  Alexandre à Babylone, 255
Lepage, Robert, 243
Levaillant, François, 66
Lewis, Matthew
  The Monk, 164, 169, 174
Lichtenthal, Pierre
  Dictionnaire de musique, 67
Lind, Jenny, 252
Liszt, Franz, 8, 61, 70–71, 75, 112–15, 116, 117, 118, 120, 122, 123, 124, 127, 128, 152, 161, 231
Locke, Ralph P., 5
London, 207, 230, 238, 270, 297
Lormier, Paul, 311
Louvre, 246, 311
Lyster, William Saurin, 330
  opera company of
    tour of New Zealand, 324, 330–34

Macdonald, Hugh, 47, 62, 158, 159, 189, 215, 287
magnetism. *See* mesmerism
Māori, 2, 21, 23–24, 25, 27, 28, 31–32, 330, 331, 334, 336
  music of, 31, 32, 33–34, 325, 329–30
Marmion, Félix (uncle of Berlioz), 71, 112, 260
McKee, Eric, 153
McLuhan, Marshall, 186
Méhul, Étienne, 146, 183, 184
Mendelssohn, Felix, 94, 95, 96, 133, 145, 214
mesmerism, 174–77, 226, 280, 287
metaphysics, 6, 7, 8, 11, 13, 69, 168, 169, 170, 274
Meyerbeer, Giacomo, 10, 96, 167, 169, 170, 180, 183, 190, 194–95, 231, 330
  Les Huguenots, 333
  Le prophète, 268–69
  Robert le diable, 165–67, 168, 179–80
military bands, 58, 64, 76–77, 79, 80, 262, 273, 321, 327–29, 334
  of Prussia, 76, 88–89, 98
  reform of
    Berlioz's views on, 78, 86–87, 269
  sight of, 89, 329
Moke, Camille, 209–10
Mozart, Wolfgang Amadeus, 190, 330
  Don Giovanni, 4
  Le nozze di Figaro, 207
Mulligan, Annie de Meurant, 323, 325, 326
muscular bonding, 80, 81, 82, 85, 98, 125, 268
museology, 247, 250, 298
museum, 13, 58, 245–47, 249, 253–54, 255, 274, 281, 284, 286, 297, 298, 300, 302, 304, 308, 311, 318, 319. *See also* exhibition
  imaginary museum (as metaphor), 72, 247, 250, 252, 292, 321
music of the future. *See* Zukunftsmusik

Napoleon Bonaparte, 11, 70, 94, 99, 100–01, 104–05, 107–08, 112, 113, 122, 126, 260. *See also* grande armée
Napoleon III (Louis-Napoléon Bonaparte), 260, 269
nationalism, 123, 260, 265, 270, 272, 328, 335, 336
Nerval, Gérard de, 238, 242
  Voyage en Orient, 254

New Zealand, 1, 2, 3, 7, 11, 13, 15, 32, 33, 137, 196, 322–23, 325–28, 329–34, 335–37
Newark, Cormac, 195, 268
noble savage, 331, 334
numinous intruder, 12, 168, 274, 292

occult. *See* supernatural
Offenbach, Jacques
  Les contes d'Hoffmann, 175, 176
Opéra (Paris), 34, 123, 128, 129, 138, 165, 191, 299, 302–03, 311, 314, 317, 322
  orchestra of the, 89
Opéra-Comique, 30, 196, 197
ophicleide, Berlioz's views on the, 207
orchestra
  as space or place, 67
  layout of the, 81, 234–37
  metaphors for the, 10, 13
    mechanical, 72, 73, 159, 208, 294
    military, 11, 71–72, 73, 90, 97–98
    natural, 72, 73
  physicality of the, 9, 10, 12, 208–09, 309
  sight of the, 12, 89–90, 129, 161–62, 231–32, 234–39, 244
orchestration, 18, 48–49, 54, 55, 56, 57
  sui generis, 11, 49, 52, 147, 170
organology, 247, 250
Osborne, George, 43, 54
Otherness, 2, 4, 6–7

Pacific, 1, 6, 11, 16, 25, 26, 27, 28, 31, 34–36, 38, 57, 324. *See also* Tahiti; New Zealand
Paganini, Niccolò, 8, 91, 100, 111–12, 113, 116, 117, 118, 119, 127, 161, 200
Page, Captain Théogene-François, 25, 26, 29, 30, 37, 38
panopticon, 137
panorama, 134, 136–38, 139, 143, 145, 157, 248, 253, 297
Paris, 11, 29, 78, 79, 81, 125, 127, 201, 240, 270, 280, 297, 300, 304
Paris Conservatoire, 54, 68, 73, 254
  instrument museum of the, 57, 247
  orchestra of the, 73, 89, 90, 97, 123, 232
Parish-Alvars, Elias, 176
performance studies, 7–8
phantasmagoria, 12, 134, 140–43, 164, 165, 280
  as metaphor, 140, 143–44, 145, 162–63
Pischek, Johann Baptist, 238
Pleyel, Camille. *See* Moke, Camille
Pomare IV, Aimata (Queen of Tahiti), 30, 31, 36, 37
Pompeii, 58, 246, 284–86

postcolonialism, 2, 5, 315, 321, 336
Pritchard, Reverend George, 30–31
programme music, 12, 129, 132, 145, 163
Puccini, Giacomo
    Madame Butterfly, 4

Queen Victoria, 268, 313
Quincey, Thomas de, 145

race, 4, 6, 7, 60, 251, 252, 297, 302, 306, 315, 316, 325, 337
railway, 195, 204, 206–07, 215, 216–19, 229–30, 251
Reicha, Anton, 254–55
réunion des thèmes, 119, 157, 216, 295
Robertson, Étienne-Gaspard, 140, 141, 164
Rossini, Giaoachino, 194
Rousseau, Jean-Jacques, 28
Rushton, Julian, 221, 307, 312

Said, Edward, 316
Saint-Saëns, Camille, 315
Saint-Simonianism, 200, 209
Sax, Adolphe, 58, 59, 90, 202, 207, 269
saxhorn, 255–56, 268–69, 271, 272
Sayn-Wittgenstein, Princess Carolyne, 316
Schivelbusch, Wolfgang, 202–04
Schmidt, Johann Philipp Samuel, 124
Schumann, Robert, 8, 95, 96, 124, 131, 132, 133, 139, 141, 152, 155
Scotland, 100, 324
Scribe, Eugène, 164, 169, 189, 231, 239, 287, 305, 311, 315
Scudo, Paul, 131
séance, 12
Senff, Bartholf, 124
Sergent, Elise ('la reine Pomaré'), 30, 37, 314
Shakespeare, William
    Hamlet, 128
Sichel, Jules, 134
sight, 10, 12, 90, 127–29, 134, 144, 147, 155, 158, 272, 273–74. *See also* camera obscura; colour; diorama; kaleidoscope; orchestra, sight of the; panorama; phantasmagoria; stereoscope; thaumatrope
slavery, 30, 55, 312
Smithson, Harriet, 113, 129, 145, 167, 175
Sontag, Henriette, 196
Spiritualism, 165, 174, 177–78, 185
Spitzer, John, 71–72

Spohr, Ludwig, 96
Spontini, Gaspare, 1, 93
Stendhal (Marie-Henri Beyle), 39
stereoscope, 157–58, 159–60, 161, 162, 163, 228
Stoltz, Rosine, 196
stopped notes on horn, 184, 228–29, 274
Strauss I., Johann, 152, 153
Sudre, Jean-François, 202
supernatural, 6, 7, 9, 11, 12, 13, 128–29, 144, 169, 170, 190, 191, 245, 251, 273–74, 309, 337, 338

Taglioni, Marie, 304
Tahiti, 26–27, 29–31, 36–37, 196, 314
Tardivel, E. C., 299–300, 304, 313
technology, 9–10, 12, 13, 134, 193, 194, 195, 200, 201, 202–04, 206–07, 208, 210, 229, 230, 242–43, 245, 251, 270, 271, 272, 338. *See also* automata; camera obscura; diorama; electric metronome; kaleidoscope; panorama; phantasmagoria; railway; stereoscope; telegraph; thaumatrope
telegraph, 12, 177, 178, 179, 185–86, 195, 203, 215, 251, 271, 280–81, 295
thaumatrope, 155–57, 163, 216
Théâtre des Variétés, 299, 300–01, 303, 305
time, 218, 293, 318
    as Other, 4, 7, 12, 255
Todorov, Tzvetan, 169
Tomlinson, Gary, 6, 168, 169
Tovey, Donald Francis, 104
travel writing, 11, 13, 14–15, 16, 19, 21, 22, 26–29, 38–39, 40, 42–43, 44–46, 47–48, 49, 54, 55, 58, 60, 62, 64–67, 107, 108–09, 128, 245, 251, 252, 253
    Berlioz's interest in, 15–16
    definitions of, 16, 19
Tunisia, 249

Urhan, Chrétien, 44, 118

Venard, Céleste ('Mogador'), 313, 314
Verdi, Giuseppe, 315, 330
    Aida, 4
    Macbeth, 170, 287
    La Traviata, 331, 333
Verne, Jules, 242
Véron, Louis, 302, 311
Viardot, Louis, 146
Viardot, Pauline, 225
violin, military associations of the, 112, 124

Virgil, 16, 245
  Aeneid, 13, 16, 252, 256, 260, 273, 274, 287, 318
virtuosity, 8, 11, 43, 68, 70, 97, 111, 112, 113, 114, 115, 117–18, 119, 120, 122, 124, 309
Vivier, Eugène, 18
Volney, Constantin François de Chassebœuf, comte de, 66

Wagner, Richard, 4, 10, 12, 98, 127, 132, 133, 162–63, 175, 190, 191, 193, 240, 241, 242, 337. *See also* Zukunftsmusik
  Der fliegende Holländer, 175
  Lohengrin, 175
  Tannhäuser, 239
Wallace, [William] Vincent, 19–21, 134, 335
  accounts of time in New Zealand, 20, 323–27
  Berlioz's account of, 2–4, 5, 13, 14, 15, 18–19, 21–24, 25–26, 31, 33–34, 38, 48, 55, 320–21, 322, 327, 328, 336–37
  Lurline, 325–26, 330, 331
  Maritana, 19, 327, 330, 331, 334, 335
Weber, Carl Maria von, 93
  Der Freischütz, 4, 65, 184, 190–91
  Konzertstück, 114–15, 116, 117
Wernicke, Herbert, 315, 317
Western art music, ideology of, 3, 4–6, 7, 8, 13, 321, 323, 325–27, 330, 335, 337
Wiprecht, Wilhelm, 88, 96
works by Berlioz
  À travers chant, 240, 241
  Benvenuto Cellini, 58, 92, 102–03, 311, 330
  'La captive', 11, 40–42, 49–52, 55, 56, 61
  'Chant des chemins de fer', 200, 215
  Le cinq mai, 74, 98
  La damnation de Faust, 12, 191–92, 194, 196, 207, 215–39, 241, 242, 243–44, 245, 294
    Part I 'Plaines de Hongrie', 220–21
    Part II 'Choeur d'étudiants et de soldats', 216–18
    Part III Scène X, 222; 'Le roi de Thulé', 221–22, 241; 'Évocation', 227–29, 294; 'Sérénade', 226–27, 231; Duet, 222
    Part IV 'Romance', 222–25; 'Récitatif et chasse', 229; 'La course à l'abîme', 229–31, 232, 234; 'Dans le ciel – Apothéose', 232–34
  Dernier jour du monde, 193
  L'enfance du Christ, 271
  Épisode de la vie d'un artiste, 129, 131–33, 135, 165, 169, 200. *See also* Symphonie fantastique; Lélio
  Evenings with the Orchestra, 1–2, 3, 4, 7, 8–9, 14, 15, 17–18, 29, 54, 88, 252, 322, 334, 335, 338
    'A Visit to Tom Thumb', 18
    Euphonia, 12, 77, 88, 192, 193, 194, 196, 197–202, 204–06, 207–10, 211–14, 215, 216, 218, 220, 225, 226, 228, 229, 232, 234, 238, 239, 240, 241, 242, 243, 244, 294
    'How a tenor revolves around the public', 220
    'The Adventures of Vincent Wallace in New Zealand'. *See* Wallace, [William] Vincent: Berlioz's account of
    'The piano possessed', 214–15, 230
  Les francs-juges, 88
  Les grotesques de la musique, 37
  Harold en Italie, 11, 44, 71, 73–75, 76, 99–100, 101, 103–04, 106–07, 108, 109–13, 115–22, 125, 271, 328, 337
    I 'Harold aux montagnes', 121
    II 'Marche des pèlerins', 103, 116–17
    III 'Sérénade', 103, 119, 155
    IV 'Orgie de brigands', 103, 110, 121–22, 123
    Liszt's transcriptions of, 113, 115–16, 121
  Huit scènes de Faust, 221
  'Hymne à la France', 265
  Lélio, 65, 128, 129, 130–31, 141–43, 161, 164, 190, 191, 234
  Memoirs, 15–16, 25, 32, 38–39, 53, 73–74, 76, 96, 106, 162, 245
  La mort d'Orphée, 8
  Neuf Mélodies (Irlande), 76
  La nonne sanglante, 12, 128, 129, 164, 165, 167, 186–90, 229, 273, 274, 287–90, 292, 337
    'Légende', 170–74, 176, 179, 180–83, 184–86, 187, 191
  Les nuits d'été
    'Au cimetière', 279
    'L'île inconnue', 34–35
  Orchestration Treatise, 8, 11, 14, 15, 38, 47–49, 53–69, 73, 78, 80, 88, 90, 97, 103, 146, 147, 178, 179, 184, 234, 256, 325, 337
  'Rákóczy March', 68
  Requiem (Grande Messe des morts), 77, 98, 193
  Le retour à la vie. *See* Lélio

Les soirées de l'orchestre. See *Evenings with the Orchestra*
Roméo et Juliette, 51, 58, 102, 220, 232, 237, 246, 279, 285, 309
'Salut matinal', 36–37
Sardanaple, 76
Symphonie fantastique, 12, 58, 62, 68, 97, 106, 128, 129–30, 138, 139, 143, 144, 145, 152, 155, 158, 163–64, 188, 190, 192, 194, 231, 242, 336, 337
    I 'Rêveries – passions', 141, 158–59
    II 'Un bal', 129–30, 152–55, 158, 162
    III 'Scène aux champs', 130, 139–40, 158
    IV 'Marche au supplice', 130, 140, 147
    V 'Songe d'une nuit de sabbat', 130, 140–41, 152, 157, 158, 159
    Liszt's transcription of, 124, 161
Symphonie funèbre et triomphale, 11, 71, 73–74, 75, 76, 78, 79–80, 81–86, 89, 90–91, 96, 98, 99, 104, 125, 328, 337
    I 'Marche funèbre', 81
    II 'Oraison funèbre', 79, 81, 82
    III 'Apothéose', 82–84, 85, 89
Les Troyens, 13, 58, 64, 189, 244, 245–46, 249, 251–54, 255–68, 269, 270–79, 281–93, 294–97, 298–99, 306–18, 320–21, 323, 330, 338

Act I No. 1, 253; No. 2 'Récitatif et air', 274; No. 3 'Duo', 287–90; No. 4 'Marche et hymne', 253; No. 5 'Pas des lutteurs', 271–72; No. 7 'Récit', 294; No. 11 'Final', 253, 262–63, 271–73
Act II No. 12 'Scène et récitatif', 273, 274–76; No. 16 'Final', 253
Act III No. 18 'Chant national', 266, 268; Nos.20–22 'Entrées', 266; No. 26 'Marche Troyenne dans le mode triste', 263; No. 28 'Final', 316
Act IV No. 29 'Chasse royale et orage', 256–60, 271, 294, 295; No. 33 Ballets, 295, 299, 311–13, 315, 316–17, 318; No. 33a 'Pas des almées', 310–11; No. 33c 'Pas d'esclaves nubiennes', 253, 255, 271, 307–10, 316; No. 34 'Scène et chant d'Iopas', 253, 314; No. 35 'Récitatif et quintette', 246; No. 37 'Duo', 273
Act V No. 42 'Scène', 276–79; No. 44 'Duo et choeur', 265, 320–21; 'Épilogue', 265, 295
'Marche Troyenne', 253, 260–65, 268, 269, 271–73, 295
Waverley overture, 327, 328
work concept, 5, 8–9, 10, 11, 71, 72, 75, 98, 113, 114, 115, 124, 125, 129, 184, 206, 207, 247, 249, 252

Zukunftsmusik, 12, 193, 239–42, 290

Printed in the United States
By Bookmasters